EGYPTIAN LITERATURE 1800 BC

questions and readings

Stephen Quirke

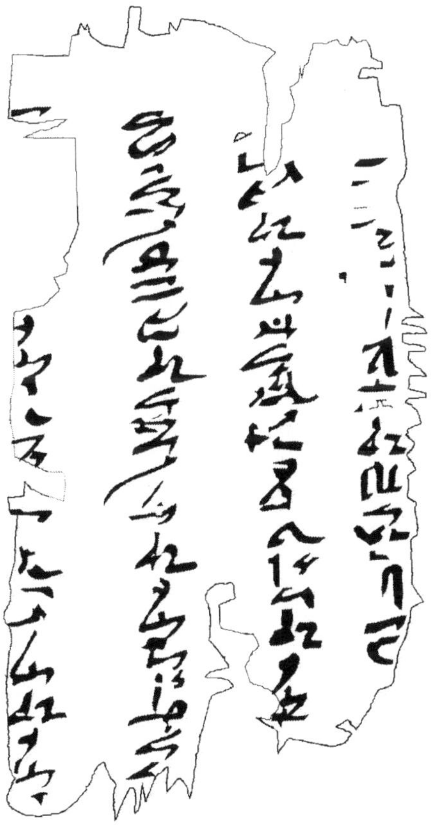

Golden House Publications
Egyptology 2

London 2004

Golden House Publications
GoldenHouse100@aol.com

second imprint

Cover picture
Papyrus found at Harageh, London UC 32773 (fragment of the Tale of the Exile of Sanehat)

Printed in the United Kingdom
By T J International

ISBN 978-0-9547218-6-2

CONTENTS

Preface

The core of the translations and discussions presented in this volume has been available online for a couple of years already, on the University College London website 'Digital Egypt for Universities', developed over 2000-2003. The internet offers one ideal vehicle for material to support student presentations or other prompts for discussion. In addition, websites can cut across disciplinary boundaries more effectively than the sharply demarcated lines of library shelving. However, the printed book offers other advantages, for easier reading, and as the more stable referent for further research. The different fates of online and printed learning materials in contemporary Egyptology have encouraged me to extend the materials that I provided online, for this print publication. I do not repeat the extensive bibliography for which the reader is recommended to the 2002 volume by Richard Parkinson, *Poetry and Culture in Middle Kingdom Egypt*. As I am an Egyptologist, my translations are academic rather than poetic, and I offer the readings as evidence against which to test the discussion of questions in the first part. Ideally these readings might also act as an invitation to a broader audience. Contemporary literary writers read, are inspired by and take into their work many other, arguably equally unknowable, aesthetic times and places, from the Athens of Aeschylus to the London of Shakespeare. They turn less often to the scarcer treasury of ancient Egyptian literature – though, of course, the exceptions include Akhmatova, Brecht, Mahfouz and Mann.

Over a decade ago Pascal Vernus recommended that I read the 1989 treatise by Bernard Cerquiglini, *Eloge de la variante*, and I am deeply indebted to him for this prompt. I am also grateful to Yvette Balbaligo for sharing enthusiasm for the project, joining me in reading some of the compositions, and commenting on drafts for the first part of the volume. Over recent years, Okasha El Daly has encouraged me to look at the potential of Arabic literature and other aspects of modern Egyptian life, to begin to move away from the Eurocentric grip on Egyptology. Other African literatures offer other escape routes. As a European and as someone outside the circle of literary studies, I acknowledge that this is not my research ground, and I look forward instead to the continued growth in Arabic-language Egyptology and African-centred Egyptology as surer paths for modernity to learn of this part of the past. In this volume, I have simply noted examples from a current introduction to Arabic literature, where I felt a possible resonance, and would like to know from readers in Arabic literary studies whether they feel the same potential.

My own initiation into the enjoyment of Egyptian literature began in the language classes by John Ray, and my greatest debt here remains to him, for teaching me so much of ancient Egyptian writing, and in particular for opening my eyes to the multiple human dimensions of its lives.

A note on transliteration and translation in this volume

I have used the following conventions for the transliteration of Egyptian from hieratic into a Latin-based script, and for the translations into English:

1. the phonetic values of the signs have been rendered according to standard Egyptological practice in English publications following Gardiner: see the table at the start of Part Two with the note on reading transliterated Egyptian
2. **bold** denotes use of red in an ancient manuscript source – this is the standard ancient Egyptian means of highlighting written words, using the contrast between exceptional red and regular black pigment: as red requires additional printing cost, it is represented in recent publications by a cheaper alternative (bold has been selected here as the more readily visible and least intrusive in translations – other options include underlining, italicising, capital letters)
3. following Egyptological practice, rounded brackets ( ) enclose words added to the original for clarity, while square brackets [ ] enclose words/letters/spaces destroyed in the ancient manuscript source; two dots .. denote a sign or letter, three dots a longer passage
4. wherever possible the transliteration and translation of a passage have been placed on the same line, in order to facilitate reading in the original

Egyptian word order differs from English and most other modern European languages, with the predominant pattern Verb-Subject-Object rather than English Subject-Verb-Object. Much greater fluency in translation would be possible with translation into Arabic, or another Verb-Subject-Object language such as Welsh or Irish. For the purposes of this volume, translations offer a guide to an existing literary content, and are not themselves intended as literary content.

His Majesty?

Translation always involves manipulation and adjustment, and perhaps always tends to veer over the cliffs of unacceptability and meaninglessness. Question Four includes some instances of the problems. A particular instance to note at the outset is the untranslateability of a frequent means of reference to the King, traditionally rendered by Egyptologists in English as "His Majesty" – *ḥm.f.* That English phrase lacks special force among current English-speakers, being reduced to a plain synonym for 'king'; therefore Egyptologists have sought a more distinctive term such as "His Person" or "His Power". According to the preliminary investigation by Oleg Berlev into the underlying sense of the words *ḥm* (*nswt*) "X (of the king)" feminine *ḥmt* used to denote the bulk of the working population in the Middle Kingdom, the word denotes the physical agency, or mechanism by which a physical effect is achieved (Berlev 1972, 33-44). Following Speigel, Berlev noted how, in the narrative relating the struggles between the gods Horus and Seth, the agents of action and speech are not expressed directly as Horus and Seth, but are instead the *ḥm* of Horus and the *ḥm* of Seth. Moving beyond previous commentators, Berlev emphasised the use of *ḥm* in combination with just one of the words for the palace of the king, *stp-s3* literally "selection of protection", an abstraction applicable to any of the physical architectural entities protecting the body of the ruler, and the one term for "palace" for which no personnel are attested, presumably precisely because it represents an abstraction. Similarly, in the offering ritual in the temple, *ḥm-nṯr* "X of the god" denotes the person acting as mechanism for delivery of material goods (clothing, food, drink) to the deity materialised in a cult image; *ḥm-k3* "X of the spirit/double" provided the same mechanism in the offering-cult for individuals after their death. The working population too, according to the ideology of kingship, acted as the agents or forces that achieve physical effects (manual labour) for the king, ensuring by agriculture and construction the prosperity of the land (as acclaimed in the 'Loyalist Teaching', translated below in Part Two, Section One, Teachings), hence the term *ḥm nswt.* In all cases, these are the physical manifestations with potential to achieve physical effects: as Berlev comments on the use of the word in the "Tale of the Herdsman" (for which see Part Two, Section Two), "the Egyptian has in mind *ḥm* (traditional rendering "slave", "servant") the social term, designating the being that creates what the master wishes" (Berlev 1972, 40). Berlev is then able to identify the definitional antonym of *ḥm* as *ḫfty* "enemy". Although the translation reads poorly, "His Power" has accordingly been adopted in this volume as the more accurate of the various options to render *ḥm.f.* "His Agent" might be more accurate still, but would probably mislead the average English-reader over the content of the phrase, separating it too fully from the "master" behind.

PART ONE
QUESTIONS

Introduction: Middle Kingdom Egypt 2025-1700 BC

Ancient Egyptian history may be defined as the timespan from the invention of writing around 3200-3000 BC to the absorption of Egypt into the Empire of Alexander the Great 332 BC. This unwieldy block was divided by the Hellenistic Egyptian historian Manetho into thirty (in some versions thirty-one) groups of rulers, or 'dynasties' (Waddell 1940). These shorter sequences comprised the reigns of kings who shared a patron deity (by their place of origin, and/or place of burial) and, sometimes but not always, belonged to the same family. Although often there are no clear reasons for why Manetho divided one dynasty from the next, his framework is so convenient that Egyptologists continue to use it. However, a change in reign, or even in dynasty, may have little to do with changes in material culture, that is, in life across social classes and geographical regions. For such wider horizons, the defining criterion is not so much who is on the throne, but how much of Egypt they control, because that determines access to resources, both human and material. Therefore Egyptologists have applied the criterion of political unity/disunity to create a series of periods grounded in the material evidence. In detail, this criterion cannot provide sharp borders for periods, because the establishment of political unity is an effect from intricate combinations of social relations organised across different levels and on different scales, from local and regional to 'national' and 'international'. However, for broad brushstroke history, the periods of unity and disunity offer a relatively stable basis for research into the past. Unfortunately, though, as in other branches of archaeology and history, the names for the periods are without exception hostage to the modern religious faith in evolutionary progress, privileging the earlier at the expense of the later, and, especially bizarre after the twentieth century, a faith in leadership, privileging the period of unity over that of disunity. The following set of names is almost impossible to redeem from implicit and ungrounded value judgements:

Early Dynastic Period	Dynasties 1-3	about 3000-2650 BC
Old Kingdom	Dynasties 4-8	about 2650-2150 BC
First Intermediate Period	Dynasties 9-early 11	about 2150-2025 BC
Middle Kingdom	Dynasties late 11 – early 13	about 2025-1700 BC
Second Intermediate Period	Dynasties late 13 - 17	about 1700-1550 BC
New Kingdom	Dynasties 18-20	about 1550-1070 BC
Third Intermediate Period	Dynasties 21-24	about 1070-725 BC
Late Period	Dynasties 25-26	about 725-525 BC
Achaemenid Persian Period	Dynasty 27	525-404 and 343-332 BC
Late Dynastic Period	Dynasties 28-30	404-343 BC

The literature considered in this volume comes from the second 'classic' period of Egyptian history, the 'Middle Kingdom', the earliest age from which there survive manuscripts bearing literary tales, laments and teachings. At this time, the written language of Egypt was Egyptian, a member of a family of languages reaching from north and east Africa across into western Asia, and therefore named Afroasiatic by twentieth-century linguists. Today the Egyptian language survives in the liturgy of the Coptic Church in Egypt, but is no longer spoken as a mother-tongue (on Coptic see Bosson and Aufrère 1999). Whatever other languages may have been spoken in Egypt, and whichever dialects might have been present in the different parts of the country, lie hidden beneath the monolingual edifice of the written record. Over the millennia, the Egyptian language changed substantially in that record, with a major shift from 'synthetic' to 'analytical' during the New Kingdom. Egyptologists have named the successive phases of the language with terms sometimes mirroring those assigned the broad historical periods, and so the language of Middle Kingdom Egypt is known today as 'Middle Egyptian' (full account in Allen 2000). The literary compositions in this volume are all written in Middle Egyptian, though some present features anticipating the next phase, 'Late Egyptian'.

With more intensive research, especially in ceramic studies, the relation between the material cultural periods and internal boundaries within them have become clearer. The Middle Kingdom can be broken down into (1) an initial phase, from reunification around 2025 BC to the establishment of a focal Residence for the king at Itjtawy around 1950 BC; (2) a central phase from 1950 to 1850 BC; (3) a late phase ushered in by major changes from the reigns of Senusret III and Amenemhat III, around 1850 BC to 1800 BC, and lasting to the end of this period of political unity, around 1700 BC. The earliest surviving literary manuscripts seem all to belong to the third of these, the late Middle Kingdom. None can be shown to have been deposited in the ground any earlier; the earliest may have been written shortly before 1850 BC, so in the central phase as defined above, but opinions have differed over the dating of the handwriting on the earliest to mid Twelfth or late Twelfth Dynasty (Papyrus Prisse and Papyrus Hermitage 1115, see Berlev and Hodjash 1997). As for other periods, our Middle Kingdom 'cultural history' is substantial, but great uncertainties remain over social structure and economy. It is not known to what degree writers and their audiences participated in the ideological assertions of centralised power, divine kingship and a redistributive economy. Much more research is needed before defining statements can be made on the social character of poetry, though African kingly courts and Asian imperial chancelleries seem to offer attractive models for comparison (see Question Four, on exploring co-texts). Fathoming ancient contexts and contents, the modern enquirer must remain acutely aware of sources as archaeological fragments from a deep time. While the content is much patchier than the longer literary narratives of India or Greece, the Egyptian fragments are as precious as the Iraqi and Syrian because they take us deep into time not through contestable channels of transmission, but directly in their material presence on stone, wood, linen and papyrus paper, to millennia before the earliest preserved Vedic or Homeric fragment. Their age cannot make them better or more important than any other human literary tradition, but together with those it guarantees the depth of our shared humanity across time as well as over space. In this way, literature helps us to replace the bogus concept 'civilization' with a more optimistic and generous assertion of the value of all human life.

The translated content here does not exhaust by any means the scope of ancient self-conscious deployment of writing. As outlined below in Question One, vastly more survives outside the 'literary core' from the Middle Kingdom and the preceding periods, and vastly more of both literary and non-literary from later periods. This volume tackles, then, just one among many areas where the past inhabitants of Egypt left their written imprint. As one of the most reflective and beautiful, this Middle Kingdom 'literary core' provides a starting-point for the encounter with ancient lives.

Question One: Survival
How does literature survive from 1800 BC?

For defining 'literature 1800 BC' (Question Two), and crucial for that definition, first the surviving record needs to be outlined, to reveal the specific place of the literary in the broader history of communication. The definition of the literary is not an exclusively theoretical question: a category such as 'literary content' acquires its definitional contours against the empirical dataset of what (else) has survived, especially where manuscripts preserving different content have survived in the same group. This chapter or Question presents the list of all surviving groups of books, establishing the extent to which the definition of literary content becomes the more form-oriented question 'what is the distinctive content of books with literary format'.

What existed? The scope of writing 1800 BC

Writing in ancient Egypt may be divided roughly into two worlds (Assmann 1991):

(1) inscription, retaining full forms for pictorial signs (hieroglyphs), and firmly fixed in place with its sights on the horizon of eternity

(2) manuscript, with signs more or less cursively derived from the hieroglyphs of inscription, less bound by place and time, and operating within the horizons of a mortal human lifespan

Although the written record, both inscription and manuscript, is grimly fragmentary for the Middle Kingdom, the range of content in the surviving materials can provide a starting-point for assessing how writing may be categorised, and whether one part of the record might correspond to modern expectations of the word literature. The thousands of manuscript fragments found at Lahun could be grouped by their content into seven major categories: administrative, legal, letters, healing, religious, literary, treatises. These categories can then be plotted against the surviving record from all inscriptions and manuscripts at all sites over the time of use of the Egyptian hieroglyphic script and its cursive derivatives, from 3000 BC to AD200:

	3000-2000	2000-1500	1500-1000	1000-500	500BC-AD200
administrative	examples	examples	examples	examples	examples
legal	examples	examples	examples	examples	examples
letters	examples	examples	examples	examples	examples
healing	examples	examples	examples		examples
religious	examples	examples	examples	examples	examples
literary		examples	examples	examples	examples
treatises		examples	examples	examples	examples

Narrower groupings of content and time-blocks would delineate the gaps more precisely, as in the following instances:

- in the literary category, love-songs are preserved only from 1300-1100 BC on manuscript
- legal documents are found only after 2500 BC
- under the category 'healing', no prescription or treatment manuscripts survive before 2000 BC
- in the category of treatises, only word-lists survive between 1200 and 400 BC: there are no mathematical or astronomical compositions from those 800 years.

A more detailed breakdown into twenty categories against eight time-blocks is online at:
http://www.digitalegypt.ucl.ac.uk/writing/scope2.html

However crude, an overarching view of written content provides a backdrop against which to consider the literary, and a reminder of the other worlds of writing beside, before and after each tabular field, worlds off which the literary feeds and against which it is to be defined.

The first appearance of literary books in the surviving record is confined to a handful of late Middle Kingdom burials and fragments in one late Middle Kingdom low-desert town. This broadening of scope of preserved written content is part of a major shift in source base between (1) the early and central phases of the Middle Kingdom and (2) the late phase, with the turning-point around the reign of king Senusret III, by 1850 BC. For the early Middle Kingdom written sources include:

1. the hieroglyphic inscriptions on temples, notably the expanded building programme of Senusret I in the twentieth century BC (a striking example is the inscription at Tod, Barbotin 1991)
2. hieroglyphic and cursive rock-inscriptions left by expeditionaries, officials travelling south into Nubia or across the desert to the Red Sea and in Sinai (López 1977)

3. cursive hieroglyphic funerary literature on the walls of coffins (dominated by, but not restricted to, the corpus of 'Pyramid Texts' in late Old Kingdom tradition and their successor the 'Coffin Texts' in Middle Egyptian, cf Allen 1996)
4. hieroglyphic inscriptions on elements from offering-chapels either at the place of burial or at a prominent cult-centre, most famously that of the god of the underworld Osiris at Abydos (Simpson 1974), but also, for example, the shrine of an Old Kingdom provincial high official at Elephantine, Heqaib (Franke 1994)
5. inscriptions in temple-size offering-chapels over the burial-places of local governors in Upper Egypt at (from south to north) Qubbet el-Hawa facing Elephantine and at Qau, Meir, Rifeh, Asyut, Bersha, Beni Hasan, usually in secondary position to depictions (cf Arnold 1977, 831-833)
6. a small number of papyri from miscellaneous sources, including the discarded batch of letters from the funerary priest Heqanakht, found at Thebes (Allen 2002), and the earliest manuscript with incantations to be recited to secure good health, now preserved in Turin (Roccati 1970)

For the late Middle Kingdom categories 3 and 5 virtually disappear, and category 2 expands under king Amenemhat III and then almost disappears in the Thirteenth Dynasty, while categories 1 and 4 continue into the Second Intermediate Period, providing groups of sources within which like may be compared with like more strictly across these longer periods of time. However, even within these object categories displaying continuity, there are significant changes in content: early Middle Kingdom Abydos inscriptions more often contain 'autobiographical' self-descriptions, including narrative, whereas religious formulae and hymns become more common later (Franke 2003).

In place of the large mass of early Middle Kingdom funerary literature within the burial-chamber, late Middle Kingdom tombs yield a smaller and more miscellaneous array of writing. Some contain inscribed items made for burial, such as the earliest shabtis with 'shabti formula' and earliest heart scarabs with 'heart scarab formula' (Quirke 2003). Only occasionally does a coffin bear the larger quantity of writing found before (e.g. the coffins of Sesenebnef from Lisht, cf Allen 1996). Other late Middle Kingdom elite burial assemblages incorporated writing in a different way, by the presence of manuscript: these range from accountancy documents in one burial (Papyrus Boulaq 18: Mariette 1872) to literary papyri in another (presumed provenance of the Athanasi papyri, and perhaps together Papyrus Hermitage 1115 and Papyrus Prisse, see below, Question One, Group One) or combinations of literary, ritual, healing manuscripts (the Ramesseum Papyri, see below, Question One, Group Two).

The extreme scarcity of complete books is compensated to some extent by the mass of discarded manuscript fragments retrieved across presumably the higher drier portion of the marginal low-desert town at Lahun, including a handful of remnants from literary compositions (Collier and Quirke 2004). In other instances, the provenance is not recorded, or precise context unclear, as at Harageh, where the Engelbach expedition discovered one fragment of the Tale of the Exile of Sanehat (UC 32773: Engelbach 1923, 32-33). Harageh comprises predominantly a series of cemeteries, but included patches of settlement, and so the Tale (a surface find?) might derive either from the houses or from the tomb-shafts; in the absence of a recorded cemetery location, it is not possible now to assess the likelihood that it might be a stray from one of the smaller areas of housing for the living. Fortunately Middle Kingdom literature continued to be read and copied for another fifteen centuries, and so we are not entirely dependant on the archaeological record of that one period alone for the reconstruction of the content (as given in Part Two). However, for questions of production and reception within the Middle Kingdom, these precious survivors provide the primary source material. Rare books and archaeological fragments make up our essential data set.

Literary compositions as fragments in an archaeological record

From 3000 BC to AD 1000 Egyptians used the giant marsh reed papyrus to make paper, and, from sheets of papyrus paper, rolls - the ancient form of books (Leach and Tait 2000). Although other materials were used as writing surfaces at various times, such as potsherds, limestone flakes, and plastered wooden boards, papyrus paper remained the principal material in Egypt from the introduction of writing until the introduction of the equally vulnerable cloth-pulp paper introduced across the Caliphate from the eighth century AD (for the latter, see Bloom 2001). Our knowledge of production methods is entirely dependent on surviving examples of the finished product: no papyrus production centre has been identified in architecture or archaeology, and no depictions or detailed records of papyrus paper production survive apart from a secondhand and not entirely lucid description in Latin by Pliny, *Natural History*. Contemporary conservation issues usefully foreground the fragility of the material (Leach and Tait 2000). Survival of papyrus book rolls depends on the physical properties of the material, on the patterns of usage (wear, reduction) and, crucially, on the specific patterns and practices of deposition (Quirke 1996), including the regionally and chronologically widely-varying burial customs (Grajetzki 2003).

The dominant use of organic material as writing surface, and the general absence of customs of deposition on dry ground, have severely limited the number of surviving manuscripts. Of these, extant literary books constitute only a small proportion, resulting in a dearth of well-preserved compositions (cf Quirke 1996, 387). From perhaps three late Middle Kingdom burials, a total of ten relatively well-preserved books are preserved; all other late Middle Kingdom manuscripts are highly fragmentary. The position is not much different for the New Kingdom, when both Middle Kingdom and New Kingdom compositions were being copied on papyrus, and only small fragments survive from books of the Late Period with copies of Middle Kingdom compositions. The principal surviving groups of literary books from all periods are listed under the next heading below, and all literary compositions known to me from the Middle Kingdom are presented in Part Two in transliteration and translation. As a direct result of the frailty of the papyrus book, the substantially preserved Middle Kingdom compositions number only fourteen, even including the long Hymn to the Nile, from the more marginal category of religious literary eulogy. Five of these survive on Middle Kingdom manuscripts, the rest being known from later manuscripts only. Moreover, of the fourteen, only eight are intact from beginning to end (accepting the first line of the Shipwrecked Official as the original first line, though this has been debated). This extremely narrow base of intact compositions stands in contrast to the archaeological record at the only large Middle Kingdom town site, near modern Lahun: there, several papyrus fragments survive, and all but one come from literary compositions not otherwise attested (the exception is a fragment from the tale of the Exile of Sanehat, UC 32106C verso: Collier and Quirke 2004, 34-35). Furthermore, several of even the better-preserved compositions are preserved in a single copy (Tale of the Shipwrecked Official, Tales at the Court of King Khufu, Dialogue of a Man and his Soul, Lament of Ipuwer). In other words, there seems to have been a substantial body of literature in the late Middle Kingdom, from which relatively little survives. This picture may never be much altered by future discoveries, given the comprehensive vacuuming of those settlement and cemetery sites most likely to produce intact Middle Egyptian literary manuscripts (Lahun town, cemeteries at Thebes).

On the survival of groups of books in ancient Egypt

Although the survival of an ancient book made of papyrus paper is little short of a miracle, books were deposited in small groups often enough for the survival of a group to be no less rare than the survival of a single book. In the modern disciplines of ancient history and archaeology, such groups of books have generally been termed ‘archives’. This local disciplinary use of the word ‘archive’ contrasts with the more precise modern usage of ‘archive’ to denote groups of writings that are no longer of direct practical use, but that are nevertheless retained for reference in special storage. Although there is no reason not to develop a local disciplinary usage for a word, it should be remembered that there is no evidence for the practice of storing any disused writings in ancient Egypt (archiving). Rather than being antecedents of the modern ‘archive’, the attested ancient groups of books may be compared instead with the modern 'library'. As both organic material and valuable recyclable commodity, papyrus paper survives in bulk from ancient or even medieval times only under very restricted circumstances. Two famous examples of the escape from time involve the large-scale though fragmentary preservation of Hellenistic and later manuscripts: the survival of Roman Period wastepaper dumps above the water-table at Oxyrhynchus; and the use of wastepaper in mass-production of cartonnage mummy-cover elements from the mid-third to late first centuries BC. Survivals within institutions are limited to the Tebtunis temple stores and the carbonised papyri from a public records office at Mendes and an administrative unit at Bubastis (Angeli 1994, 87-96). Other carbonised papyri from Tanis may belong either to a private house or to a temple workshop (see Group Nine below). As a result, our knowledge of ancient libraries in Egypt, including those at Alexandria, remains acutely limited.

The House of Books in ancient Egyptian written sources and architecture

Ancient Egyptian inscriptions and manuscripts include numerous references to groups of books as the House of Books (Schott 1990, 452 index). In the surviving architecture, just one House of Books is identified as such by hieroglyphic inscription: this is a chamber on the south side, eastern half, of the outer columned hall in the temple of Horus at Edfu. However, the chamber seems too small to have contained an entire temple library, and so this single extant example may be misleading, illustrating not the large-scale storage of books, but the use of the term 'House of Books' to refer to any scale of book-storage. The inscriptions of the Edfu chamber include a catalogue of books, and identify the room itself (Schott 1990, 69) as:

pr mḏ3t n ḥr ꜥpr m b3w ḥr-rꜥ

'the house of books of Horus, equipped with the Powers of Horus-Ra'

The term 'powers of Ra' is used in the Ptolemaic Period as a name for content of sacred and medical books (Schott 1990, 68-70 no.121). The size and location of the chamber indicate that it may have been the storage-place for ritual books that were in repeated use during temple rituals. The term *pr* 'house' might refer to a receptacle of any size, as with the 'house of bow and arrows' attested from a hieratic inscription on a label probably from a box, found in the tomb of king Thutmose IV of the Eighteenth Dynasty. A 'House of Books' might then refer simply to a box, such as that in which the Ramesseum Papyri were found (below, Group Two). This takes us far from the usual modern meaning of 'library' as a large collection of books arranged in a manner making them accessible to readers.

No architectural remains, then, have been securely identified as a large ancient Egyptian library. Presumably the most important would have been in the palace(s) of the king. Others might be expected in the principal temples at Iunu (Heliopolis), Memphis, perhaps Khemenu (Hermopolis/Ashmunein), and from the New Kingdom Thebes and from the Twenty-first Dynasty Tanis.

Surviving groups of ancient Egyptian books

In modern times, modest groupings of papyri have been uncovered, mainly from burials. This leaves us heavily dependant on the pattern of burial customs, with little chance of preservation of manuscript groups except in those periods at which daily life objects were placed in the tomb. Contrary to general popular and even Egyptological assumption, at most periods daily life objects were not included in burial equipment: the major exceptions are the First Dynasty and the Eighteenth Dynasty, with a shorter, as yet little-studied, phase in the late Third Intermediate Period and early Late Period (Grajetzki 2003). Even when the burials received objects other than those made specially for the tomb, the burial equipment represents a cultural selection, and in neither the First nor the Eighteenth Dynasty did the regular selection include books from life. From the First Dynasty, there are only the fragments of a blank papyrus roll from the tomb of the high official Hemaka at Saqqara (Emery); from the mid-Eighteenth Dynasty onwards, the elite daily activity of writing was represented in the tomb by a book specially made for burial, containing religious formulae for surviving death, the so-called Books of the Dead (already on coffins and shrouds earlier, but regularly on papyrus in the burial equipment from the joint reign of Thutmose III and Hatshepsut onwards, from about 1450 BC: the earliest example may be that of the vizier Useramun, published Munro 1990). Fortunately, the Eighteenth Dynasty practice of including objects of daily life in the tomb has its roots in fundamental changes to burial customs during the late Twelfth Dynasty (Bourriau 1991); in the late Middle Kingdom, Second Intermediate Period, and early Eighteenth Dynasty, the widely varying selection of objects placed in middle-ranking elite tombs did occasionally include books (see Groups One to Four below), and in the early to mid-Eighteenth Dynasty, rather more often, plastered wooden writing-boards including a number with excerpts from literary compositions. This never seems to have become a regular practice, and so long-term preservation depends upon that highly sporadic burial custom for the deposition of daily life books. Soil conditions are suitable for preservation of organic materials such as papyrus paper at only a few locations. Here again, the contours of the archaeological record for the late Middle Kingdom are against the survival chances of a book. Most Delta cemetery sites are on wet land, and preserve no papyri, while the royal pyramid complexes and higher elite cemeteries of the period tend to be close to the fields, and their tomb-shafts too close to the water-table, at sites such as Hawara and Dahshur. Conditions at Saqqara are more favourable; by contrast, the cemeteries on the West Bank at Thebes are both dry and, equally important, remote from the modern larger concentrations of population.

The following ten groups of papyri are the only such known to me, offering at least some examples of ancient small-scale 'book collections' (their possible status as private 'libraries' may seem natural to modern commentators, but it is a culturally-specific assumption):

1. a group of late Middle Kingdom literary papyri collected by Athanasi (about 1800 BC)

2. a miscellaneous group of late Middle Kingdom papyri from a tomb under the later Ramesseum precinct (about 1800-1750 BC)
3. an early Eighteenth Dynasty group (about 1500 BC)
4. a late Eighteenth or early Nineteenth Dynasty group (about 1325 BC)
5. one or more groups of Memphite papyri collected by Anastasi, d'Orbiney, Sallier (about 1200 BC)
6. one or more groups of Deir el-Medina papyri excavated by Bruyère and/or collected by Chester Beatty (deposited after about 1150 BC)
7. a group of Third Intermediate Period papyri from el-Hiba (about 950 BC)
8. a group of Late Period papyri collected by Wilbour (about 350 BC)
9. a large number of papyri from a Roman building at Tanis (about AD 150)
10. a large number of papyri from the temple precinct at Tebtunis (deposited about AD 200)

This list excludes the more numerous and larger groups of documentary papyri that survive, such as the papyri from Deir el-Medina, and groups of accounts (Abusir Papyri of the late Old Kingdom, Reisner Papyri of the early Middle Kingdom) and legal documents (Lahun lots I+II of the late Middle Kingdom, and the Tomb Robbery Papyri of the Twentieth Dynasty). Most documentary papyri were discovered in more or less fragmentary condition as discards: exceptions are the Reisner Papyri, found in an early to mid-Twelfth Dynasty tomb at Naga el-Deir, and the Tomb Robbery Papyri, apparently cached near Medinet Habu at the end of the Twentieth Dynasty. Discarded papyri on town sites extend the range of surviving content, but in much poorer condition than the ten groups cited above. For the Middle Kingdom, only the town-site at Lahun has preserved such fragmentary rubbish-heaps, and this was excavated in 1889, too early in the history of archaeology for any precise information to be recorded on findspots. Two literary manuscripts from Lahun may come from a large batch of manuscripts discarded in one of the palatial mansions there, but the circumstances of discovery are far from clear (Gallorini 1998 on 'Lot VI' and 'Lot LV' as possibly part of one group retrieved in the spring and then the autumn seasons of excavation: Lot VI included the Tale of Horus and Seth, and Lot LV the Hymns to Senusret III with Tale of Hay on the back, see Part Two below for transliterations and translations). Whereas fragmentary papyri may have been discarded by more than one person over an unknown period of time, the ten groups considered here appear to represent single and consciously-made selections of written material, although it must be conceded that the depositers left no explicit reason for their action.

Group One: literary papyri of the late Middle Kingdom collected by Athanasi

Richard Parkinson has investigated the modern history of this set of literary manuscripts (Parkinson 2003). In 1837 the Greek Egyptian Athanasi put on sale in London a collection including the following group of literary manuscripts dating to the late Middle Kingdom, about 1800 BC. The main items were later acquired by Richard Lepsius for the Egyptian Museum, Berlin:

- papyrus with copy of the Tale of Sanehat (Sinuhe), now Berlin 3022
- papyrus with copy of the Tale of Khuninpu ('Eloquent Peasant'), now Berlin 3023
- papyrus with sole surviving copy of the Dialogue of a Man with his Soul, and with part of a narrative involving a herdsman, now Berlin 3024
- papyrus with copy of the Tale of Khuninpu ('Eloquent Peasant'), now Berlin 3025

Fragments of all four became separated in the early modern history of the manuscripts, perhaps simply from repeated unrolling in the sales rooms, and entered the Amherst collection; these are now in the Pierpont Morgan Library, New York. A fifth manuscript, Papyrus Butler, also derives from the Athanasi collection, according to the research by Richard Parkinson: it contains a copy of the Tale of Khuninpu and on the reverse the only surviving copy of a portion of a similar composition, a hunter's lament.

Without any documentation on the finding and removal of the material from the ground, it is impossible to determine what other manuscripts or other items might have been in the same find, or what the circumstances securing survival might have been. Nevertheless, on the analogy of the Ramesseum Papyri (Group Two below), and from comparison of the handwriting and use of end-notes, the four-to-five manuscripts are generally considered to represent a single group deposited in a late Middle Kingdom burial. The most likely place for the discovery of a group of well-preserved Middle Kingdom papyri at that date is Thebes West: few of the Middle Kingdom cemetery sites farther north had yet been explored. This would confirm the indication in the Sotheby's Sale Catalogue of 1837 for the Athanasi Collection, that they were among papyri from the tombs at Thebes, although such auction-house labelling tends to be applied rather vaguely to groups of items, not all always from the provenance claimed, and so requires corroboration. In his article on the history of the group, Richard Parkinson notes stronger confirmation in the find of Middle Kingdom literary papyrus fragments during the Austrian Institute excavation of the tomb-temple of Ankhhor in the Asasif area of Thebes West.

The longest and most perfect Middle Kingdom literary book, Papyrus Prisse, is also supposed to have been found in Thebes, though it was purchased a decade after the Athanasi sales, and no reliable information survives concerning the circumstances of the find (Dewachter 1985, 63, noting that it could be from any part of the Theban necropolis, and 65, publishing a letter from its first European owner on its acquisition). It contains the only surviving copy of part of the Teaching of Kagemni and a refined version of the Teaching of Ptahhotep, in handwriting very similar to that of Amenyaa, who wrote and 'signed' the single extant copy of the Tale of the Shipwrecked Official (possibly then another ancient group, albeit comprising just two mansucripts, cf Bomhard 1999). Although the quest for the name of an ancient owner of literary papyri is virtually irresistible, the case of the Ramesseum Papyri indicates that it would be hazardous to expect ever to recover the identity of the ancient owner. Most late Middle Kingdom burials seem to have been without name, and for the Ramesseum Papyri the one object that might have provided it, the coffin, did not survive. Even in middle-ranking burials most coffins were uninscribed, and the lack of name may extend to burials of relatively great wealth.

Group Two: late Middle Kingdom manuscripts from a tomb under the Ramesseum precinct

In 1896 on the West Bank of the Nile at Thebes, Petrie and Quibell uncovered a late Middle Kingdom shaft tomb cut into the rock on the area to be covered at ground level four centuries later by the mud-brick store-rooms of the temple to the cult of Ramses II at Thebes, the Ramesseum. Although the coffin(s) of the original occupant(s) of the tomb did not survive, the excavators found in the tomb-shaft a characteristically miscellaneous assortment of late Middle Kingdom figures around a box full of fragile manuscripts (for late Middle Kingdom burials see Bourriau 1991, Grajetzki 2003: 57-61). After conservation by Hugo Ibscher in Berlin, the manuscripts were listed by Alan Gardiner as follows (Gardiner 1955: all are in hieratic unless noted to be in the more formal 'cursive hieroglyphic' script):

A. the Tale of Khuninpu ('Eloquent Peasant') on one side, Tale of Sanehat ('Sinuhe') on other side (Berlin 10499)

B. copy of a ritual for a statue of Senusret I ('Dramatic Ramesseum Papyrus') (British Museum EA 10610, in cursive hieroglyphic script)

C. copy of administrative despatches from fortresses in Nubia on one side ('Semna despatches'), incantations for good health on other (British Museum EA 10752)

D. copy of wordlist ('Onomasticon') (Berlin 10495)

E. copy of a funerary ritual (British Museum EA 10753, in cursive hieroglyphic script)

1-18 = British Museum EA 10754-10771, in detail:

1. only surviving copy of a 'Lament of Sasobek'
2. miscellaneous didactic maxims

3 and 4. prescriptions and incantations for good health

5. prescriptions for good health, in cursive hieroglyphic script
6. hymns to Sobek, in cursive hieroglyphic script
7. incantations (perhaps funerary formulae), in cursive hieroglyphic script

8 to 12 and 14 to 16. incantations for good health

13. incantations for good health, with list of 77 days for purification (for embalming?)

17. incantations for good health on the five days at the end of the year

18. administrative despatches from fortresses in Nubia (as Papyrus C above, 'Semna despatches')

The division into different numbers for the incantations for good health requires reexamination; it is possible that some manuscript fragments might join to form longer rolls.

For the objects found around the box, see Quibell 1898: 3 and pl.3. The box in which the manuscripts were found has not been identified in any museum receiving a share in finds; it is described by Quibell in the following terms:

> 'a wooden box about 18x12x12 inches. It was covered with white plaster, and on the lid was roughly drawn in black ink the figure of a jackal'.

Beside the papyri, the box itself contained 'also a bundle of reed pens, 16 inches long and a tenth of an inch in diameter'.

Group Three: a group of early Eighteenth Dynasty treatises

The three most important extant mathematical and medical books from ancient Egypt probably come from a single burial on the West Bank at Thebes, though acquired by three separate visitors to that area in the mid-nineteenth century: the surgical treatise Papyrus Edwin Smith; the book of prescriptions

Papyrus Ebers; and the Rhind Mathematical Papyrus (Spalinger 1988, 255-258). A leather roll with mathematical formulae may derive from the same source. No information is available on the circumstances of the find, or other objects or manuscripts found with them.

Group Four: a group of late Eighteenth Dynasty literary manuscripts
In the Pushkin Museum of Fine Arts, Moscow, and the British Museum, are preserved fragments of several magnificent literary books of the late Eighteenth Dynasty, about 1350 BC, the main part published by Ricardo Caminos in 1956. There is little information on their provenance; in content, northern themes are prominent, centred on the Fayum, but in 1913 Vladimir Golenischeff published a reference to part of a large group of papyrus fragments acquired 'autrefois' in Luxor. Although purchased at Luxor, the group has no archaeological context, and therefore, despite the Egyptological tradition of accepting a probable provenance, its provenance is not yet known (cf Malek 1999, xvii). An alternative to Thebes may seem an unlikely and unnecessary suggestion for organic material such as papyri, but manuscripts were early in the nineteenth century a prize for collectors, and already in 1895 local movement of antiquities is attested within a region: Petrie purchased at Quft a stela fragment set up in the Second Intermediat Period at Dendera (UC 14326, purchase recorded in the Petrie 'Journal' published by Adams 2002, see there pp.9 and 11). By 1913 it might not be surprising to find antiquities moving across regions between major sale centres, notably from Giza and Cairo to Luxor or vice versa: in 1912 an excavation worker from Quft brought an inscribed block from there to Petrie at Hawara in 1912, (UC 14481+14581, Petrie 1912, 36). Therefore, the precise year of acquisition and the specific history of the antiquities trade need more detailed research from the literary studies circle, in both London and Moscow. Whether from Thebes or from Memphis, or from another site, the survival of a group of papyri of late 18th to early 19th Dynasty date is unparalleled, and requires comment. Post-Amarna Period burials tended to exclude daily life objects (Grajetzki 2003, 90-91), though there are exceptions down to the early reign of Ramses II, and the Sennedjem ostracon with a copy of the Tale of Sanehat would provide a closely contemporary parallel for a literary composition among burial equipment at that date (Toda translation by Daressy 1920, 154, recording also cubit measure, wooden staff with name of Sennedjem, and a pair of reed sandals, confirming the presence of objects 'of daily life' alongside the objects made for the burial). The other possibility is that the group was found on a settlement site; however, at such sites papyri survive, where at all, substantially less well, and, though fragmentary, the Moscow literary papyri amount to far more than has been found at the extant dry late 18th Dynasty town sites (Amarna and Gurob). Again, the date of acquisition might provide circumstantial evidence towards pinpointing findplace.
As objects of daily life, they might have been placed in the tomb in either Thebes or Saqqara at that date, but there is no archaeological context recorded for the group. I know of no parallel for the inclusion of literary papyri among late Eighteenth to Nineteenth Dynasty burial goods, but contemporary grave assemblages might include other writing-surfaces bearing literary compositions: a large ostracon with part of the tale of the Exile of Sanehat is listed alongside a cubit rod and sandals in the inventory of finds from the tomb of Sennedjem, early 19th Dynasty, Cairo CG 25216, and so presumably came from the burial-chamber (list by Toda, most accessibly reproduced by Daressy 1920, 154). The manuscripts are in Moscow where not otherwise stated:

1. eulogy of the king as hunter (identified by first editor as separate compositions 'Sporting King', 'Fishing and Fowling': for the tentative identification as a single composition, see Part Two, Section Three)
2. a mythological narrative (a composition datable to the New Kingdom by the vocabulary, according to Korostovtsev 1960a)
3. copy of the Tale of Sanehat (Sinuhe)
4. copy of the Teaching of Ptahhotep (more substantial portions in British Museum EA 10509)
5. copy of the Teaching for king Merykara

As there is no context for the acquisitions, it is not possible to determine whether other manuscripts of the same or other content categories might have been in the same group.

Group Five: one or more sets of books from Ramesside Memphis
In the 1820s the collector Sallier in Aix-en-Provence and a European diplomat in Egypt, Giovanni Anastasi, acquired literary manuscripts linked by the names of the copyists and by the contents to one another and to the cemeteries of Memphis at Saqqara. A papyrus belonging around the same time to one Madame D'Orbiney is linked to the group on the same grounds. All these manuscripts are now preserved in the British Museum.

1. Papyrus Anastasi 1, a copy of the Late Egyptian 'Satirical Letter' (British Museum EA 10247)

2. Papyrus Anastasi 2, 3, 4, 5, 6, didactic excerpts and hymns ('Late Egyptian Miscellanies': British Museum EA 10243, 10246, 10249, 10244, 10245)
3. Papyrus Anastasi 7, copy of the Middle Egyptian 'Hymn to the Nile flood' (British Museum EA 10222)
4. Papyrus Anastasi 8 and 9, copies of formal letters (British Museum EA 10248)
5. Papyrus D'Orbiney, sole copy of the Late Egyptian 'Tale of the Two Brothers' (British Museum EA 10183)
6. Papyrus Sallier 1, copy of the Middle Egyptian 'Teaching of king Amenemhat I', and sole copy of the Late Egyptian 'Tale of the Quarrel of the rulers Seqenenra Taa and Apepi' (British Museum EA 10185)
7. Papyrus Sallier 2, copy of the Middle Egyptian 'Teaching of king Amenemhat I', 'Teaching of Khety', and 'Hymn to the Nile flood' (British Museum EA 10182)
8. Papyrus Sallier 3, copy of the narrative eulogy of Ramses II at the Battle of Qadesh (British Museum EA 10181)
9. Papyrus Sallier 4, on one side a 'Calendar of Lucky and Unlucky Days', on the other side didactic excerpts and hymns ('Late Egyptian Miscellanies') (British Museum EA 10184)

Without further information on the archaeological context of the find or finds, it is not now possible to determine whether these manuscripts all came from a single burial, or other context (Spalinger 2002, 106-133 for detailed discussion of some aspects of the relationships between the manuscripts). At the date of the copies, about 1200 BC, daily life objects were generally no longer included in burials (Grajetzki 2003). Therefore it is perhaps more likely that the papyri were deposited in some other manner, perhaps in a sealed pottery jar buried in a dry place for safe-keeping (the means by which the Tomb Robbery Papyri were preserved a century later, Grandet 1994, volume 1, 4-10, and compare Group Seven below).

Group Six: a set of manuscripts from Ramesside Deir el-Medina

The following papyri from Deir el-Medina, now preserved in the French Institute, Cairo, in the Ashmolean Museum, Oxford, in the Chester Beatty Library and Gallery, Dublin, and in the British Museum, are generally now considered to derive from a single find (Pestman 1982).

1. Papyrus Chester Beatty 1, sole copy of the Late Egyptian 'Tale of Horus and Seth', and of a group of Late Egyptian love songs (preserved in Dublin)
2. Papyrus Chester Beatty 2, sole copy of the Late Egyptian 'Tale of Truth and Falsehood' (British Museum EA 10682)
3. Papyrus Chester Beatty 3, sole copy of a Dream Book, on other side a copy of the narrative eulogy of Ramses II at the Battle of Qadesh (British Museum EA 10682)
4. Papyrus Chester Beatty 4, hymns and didactic excerpts (British Museum EA 10684)
5. Papyrus Chester Beatty 5, copy of the Middle Egyptian 'Hymn to the Nile flood', and didactic excerpts (British Museum EA 10685)
6. Papyrus Chester Beatty 6, prescriptions and incantations for good health (British Museum EA 10686)
7. Papyrus Chester Beatty 7, 8 incantations for good health (British Museum EA 10687, 10688)
8. Papyrus Chester Beatty 9, copy of the Offering Ritual for Amun in the name of king Amenhotep I, and on other side incantations for good health (British Museum EA 10689)
9. Papyrus Chester Beatty 10, aphrodisiacs (British Museum EA 10690)
10. Papyrus Chester Beatty 11, incantations for good health including the Tale of Isis and Ra, and a hymn to Amun (British Museum EA 10691)
11. Papyrus Chester Beatty 12, 13, 14, 15 incantations for good health (British Museum EA 10692, 10693, 10694, 10695)
12. Papyrus Chester Beatty 16, incantation for purity (British Museum EA 10696)
13. Papyrus Chester Beatty 17, excerpts from the Late Egyptian 'Satirical Letter' (British Museum EA 10697)
14. Papyrus Chester Beatty 18, didactic excerpts and incantations for good health (British Museum EA 10698)
15. Papyrus Chester Beatty 19, copy of the Teaching of Khety (British Museum EA 10699)
16. Papyrus Ashmolean, the will of a woman named Niutnakht (completed by Papyrus IFAO Deir el-Medina 2, part of the Will of Niutnakht)

The papyri in the French Institute of Oriental Archaeology, Cairo expand the contents of the group to include personal letters and accounts documents, including the following:

1. Papyrus IFAO Deir el-Medina 1, copy of the New Kingdom 'Teaching of Any', and on other side incantations for good health
2. Papyrus IFAO Deir el-Medina 3 -16, 21-22, letters
3. Papyrus IFAO Deir el-Medina 17, list of bronze tools

From the French Institute records, it seems that the bulk of these manuscripts were retrieved in 1928 during the excavations by that institute at Deir el-Medina. However, it is not certain that all items derive from that one find.

Further research into the genealogies involved is needed, to reconstruct the history of this group of papyri. However, from the research by Posener and Pestman broadly it seems that in the late 19th Dynasty (late 13th century BC), the literary papyri in this group were collected, and some compositions copied, by a member of elite officialdom, a man called Qenherkhepshef, Secretary to the Project for the King's Tomb (Pestman 1982). The title designates the head accountant for the teams cutting, plastering and drafting designs on the walls of the tomb of the reigning king in the Valley of the Kings (Černý 1973, 225-230). Over the next century his successors began to add documentary papyri (accounts, legal documents, letters), and to tear rectangular sections from the literary books for reuse as writing material for such documents. The group may have been stored in a tomb-chapel, before being moved to their final resting-place; it has been suggested that they are the books mentioned in the following private letter of the 12th century BC, from Thutmose, another Secretary to the Project for the King's Tomb to his son and assistant Butehamun (after Wente 1990, 191, from papyrus British Museum EA 10326, lines recto, line 19- verso, line 1):

ḫr nḥ.k r mdw r-ḏd	Now you wished to say,
tw.ỉ ꜥnḫ.kwỉ r tꜣ mdw	"I am alive to the matter of the
n nꜣ sšw nty wꜣḥ tꜣ ꜥt r-ꜥ rdwy	writings which were placed in the staircase chamber".
ḫr m-dỉ nꜣ sšw ỉ.ḥw tꜣ pt r.w	Well, about the writings that were rained on
m tꜣ ꜥt n sš ḥr-šrỉ pꜣy.ỉ	in the chamber of the scribe Horsheri of my family,
ỉw.k ỉn.w r-bnr	you brought them out,
ỉw.n gm.w r-ḏd bw pwy ft	and we found that they hadn't been washed off -
ỉw.ỉ ḏd n.k ỉw.ỉ sfḫ.w ꜥn	I told you I would untie them again.
ỉw.k ỉnt.w r-ẖry	You brought them down below,
ỉw.n wꜣḥ m tꜣ ꜥt	and we placed (them) in the chamber
mꜥḥꜥt ỉmn-nḫt pꜣy.ỉ ỉt	of the chapel of Amennakht my forefather.
nḥt.k r-ḏd tw.ỉ ꜥnḫ.kwỉ	And you wished to say "I am alive (to it)".

Group Seven: three Third Intermediate Period books from el-Hiba

In 1891 the Russian Egyptologist Vladimir Golenischeff acquired a group of Third Intermediate Period papyri at Cairo, said to have been found together in a pottery jar at el-Hiba (cited from the 1897 publication by Golenischeff, in Korostovtsev 1960b, 5-6: 'shortly before my arrival in Egypt in the autumn of 1891, some fellahin near the settlement of el-Hiba facing thc town of Fashn in Upper Egypt found a large pottery vessel containing several ancient Egyptian papyrus rolls ... On closer inspection of the fragments it became clear that they originally belonged to three separate manuscripts'). They are now preserved in the Pushkin Museum of Fine Arts, Moscow:

1. sole copy of a Late Egyptian 'Tale of Wenamun' (Papyrus Pushkin 120)
2. sole copy of a Late Egyptian 'Literary Letter of Lament' (Papyrus Pushkin 127)
3. best-preserved surviving copy of the wordlist the 'Onomasticon of Amenemope' (Papyrus Pushkin 169: see below Question Four, for an outline of the contents)

It is not recorded whether the find was made in the town, or in the cemeteries of el-Hiba. The site marked the Residence of the Libyan generals who ruled Upper Egypt under the Twenty-first Dynasty (1070-945 BC). The survival in a pottery vessel finds a close parallel in the ancient references to the Tomb Robbery Papyri as being stored in a jar (Grandet 1994, volume 1, 5 with n.40 on p.15).

Group Eight: a set of Late Period papyri collected by Charles Wilbour

The papyri from the collections of the American traveller and scholar Charles Wilbour are now preserved in the Brooklyn Museum, New York. They include one of the largest sets of fragments thought to derive from one source; unfortunately the location and the date of acquisition of this find are unknown, and it is not certain that all items were found together. Several more substantial manuscripts were still in their original rolled condition, until their unrolling and framing in 1966. The contents indicate a substantial group of manuscripts all dating to the Late Period or Late Dynastic Period, (664-

525 or 404-343 BC, or a little later: for the earlier date of at least the literary composition, mid-sixth century BC, see Verhoeven 1999). Few of the manuscripts have yet been published. The following list is that provided by de Meulenaere 1982:

1. Ritual for the confirmation of royal power at the New Year (Brooklyn 47.218.50)
2. Compendium of sacred knowledge relating to the cities and provinces of the Delta (Brooklyn 47.218.84)
3. a Late Period literary composition, predominantly didactic (Brooklyn 47.218.135)
4. Treatise listing and defining types of serpent, with prescriptions for treating their bites (Brooklyn 47.218.138)
5. a series of incantations, with coloured illustrations (Brooklyn 47.218.156)
6. 'several medical treatises'

The date of these manuscripts is of particular importance for the history of the library in Egypt, as they appear to date to one century or more before the founding of the great library at Alexandria. Therefore they convey some impression of the scope of collections of writings, and the systematicity of writing, in Egyptian, that would have been in existence at the time that Ptolemy I and II created the Greek-language library in their new city.

Group Nine: a group of books from a Roman Period building in Tanis

In 1884 Flinders Petrie uncovered on the eastern side of the great temple at Tanis a structure which he labelled 'House 35', and identified as a private house, full of objects and papyri (Petrie 1885: 41-50, frontispiece and pl.12, nos.12, 39-40). Despite the Delta damp, fragments of about 150 manuscripts on papyrus paper had been preserved by carbonisation, from a fire that had destroyed the quarter in the mid- to late second century AD. Petrie seems to have recorded no plan of the building, and the correct identification of the building remains uncertain. The objects range across all categories, from two burnishers in semi-precious stones to a statue in mixed Greek-Egyptian style inscribed in demotic for a man named Ashaikhet (misread initially as 'Bakakhuiu', giving rise to the misnaming of the find as 'the house of Bakakhuiu'). Most of the objects are now in the British Museum. The combined evidence has never been assessed in detail: is this a centre of production, such as a temple workshop, or the remains of the contents of a rich household of the late second century AD?

The manuscripts are now preserved in the British Library, except for two in the British Museum; only the two in the British Museum have been published, one with a hieroglyphic sign and word list as the 'Tanis Sign Papyrus' (British Museum EA 10672), and the other with a tabulation of religious knowledge as the 'Tanis Geographical Papyrus' (British Museum EA 10673). The others are only known, along with information on the archaeological context, from the publication references:

> 'This house stood over a large underground cellar without windows, which was reached by a staircase from the ground-floor rooms. These steps descended first toward the north, then stopping at a flat landing another flight descended to the south, on the east side of the upper flight. This lower flight had a cupboard opening on to it, which was formed in the wall beneath the upper flight. In this cupboard the waste papyri were stowed in baskets along with other rubbish, as brown jars, and a piece of bronze.' (Petrie 1885: 41)

> 'Of the papyri found, but little has been yet read. There were about a hundred and fifty saved from this house; they appear to have been all waste papers, roughly shoved into six plaited baskets, without any care or order. They are of all kinds - hieroglyphic and hieratic, with vignettes and rubrics, fine uncial Greek, demotic memoranda, receipts, and legal papers of various sorts; some rolls, some documents of a few columns, some mere scraps of a few lines. The rolls have been flattened and crushed by the other papers, the folded slips have been twisted across, and the whole has served as a nest for mice, who have brought in almonds and hazel nuts, the broken shells of which I found amid the documents. Unhappily most of the basketfulls had been burnt to white ash in the conflagration of the house; but about a quarter of the whole bulk remains, reduced to black tinder, but still legible. The greater part of this, however, is made up of fragments of larger rolls, and nearly all the papyri have suffered more or less by cracking to pieces at the folds. Bad as is the condition of these remains, yet it is far better than if they had not been burnt, as in the neighbouring house some unburnt examples were found which have so completely rotted from damp that they fall to powder with the gentlest handling. We cannot hope to obtain better papyri than these thoroughly-burnt examples from such a wet district as San. That these papyri are of various ages is shown by the names that have been already observed - Hadrian, the Emperor Titus, and on a demotic papyrus one of the Ptolemies.' (Petrie 1885: 42)

'In the house of Bakakhuiu nothing from Greece or Italy was found; the only foreign influence was Syrian, and the papyri were nearly all demotic, only a small proportion being in Greek, such as would naturally accrue in course of business.' (Petrie 1885: 46)

'The best preserved papyri are stiff, with a shiny surface, as if blackleaded; the ink is black, or yellowish where it was originally red. They have been thoroughly charred; most in fact have had the largest part burnt away. All, except two, are from the house of Bakakhuiu, whose numerous rolls contained religious as well as legal texts. Some were, perhaps, connected with the plans of a new or restored temple. The geographical and other lists in the papyrus, which Mr. Petrie has copied (No. 103), with the scraps of a similar one (nos.130 and 131), where the entries of nomes, feasts, marshlands, etc., are corrected by notes in minute hieratic at the foot, and especially the columns of hieroglyphics in papyrus 118, in which the gods grant divine gifts to a king or emperor, whose cartouche is unfortunately left blank, seem as if they were sketches and notes to be expanded on some temple-wall at Tanis.' (Griffith and Petrie1889: 2; the plates indicate that the 'Sign Papyrus' was Papyrus No.80, and on p.3 it is confirmed that it too 'was found in the house of Bakakhuiu').

Group Ten: the Library of Tebtunis Temple in the Roman Period?

In 1931 Carlo Anti discovered in a cellar of structures at the temple enclosure wall at Tebtunis in the Fayum a great mass of papyrus manuscripts; many from the same find were acquired by contemporary collectors (Osing 1998, 19-23). Items excavated by Anti are preserved in Florence, and the larger part of the remainder is in Copenhagen; a joint project with an international editorial board now oversees the publication of the documents.

The manuscripts are in Egyptian scripts (hieroglyphic, hieratic and demotic) and in Greek, and date principally to the second century AD; they may have become waste paper by the time of their deposition in the third century AD. They provide a detailed impression of the contents of a temple library in the latest period at which Egyptian scripts were still in regular use.

It is estimated that the find comprised remnants of around five hundred manuscripts:

- about 300 demotic, mainly literary compositions and treatises
- about 100 in hieratic, mainly relating to cult and religious knowledge
- about 50 hieroglyphic manuscripts, all in particularly fragmentary condition
- about 50 Greek papyri, mainly private documents, some temple accounts, giving a date range from about 27 BC to AD 210.

The painstaking task of editing and publishing these fragmentary manuscripts is already transforming modern appreciation of ancient Egyptian writing and knowledge in the Roman Period. The documents published or cited in preliminary reports so far include the following extensive and important manuscripts:

1. 1 hieratic and demotic astronomical treatise
2. 1 hieratic copy of the 'Book of the Fayum' with hymns to Sobek
3. 3 copies (2 hieratic, 1 hieroglyphic) of the same tabulation of religious knowledge as in the 'Tanis Geographical Papyrus' (Osing 1998; Osing and Rosati 1998)
4. 1 hieratic copy of an extended version of a word-list (nouns and verbs) and parts of the tabulation of religious knowledge (Osing 1998)
5. 1 hieratic copy of a related collection of sacred knowledge with sets of words, dominated in its surviving condition by lists of deities (Osing 1998)
6. 2 hieratic copies of the daily cult of Sobek lord of Bedenu (PSI I.70 and Papyrus Carlsberg 307) (Osing and Rosati 1998)
7. 2 hieroglyphic copies of inscriptions on the walls and facades of tomb-chapels from 2000 BC at Asyut (PSI I.3 and PSI I.4) (Osing and Rosati 1998)
8. 1 hieratic copy of a mythological manual of nomes in hieratic (PSI I.72) (Osing and Rosati 1998)
9. 1 hieratic copy of a manual of a 'pure-priest of Sekhmet' (PSI I.73) (Osing and Rosati 1998)
10. 17 of the 40 or more extant copies of the 'Book of the Temple', a treatise on the architecture of the ideal temple, and the titles and duties of its staff (cited in Quack 2000)

Categories of content within groups of books

Despite the inadequate documentation on the circumstances of discovery, the small numbers of manuscripts in Groups One to Eight, and the minute size of this sample when set against a timespan of three thousand years, these groups provide our only direct source for information on the kinds of content assembled within one 'reading space' at different periods. The content for the earlier groups may be summarised as follows, for reconsideration below under Question Four, in the discussion of ancient reception:

Middle Kingdom groups of books

Group One: literary (tales, laments)

Group Two: literary (tales, laments), ritual (Sobek hymns, funerary liturgy, statue ritual), wordlist ('onomasticon'), healing (prescriptions, incantations); note too the secondary presence of administrative content either reused or as later minor jottings

New Kingdom groups of books

Group Three: mathematical, healing (treatments, prescriptions)

Group Four: literary (eulogies, tales, didactic teachings, reflective teachings)

Group Five: literary (satirical, teachings among miscellanies, reflective teachings, Qadesh kingship eulogy), religious literary (calendar of lucky and unlucky days, hymn to Nile Flood, hymns among miscellanies), copies of letters

Group Six: literary (satirical, tales, Qadesh kingship eulogy, teachings, reflective teachings, love songs), healing (prescriptions, incantations), legal, letters, administrative; note too the apparently secondary presence of a Dream Book reused for copying a literary composition on the back (Papyrus Chester Beatty III) and of a ritual reused for healing incantations

Third Intermediate Period and Late Period groups of books

Group Seven: literary (tales, laments), wordlist ('onomasticon')

Group Eight: ritual, healing, literary (teaching), knowledge compendium

Allowing for the chronically imperfect documentation, Group Three contains treatises only, while Groups One and Four are exclusively literary in the present state of our knowledge. These groups provide, then, some evidence for the conscious ancient separation of content, already implicit in the different manner of laying out the written content on manuscripts. The other groups present varying combinations of content, to be researched.

Survival of Middle Kingdom literary books outside Groups One and Two

In order to appreciate the archaeologically fragmentary character of the surviving record, it is worth noting in addition to the Groups just how few other books have survived. For one pair of papyri, a common provenance has been proposed (Papyrus Prisse, with the Teachings for Kagemni and of Ptahhotep, and Papyrus Hermitage 1115, with the Tale of the Shipwrecked Official). Otherwise all books survive as sets of fragments:

Uncertain origin, perhaps from tombs:

Papyrus British Museum EA 10371+10435 (Teaching of Ptahhotep)
Papyrus Buenos Aires (Tale of Sanehat)
Papyrus Harageh 1 (Tale of Sanehat: probably from a tomb, as the site is dominated by cemeteries)
Papyrus Lisht (one or two tales of travel: probably from a tomb, stray find)

From the large town site near Lahun

Tale of Hay (UC 32157); Tale of Horus and Seth (UC 32158 and related fragments); Tale of Neferpesdjet (UC 32156A); narrative fragments (UC 32105A, B; UC 32105E, UC 32107A; UC 32271B); didactic fragments (UC 32117C) – all reproduced in transliteration and translation in Part Two

There is also the unprovenanced letter-format sheet Papyrus Pushkin 1695 with the opening lines of two literary compositions, one on each side.

This summary covers only the Middle Kingdom survivors. In addition to these, though not a direct source for Middle Kingdom reading and writing practices, there are the copies of Middle Kingdom literary compositions on manuscripts of later date, from Second Intermediate Period to Late Period. Thanks to the later copies, several other Middle Kingdom literary compositions have survived, notably in Groups Four to Six above, from the New Kingdom. Another practice ensuring preservation of at least literary excerpts on a large scale is the Ramesside, predominantly Theban, practice of writing short passages on limestone flakes and potsherds ('ostraca'). Rarer in the extant record, but extending to early Eighteenth Dynasty and Twenty-Sixth Dynasty, are wood and plastered wood writing-boards, stone writing-tablets, and larger fragments of jars or entire pottery vessels. Several compositions survive only through these later and more partial sources.

Question Two: Definition
What is literature 1800 BC?

As outside Egyptology, the term 'literature' is sometimes applied to all self-conscious use of language (cf Jasnow 2002), sometimes restricted to a narrow set of compositions, principally tales, teachings and laments (cf Parkinson 1996b, 302). Whereas the definition of 'literature' remains contentious, the literary book has a rather clearer profile in ancient Egypt, as a category of manuscript with distinctive physical appearance. Therefore, the literary book and its contents authorise our pursuit of the narrower definition, if only on material grounds. Changes to the scope of contents within this materially distinct category over time encourage us to question its definition against its written, as well as its indirectly attested oral, contemporaries at each period, in the spirit of the 'open canon' proposed by Edward Said (Gorak 1991).

On the criteria for defining literature

- function, form, content within the margins of the literary book

Among the wide range of implicit and explicit criteria for defining literature, and perhaps in part as a means of rationalising the ways in which Egyptologists treat the content deemed 'literary', in his recent authoritative summary Antonio Loprieno offers the flexible definitional criteria of fictionality, intertextuality, and reception (Loprieno 1996). Previously, an implicit evaluation of content probably underlies the manner in which, from the mid-nineteenth century, Egyptologists have regularly labelled certain compositions as 'literary'. If the literary book, rather than the composition, is the prime separable category, the question of definition becomes more tangibly, what is distinctive about the content of these manuscripts. Below, the definition of the 'literary' is considered briefly under the headings of function, form and content, though clearly none of these is likely to lead to a definition to the exclusion of the others. Rather than imposing a single criterion, a modern reader/researcher might seek instead to locate a particular composition, or a particular category such as 'literary book', or a particular genre such as 'narrative literature', on the more fluid and socially-assessed spectrum from least to most self-conscious communication. For the communicated words operate within an intersubjective and so intricate relational field both in antiquity and in modernity. Throughout both those long periods, the most important activity in receiving a work as literary, and in appreciating a literature, may be the activity of reading as widely as possible both perceived literary and perceived non-literary writings. The social and political dimensions of this activity are inescapable: a reader is as much the defining agent in literature as an author, interlocked in a complicity of author and reader in establishing literary circles (Morse 1984). Literary history is therefore embedded in, or an aspect of, social history.

Content

Defining Ancient Egyptian literature is part of a wider modern reception of ancient written communication. It depends on the breadth of reading by the modern receiver, and this depends in turn on the proportion of surviving writing. Despite the very small number of surviving compositions perceived as literary, content is the first criterion especially for implicit definitions of literature, and individual compositions can be grouped by content both within a general field of literary composition, and against an external field of non-literary composition. Shared theme, vocabulary, and mode can be used to delineate provisionally separated groups of compositions as Tales, Teachings, and Laments, and to divide further the Teachings into those dominated by the imperative ('didactic Teachings'), and those with higher proportion of description ('reflective Teachings'). As with form (below), content or generic mode alone fails to define a literary terrain: narrative is found in legal documents as well as in 'compositions written with the primary function *to be read*'. From the recent excavations by Dieter Arnold at Dahshur, James Allen has succeeded in reconstructing the inscription on the east external wall of the chapel of Khnumhotep as a narrative with an opening close to that of the Shipwrecked Official (presentation at a British Museum conference on the Second Intermediate Period, July 2004). At a more localised level of language, semantic intensity might be used to identify content as literary on the principle that the more information is contained within each word, the more literary the composition (cf Lotman 1970, 17-18). However, density in meaning is also an insufficient criterion when it comes to defining the distinctive content of literary manuscripts of the Middle Kingdom: hymns are semantically concentrated poems, but with a purpose – they can also be more or less strongly tied to a liturgical or other non-reading purpose – and tend to occur in hieroglyphic inscription and cursive hieroglyphic manuscript in the Middle Kingdom, rather than in the hieratic manuscripts with tales, teachings and laments. Moreover, the evaluation of content categories differs between societies, and may change radically over time. As an example of the former (difference between societies), the Thousand and One

Nights entered classical literary canons through translation into French, out of a world in which it ranked outside the accepted boundaries of the literary (Allen 2000, 169). For the second case (change in attitude within one society over time), the European reception of ancient Egyptian narrative literature provides an example of reevaluation, moving from the early publication of tales as "*contes populaires*" to the refined appraisal of the same compositions as literary masterpieces created in a royal court (e.g. Parkinson 2002).

Function

A recurrent and convenient definition would apply a binary structure of 'functional' versus 'non-functional': literary compositions would be those with no functional application, and so stand apart from all other content, from letters and accounts, to rituals for temple or festival rites, and mathematical and medical treatises. By negative definition, the literary compositions comprise the material left once such functional communication has been excluded. However, even a composition written only to be read, with no other functional daily application, bears those communicative and social functions of being read and constituting a readership. Therefore it might be more accurate to recast the definition of literature as those compositions written with the primary function of being read. This defines the category 'literature' by usage, and change in use will either broaden or narrow the terrain of literature:

- a composition may be written with functional intent, but be received as literature, perhaps in a later generation (Vernus 1996, 558-559): two celebrated examples are the triumph stela of king Kamose, with hieroglyphic inscription to perpetuate the kingship of his reign, copied within a century in hieratic on writing boards apparently as examples of fine composition (Smith and Smith 1976); and the kingship eulogy celebrating the narrow escape of Ramses II at the Battle of Qadesh, copied on papyrus at both Memphis and Thebes later in the Nineteenth Dynasty, see Spalinger 2002)
- a composition may be written primarily 'to be read', that is 'as literature', but be copied in order to instruct apprentices in spelling or style, that is 'as teaching copies': the only clear examples of this practice known to me are the Nineteenth Dynasty sherds from the Ramesseum that bear neat proficient copies of Middle Kingdom compositions on one side, and large signs in untrained hands on the other side (not generally noted in the first edition, but cf Spiegelberg 1898, pl.10, no.84): however, the scrawled signs have not yet been identified as efforts at rendering precisely the same text as the neat copies on the same sherds, and therefore it remains an assumption that the ostraca imply use of literary compositions in schooling

The role of exemplary verbal communication in teaching tends to undermine a rigidly functional definition of literature. In ancient Egyptian 'teachings', 'freedom from function' is as doubtful as 'fictionality': the teaching places emphasis on didactic function, and there is no clear means of assessing whether the ancient audience received the teachings as 'fictional' (that is, whether they thought, for example, that the Teaching of Ptahhotep was *not* a collection of sayings originating in the reputation of a high official from a bygone age – or whether this question was important to the ancient audience). Any words exemplifying a socially endorsed talent or quality may play a role in the continual construction of social boundaries, and so the main function of literature may be to keep social classes distinct. In this vein, for modern European literatures the relation between literary canon and educational programme may be problematised, with regard to the maintenance of social barriers in stratified societies. The formula for criticism might be 'literature is the set of texts you teach at school' for Bronze Age Egypt too. More broadly, the political never lags far behind the aesthetic (Bourdieu 1979, Eagleton 1990, and see below, Question Four, on the related question of the term 'propaganda' as used in Egyptology). These considerations destabilise any definition of literature (or art) as non-functional, though the compositions might perhaps be defined by the specific means used to achieve that socio-political function.

Form

The compositions thought to have been written with the primary function of being read share formal features, from material to transmission history; most are known from copies on papyrus rolls, often with a particularly calligraphic style of handwriting, and often with special framing features such as introductory or end phrases, or the red points added at rhythmic intervals above the line after the last word of a phrase ('verse points'). In transmission, many Middle Egyptian literary compositions are found first on Middle Kingdom (about 2025-1700 BC) papyri, then on New Kingdom (about 1550-1069 BC) papyri, writing boards and, sometimes abundantly, ostraca, and then more rarely if at all on Late Period (about 700-525 BC) papyri and writing boards (Quirke 1996).

The formal criteria have the advantage of including within a definition of literature some compositions that a modern reader might not privilege with the term - as in medieval literature, New Kingdom literary manuscripts may include hymns and prayers alongside didactic or lyrical passages.

Formal criteria have the disadvantage of insufficient definition: both transmission history and calligraphic writing style are paralleled for compositions with a primary function other than that of being read, as are the 'verse points' (found, for example, among New Kingdom incantations to be recited for good health) and the introductory phrase *ḥꜣt-ꜥ m* 'beginning of' (found in good health manuscripts) and final phrase *iw.f pw* 'this is its end' (first found in mid-Twelfth Dynasty funerary literature, about 1900-1850 BC). The significance of the latter has been expounded in particular by Richard Parkinson (from Parkinson 1991b, 94-96). Given the range of content united by those three formal criteria, it may be said that they contribute to a definition of Ancient Egyptian literature, rather than fixing the definition.

The layout of writing on the page provides a bridge between form and function. The selection of certain page-heights and line-spacings, and the combination of vertical and horizontal lines of writing on Middle Kingdom literary manuscripts, imply intentional difference, and also have an impact on the shapes of signs. As a result literary books constitute a category distinct from other written products, and can be recognised by their visual features even without reading the content: they look different. While literature remains relatively intangible, a narrower or broader segment on the spectrum of self-conscious writing, the literary book exists in the surviving record for the Middle Kingdom as a visually separable material product of its society.

A practical opportunity to test formal categorisation arose with the publication of very fragmentary manuscripts of assorted content, excavated at Lahun.

Categorisation in practice: Lahun Papyri

In the 1990s Mark Collier and I read through all the fragments of papyrus retrieved by the excavation under Flinders Petrie at the Middle Kingdom townsite north of al-Lahun in 1889, and now preserved in the Petrie Museum at University College London. The bulk of the collection was dominated by the almost equal use of red and black pigment, by guidelines, by names of commodities, and above all by numerals, and could therefore be identified on formal criteria and on contents as administrative accounts. As the largest category, with some of the most difficult sheet-sizes for reproduction, and some of the most broken groups of fragments from single manuscripts, these were set to one side for publication after the remainder of the collection. Among the remainder, the letters were most easily identifiable, because the writers selected sheets of varying size but distinctive disposition of writing on front and back, and because they used a small set of phrases to identify recipient and writer and to frame the blocks of words assembled to communicate a written message (Collier and Quirke 2002). With this largely homogeneous group of official and private letters extracted, almost a hundred manuscripts and manuscript fragments remained between the two blocks ‘Letters’ and ‘Administrative Accounts’. These ranged in size from reassembled rolls 35.7 cm high and 107 cm long (UC 32057) to scraps 2.1 by 2.3 cm (UC 32118A), and in content from legal testaments (UC 32037, 32058) to a narrative tale featuring the seduction of the god Horus by the god Seth (UC 32158+32148B+32150A). Medium (preeminently papyrus paper), page size, use of sheet or roll, selection of script, and formal layout (distribution of writing over a page) differ between the various categories of writing: letters, administrative accounts, offering-rituals, incantations and prescriptions for good health, legal documents, model letters, and together mathematical exercises and literary compositions. For this reason even a small Middle Kingdom papyrus fragment may usually be assigned to a particular category, as experienced with hundreds of mainly small fragments of papyri from the ancient townsite at Lahun (Collier and Quirke 2004).

In this categorising operation to publish the collection, then, the formal criteria offered a starting-point for identifying ancient categories of content, in combination always with an assessment of the word-content, from all available parallels for each individual feature. As an example, in the case of one tiny fragment, UC 32118A, both the hieroglyphic forms of individual signs and the frame of horizontal and vertical lines can be paralleled among better-preserved Middle Kingdom manuscripts where the content involves the securing of good health (so-called ‘medical’ or health manuscripts), and both are absent or rare in other categories. The single surviving phrase *ḏd.ḫr.k* ‘you should say’ is common in those manuscripts, whereas it is absent in the surviving legal documents, and relatively scarce in other categories such as literary narratives. However, given its diminutive size, the categorisation of UC 32118A under ‘health manuscripts’ remains highly uncertain: at a later date, religious manuscripts and especially funerary religious papyri are much more common, and the formal criteria and written content would be equally at home there. The ascription to this ‘medical’ category rather than the closely-related category of religious writing depends on our assessment not only of the fragment and the categories, but of the whole corpus of writing at Lahun, where funerary papyri are absent. A combination of formal criteria seemed decisive: the frame of vertical and horizontal lines is not securely attested for written signs on this scale at this period, whereas it is attested for a slightly larger Lahun fragment, UC 32117E. The latter is locked more securely within the circle of 'health manuscripts' by the phrase 'every serpent' found on compositions concerning treatment of scorpion and snake bites, a necessarily prominent branch of healing in Egypt.

Lahun fragments UC 32107E+H and 32117E demonstrate the ease with which a literary manuscript may be identified. They bear the lower ends of vertical lines with hieratic signs of an expansive form not attested outside literary manuscripts: the spacing between the lines is also characteristic of extant late Middle Kingdom literary manuscripts. A red versepoint on UC 32107H reinforces the ascription to the literary category. These are striking instances of formal categorisation, for scarcely more than a word can be read in any of the few preserved lines. Formal categorising can be made explicit, then, even if only for the purpose of establishing a visible category to be contested. For the Lahun papyri in the Petrie Museum, of twenty-two smaller items of uncertain grouping, most lay on the border between letters and administrative records: only three pieces were considered possibly literary (UC 32133F, measuring 5.3x3.7 cm, and two fragments in the group UC 32284, measuring 6.8x5.7 and 5.0x2.9 cm). The uncertain categorisation of the twenty-two items must be considered within its context of several thousand fragments. The operation highlighted for me the material presence of the literary book as a distinctive object category, in formal features such as the handwriting style, spacing of signs and lines, and sometimes the combination of vertical and horizontal lines for segments of writing. For each of these formal features, the closest category to literary writing would be legal writing, especially the writing of legal reports. Indeed fragment UC 32107A changed sides several times during preparations for publication, between the legal and the literary sections (it ended up in literary, and the translation as a possible 'Nakhti tale' is given below in Part Two). Legally-binding reports also share features of content with literary compositions – temporally and spatially defined plot, consequent prominence of narrative, focus on the question of truth/fictionality, and tension between plot resolution and the lack of it (cf Blumenthal 2003). The world of the law enters into the world of literature again in the discussion of readership and authorship below, as the administrative official emerges as central player.

Problems outstanding

Certain compositions defy function-led categorisation, reflecting the small scale of manuscript survival. Eulogies and hymns might have been composed for performance: the Hymn to the Nile Flood and the eulogies of kings may have come to life within Nile Flood festival and palace ceremony. For that reason they belong to 'functional' categories, even though they share features of form and content with the 'narrowly literary' tales and teachings and laments (Parkinson 1999b, 187-190). However, the boundaries can be redrawn by research or new discoveries: previously considered a tale within narrowly defined literature, the extended New Kingdom Tale of Horus and Seth has been identified by Ursula Verhoeven as a written version of myth not for narration at any time of the year, but specifically in the setting of a principal annual kingship festival (Verhoeven 1996). To date, no such specific functional and temporal setting has been identified for Middle Kingdom tales, didactic and reflective teachings, and laments. These categories of content appear in the distinctive 'literary books' with their special layout as indicated above. Therefore, it seems reasonable, if conservative, at present to continue to consider these as a distinct group, as 'narrowly defined literature'. Didactic teachings may be most at risk in this literary stock, as codes of conduct for specific social roles. However, the dearth of information on schooling spares these the expulsion from the 'literary' suffered by most religious compositions. A significant factor in the differential drawing of this line is a relative modern Western antipathy to the religious, and privileging of the 'secular'. In order to keep a border open between literary and 'religious literary', on the precedent of other anthologies, I include the Hymn to the Nile Flood and two sets of fragments with eulogies of kingship, as a liminal section at the end of this volume. After some vacillation, I also include in that section the Lahun Hymns to Senusret III, even though they seem to have been composed for use in festival, to judge from layout, use of rubric, including one *inyt* 'refrain', and a broken passage perhaps describing the festival procession (UC 32157: Collier and Quirke 2004). These compositions form a bridge out to the far vaster surviving corpus of funerary literature and hymns, just as the narratives and teachings lead us into the autobiographies or 'self projections' on hieroglyphic inscriptions of the Middle Kingdom. However tightly the literary border is drawn, the words invite us out to all other ancient writings (for the broader oceans of co-text as resource for penetrating the narrow literary set, see too Question Four).

Other perspectives on Egyptian literature

Western Egyptology suffers from the Eurocentrism characteristic of all orientalist disciplines, and shares their political partisanship cloaked by the claim of academic political innocence (Said 1995). In general, current literary studies are perhaps particularly locked into European academic tradition, despite notable exceptions (e.g. Assmann and Bommas 2002 using *qala qalaun* as the motif by which to perceive one feature of Middle Kingdom funerary liturgies). Despite the historically relatively late date, and the geographically and culturally distinct homeland, classical Arabic literature and literary criticism offer a point of new departure, to check Eurocentric assumptions and rethink categories. Okasha El Daly has pointed out to me a recent contribution by Louis Baqtar to Arabic-language research into ancient Egyptian literary composition, encompassing European Egyptological tradition and Arabic translation (Baqtar n.d.). Contemporary Egyptian Egyptological presentation of ancient Egyptian literature advances us one step ahead. However, the decisive step comes after this, with the reappropriation of ancient Egyptian content by contemporary literary studies in the Arab World with their own perspectives. The Arab World, and especially modern Egyptian access to this literature can claim to be not only different, but linguistically and geographically closer than Western European reception can be: Arabic reception does not render the European contribution void, but it does promise to refresh perspectives on ancient literatures, and should encourage a greater degree of humility in Western Egyptological researches. I have never studied Arabic literature and history, and can only cite from a secondary summary such as that by Roger Allen: even from a cursory reading, several parallels seem to me particularly alluring, as points on which a European Egyptologist might wish to begin asking questions of Egyptian Egyptologists and Egyptian and European scholars in Arabic literature (Allen 2000). Classical Arabic poetry offers for certain motifs and 'genres' a resonance entirely lacking in English and other European literary traditions. The eulogy genre *madīh* allows appreciation of compositions at or outside our literary borders (Part Two, Section Three), and the *fakhr* 'boast' mercifully loses in Arabic the unfailingly negative reception assigned to much rhetorical content in English-language studies of both literary manuscript and 'autobiographical' inscriptions from ancient Egypt. A more systematic encounter with Arabic literary tradition would above all serve to remind the European researcher that the questions of definition, production, reception of ancient Egyptian literature can also be asked from within Egypt.

Question Three: Authoring
How is literature composed 1800 BC?

Problems with the words 'text' and 'author'

Like any other word, 'text' and 'author' come with the baggage of time and place. This is not avoidable, as vocabulary must always be defined by context and history. However, use of a word can become problematic, if it is prominent in a study in which its history and cultural embeddedness are not recognised. Cerquiglini 1989 challenged the contemporary instinct to assume that all writing shares properties peculiar to modern printed text, blind to the specific histories behind its production, circulation and consumption. Cerquiglini wrote in deliberately polemical, provocative vein, and reviewers raised problems with his observations (for example Varvaro 1989). The combination of polemic and reaction is productive for the researcher and reader approaching writing from pre-print societies, including ancient Egypt.

Problems with text and the phantom Urtext

1. the assumptions to which Cerquiglini objects

The philological tradition of editing ancient and medieval writing makes the assumption that there is an original stable text to be recovered, in the pristine form in which it appeared from the hand or mouth of the author. This is the 'Urtext' (rather mystical German expression for 'original text', as baneful as the Ursprache of linguistics: 'primeval text' captures the implications better perhaps). It has to be reconstructed from the copies which are all, the philologist may feel, more or less degraded by errors made in copying. However philologists make two critical unwarranted assumptions in their editing: that copyists tend to simplify (presumably having less genius than the author), and that two copyists are unlikely to make the same error at the same place (against the evidence of most school classrooms, as Cerquiglini notes, p.77).

2. objections by Cerquiglini to these assumptions

Objection: the modern concept of perfectly finished and precisely replicable work is a specific historical product of the fusion of two procedures around 1800:

1. improvements in the technology for reproduction, from early printing in 15th century Europe to advanced printing presses by 1800
2. corresponding increase in authorial control over the reproduction of image and printed word in 1790s-1800s, accompanied by new copyright laws in 1790s (cf Woodmansee 1984; Woodmansee and Jaszi 1994)

By contrast, in 11th-12th century French literature, the word textus (Latin for 'woven', and so 'finished') was only used for the Bible: by implication, the rest of literature was still being woven.

Objection: implicitly, perhaps unintentionally, the modern concept of fixed text emphasises the conservatism of writing, in fixing content. However, for Cerquiglini oral tradition is arguably far more conservative, and writing can be seen as liberating and radical.

Objection: originality is problematic as an author may produce more than one 'original version'. European critical audiences are familiar with the different versions of Macbeth and King Lear by Shakespeare, and the different versions of operas produced by Rossini and Verdi for different audiences (sometimes in different languages).

Variations may be intentional: if a particular tradition of writing is lessed fixed, the person transmitting a composition may be expected to embellish the content. When there are two versions of a phrase among the copies of a composition, the more difficult version may or may not be the original version: it cannot be assumed either that every 'more difficult reading' is the original, any more than that every 'more difficult reading' is a 'corruption' by a later copyist. Two copyists could easily make the same error in the same place, because certain linguistic sequences lend themselves to the same errors by same-language writers.

3. rejoinders to the Cerquiglini objections

It is correct to search for the original context and for variations in the value placed on originality, embellishment, and faithful reproduction of any original; however, it cannot be denied that ancient and medieval copyists at least sometimes strove to reproduce at least some compositions as exactly as possible, because they record in explicit terms their faithfulness in copying.

It is correct to emphasise that writing is not always conservative; however, any communication - spoken or written - can be deployed either to conservative or to mould-breaking ends.

Although production of manuscript originals and copies involves variations, both intentional and by error, writing does produce a single object; even if the writing is variable until 1800, the reader experiences a single, fixed copy.

4. stabilizing the reproduction of writing in ancient Egypt

There are limited sources for the method of control of manuscript copying, all from the paratext (features at the margins of the main body of a composition):

1. margin corrections occur in manuscripts with religious and literary compositions (see for example the Book of the Dead of Nu, Lapp 1997)
2. formulaic opening and concluding phrases occur in manuscripts with religious, technical (healing, mathematical) and literary compositions

The formulaic opening phrase *ḥ3t-ˁ* m 'beginning of' occurs in the literary genre of Teachings, and in religious compositions and healing treatises; this indicates ancient consciousness and emphasis that a composition had a set beginning.

The formulaic end-note *iw.f pw* 'this is its end' and longer variants occur in literary and religious compositions from the mid-Twelfth Dynasty onwards. Richard Parkinson emphasises the importance of these end-notes as markers of an ancient consciousness of the unity and integrity of a composition (Parkinson 1991b, 94-96; Fischer-Elfert 1996, 501). The earliest end-note to a literary manuscript is that written by Amenaa for the Tale of the Shipwrecked Official (late Middle Kingdom, Papyrus Hermitage 1115, lines 186-189):

> *iw.f pw ḥ3t.f r pḥwy.fy mi gmyt m sš*
> [*m*] *sš sš iḳr n ḏbˁw.f imny s3 imn-ˁ3 ˁnḫ wḏ3 snb*
> 'This is its end, from beginning to end as found in writing,
> [as] written by the writer excellent in his fingers, Ameny's son Amenaa, may he live, prosper and be well.'

End-notes are found in the manuscripts of Question One, Group One, and in some other preserved ends of literary manuscripts (e.g. Tale of Hay, UC 32157 verso), but not in those of Group Two: if its presence was a variable rather than a universal feature, it cannot be considered indispensable for the category 'literary manuscript'. More elaborate versions in New Kingdom funerary manuscripts assert that nothing has been added to or subtracted from the version found in writing. These demonstrate a negative consciousness of copying comparable to the negative evaluation of copying that is implicit in modern philology.

Despite this endorsement, in at least some ancient sources, of a philological preference for invariance, the degree of variation in compositions is itself a variable. It cannot always be assumed that variation equates with degradation of some perfect original. In some instances it may be, as the end-notes imply. In other instances, variation may be produced for enjoyment, much as variations on established and familiar themes are encouraged in some modern literary genres (thrillers, crime drama), in journalism, and in popular music. As in other arts including the visual arts, there may be two magnetic poles (from Lotman 1970):

1. an aesthetic of difference (where difference from other products is enjoyed - compare 'realism'/ 'portraiture' in figurative art)
2. an aesthetic of similarity (where the similarity to an ideal or to other products is the source of enjoyment - compare 'idealism' in figurative art)

Cerquiglini 1989 asserts enjoyment of variants as the essence of French medieval vernacular literature. Egyptian literary and religious compositions that may also relish variation on themes include sun hymns, eulogies of kingship, and the praises of writing in the New Kingdom, and, at all periods, autobiographical hieroglyphic inscription in narrative and in nominal and adjectival mode. Within religious corpora defined by the medium on which they survive, there may be different degrees of desired variation: the Pyramid Texts, Coffin Texts and Book of the Dead include more fixed compositions, sometimes with the end-note signifying consciousness of integrity, implying desire for less change, and the looser compositions generating ever more variations.

In sum, variation is an object for research. Copy errors form only one part of the picture. The implications of our attitudes to copyists are considered again below, in Question Four, in considering ancient reception.

Problems with authors – does the author exist?

1. the assumption to which Cerquiglini objects

Common sense dictates that every text must have its author - a single person in a single time and place.

2. objections by Cerquiglini to these assumptions

For two generations the concept of 'author' has been under heavy fire (see the English translations of seminal essays by Barthes and Foucault: Barthes 1977, Foucault 1989)

Like 'text', the modern 'author' has emerged in specific historical places and times, from the fusing of two ideological assumptions:

1. the fixed text (see above)
2. the individual genius, from Romanticism

The arrival of the computer as dominant tool in producing and copying communications has destabilised the concept of author: computer screens have taken us closer to the conditions of generating and circulating writing in the world of the manuscript.

In place of the single authorial person, place and time, there may be a looser field of writing, in which the copyist is more a participant than a passive consumer.

3. rejoinders to the Cerquiglini objections

Certainly each society and period has its own concepts of communication and creativity; however, there are medieval as well as classical Greek and Latin authors - the medieval world itself has a self-conscious author of the rank of Petrarch, and a recurrent medieval Latin theme of accessus ad auctores 'access to the authors' (Varvaro 1989: 476)

4. finding (or making?) authors in ancient Egyptian literature

There are ancient Egyptian references to personal names both within and in connection with compositions. The names are attached to literary compositions in different ways, in part apparently according to genre:

1. Teachings and Laments in the form of Teachings may have an explicit introduction such as 'Teaching made by N', or in the New Kingdom 'start of the Teaching made by N', in some instances with a name dating to a period earlier than the language in which the surviving versions of the composition are written: the Teachings of Ptahhotep and Hardedef are in Middle Egyptian, though the names belong in the Old Kingdom, period of Old Egyptian
2. Laments and Tales may begin 'There was a man called N' (Khuninpu, Neferpesdet); other compositions begin with the titles and names of one individual (Sanehat), or are dominated by one protagonist (Laments of Ipuwer and Neferty).

These named individuals are not identified as the authors in the kind of paratext taken for granted in modern book production, where title-pages, book-covers, book-spines, and library reference cards provide standardised fields for place and date of publication, names of authors, publishers and editors, titles of works etc (Genette 1987). In ancient production, the names remain instead within the composition, and therefore they leave a range of possible interpretations on the evidence of parallels from world literature. For example, a name may be that of the 'author', or it may be a literary device created by an unnamed author for specific literary effects. Both authorship and literary device seem to be acknowledged in the sources for ancient reverence for individuals whose names appear in Teachings and Laments, as outlined below.

A passage on a Ramesside manuscript sheds light on attitudes to names in compositions in at least that period of ancient Egyptian history (about 1200 BC, Papyrus Chester Beatty 4, British Museum EA 10684, verso, column 6, line 11 to column 7, line 1, published Gardiner 1935a). According to this literary passage, a certain Khety is said to have written the Teaching of king Amenemhat I for his son king Senusret I, rulers in the 20th century BC:

[wḥm?] ꜥnḫ mꜣꜣ ỉtn	[Repeating?] of life and seeing the sun-disk
n sš ẖty	for the writer Khety,
ỉw pr-ḫrw t ḥnḳt	with voice-offerings of bread and beer
m-bꜣḥ wn-nfr	before Wennefer,
ḳbḥ ỉrp mnḫt n kꜣ.f n ỉst.f	cool water, wine, cloth for his spirit and for his staff,
pꜣ ỉḳr stpw ṯsw	the one excelling in choice of phrases,
dỉ.ỉ rn.f r nḥḥ	I give his name for eternity,
mntf ỉr šfdw m sbꜣyt	It is he who made a book of the teaching

n nswt [bꞽty s]-ḥtp-ꞽb-rꜥ	of the dual [king S]ehetepibra
ꜥnḫ wḏꜣ snb	may he live, prosper and be well!
ꞽw.f ḥtp ẖnm.f ḥrt	when he set, joined the sky,
ꜥḳ[.f] m nbw ẖrt-nṯr	and entered in with the lords of the cemetery,
nꜣ [...] dꞽ.f [...]	those [...] he gives [...]
r-gs s-ḥtp-ꞽb-rꜥ	beside Sehetepibra
ꜥnḫ wḏꜣ snb	may he live, prosper be well!

This intriguing and unparalleled ancient attribution raises a range of possibilities in literary production, notably that someone might write a Teaching which bears the name of another person. This is not evidence of an intention to deceive readers into believing that someone else wrote the teaching, any more than in modern literary examples such as the Memoirs of Hadrian by Marguerite Yourcenar.

Cerquiglini cites the instance of the modern 'fabrication' of an author 'Marie de France' for the Lai de Lanval out of the phrasing within three separate medieval French compositions (Cerquiglini 1989: 49-52):

1. the start of the first of twelve songs after the Lai de Lanval on one manuscript begins 'Oez, seignurs, ke dit Marie, Ki en sun tens pas ne s'oblie'
2. the note at the end of a set of Fables records 'Me numerai pur remembrance: Marie ai num, si sui de France'
3. a passage in the Espurgatoire saint Patrice reads 'Jo, Marie, ai mis en memoire, Le livre de l'Espurgatoire'

From these disparate references the name 'Marie de France' has been created, to fill the empty slot for author of the Lai de Lanval, along with the other compositions. The layer of speculation is easily overlooked when 'Marie de France' becomes the principal means for indexing the compositions under 'author name' in library cataloguing systems and book market distribution.

This example is curiously reminiscent of the case of Khety in recent Egyptological commentary. The following evidence has been marshalled to create a modern-style author Khety:

1. Khety is said to have written the Teaching of king Amenemhat I, in the Ramesside papyrus cited above
2. in another 'hymn to writing' on the same Ramesside manuscript, translated below, names of ancient writers include Khety and he is called *pꜣy.sn tpy* 'their leader'
3. a Middle Kingdom composition now often called the Satire of Trades bears the opening phrase 'teaching made by the man of Tjaru (?) called Duau Khety'
4. several Ramesside manuscripts group the Teaching of king Amenemhat I with the Satire of Trades and a third composition, the Hymn to the Nile, and the first two are still being grouped together in the Late Period (Quack 2003)

As a result Khety has been proposed as author for all three compositions (Derchain 1996: 83-84). Although this is one possibility, all this evidence is circumstantial, and two main objections may readily be raised:

1. Khety is a popular Middle Kingdom name
2. none of the manuscripts grouping the three compositions makes any claim for or against their joint authorship, nor does any other surviving ancient source.

There is no Egyptological consensus over this ascription; in general, opinion seems sceptical (Quack 2003, 184, with nn.16-18). However, the case provides an interesting parallel to the medievalist conjuring of a Marie de France out of circumstantial evidence; this similarity may reveal shared underlying tendencies and attitudes across the two philological disciplines, the study of ancient and of medieval manuscripts. Are modern readers, including researchers, desperate for an author? What in modern ideology lends urgency to the quest for authors?

A single ancient Egyptian attitude to names in compositions is difficult to construct from the fragmentary evidence. In the 'hymn to writing' on Papyrus Chester Beatty 4 (translated with discussion below), persons named in Teachings, such as Ptahhotep, appear alongside Khety, identified elsewhere on the same manuscript as author of the Teaching of Amenemhat I (see above). At first glance, this seems to be a mingling of 'real' and 'fictive' writings (see the commentary by Assmann 1996: 75-76). No definitive solution can be proposed: among the range of possibilities, it might be suggested that two routes to immortality by writing were identified:

1. a writer achieved immortality by writing down, and being known to have written a composition, whether or not his name appeared within it (this seems to be the Ramesside Period understanding of the Teaching of Amenemhat I 'by Khety')
2. all Teachings derive from collections of sayings and/or writings ascribed to named individuals, and all these individuals achieve immortality when their Teachings have been written down

(whether by themselves or by others) and are being copied and recited, rather as Socrates achieves immortality today through Plato

However, this is a modern rationalisation of the evidence. Other possibilities, including multiple and mutually exclusive attitudes to authorship, need to be considered. Researchers and readers need to remain aware of the range of possible relations between named individual and written composition. These should be considered in connection with the range of possibilities from fixed to loose composition ('text'). Content offers a more secure object of study for modern research, than the elusive author.

Reverence for individuals whose names appear in literary compositions

From the Ramesside Period, two manuscripts and one inscribed relief provide the most explicit ancient evidence for reverence of men to whom Teachings are ascribed (recent discussion of all three in Fischer-Elfert 2003). These contribute to understanding the ancient Egyptian sense of name in relation to composition. However, this is not an ancient version of the modern ideology of authorship. The difference between the ancient and modern understanding of 'author' can be seen in the New Kingdom papyrus specifying a man named Khety as the person commissioned by Senusret I to write the Teaching of Amenemhat I, cited above in the discussion of problems involved in automatic application of the word 'author'. In relation to that source, there is no evidence as to whether the Middle Kingdom audience believed the Teaching to have been written by Amenemhat I or by Khety.

The three Ramesside sources

1. the eulogy of writers in a 19th or 20th Dynasty series of short compositions (British Museum EA 10684, Papyrus Chester Beatty 4, published Gardiner 1935a)

One in a group of Ramesside manuscripts from Deir el-Medina, this book-roll bears the longest surviving ancient Egyptian passage in praise of writing and writers as the safest means of ensuring immortality. It occurs within a larger composition urging an apprentice to persevere with writing, in the tradition of the Teaching of Duau Khety (Satire of Trades). According to this passage, whereas offering-chapels and families may not survive a thousand years, a writer is kept alive by his writings. This is not exactly the same as bodyless immortality of the name, where immortal existence consists of the memory of a person among others. The ancient Egyptian belief in immortality included the belief that the dead needed food and drink, and this was provided by the recital of the 'offering formula': the passage below reveals the concern that monuments might be destroyed, and families and friends might not be present in future generations, and that therefore individuals required a wider audience to pronounce the offering formula for their names.

In Egyptology the passage is celebrated in particular for its list of famous names from the past, associated with writings (Paragraph 7 below, cf Fischer-Elfert 2003, 125-127). Of eight names, up to five are known from surviving compositions (Teachings of Hordedef and Ptahhotep; Khety perhaps from the Satire of Trades and/or the Teaching of Amenemhat I; Khakheperraseneb from excerpts on one source; Prophecy of Neferty).

Papyrus Chester Beatty 4 (British Museum EA 10684), verso, column 2, line 5 to column 3, line 11 after Gardiner 1935a, I, 38-39 with II, pl.18-19

The divisions into paragraphs follow the stanza-lengths indicated by rubric in the original.

Paragraph 1

ỉw swt ỉr ỉrr.k nn	**If you would only accomplish this,**
ỉw.k *šsꜣ.tỉ n sšw*	**becoming** expert in writing:
ỉr nꜣ n sšw rḫyt	Those writers of knowledge
ḏr rk ḫprt ḥr-sꜣ nṯrw	from the time of events after the gods,
nꜣ n sry ỉ.ỉyt.s	those who foretold the future,
ḫpr rn.sn mn r nḥḥ	their names have become fixed for eternity,
st šmt skm.sn ꜥḥꜥ.sn	though they are gone, they have completed their lifespan,
smḫm hꜣw.sn nb	and all their kin are forgotten.

Paragraph 2

bw ỉr.n.sn *mrw m ḥmty*	**They did not make for themselves** a chapel of copper,
wḏ ỉry m bỉꜣ n pt	or a stela for it of iron from the sky.
bw rḫ.sn wꜣḥ ỉwꜥt	They did not manage to leave heirs,
m ẖrdw[.sn] ḥr dmw rn.sn	from their children, to pronounce their names,
ỉr.n.sn ỉwꜥt m sšw	but they have achieved heirs out of writings,
m sbꜣyt ỉrw	out of the teachings in those.

Paragraph 3

__di n.sn__ [mḏꜣt] m ẖry-ḥbt
ꜥꜥnw m sꜣ-mr.f
sbꜣyt nꜣy.sn mr
pꜣ ꜥr pꜣy.sn šri
sꜣ inr n st ḥmt
m šꜣꜥ m wr r kty dit r msw.f
r sš ntf pꜣy.sn tpy

They are given the book as ritual-priest,
The writing-board as loving-son.
Teachings are their chapels,
the writing-rush their child,
and the block of stone the wife.
From great to small, (all) are given as his children,
for the writer, he is their leader.

Paragraph 4

__iry.tw n ꜥꜣ ḥwt__ st fẖ
ḥmw-kꜣ.sn m iwt
iw nꜣy.sn wḏ ḥsꜣw m iwtn
is.sn smẖm
dm.tw rn.sn ḥr nꜣy.sn šfdw
irw ḏr wnn.sn nfrw
sẖꜣ.f irt st n ḥnty r nḥḥ

The doors of their chapels are undone,
Their ka-priests have gone.
Their tombstones are smeared with mud,
their tombs are forgotten,
but their names are read out on their scrolls,
written when they were young.
Being remembered makes them, to the limits of eternity.

Paragraph 5

__irt sš imi sw m ib.k__
ḫpr rn.k m mitt
ꜣḫ šfdw r wḏ
m ḳd r inhꜣt smn.ti
irt nn ḥwt.w mrw
n ib n dm rn.sn
smwn r.f ꜣḫ m ẖrt-nṯr
rn m r n rmt

Be a writer - put it in your heart,
and your name is created by the same.
Scrolls are more useful than tombstones,
than building a solid enclosure.
They act as chapels and chambers,
by the desire of the one pronouncing their name.
For sure there is most use in the cemetery
for a name in the mouths of men.

Paragraph 6

s ꜣḳ ẖꜣr.f m iwtn
hꜣw.f nb ms n tꜣ
in sš r dd sẖꜣ.tw.f
m r n dd n r
ꜣḫ šfdw r pr ḳd
r ḥwt ḥr imntt
nfr st r bḫnw
grg r wḏ m ḥwt-nṯr

A man is dead, his corpse is in the ground:
when all his family are laid in the earth,
It is writing that lets him be remembered,
in the mouth of the reciter of the formula.
Scrolls are more useful than a built house,
than chapels on the west,
they are more perfect than palace towers,
longer-lasting than a monument in a temple.

Paragraph 7

__in iw wn dy mi__ ḥr-dd.f
in iw ky mi ii-m-ḥtp
bw ḫpr hꜣw n.n mi nfrti
ḫty pꜣy.sn tpy
di.i rḫ.k rn n ptḥ-m-ḏḥwty
ḫꜥ-ḫpr-rꜥ-snb
in iw ky mi ptḥ-ḥtp
kꜣ-ir.s m mitt

Is there anyone here like Hordedef?
Is there another like Imhotep?
There is no family born for us like Neferty,
and Khety their leader.
Let me remind you of the name of Ptahemdjehuty
Khakheperraseneb.
Is there another like Ptahhotep?
Kaires too?

Paragraph 8

__nꜣ n ḫryt srt iy__
pr m r.sn ḫpr
gm.tw m ṯsw
di n.sn msw n ktw
r iwꜥt mi ẖrdw.sn
imn.st ḥkꜣw.sn r tꜣ-tmm
šd m sbꜣyt
st šmt smẖ rn.sn
m sš r dd.tw sẖꜣ.tw.w

Those who knew how to foretell the future,
What came from their mouths took place,
and may be found in (their) phrasing.
They are given the offspring of others
as heirs as if their (own) children.
They hid their powers from the whole land,
to be read in (their) teachings.
They are gone, their names might be forgotten,
but writing lets them be remembered.

2. The second source is a sketch of men of the past, identified in cursive script alongside each figure, on a Nineteenth or Twentieth Dynasty papyrus (Papyrus Athens 1826, publication in preparation, see Fischer-Elfert 2002 for details of content, Fischer-Elfert 2003, 124 for photograph). The sketch is introduced by the following passage: 'list of the names of those excellent spirits, great officials, whose names, when placed at the neck of a rat, no cat can catch it, when placed at the neck of a bull, none can butcher it, when placed at the neck of X son of Y, no male damned, no female damned can fall on him'. This instruction may sound funerary, but the rest of the papyrus preserves words to be spoken against nightmares, and so probably the book was compiled to defend the living sleeper, rather than the dead, against misfortune; it would have been, then, a book for use in the world of the living, not a funerary amulet made for a burial. In the sketch there are twenty-two figures in two rows, the first ten standing, the rest seated on the ground. The names beside the figures are written in a very cursive hand, at several points defeating decipherment:
Standing: 1. Imhotep; 2. Hordedef; 3. Fay; 4. Item-...ef; 5. Sam-...f; 6. Ipy; 7. Djadjamankh; 8. ?; 9. Nefer; 10. Ashakhet (?);
Seated: 11. Ka?, 12. Hepu; 13. Hotep; 14. Saiset; 15. Seha or Sia?; 16. Permut?; 17. Ankhpehty or Hekauser?; 18. Ptah; 19. Khety?; 20. Sanebthut?; 21. Neferseshempen; 22. Puy
Of these, Imhotep, Hordedef and the possible Khety appeared in the praise of writing and writers in the preceding manuscript, and Djadjamankh is the name of a protagonist in a cycle of short stories set At the Court of King Khufu. The others could owe their presence in the list to their role as "great officials" rather than any role in writing; at least there is no clear connection between the names as given here and extant literary compositions.

3. The third Ramesside source is an inscribed relief block, presenting a series of figures of whom a small proportion bear names found in literary compositions. The relief is known in Egyptology as the Daressy Block, after an earlier recorder. The fragment of relief, in two blocks, preserves the lower left corner of a wall from a tomb-chapel, and in the absence of parallels it is impossible to estimate the original extent of the sequence. On the extant portion, an upper row of throned figures represented kings, but their names are lost. Below these thirteen throned individuals, two more registers present twenty-six mummiform men facing right, thirteen on each register, every figure identified by a vertical line of hieroglyphs to the right of the relevant figure. From right to left, the names are as follows:
Row 1.
Viziers: Imhotep, Iymeru, Ptahshepses, Kaires, Usermont
Greatest of Directors of Crafts (High Priests of Ptah): Ty, Ptahmes, Sehetepibraankh, Nepipu Redini, Paired, Nefertem, Sennefer, Pahemnetjer
Row 2.
Reporter Buy; Master of Distribution Sakhety; Lector Saamun; Master (Lector) Iuny; Lector Khakheperraseneb
Overseers of embalmers: Meniankhnefer, Senbef, Khafkhufu, Teti Senbef, Sekhemiah, Wadjmes, Khamhat, Rames
The two rows of named individuals are separated by a horizontal line of hieroglyphs giving titles and names of eight more individuals without depiction :
Miscellaneous titles: ..-Djehuty; Overseer of Singers Ipuwer; Greatest of Seers in the House of Ra (High Priest of Ra at Iunu/Heliopolis) Amenemipet; High Steward of Memphis Amenhotep
With title pair 'King's Secretary, Lector in the Good House': Horankh, Imhotep, It, Hor Intef
The line appears to end with a reference to the deity Amun-Ra rather than another titled official.

Of the thirty-four names on the preserved part of this unparalleled relief, three occur in the same form within stanza 7 of the roughly contemporary composition 'In praise of writers and writing' (next section below): Imhotep, Kaires and Khakheperraseneb. By emending other names (Sakhety to Khety, ..-Ra Djehuty to Ptahemdjehuty), two more might be identified in the same source. Another, Ipuwer, is found in the Middle Kingdom literary composition the Lament of Ipuwer, and another again, Amenemipet, recalls the New Kingdom Teaching of Amenemipet. However, some or all of the emendations and associations may be the result of modern interpretation anxious to overlay as much literary history as possible onto the block. Religious and administrative functions seem stronger on the relief taken as a whole, as far as it survives. The upper right series of names starts with the five viziers; then the block of eight High Priests of Ptah is aligned above the block of eight Overseers of Embalmers, and the two sets of eight figures are divided by the names of the group of four Lectors in the Good House ending the horizontal line. The dominant themes are high officialdom, presumably at Memphis, and the task of embalming (the Good House being the place of embalming), in keeping with a funerary monument from Saqqara, the burial-ground for Memphis. The majority of these names have no known literary associations, and the names Amenemipet and Imhotep are perhaps also too common to assert a specific historical literary association (note the two occurrences of the name Imhotep here, with different titles); there is an early Eighteenth Dynasty vizier Imhotep to take into account, in addition to the Third Dynasty high official assumed to be the 'literary' figure revered in the other two sources. On the other hand, Ipuwer and Khakheperraseneb seem more plausibly literary figures, because their titles do not place them in such solid blocks. In sum, the web of references woven in this group of figures needs careful decoding in order to identify the different motivations for inclusion of named title-holders and the relations between those motivations. The loss of archaeological, architectural context for the relief may otherwise lure the modern writer into asserting more literary history than the extant record can support here (so too Fischer-Elfert 2003).

On names and literary compositions: in sum ...

Either of two conclusions might be drawn from the general lack of external (paratextual) or internal data on authorship. Perhaps authorship was known to the ancient audience from general oral tradition, or from written sources that have not survived. Or else authorship was not as important to the ancient Egyptians as it is to modern audiences. In a manuscript tradition, reproduction depends on copying by hand, and this activity may undermine the closed circle of authorship. In classical Arabic literature, the culture of manuscript copy fostered a focus on *sariqat* or the ellision of one name by another, with an anxiety over the attribution of compositions to names other than their authors by plagiarism or by forgery (Kilito 1985, 24-25). Authorship finds less secure home in the manuscript. In turn, the copyists lead us into the world beyond the genesis of a composition, the world of its reception and dissemination in a society.

Question Four: Reception
How is literature received 1800 BC?

Who can read 1800 BC? Evidence for literacy as part of the history of reading

Literacy remains an elusive subject for ancient Egypt (Baines 1983; Baines and Eyre 1983; Lesko 2001). Estimates of 1-5% of the population as literate are based on the very limited available evidence. Generalisations covering the whole country, even within any one period, inevitably mask differences between regions, and, most importantly, between urban and rural populations. They may seriously underestimate the proportion of the population able to read and write in towns; low literacy estimates are a regular feature of 19th and 20th century attitudes to ancient and medieval (pre-Reformation) societies (as observed in the polemical work by Cerquiglini 1989: 35). From the late Middle Kingdom town-site at Lahun (about 1800 BC), Flinders Petrie acquired in 1889 around eighty separate groups of fragmentary papyri: these thousands of fragments represent a fraction of the written output of a town of perhaps 5,000 inhabitants across a period of perhaps five decades. Although few findspots were recorded, the papyri seem to reflect levels of literacy in both the palatial town houses of the elite, and the smaller houses covering most of the site (Gallorini 1998). The estimate of literacy in manuscript-reading and manuscript-writing for this urban population may need to be revised upwards to around 15% for the former, perhaps not so much less for the latter. The Letters to the Dead from Qau and Hu (Gardiner and Sethe 1928) present the earliest evidence for daily writing in those provinces of Upper Egypt; without their chance survival, the archaeological record of literacy might begin there with substantially later and more formal writing (hieroglyphic inscription).

Literacy estimates raise evident dangers in simplifying social relations to two opposing blocks of 'literate' and 'non-literate'. As observed by Cerquiglini 1989: 36-37, calculations of low literacy levels have been less distorting than the simplistic impression and manipulation of this oral-written opposition. Lesko 2001 notes the need for awareness of the grades of literacy. Problems with reductive approaches to literacy include the following:

1. ancient Egypt always had at least two scripts in operation (Assmann 1991), one for securing eternity, deployed together with formal art (hieroglyphic script), one for more day-to-day purposes (cursive scripts: first hieratic, and from about 700 BC demotic). Therefore there would have been at least three blocks: those trained in hieroglyphs, those trained in cursive writing, and those without training. This recalls the three groups into which ancient Egyptian writings often divide the population: *ḥnmmt - pꜥt - rḫyt*. The focus of that tripartite division, whatever its relation to writing in practice, seems to be the person of the divine king with humanity clustered in concentric circles of decreasing access radiating out from the king (Berlev 1972, 97-98).
2. literacy is not a one-dimensional single subject, but covers different grades (from illiterate to proficient) and practices (reading, writing, composing, copying). This fine typology needs to be considered in relation to another fundamental skill in literate societies - numeracy.

The pursuit of literate versus illiterate percentages of the population may distract researchers from study of the impact of writing on society. What comments are found in ancient Egyptian writings themselves on the ability to read and the ability to write? How could those not trained to write acquire the skill? These questions raise the particular issue also of gender and literacy. What part did writing play in the life of the non-literate individual? Do written and other archaeological sources reveal strategies used by the non-literate to adapt to areas of life dominated by the literate?

Computer literacy in contemporary society may offer a convenient model to replace the simple opposition 'literate versus illiterate', because it is not aligned with economic and social status as directly as (il)-literacy. Senior managers are among the population groups relatively ignorant and fearful of newer communications technologies, and, similarly, traditionally privileged elders are disempowered by computer literacy levels by comparison with traditionally demoted groups such as younger teenagers. In contrast to the romanticist division in 'literate versus illiterate', computer literacy is perceived more openly in terms of a spectrum with acceptance of knowledge as functionally oriented rather than somehow morally significant (the elite portrayal of the non-literate as idiot). In the more generous social perception of computer literacy, the most expert is a technically trained and talented individual, a computer programmer, but the social elite is not a group of computer programmers. On the next rung of the communications proficiency ladder, higher salaried urban office-workers may be familiar with particular software packages, whether in multimedia, graphics or just writing, without having the expertise to adapt the off-the-shelf products. Many more workers may use the simplest electronic communications tools, either at the range of internet, e-mail and plain image files, or in the still-frequent use of desk-top computers as 'e-typewriters'. A high proportion of socially and economically advantaged individuals remain excluded from the world of new technology. Along such spectral lines, a refined typology of pre-modern literacy might range from full literacy in sacred script, through literacy in writing cursive, to reading and recognising particular ranges of cursive writing, to mark-making/-reading to non-literate persons. A primary research question remains, whether reading and writing formed, for the bulk of the urban and the rural population, even indirectly, part of life, and, if so, in what ways.

How are words read 1800 BC? co-texts and categories

Все слова пахнут профессией, жанром, направлением, партией, определенным произведением, определенным человеком, поколением, возрастом, днем и часом.
Каждое слово пахнет контекстом и контекстами, в которых оно жило своею социально напряженной жизнью, все слова и формы населены интенциями.

All words smell of a profession, a genre, a movement, a party, a particular origin, a particular individual, a generation, an age, a day and hour.
Every word smells of the context and contexts in which it lived its socially charged life, all words and forms are inhabited by intentionalities.
Bakhtin 1977, 106

Exploring co-texts

Words have meaning and life not as the atomised automata of dictionary definitions, but within the flow of the living language of human language-users with all their varying competences and pressures. The resonance of a word in every new context draws on all the other occasions it has been used before, in the consciousness and sub-conscious of the speaker/writer. The sum of the contexts of those other occurrences may be called the co-text – a partly conscious and partly implicit pre-echo and echo for the resurrected word (cf Kilito 1985, Chapter One on the metempsychosis of the poem, pp.17-23, especially on p.19, the words of Ibn Rashiq, "were the word not repeated, it would disappear", in commentary on the earlier Arabic poetry of Antara). In study of writings from a distant past, in any reading of another language, the foreign reader risks preselecting the range of compositions to such a degree that the new reading loses all substantive connection with the 'co-text' of those for whom that language was the mother tongue. In the contemporary university training of modern Egyptologists, the selection of compositions ranges according to the biographies that have constructed the institution: for example, English universities have tended to teach less of the religious corpora, by comparison with German universities. Curricular differences alert us to the partiality of readings, and the danger of losing the co-text and therefore, in essence, the very words.

In a recent article, Detlef Franke reacted strongly against a Western Egyptological trend to construct a class of ancient free-thinking intellectuals as the creators and receivers of literature (Franke 1998). These literature-men seem suspiciously close not only to the artistic genius in European Romanticism, but, more worryingly, to a heroic self-image of Egyptologists themselves, as if Egypt would have had proto-Egyptologists as its literati. The construction depends on interpreting a certain designation *nḏs* 'little man'/ 'fellow', found in several literary works, as a word evoking a socio-historical middle class pioneering a free position outside official administrative structures. Certainly a class outside administration may have been in existence (cf Quirke 1991, but see Andrassy 1998). However, the role of any such group in the production of written literature seems highly questionable, as the interpretation of the word *nḏs* as a social technical term lacked grounding in the full range of written sources for the designation in First Intermediate Period and Middle Kingdom writings. Curiously, given the smaller scale of Russian-language Egyptology, the same interpretative issue had arisen, and had been confronted, and an exhaustive list and assessment of sources provided a full generation earlier by Oleg Berlev in his study of social relations in the Middle Kingdom, as Franke emphasised (Berlev 1978). In hieroglyphic inscriptions the term *nḏs* 'little man'/ 'fellow' was used from the end of the Old Kingdom to the early Twelfth Dynasty (dated examples down to the reign of Senusret I) and then again from the late Second Intermediate Period into the New Kingdom; Berlev suggested that the presence of the word could therefore be used as an indirect dating criterion for literary compositions. Whether or not that implication is accepted, Berlev showed from consideration of all available sources in their contexts that the word did not carry specific social reference, but was deployed in the plural in vaguer antonymy with various words for 'great ones', on the model 'rich' vs 'poor'. The autoreferential use of the word, where a single individual describes himself as *nḏs*, is revealingly different to the use of *nḏs* in the plural:

whereas the plural denotes a group diametrically opposite to 'great ones', and in need of protection, in the singular the word could be used precisely by such 'great ones' to refer to themselves as strong and valiant. From the list of all instances of autoreferential use, Berlev was able to demonstrate that, far from 'independents' outside administration, it was high-placed officials who were generally the ones to call themselves *nḏs*. He found no certain instance where *nḏs* was deployed to evoke size, as the English translation 'little man' might imply: rather, it carried an association of minority in age, being deployed as an opposite to *iȝw* 'old man'. Since youth is optimal fighting age, this would explain why it could be used with the connotation of able-bodied and valiant fighter, in the autoreferential use of the word, and why it was such a prominent feature of the written record in the First Intermediate Period and then again from the Second Intermediate Period, when the individual presumably needed military prowess more than in periods of strong central control. Through meticulous assembling of all available sources, and contextual source-critical analysis, Berlev was able to capture the Middle Kingdom deployment and reception of a word, and his approach provides a model to follow for every item in thick reading. Understandably, then, Franke laments the general lack of engagement with the sources and the study of them by Berlev in more recent Western European discussion of the term.

A comparable example of Egyptological assumption may be the automatic reading of the designations for the two protagonists in the Tale of the Shipwrecked Official. One is *ḥȝty-ʿ* 'mayor', the other *šmsw* 'follower'. The latter attempts to reassure the former on return from an unsuccessful expedition, as they pass the First Cataract at the southern boundary of Egypt. The conversation between them tends to be read as the reassurance of a subordinate to his master. However, 'follower' and 'mayor' are two administrative designations at different relative levels on the hieroglyphic and cursive rock-inscriptions left by just such expeditionaries precisely in the Middle Kingdom, many at the First Cataract itself. Along with the rest of the evidence for the two terms, the mass of expeditionary co-text has not been exploited in the Egyptological reception of the Tale. Certainly it is possible that the 'follower' is 'follower (of the mayor)', as generally assumed: the explicit title *šmsw n ḥȝty-ʿ* 'follower of the mayor' is attested from the late Middle Kingdom, and a 'follower of the estate' appears among staff of the mayor at Qau (Berlev 1978, 211). However, the Tale includes the account of an earlier expedition after which the shipwrecked official was appointed 'follower' by the king at the palace, and allotted servants for the post: Berlev pointed out that this can most be plausibly read as an appointment to the position attested in the late Middle Kingdom as 'follower of the ruler' (Berlev 1978, 215-216 noting the close parallel in the autobiographical inscription of Khusobek from the reign of Senusret III). In expedition rock-inscriptions a 'follower (of the king)' may be senior to the 'mayor', as palace military officials ranking higher than even the leaders of the local administration. The assumed relation between the protagonists in the Tale might then need to be inverted. A third possibility might be that the two men were colleagues of comparable standing, in accordance with the term *ḫnms* 'colleague', 'friend' used by the mayor to address the follower at the close of the Tale. Since we do not know the standing of this 'follower' within the palace hierarchy, or the place and so strategic importance of the mayorship, we may not be able to solve the problem of the social relation between the protagonists. Our literary history may suffer from this failure, but our literary reading may be greatly enriched, as in the performance of drama, by having to try out all three possibilities – equals, high to low, or low to high. The Teaching of Ptahhotep contains the rules for behaviour in each of the three cases, indicating that the anxiety was shared in antiquity. The reception of the words 'follower' and 'mayor' must have changed within ancient time, specifically in this instance from the period before the reign of Senusret III, when vaguer titles were the norm, to the period of the late Middle Kingdom, when titles became much more precise. Antiquity cannot be treated as a homogeneous dehumanised block.

It would, of course, be unfair to accuse philology of a general systems failure to read the expansive co-texts, such as the hundreds of hieroglyphic inscriptions recording expeditions with titles and names of individuals. Berlev and Franke evidently did, and both Galán and Bárta have provided illustrated translations of literary compositions to restore at least part of this co-text, with strong visual support (Galán 1998, Bárta 1999). In all these studies, the self-conscious perception of historical time by a researcher is of crucial importance. Periodisation establishes accurate sight-lines for research into words, including but not restricted to names and titles. Each period represents a new alignment of productive forces, more or less concentrated, with new relations of power, and specific networks of access to resources. Across several thousand years, into the Bronze Age, we are unlikely to find enough data to chart yearly or even generational developments in detail, but the broader periods are now coming into clearer focus. The early, central and late phases of the Middle Kingdom can be distinguished, and the dated written sources from each can be studied and compared with content of literary compositions that are not yet so closely dated. As a result of comparative research (Grajetzki in press), most second millennium BC Egyptian literary compositions can be dated to broader periods (Middle Kingdom, Second Intermediate Period, New Kingdom) and some to the narrower periods (early Middle Kingdom, central Middle Kingdom, late Middle Kingdom). More specific datings would be useful, but are rarely obtainable. Sometimes Egyptologists attempt to date over-specifically within periods of material culture on insufficient evidence, and in so doing they risk losing the benefits of knowing the succession of broad phases of the culture, that is of longer duration and material cultural history against short duration or event-by-event history. The literary history of this remote antiquity cannot be event-by-event in the annalistic manner of publication dates for modern works, but this should not be seen as an obstacle to the project of writing a literary history for the second millennium BC, or claiming a place for its literature within world literature. The broader periodisation already sets literary production within material cultural worlds for which Egyptian archaeology and philology have accumulated large data sets and traditions of interpretative tools.

Categories of space: the city as a definitional category of social identity 1850 BC

Alongside time, interweaving, space provides defining coordinates of human existence variously mediated and moulded in the linguistic expression of that existence through speech and writing. So basic is the spatial dimension, that the reading of any literary composition from another society requires appreciation of the difference between 'our' perception and experience and 'theirs'. For Bronze Age Egypt, the definitional spatial category seems to me the large-scale settlement, the 'city'. City is a word of widely varying definition even within contemporary experience: inhabitants of New York and Los Angeles might find it difficult to agree on a definition, and even the most urban parts of London fail the classic characterisation of the modern city by Georg Simmel on such counts as speed of transport or width of roads. Five centuries later than the Middle Kingdom, a series of inscriptions at Amarna in Middle Egypt define the limits of a new royal city, and these Boundary Stelae in the cliffs define that city as the entire area between them (Murnane 1993). This is in agreement with the onomastica that summarise Egypt as a sequence of 'cities' (below), and the religious tabulation of the Two Lands as a sequence of 'city-provinces' each with one dominant city (Schwab-Schlott 1981). The land is equal to the sum of its cities, defined as the territory between the eastern and western deserts either side of its Two Banks of the Nile, including the broad Nile Delta with its several branches. The main Middle Egyptian term for Egypt as Black Land may be written with concluding city-sign (Goelet 1999). The land is the sum of settled space. In contrast to the modern Western depiction of ancient Egypt as a civilization without cities, it appears as a densely populated territory within which the urban space asserts its hegemony. The city may be organic, growing up over time (*niwt*), or it may, like Amarna, be founded by administrative executive decision (*ḥwt*). Most organic settlements may have been located on the higher land above the level reached by the Nile flood; during the late summer flood these urban spaces would have been transformed into islands within the long flood-lake, surrounded by waves instead of fields, until the floodwaters drained down into the Mediterranean. By contrast, new towns in Upper and Middle Egypt would probably have been founded most often along the desert edge, though within reach of water, so on the low desert rather than on the high cliffs along the Nile Valley. Here, in towns such as Middle Kingdom Lahun and New Kingdom Amarna, the experience of urban space would have been entirely different, with the fields (in floodtime, water) on one side, and the desert on the other.

There is though a narrower sense of the concept of city alongside this broader reference to the symbiotic space of city-with-support. An indigenous vocabulary defines various extramural and intramural spaces within each segment in the chain of city-provinces. By oppositional definition the word for city *niwt* may be set against a word *š3* and a word *sḫt*. More refined lexicographical research is needed into these sets of terms, but provisionally it may be argued that the 'not-city' or countryside in the sense of arable land is covered by the word *š3*, while *sḫt* would be the word for countryside in the sense of non-arable land, in the context of the Nile the marshes. The untamed marshes lie not next to the river at the middle of the valley, but to the lower edges of the valley profile, along the desert, where floodwater lingered longer after the annual Nile flood in late summer. In the standardised mid- to late Ptolemaic Period processions of Nile-flood deities, each province of Egypt comprises *mr* 'waterway', *w* 'arable land', and *pḥw* 'backwaters' (Beinlich 1977); here *pḥw* 'backwaters' presents another word for the marshland, with one 'classic backwater' area in each administrative district of the land. The schematic profile of the Upper Egyptian Nile Valley below may help to reinsert these terms in a living topography (Butzer 1976, 15-25). Without such a section, those of us not inhabiting the space may be misled by the homogenising flatness of our maps, and lose the specific topography and psychology of urban experience within the Nile Valley.

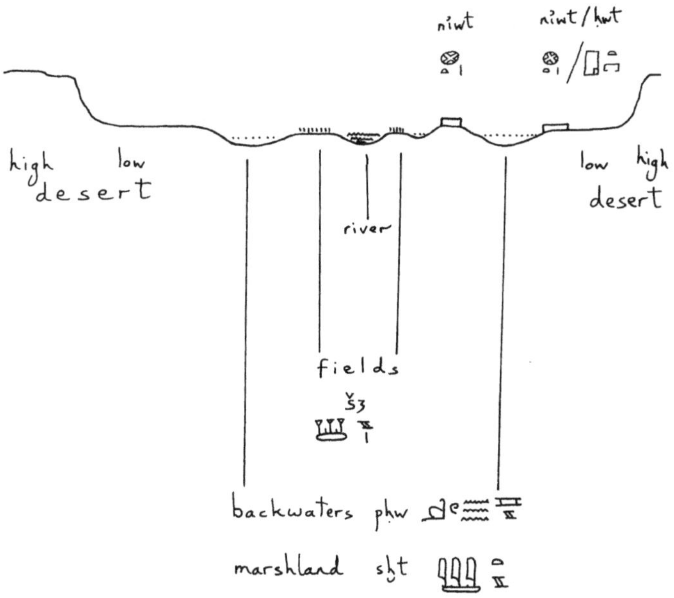

If the terms 'city', 'field' and '(marsh)-margins' are accepted as three categories of inhabited space in the Nile Valley, they correspond strikingly enough with a distinction cited by Doris Abouseif from Ibn Khaldun on bedouin – farmer/village – citydweller/city as the definitional categories of inhabitants throughout the Egyptian Nile Valley in medieval civilization (Abouseif 2000). Wealth/social status/social **class** may be identified as a dominant factor of identity in this horizontal sectioning, transposing it into a hierarchy, a vertical stratigraphy. Arable land - marshland - low desert all belong within a symbiotic city space, but in decreasing symbiosis and with increasing opportunity for **class** opposition. Symbiosis as integration of separate elements cannot avoid fostering also a terrain for conflict and hierarchy. Here desertdweller becomes the enemy; the marshdweller as hunter-gatherer is a marginal outsider, even if, like Khuninpu (in Part Two, Laments), he is a trader of means, with pack-animals and local and imported produce. Even the farmer, though the social agent most regularly feeding the city, can be seen to be occupying a slot outside the city walls, and so even he remains an extramural member of the urbanised land.

This mesh of security and conflict can be read in the Lahun cycle of hymns to king Senusret III evoking cliff and foreigner (**race**), always keeping an eye on the sectional view of Valley (UC 32157: Part Two, Section Three). Lands beyond the cliff face may be a source of exotic resources, or home to enemies:

> How great is the lord for his city! Indeed he is a rampart, of bronze of Syria (line 4)
>
> How great is the lord for his city! Indeed he is the Powerful Goddess against enemies treading on [his?] border (line 10)

The spatial dimension of human experience is central to this, as to other compositions.

Egyptian words defined against one another, by Egyptians: the Onomastica

Onomasticon is the Latinised writing of a Greek word (plural: onomastica) used by Egyptologists to refer to ancient Egyptian compositions comprising lists of words by category. These are not dictionaries or explicit encyclopaedia, as they do not include explanations for the words. However, the order and selection of words provide an implicit guide to the categories into which the Egyptians divided the world. One example among the Tebtunis papyri of the 1st and 2nd centuries AD includes verbs as well as nouns (Osing 1998): all other onomastica contain nouns only. The oldest is a fragmentary example of about 1800 BC, one of the Ramesseum Papyri (above, Question One, Group Two). All onomastica would have provided instruction in both broad vocabulary and standard spellings, but there are no sources on the precise way in which they were used. The Onomasticon of Amenemipet is the only composition with the beginning preserved, including a named compiler or author (whether historical or fictitious), and it is the onomasticon known from the greatest number of sources, from Ramesside Period to late Third Intermediate Period. One of the best preserved copies is a Third Intermediate Period papyrus from Hiba in Middle Egypt, acquired by Wladimir Golenischeff and often known as the Golenischeff Onomasticon (above, Question One, Group Seven): it served as the basis for the main modern edition of the composition, Gardiner 1947. Below, for comparison, I provide a summary of the one surviving late Middle Kingdom onomasticon and the Onomasticon of Amenemipet.

1. Ramesseum Onomasticon of the late Middle Kingdom

My summary here follows Gardiner 1947, 6-23 with pl.1-6. The beginning is lost; thereafter every tenth line is identified by number, and at lines 324-325 a total is given with the observation that there should have been 343 items but in fact only 323 are present. There is also a missing item between 230 and 240, and another between 250 and 260. Following the main list comes an unnumbered set of lines recording twenty different types of cattle. Down to line 90 no complete word survives, though liquids and plant names were certainly in this portion of the list. At lines 91-92 are two types of oil, before another damaged portion contained liquids, plants, wickerwork (nos.108, 113-114), minerals and seeds. The better preserved series contains the following groupings:

122-133 birds
134-152 fish
153-161 birds
161-162 uncertain
164-170 animals (including gazelle and giraffe)
171-187 seventeen fortresses from the Second Cataract in Nubia to Gebel el-Silsila in Upper Egypt
188-216 twenty-nine towns from Elephantine to a town north of Akhmim, in the area between Upper and Middle Egypt
216A a short vertical line specifying 'items placed on water', apparently the title to the following
217-253 loaves and cakes
254-265 cereals
266-270 materials in grains (including salt and perhaps cereal product residues)
271-311 meat
312-323 fruit

2. Onomasticon of Amenemipet, probably late New Kingdom

Title

ḥꜣt-ꜥ m sbꜣyt wḥꜥ ỉb	Beginning of the teaching, explaining to the heart,
mty ḫm rḫ wnnt nbt	instructing the ignorant, to know all that exists,
ḳmꜣ.n ptḥ sḫpr.n ḏḥwty	created by Ptah, brought into being by Thoth,
pt m šsrw.s tꜣ ỉmy.f	the sky with its features, the earth and what is in it,
ḳꜥḥ ḏw ỉwḥ m nwn	the bend of the mountain, what is washed by the waters,
m ꜣḫt nbt ḥꜣy.n rꜥ	consisting of all that is useful, illumined by Ra,
srwdt nbt ḥr-sꜣ tꜣ	all that is made to grow upon earth,
mꜣỉ.n sš mḏꜣt nṯr m pr ꜥnḫ	reported by the writer of god's books in the House of Life
ỉmn-m-ỉpt sꜣ ỉmn-m-ỉpt ḏd.f	Amenemipet son of Amenemipet, who says:

There follow in the best preserved manuscript, the Golenischeff Onomasticon, the following categories of words:

1-62 sky, water, earth
63-229 gods, spirits, kings, officials
230-312 people and groups of people including foreigners and foreign lands (238-294) and age groups (295-304)
313-419 category town (*dmyt* 313), list of towns of Upper and Lower Egypt
420-473 buildings and their parts, and types of land
474-578 agricultural land, grain, produce
579-610 parts of an ox and kinds of meat
The Golenischeff manuscript ends at word number 610: one fragmentary Third Intermediate Period papyrus continues with names of plants and trees (British Museum EA 10795, unpublished).

As examples of the categories, three sections are given below with the numbers allotted by the principal modern editor Alan Gardiner.
Selection One: distinctions between superhuman beings (63-68) and the human beings most intimately connected with the divine king (69-75)
63 god (*nṯr*)
64 goddess (*nṯrt*)
65 transfigured man, the blessed dead (*ꜣḫ*)
66 transfigured woman, the blessed dead (*ꜣḫ*)
67 king (*nswt*)
68 goddess of kingship (*nsyt*: this word is never used of queens, only of goddesses)

69 wife of the king (*ḥmt nswt*)
70 mother of the king (*mwt nswt*)
71 child of the king (*ms nswt*)
72 leader of nobles (*iry pʿt*: a title used for the Crown Prince in the Ramesside Period)
73 first minister, usually translated 'vizier' in Egyptology (*ṯ3ty*)
74 sole companion (*smr wʿty*)
75 eldest son of the king (*s3 nswt smsw*)

Selection Two: designations for groups of human beings
230 people (*rmṯ*)
231 nobles (*pʿt*)
232 populace (*rḫyt*)
233 entourage (of the sun-king) (*ḥnmmt*: spelled with the sign for sun disk and rays)
234-235 archery officers (*ṯs pḏwt*)
236 infantry (*mnf3t*)
237 cavalry (*t-nt-ḥtr*)
Following these, entries nos.238-294 list foreign peoples and lands: 238-242 in the west; 243-252 Hittite Empire and its allies in the Battle of Qadesh; 253-294 Syrians and Nubians

Selection Three: designations for differences between human beings by age
295 adult man (*s*)
296 youth (*mnḥ*)
297 old man (*i3w*)
298 adult woman (*st*)
299 young woman (*nfrt*)
300 mixed people (*tp šbn*: this term might be used in administration to denote a group of people of different ages and both genders)
301 lad (*ʿḏd*)
302 infant (*nḫn*: perhaps the new-born child, neonate - the English word infant comes from Latin infans 'not speaking', and a similar distinction might have applied in Egypt, but this is not documented)
303 boy (*rnn*: literally 'he who is nursed')
304 girl (*rnnt*: literally 'she who is nursed')

Although this Onomasticon dates centuries later than the Middle Kingdom, like the Ramesseum Onomasticon it alerts us to the different ways in which the world and being(s) are categorised, in the specific ways by which nouns are deployed by humans in social communication. Study of these sources, as well as of the determinatives, can help to take us out of the assumptions of our own times and word usages, and closer to the time and place of Middle Kingdom literary compositions.

Between production and reception: copying as creation

Redeeming the copyist

Appreciation of pre-print literatures can be blocked by modern assumptions concerning text and author. The Cerquiglini volume from which the notes on author and text above are drawn is a polemical reaction against the modern philological method developed by Karl Lachmann, the method behind most modern editions of ancient writing, notably classical Greek and Latin works, and the Bible (Cerquiglini 1989). Modern readers read ancient or medieval writing not directly from source, but from versions standardised by modern philologists out of all available, often highly variable copies. There is a danger that the philological editor sees the copy, or more personally the copyist, as the enemy that stands between editor and pure text from original author. Yet copying carries other, entirely positive effects. In the world before print, in manuscript production, and in the world after print, with computer screens, copying can be as creative an activity as authorship; copyists participate in their literature more actively than the consumer of printed books. In the hunt for ancient reading (see next section), copyists may be the principal identifiable readers. An offhand dismissal of copying activity as inherently flawed would deprive us of access to ancient readers, and would oversimplify the complex relations between writing/writer and copying/copyist. Instead of distortion and corruption, differences between manuscripts may be intentional in an active reception of manuscript: permitted variation may be attested for the Teaching of Ptahhotep, known in two versions already in the late Middle Kingdom. However, at the end of some copies of literary and religious compositions, the copyist claims to have copied exactly as found in writing, and this feature confirms that an ideal of exact reproduction existed in ancient Egypt alongside variance (above, Question Three, problems of text. There may have been greater emphasis on immutability in certain contexts or for certain compositions; replication is a variable to be studied across all composition types, rather than a universal principle to be assumed.

Copyists might have been bibliophile readers, or talented calligraphers commissioned to produce copies, or both. In the absence of explicit written sources from the Middle Kingdom, it is tempting to resort to evidence centuries, even millennia later, to obtain an impression of the experience of book-production and -circulation in a manuscript-world within the same geographical landscapes. Around AD 170, in the great provincial city Oxyrhynchus (today Bahnasa), a private letter ended with two afterthoughts (Papyrus Oxyrhynchus XVIII 2192, after Legras 2002, 152):

> "Have copies of Hypsikrates, *Figures of Comedy*, books 6-7 made, and send them to me. For according to Harpokration, they are present among the books of Polion, but others must have them too. He also has the prose summaries of Thersagoras, *Myths of Tragedy*."
>
> "The book-seller Demetrios also has these books, according to Harpokration. I wrote to Apollonides to send me some of my own books, that Seleukos himself is going to show you soon. If you find any that I do not have, have them copied and send them to me. Diodoros and his friends also have some that I lack."

Harpokration is known as the author of a treatise on Attic rhetoric, *Ten Orators*, and Polion and his son Diodorus are attested as Alexandrians of learning, indicating that this letter derives from correspondence among a cultivated elite (Legras 2002, 152-153). The Hellenised elite of Alexandria and provincial cities in the Roman Period cannot serve as a direct guide to the social relations and material culture of the Middle Bronze Age. Nevertheless, they stand a step closer in the history of communications, and reintroduce the ancient readers and the social mechanics of obtaining books, into a circle otherwise too easily limited to writer and copyist and modern commentator.

Two demotic letters on a similar topic survive from Tebtunis, dating to a slightly earlier period, the second or first century BC (Zauzich 2000). In one (Papyrus Carlsberg 21), a man called Maihesa writes to a man called Panisi:

> "I have had Hor son of Maara my brother bring you the book of the physician and the scroll of the box, making two books, that you gave me before today. Do not register any (complaint-)document because of the delay that arose – I couldn't find anyone reliable (to bring them to you)"

The last phrase "I couldn't find anyone reliable" is a reconstruction by Zauzich from the signs in a line broken along the middle, and suits the gist of the letter: evidently, Maihesa had failed to return two books and has been threatened with legal action, prompting their immediate return with this apology and plea not to start proceedings. The "scroll of the box" may have been a collection of prescriptions, in which case the pair of books might be compared to the surgical treatise Papyrus Edwin Smith and the encyclopedic prescription book Papyrus Ebers one and a half millennia earlier (above, Question One, Group Three).

The second Tebtunis letter (Papyrus Carlsberg 22) is more heavily damaged, and the names of both sender and recipient are lost. Nevertheless, the message reveals the title of the person to whom the letter was sent, and the theme:

> "Everyone coming here, I ask concerning the well-being of the writer of god's books, and they tell me, no harm, and my heart finds it right (so). The corpus (?) that you seek, write to me about it: if there is a book [...]"

On the reverse a line of address survives: "to be handed to the writer of god's books". Although the word for whatever the recipient seeks is unclear, it is plausible to consider this message as an offer to supply him with manuscripts from which he could fill a gap in his own collection of writings. The title "writer of god's books" would refer at this date, around 100 BC, to someone mastering hieratic and hieroglyphic scripts, and the contents of books written in them, from rituals and compendia of religious knowledge, to medical treatises (for the range, compare perhaps the later Tebtunis papyri, above, Question One, Group Ten). This would then be another glimpse of the world of readers, writers, copyists in action and in social context at Tebtunis, a town at some distance from the primary urban centres of its day.

The rediscovery of these named ancient individuals as book-owners, book-copiers and book-borrowers introduces character, rehumanising the world of writing, but the encounter may also reinforce deep-rooted mistrust of handwritten copy, a sentiment endemic in philology. In historical practice, the degree of editorial control to prevent copying errors is a variable both within manuscript production and within print production. Manuscripts with Arabic editions of classical Greek compositions reveal exceptionally tight control of copying (Salama-Carr 1990). Even medieval European manuscript copyists achieved far greater accuracy than early modern printing methods (Cerquiglini 1989, 19). Procedures of editorial and authorial checking and revising are cultural historical products, requiring research and assessment. Contrary to modern assumptions over the print revolution, no clear-cut qualititative transformation divides manual from mechanical production of written content. Quality and intention of copying cannot be assumed from the degree of mechanisation, or the place of the copy in the broad history of writing and printing. Where an ancient copyist has lapsed despite an intention or an order to produce an accurate copy, the resulting copying errors can still be treated more sympathetically than the modern editor usually manages, for they provide a wealth of information on language in action, invaluable for languages where native speakers are no longer available for researchers.

Sometimes a surviving manuscript seems to deliver a trial writing rather than a finished product, as if it represented not the copy, enemy of Romantic original talent, but that Romantic prize the autograph. Middle Kingdom papyri in this category might be the assorted sayings collected on Papyrus Ramesseum II, and perhaps the start of a Tale of Neferpesdjet (washed out after finishing, or given up before completion? by copyist, or by author?). From its dimensions of 29x21 cm, I would suggest that Papyrus Pushkin 1695 had been cut for use as a letter, but was then (re-?) used for two literary titles, one on each side: given its regular single letter-sheet size, it would have been awkward to paste on more letter-height sheets to continue the composition more than a few lines. It may be a record of a favourite composition, but perhaps each title represents trial literary openings, in the manner of Ramesside ostraca with practice opening lines 'beginning of the teaching made by' (e.g. Spiegelberg 1898, pl.1, nos.3-4; another example may be the ostracon from Abydos Simpson 1995 A4). As with the Tale of Neferpesdjet, perhaps the work never progressed beyond that initial line or two.

Reading

If literary compositions may be defined as writing created principally in order to be read, it must be conceded that the activity of reading in ancient Egypt remains to be researched in detail. For other societies, the sociological study of reading has drawn productive distinctions:

1. in the range from the most private unspoken reading to the most public recitation of writings, above all drama
2. from intensive reading of select compositions (where a few writings are known intimately, as in Christian traditions of reading the Old and New Testaments) to extensive reading of a broader number of compositions (associated with private unspoken reading and the accumulation of libraries) (cf Chartier 1992)

Worlds of reading and writing all form part of a less tangible arena of communication, to include gesture as well as speech. These must be taken into account when assessing the profile of reading within a particular society at any period.

Richard Jasnow is among recent scholars to ask, and find it difficult to identify sources to answer, the question of who was reading literature in antiquity (Jasnow 2002, 208 n.5). Names of copyists in the peritext of manuscripts offer one answer, as might the names on items with which ancient manuscripts were buried. On the latter, though, Willy Clarysse expressed caution over the possibility of extrapolating sociological data from funerary contexts. On the presence of Greek literary manuscripts in burials a millennium and a half after the Middle Kingdom, he noted: 'Apart from the question whether these books in the tomb were really personal copies of the deceased and not an imitation of the Egyptian practice of giving a funerary papyrus to the dead, we hardly know anything of the persons in question, not even their names' (Clarysse 1976, 47). The practice of placing a funerary papyrus in the tomb (in most cases a Book of the Dead) did not become regular before about 1450 BC, and so this precise factor could not be at play three to four centuries earlier, in the Middle Kingdom. Nevertheless, it is fair to apply to the earlier period the broader point of method, that the deposition of books in burials needs to be interpreted within the contemporary funerary customs before a personalised relation is assumed, for we know next to nothing about circulation of manuscripts. In the late Middle Kingdom, several papyri seem to have been deposited in tombs (see Question One, Groups), but not all are literary, and some are accountancy records: in one case only can a personal link be documented, where the title and name secretary of the main enclosure Neferhotep appear on both the coffin and one of two accounts papyri in the tomb (Papyrus Boulaq 18, smaller manuscript: Mariette 1872). Given the range of content types, it might be argued that the underlying intention was to secure the presence of writing, in which case any personal ties to the books might not necessarily have been so crucial. By comparison with the names of copyists, the names in burials may lead research no farther.

Clarysse expressed regret, in the article cited above, that the Greek literary papyri from Egypt provided no equivalent to the extraordinarily well-documented instance of the Ramesside family that owned the Chester Beatty Papyri (Question One, Group Six: Pestman 1982). Although the genealogical details remain to be ironed out between various family members with the same name, and although the ascription of all papyri to one ancient grouping remains uncertain, in a sense it seems enough that the several literary items are linked to the Ramesside community of Royal Tomb cutters and decorators at Thebes (known in Egyptology by the Arabic name for the site, Deir el-Medina). The involvement of the secretary to the Royal Tomb project, Qenherkhepshef, in the circulation of 'literary' content seems demonstrable from his own copy of parts of the kingship eulogy celebrating the prowess of Ramses II in the face of disaster at the Battle of Qadesh (Spalinger 2002, 329-330, noting the focus on kingship in the 'literary' scope of the Chester Beatty Papyri). Here we have the copy, the associated books, and, from the great wealth of writing preserved from Deir el-Medina, the administrative position and even personality of an ancient reader. By his title, Qenherkhepshef belongs to a higher circle of national bureaucracy, and must have been as proficient in mathematics as in reading. When his title is compared with other Ramesside copyists attested from their colophon-'signatures', the accountants emerge as the main Ramesside readers (notably in Question One, Group Five manuscripts). In Egyptology the character of their work and the prominence of numeracy alongside or over literacy tend to be obscured by a strategic use of the orientalist term 'scribe' to translate the Egyptian word *sš*. The word *sš* covers the several areas of work, where a man used a reed brush to draw or write hieroglyphs or cursive scripts derived from hieroglyphs. Special uses are marked by qualifying terms. As *sš sp<u>h</u>r* 'copyist' the 'reedman' is at work copying sacred manuscripts: a classic instance is Nebseny, a mid-Eighteenth Dynasty copyist in the Ptah temple, whose magnificent and lengthy Book of the Dead is, exceptionally, in black and red outline, with unusual addition of liturgies indicating exceptional degree of access to sacred writings (British Museum EA 9900, compare against the regular production of the period, Munro 1988; for Middle Kingdom examples of the title, see Ward 1982, 165 no.1428). For the more widely attested *sš ḳdwt* 'draughtsman' the task may be more generally to prepare any composition in outline according to the rules of formal art and script (Middle Kingdom examples of the title in Ward 1982, 166 no.1444). Yet these ideological occupations are far outnumbered by the main work in the word *sš* 'writer', that of accountancy. In most titles, *sš* can be translated fairly as 'accountant'; for example, the large quantity of Lahun temple papyri preserved in Berlin and Cairo demonstrates that the main correspondent in those business files, the temple *sš* Horemsaf (*sš ḥwt-n<u>t</u>r*), was the temple accountant (Luft 1982). In the Middle Kingdom manuscript of the Tale of the Shipwrecked Sailor, the copyist identifies himself in the colophon as the *sš* 'writer' Amenyaa, and it must be asked of the contemporary co-text in hieroglyphic inscription, funerary writing, and documentary writing, whether this is not most readily translateable 'accountant'. It is not a surprise to find officialdom as the readership of ancient literature, but the impact and effect is almost the opposite of that obtained by the Egyptological interpretation of *n<u>d</u>sw* 'little men' as heroes of a 'bourgeois' literary flowering or intellectual breakthrough.

In orientalist imagination, ancient Egypt was populated by scribes and priests. Precisely these two roles are identified as the key groups of readers in ancient Egyptian hieroglyphic inscriptions from offering-chapels, mostly from Abydos, in the formulae that start "O you who live on earth", known in Egyptology as the Appeal to the Living (Berlev 1962). Twelfth Dynasty examples of the formula tabulate the expected readers with prominence of place for *sš* and temple ritual staff such as the *ḥm-n<u>t</u>r* "god's servant". At first glance, the orientalist view might seem confirmed here. However, Lahun temple papyri (in Cairo and Berlin) demonstrate that the holders of temple positions served sporadically by a system of monthly rotation of staff, divided into four pools called 'watches' (Greek *phylai*). Therefore hte inscriptions are appealing to passing individuals not by fixed permanent titles (as in the orientalist ontology of scribal and priestly life), but rather by the role that brings the individual to the offering-chapel in which the stela was placed. It is worth rereading in this light the contributions to *L'uomo Egizio*, a remarkabe anthropology of ancient Egypt assembled by Sergio Donadoni (Donadoni 1990): the chapter headings 'priest', 'official', 'scribe', 'farmer' may be absorbed less as castes or fixed groups, more as the socio-economic roles an individual might be called upon to play. As roles, rather than ontologised personifications, the headings are not mutually exclusive. The ka-servant (offering-priest in cult of an individual) Heqanakht may spend part, probably most, of his time as farm-manager, as temple pure-priest, as accountant for a project of kingship, even as soldier, and only a lesser part performing the rituals that entitled him to the income of ka-servant. In these conditions, priesthood and scribal class do not exist as classes : both become aspects of a broader category, officialdom, though in Middle Kingdom terms within the realm of the temple rather than the king's domain (late Middle Kingdom stela of Nebipusenusret, British Museum EA 101, referring to 'every office of the temple, every office of the king's domain'). In the offering-chapel inscriptions, it seems likely that the tabulated reader-groups would belong to the domain of the nearest temple, that of Osiris at Abydos. On the model of the Lahun papyri, the *sš* would be the temple accountant, the one permanent position among the temple staff.

The primary task for those researching ancient literary readership may then be to identify observable internal differentiation within officialdom in each age for which literary manuscripts are attested (cf Parkinson 1996a, 137, 140 on the *srw* 'officials', and for the Fayum in the Ptolemaic and Roman Periods van Minnen 1998). In the history of officialdom, it seems very doubtful that reunification of Egypt and consolidation under Twelfth Dynasty kingship altered the social profile as compared with Old Kingdom officialdom, as radically as assumed in Egyptological literary studies and commentary on the impact of the First Intermediate Period (e.g. Assmann 1990, 54-57). If we suspend use of the translations 'scribe' and 'priest', and examine instead from the sources the precise internal differentiation, or lack of it, in literate officialdom, we may achieve a less prejudiced reconstruction of ancient society and its literary self-expressions.

Receiving literature anciently: words good or beautiful?

Propaganda? political dimensions of literary writing

Studies of humans need a chronological as well as geographical framework, not only for accuracy, but to retain the humanity of their objects of study: human experience is human by its time and space coordinates as conditions of human life. Chronology can, though, become chronicle, and sources for cultural history then find themselves forced into an alien mould, political history. In the study of literature from ancient Egypt, the nineteenth century brought an initial phase of recovery and decipherment, and identification as literary, followed by the phase of hunting for political data in the literary. For Egyptology, the classic work by Georges Posener, *Littérature et politique*, set the seal on a political interpretation of Middle Kingdom literary output (Posener 1956). The Teaching of Amenemhat I and the Prophecy of Neferty, heralding a renaissance at the accession of a king Ameny, were to be read as propaganda, weapons of persuasion to turn the fractured elite into supporters of the new Twelfth Dynasty founded by Amenemhat I. The Tale of the Exile of Sanehat could be read similarly, and a political agenda of training a new loyal bureaucracy could be uncovered in the Loyalist Teaching and even the attack on non-literate workers in the Satire of Trades (Teaching of Duau Khety). Despite its origins in the Counter-Reformation, propaganda became a very twentieth-century secular motif, between the agitprop of the October Revolutionaries and the wartime propaganda machines of Goebbels and his Allied opponents. Small wonder then that twentieth century scholars found it convenient to redeploy the word into ancient settings. At the same time, the very strength and specificity of the word in contemporary political vocabulary have, though, brought substantial resistance, with more recent questioning of the applicability of the word to a world without elections and so without defined political blocks to be persuaded. Most seriously, the use of the word propaganda, and the hunt for politics, have been considered detrimental to any aesthetic appreciation of a composition (cf Parkinson 2002). If a work is received today as primarily propagandistic, arguably it loses its literary character for the receiver: aesthetically, literarily, it has died.

It can be countered that famous works of literature belong in well-documented political contexts, from the Odes of Horace and the Aenead of Virgil, to the Henry V of Shakespeare and the 1984 of George Orwell. The political persuasiveness of a piece may not detract from, but rather be integrated into its overall literary impact. However, this counter-argument perhaps only becomes effective if the reception of the piece remains primarily aesthetic, if it remains recognisably within a world called literature rather than one called politics. Egyptologists could return to the political content if they first recognised the literariness of the terrain, and then accepted that the compositions are not dated, and so very difficult to link to political history, or the chronicle of one event after another. Until, as in Parkinson 2002, that new phase of literary or aesthetic appreciation is more solidly underway, the political hue of any literary composition is bound to remain obscure, and a source of poor history-writing. There may, too, be a deeper and darker side to the free use of the word propaganda by 'Western' scholars for 'Eastern' histories. Bahrani has commented on standard interpretations of Assyrian palatial architecture and inscription:

> "Reading all Mesopotamian cultural remains as nothing more nor less than the propagandist utterances of the king reduces this Mesopotamian identity to the epiphenomenon of articulate ideology and thus serves the rhetorical stragegy of "Oriental despotism." In this way, current scholarship repeats and diffuses the prototypes of imperialism."
>
> (Bahrani 1998, 169)

The same motivation, conscious or not, seems alive in the tendency of Egyptologists to apply the term 'propaganda' to ancient Egyptian art, including literature.

One way through the problem may be offered by conceiving of the political content not as a dominant and isolated factor, as in perceived propagandistic motivation, but as part of a multidimensional web of 'reality features' and 'interpretative dimensions' either filtered all together through the aesthetic, or with the aesthetic as another component. Jan Assmann sets the political dimension among other dimensions of interpreting the world in ancient Egypt, as plotted on a table against the features of the world (Assmann 1990: 38):

area of reality → interpretative dimensions↓	**the sacred**	**cosmos**	**state/rule**	**society**	**human**
religious	(theology)	sacred aspects of cosmic features	divine kingship	religious aspects of social cohesion	religious anthropology (ka, ba, akh etc)
(bio)-cosmic	cosmic dimension of deities	(cosmology)	cosmic dimension of kingship	cosmic aspect of social order	cosmic aspect of human, immortality
political	city deities	sun-course as exercise of power	(politology)	political aspect of social order	political aspect of human
social	society of deities – 'mythology'	cosmos as system of activities	social/ protective function of kingship	(sociology)	social aspect of human
anthropological	anthropo-morphism/ -centrism	age cycle of cosmos	anthropolog. role of rule	anthropolog. role of society	(anthropology)

This table provides a means of defusing the political issue, abandoning the overly baggage-laden propaganda word (as Parkinson urges), but allowing future research to consider the degree and role of political content.

Without precise dates of composition, the political is likely to remain the least accessible of the features of this web, but it does not disappear entirely. In a study of the recurrence of the term 'repeating of births' or 'Renaissance' under Amenemhat I, Sety I and Ramses XI, Andrzej Niwiński suggests that the creation of a Residence at Itjtawy would have reshaped the creative productive forces of the country, producing new alignments of social and economic power, and that this may have its impact on literary production too (Niwiński 1996). Admittedly, the evidence is scant and his datings of change can be contested: thus, the Third-Fourth Dynasty seems more a turning-point than the Fifth, the Amarna Period as much a turning-point as the post-Amarna Period, and the post-Ramesside 'repeating of births' has been more satisfatorily explained, to my mind, by Jansen-Winkeln, as predating establishment of a king Smendes at Tanis and related Libyan general Herihor at Thebes (Jansen-Winkeln 1992). Moreover, his politicisation of the aesthetic risks a return to the flat reading of literature as an art of persuasion and nothing more. Still, it seems plausible that all Middle Kingdom literary compositions postdate the founding of the new Residence at Itjtawy in perhaps year 20 of Amenemhat I = year 1 of Senusret I (Arnold 1991), and in this sense the start at least of Middle Kingdom literary output does amount to a 'literature of the Residence'. There may even be authors at the highest level of the court of Senusret I, if the treasurer Mentuhotep has been correctly identified as author of the Loyalist Teaching (Berlev 1972, 30). The political dimension is there. However, no exploration of a political dimension can begin before the preeminently aesthetic or literary qualities of the compositions have been fully acknowledged, and this still seems incompletely established among Egyptologists.

Literature – Belletristik – Eurocentrism?

In reasserting the literariness of ancient Egyptian literary writing, the term *belles lettres* has been a useful substitute for 'literature' as a label for aesthetic writing. Since 'literature' has the broader sense of 'advanced writing' in phrases such as 'scientific literature', 'secondary literature', or 'the Egyptological literature', it seems fair to make use of *belles lettres* as a term that distinguishes literary writing from those uses. In addition, its slight foreignness may activate warning signs against assuming that the literary borders and contours of ancient Egypt are precisely the same as those in modern literature. Finally, the term provides a literal translation of the ancient Egyptian *mdt nfrt* (Vernus 1996, 558). Despite these advantages, I see two risks in the use of the French term in English language Egyptology (noting the association of foreign-language word and ideological and political power, as Voloshinov 1995 [1929], 290). First, the use of a foreign language can reinforce specific social boundaries, and remove the aesthetic from the very horizon of universal humanity that makes these ancient writings so powerful still today. The aestheticisation and refinement may be desired, but any social implications should be made explicit, and, if not desired, combated in some way. The second, scientifically and historically more disturbing problem lies in a lack of historicised awareness among Egyptologists; perhaps this is a term that we think we know, and for which we need to doublecheck our ground. Fortunately, the history of the term has been explored by Philippe Caron, and some notes from a reading of his theses may be presented here, for the context of Middle Kingdom Egypt, though that is a land and place with social and communicative structures barely comparable with either the world of modern literature, or the home ground of *belles lettres*, France in the century or so from 1640 (Caron 1992). When Caron voices the need for this historical enquiry into the meaning of *belles lettres*, his warning could be applied to Egyptological use of the term as part of this modern ahistorical experience of vocabulary: "A tout instant la recherche est guettée par le risque de plaquer sur un siècle passé les automatismes linguistiques et conceptuels de la période que nous vivons" (Caron 1992, 361). Unless we pursue the term, it may become an obstacle instead of an aid to understanding the other past.

Prior to the mid-seventeenth century, the phrase *bonnes lettres* dominated references to broad spheres of learning (pp.150-154): this Egyptologically less familiar term would provide another literal translation for ancient Egyptian *mdt nfrt*. Although there was no declared antonym, the implicit opposite to this essentially high Renaissance term was clearly the writing and learning of the period between classical Roman antiquity and the Renaissance; the Middle Ages provided the temporal block against which Renaissance scholarship defined itself. In the heyday of *bonnes lettres*, the sixteenth century, the term *belles lettres* is not attested (p.103). The age of the *bonnes lettres* knew only two literate groups in French society, the clergy and 'la bourgeoisie et la noblesse parlementaires'; this changed with the establishment of a centralising royal Court under Louis XIII (p.363). "D'une conception quasi mystique de la parole, on passe à une langue-ornement, destinée à plaire au Prince at à attirer sur l'auteur les bénédictions du pouvoir et les suffrages du grand monde" (p.364). "Le passage de *bonnes* à *belles* est symptomatique d'un changement idéologique qui privilégie le canon esthétique au détriment de la valeur morale" (p.153). In turn, over the course of the eighteenth century, *belles lettres* gave way to 'literature', and Caron explains the success of the latter term as part of a paradigm shift from aesthetic to historicist focus in European civilization, moving from absolutism past the bourgeois revolution (p.190-191). On literature he comments: "Le mot était moins marqué par les préoccupations d'une époque. Il ne préjugeait pas de la fonction prédominante des textes du canon littéraire. Il était en outre d'une plus grande maniabilité distributionnelle. Toutes ces raisons l'ont fait préférer pour traduire le nouveau partage conceptual qui était à l'oeuvre" (p.191).

In the seventeenth and eighteenth centuries AD, in France, the precise reference of the term *belles lettres* varied from one authority to another, as tabulated by Caron from its heyday down to about 1750 (p.114) and from selected works of 1726-1785 (p.123). Ancient rhetoric and poetry provided a stable core, usually with ancient history and the grammar of Latin and Greek; an outer circle less consistently included within the term comprises the four terrains of 1. philosophy, 2. painting, 3. polymathic learning, and 4. French rhetoric, poetry, grammar and history. The mid-eighteenth century works all retain poetry and rhetoric, usually including also history and grammar, less often philosophy, and only rarely novels and other varieties of prose. These specific topics define the parameters, albeit variable, of the term *belles lettres* in its home. This may be useful comparative material if we decide to deploy the term for ancient Egyptian writing. The groups of second millennium BC papyri that include literary compositions tend to combine the three 'narrow literary' categories or genres of tales, laments and teachings, with other literary content, religious literary and ritual manuscripts, and the themes of knowledge and healing (notably the Ramesseum Papyri and the Chester Beatty Papyri). If Aristotelian and later European categories and titles such as poetry, rhetoric, grammar, philosophy dominate the territory of seventeenth and eighteenth century *belles lettres*, there may not be much ground left for the Egyptological deployment of the term, at least, not if we wish to avoid massive reinforcement of Eurocentric assumptions in our study of ancient Egypt and its literature.

The conflict between mystical *bonnes lettres* and aestheticised secular *belles lettres* might be taken as productive ground for pursuing the Egyptian term that both can translate, *mdt nfrt*. At first sight, an ancient Egyptian accountant like Qenherkhepshef or the treasury secretaries of the Anastasi and Sallier papyri could be considered closer to the world of *bonnes lettres*. On the other hand, the new Residence at Itjtawy might be compared with the courts of Louis XIII and XIV. However, without extremely sensitive handling of starkly different backgrounds, any transhistorical comparisons falter and fail against the detailed historical contextualisation provided by Caron. The absorbing spectacle of local and centralised elites in seventeenth century France is too distant from the world that produced ancient Egyptian literary books and the men who read them, up to the high officials, men such as the treasurer Mentuhotep under Senusret I, possible 'author' of the Loyalist Teaching (uncertain but see Berlev 1972, 30). In passing, it is worth exploring the way we react to the different social groups of individuals. If Egyptological philologists have shown a predilection for *belles lettres*, they may be unlikely to welcome the idea that the less aestheticised promoters of *bonnes lettres* were closer to the ancient Egyptian producer/consumer of literary compositions. If Egyptologists find satisfaction in noble ancestry or an ancestry of genius, they may resist the discovery that ancient readers spent their professional lives doing sums – except presumably those Egyptologists who study ancient administration. By default we probably generally replicate the same moralising hierarchies inculcated in our own education and reinforced in daily communicative practice. Content is evaluated on a scale privileging the purely aesthetic: a pure thinker separate from the world is likely to be considered superior to a thinker muddied by engagement in social/economic/political realities (compare the different reception of members of the Bakhtin circle in non-socialist and post-Soviet reception, Hirschkop 1999, 129-130). Academic professionals may have found comfort in projections of themselves back into time to be discovered as prototypical Western-style free-thinkers creating literary masterpieces: what horror if the creators of that literature turned out to be the accountants. The modern successor to ancient genius would then have been identified as the administrative department, very antithesis of the university lecturer. The writers, copyists and readers of ancient Egyptian literature are the *kuttub* 'bureaucrats' as they were in the early world of classical Arabic *adab* 'literature' or 'learning' (Allen 2000, 139-141). Their leaders would be the *srw ꜥ3yw* 'high officials' as expressed in one of those rare Ramesside sources for reverence of great men (Fischer-Elfert 2002, and above under Question Three). That term becomes common in the late New Kingdom, in legal documents as well as in courtly inscriptions. For the Middle Kingdom the noun *sr* 'official' is more often qualified by the adjective *wr* 'great', though usually with reference to the sun-god and to Osiris, rather than to high officials (according to the index-cards of the Dictionary of the Egyptian Language published online by the Berlin Academy of Sciences at http://www.bbaw.de/forschung/altaegyptwb/dza.html). Does this imply less internal differentiation of the elite during the Middle Kingdom than in the Ramesside Period? How does this affect our understanding of the readership, and the content, of Middle Kingdom literary compositions? An indispensable part of research into Middle Kingdom literature is a sociology of the Middle Kingdom official, on the lines drawn so clearly by Dorothy Thompson for the Ptolemaic Period (Crawford 1978).

In sum, two areas offering fertile ground for future research can be identified, as (1) the question of homogeneity or factionalism within the ancient elite, and (2) the linked question of the relation between numeracy and literacy in training and practice among the ancient elite. These questions need first to be raised with reference to the sources from one period, before the periods may be compared to construct a longer historical context for writing, including literary writing. From the Ptolemaic and Roman Period Fayum, Minnen has charted one world differentiating its officialdom, identifying besides the 'priests' and 'school grammarians' (the stereotypical writing-producers and – consumers assumed for Egypt by Western commentators) "officials of various kinds", and other social factions such as the veterans (van Minnen 1998, 108-112). In the detail on book-owners such as the local tax-collector, or the family of the veteran Caius Iulius Niger at Karanis, the Greek Fayum evidence reveals a varied literate elite in the large 'villages' of Egypt – population centres which, we should remember, would have ranked higher than most 'cities' in the less urbanised Western Empire. These far later Egyptian sources can help us to remove our assumptions on 'priesthood', and to take on board the caution of Minnen against assuming predominant role for either school or library in the circulation, consumption, production of literary compositions (van Minnen 1998, 109 with nn.29-30). Other worlds, including the courts of Louis XIII and XIV and the Tsar and the Caliph and the Emperor of China and the Oba of Benin, also allow us to widen our knowledge of the possible, and provide fresh examples for devising methods for analysis. Yet they cannot fill in the gaps in our knowledge of Egypt, or act as a flawless mirror to a Bronze Age kingdom. After reading on the other worlds, the time comes to return to the contemporary writings and the contemporary material culture of these Middle Kingdom literary compositions, and to read them.

A Middle Kingdom introduction to writing - Kemyt?

Numerous New Kingdom sources preserve parts of a Middle Egyptian composition, of which the first half seems designed to introduce an apprentice to writing-style, including letter formulae and the spelling of words. The various sources for the composition are themselves written in a curious and distinctive style; entirely contrary to usual New Kingdom writing practice, it evokes instead 'Old Hieratic', the standard cursive script of the late Old Kingdom to early Middle Kingdom. The unusual handwriting misled the first Egyptologists studying ostraca with this composition into dating them to the Middle Kingdom: only with the discovery of more examples in the French excavations on the Ramesside settlement site at Deir el-Medina did it become clear that most are from that site and date to the Nineteenth and Twentieth Dynasties.

The composition has been identified as a work cited in other ancient Egyptian literary compositions as *kmyt* 'the compilation' from a quotation of the final phrase within the Middle Kingdom composition entitled the Teaching of Duau Khety (its Section 2):

šd r.k pḥwy kmyt	Read for yourself the end of the Compilation
gmy.k ṯs pn im.s m ḏd	and you can find this phrase in it saying
ir sš m st.f nbt nt ẖnw	'The scribe, whatever his place at the Residence
nn ḥwr.f im.f	He cannot be poor in it'

The phrases that constitute the first part of the composition are typical of formulaic openings to letters in the late Old to early Middle Kingdom; they have been called in Egyptology the Memphite Formula. Apart from the parallels in actual letters, parts are attested on two Middle Kingdom sources:

1. an early Middle Kingdom pottery stand from the cemeteries at Naga el-Deir in Upper Egypt (Simpson 1981)
2. a fragment of papyrus from the late Middle Kingdom town at Lahun (UC 32271A: Collier and Quirke 2004, 50-51)

The Lahun papyrus shows that already in the late Middle Kingdom the copyists were emulating the early Middle Kingdom forms of signs, radically different from any in extant contemporary late Middle Kingdom manuscripts.

The second part of the composition is more miscellaneous, and is not known from any pre-New Kingdom source, though its vocabulary and language also seem to belong in the Middle Kingdom. Wente 1990, 16 interprets the Egyptian word *ꜣw* 'extended' as a personal name of a man, Au; in the translation below, it is given as 'extended one', and its meaning left to the reader to decide. Possibilities include the meaning 'deceased', as attested in late Middle Kingdom juridical documents. Whatever the meaning, there seems to be a dialogic exchange from the position of the woman in Section 8, to the address to the woman in Section 9. This would anticipate the exchange of love songs between man and woman in Ramesside cycles of poems. A reference to the Residence in Section 17 may point to a date of composition for that part after the foundation of the new Residence at Itjtawy, late in the reign of Amenemhat I of Dynasty 12. However, it is not clear at what date the various parts were brought together to form the whole as attested in the New Kingdom.

Transliteration and translation

Wente has provided an introduction and translation into English, from the original assembling and study by George Posener of the innumerable New Kingdom ostraca (Wente 1990, 15-17). Here, the sections are numbered as in the Posener edition, from 'pause' signs in the original sources. Some may reflect later interpretations of the passages, as they seem at places to interrupt a grammatical sequence.

Section 1

bꜣk ḏd ḫr nb.f	The servant says before his master,
mrrw.f ꜥnḫ.f	whom he so wishes to live,
wḏꜣ.f snb.f	to be well, to be healthy,
m ꜣwt ḏt r nḥḥ	in the lengths of time for eternity
mi mrr bꜣk im	as the servant there wishes

Section 2

m3ʿ ḫrw.k ḫr b3w iwnw
ḫr nṯrw nbw
di.sn n.k ʿnḫ.k
ir.sn n.k ḫt nbt nfrt rʿ nb
mi mrr b3k im

May your voice be true before the powers of Iunu
before all gods,
may they grant you that you live
may they make all good things for you every day,
as the servant there wishes

Section 3

iw ḫrt.k m ʿnḫ ḥḥ n sp
iry n.k mntw nb w3st
mi mrr b3k im

Your condition is as life a million times
may Mont lord of Thebes act for you
as the servant there wishes

Section 4

snḏm ptḥ rs inb.f ib.k
m ʿnḫ nfr wrt
i3wt nfrt sbt r im3ḫ
wn r im3ḫ.k nfr
ḫr k3 n mntw nb w3st
mi mrr b3k im

May Ptah south of his wall gladden your heart
with a good life greatly,
a good old age, proceeding to reverence,
being in your beautiful reverence,
before the spirit of Mont lord of Thebes
as the servant there wishes

Section 5

m ḥtp nfrt wrt
ḫr nn r sšw
rdi.n wi wpwty n ḥm.k ḥr.s
iw.i r irt ḥst.k

in peace well and greatly,
Now for the writings
on which the messenger of Your Person has placed me,
I will do what you praise

Section 6

ḥtp.k r nbt b3st
snḏm ib.i pn
rdit iwt 3w
m3.n.i sw m ḫmtnwt.f rnpt

May you be more content than the Lady of Bast,
this my heart is gladdened,
to have the extended one come,
whom I saw in his third year

Section 7

wrḥ m ʿntyw n pwnt
ḫnm t3 nṯr
sd m d3iw n ir.i
i3dw m3.n.f ḫnty

Anointed with the myrrh of Punt
with the scents of the Land of the God,
clothed in a kilt of my making,
(only) a child when he saw the Palace

Section 8

ḏd.s is 3w
m3.n.k ḥmt.k
iw mr rm.s ṯw
iw rmm.s ṯw
ḥr rmw.k m grḥ
3pdw.k m hrw

She says 'go, extended one,
you have seen your wife':
it is bad that she weeps so over you,
and she does weep so over you
over your fishes in the night
and your birds in the day

Section 9

mi r.t m ḫd
sḏd.i n.t nn
mdw rḥw snw iry
gm.n.sn wi ḥr rs n niwt

Lady, come north -
I tell you these,
the words of the companions and brothers there,
when they have found me to the south of the city

Section 10

ib.i nḏm st w3t
tp ḥr m3sty
mi nmḥ ḥr m3ʿ n kt niwt

My heart is glad in a far place?
- head on lap
like an orphan on the shore of another city

Section 11

ii.n.i m niwt nt sn.i
sw3.n.i ḥr tp ʿ3 wr niwt

I came from the city of my brother,
I passed the great head of the city,

gm.n.i it.i hrw n ḥb.i	I found my father the day of my festival,
iw mwt.i sbt r nht	my mother had gone to the sycamore

Section 12

ink mryw n it.i	I am one loved of my father
ḥsyw n mwt.i	praised of my mother,
mrrw snw.f snwt.f	one whom brothers and sisters love.
nn sp tꜣḥy.i n it.i	Never would I dispute my father,
n sšny.i n mwt.i	nor did I quarrel with my mother

Section 13

wḥm ḏdt n imy-r	Repeat what is said, to the overseer,
n mrwt dꜣir ẖrt	for love of removing problems.
ink gr ẖnty	I am the silent one of the Palace,
dr srf m ḳmꜣw sp	removing the heat, in creating the moment.

Section 14

šw m ʿšꜣt ẖrw.i sš im	Free of excess in my voice, the secretary there,
iḳr n nb.f	one who is excellent for his master,
ḥmww n wnwt.f	the craftsman of his hour

Section 15

wḥs n sšw	Persevere (?) in writing,
irr.k sꜣ	and when you have a son,
sbꜣ r sšw	instruct in writings,
ꜣẖw m ḥꜣt.i	the benefit from before me,
sbꜣ.n wi it.i r sšw	as my father instructed me in writings,
ꜣẖw m tp ʿwy.fy	a benefit from upon his hands.

Section 16

nḏr.f ʿ.f ḥr ḥw-ʿḏꜣ	He exercises his arm on the bad pupil:
gm.n.i ḥsyw im	I have found (how to be) praised there,
ḥw ḥr.f m-ẖt sꜣrt	He is struck after need,
m-ẖt wbꜣ n ḥr.i	after opening up to my sight,

Section 17

šmsw pw ḥnʿ nḏt	He is the guard with the milling woman.
irr.k sꜣ sbꜣ r sšw	So make a son, instructed in writings
ir sš m st.f nbt nt ẖnw	For a secretary in any place of his of the Residence,
n ḥwr n.f im.f	he cannot be poor in it.

End note

iw.s pw nfr m ḥtp	This is its end, perfect, in peace.

PART TWO

READINGS
of
SURVIVING MIDDLE KINGDOM LITERARY COMPOSITIONS

How to read transliterated Egyptian

Today the language written in Egypt before the arrival of Arabic is concealed by the modern, especially European perception of its script, Egyptian hieroglyphs, as the ultimate mystery in the history of communication (Iversen 1993). Readers today may be surprised to learn that, though some signs communicate the picture (for example, a tree hieroglyph means 'tree'), others communicate sounds (for example, the common owl hieroglyph denotes the consonantal sound 'm'). In other words, the Egyptian hieroglyphic script is not a sequence of silent pictures, but a strongly integrated combination of sound-signs and idea-signs that conveys the Egyptian language more efficiently than the alphabet later managed (Fischer 1986). It is not a difficult system to learn, but it has to be learned together with the language for which it was invented, Egyptian.

The written language had twenty-five consonants, five of which are weak, something between a vowel and a consonant (Loprieno 1995 for details on the Egyptian language). In the late nineteenth century, German philological Egyptologists established the system now used in Egyptology for transliterating the sound-content of hieroglyphs into a Latin-based script, and a phonetic order for them, starting from weaker consonants, then labial consonants, voiced, sillibants and through to dentals at the end:

ꜣ i̓ y ꜥ w b p f m n r h ḥ ḫ ẖ z s š ḳ k g t ṯ d ḏ

The series of sounds underwent certain changes over the millennia: for example, z and s are no longer strictly distinguished in second millennium BC writing, as they had been in third millennium BC writing, and there seems to be an 'l' lurking behind some sounds written with *ꜣ n* and *r*. There are also regional differences beneath the monolingual imprint of the hieroglyphic script: in regular second millennium BC writing, *ṯ* 'tj' tends to reduce to *t*, and *ḏ* 'dj' to *d*, but northern dialects may have developed differently, with *ṯ* softening to *z* or *š* – as in the placename **Tj**ebennetjer rendered by Greeks at the end of the first millennium BC as Sebennytos.

In contrast to European languages, vowels are not so radically important to reading, and so were not written in the hieroglyphic script, just as modern Arabic and Hebrew newspapers and books are written without vowels, with no difficulty for the reader who knows the language. Research continues into the quality and placement of vowels in Egyptian as it was spoken in remote antiquity: a word written m+n could in theory have been pronounced in many different ways (man, min, mon, mun, mana etc). The clues to the dominant ancient pronunciation tend to be indirect, from words written in other ancient languages of western Asia and the eastern Mediterranean, and from the latest phase of Egyptian written in the alphabetic script derived from Greek with adapted demotic signs, Coptic. While those debates continue, English-speaking Egyptologists tend to pronounce the words by changing the weak consonants into vowel sounds, and supplying 'e' between other consonants where needed. Arabic-speaking Egyptologists have the advantage that they regularly read consonant-only writing, and so can provide more fluent readings for a series of transliterated consonants. Whereas an Arabic-speaker can pronounce all the consonants of the Egyptian language (even 'p' is familiar from names of a country like Pakistan where the Arabic alphabet is used), an English-speaker needs to listen to Arabic for a flavour of several essential sounds not regularly found in the English language.

The table below provides a general guide for English-speaking readers for reading aloud any transliterated Egyptian passage. Poetry must be read aloud, even poetry in a foreign language, if any of its literary qualities are to be appreciated. The translations in Part Two are given with the transliterations, on the same line wherever line-length permits, to encourage readers to read aloud, to come one step closer to another experience in world literature.

Two examples for roughly reading a line of Egyptian from transliteration:

Transliteration	Rough sound	Translation
spr.f r pr.f ind	seperef erperef ined	he reaches his home in utter poverty
ꜥšꜣ n.i m mnmnt.i	'ashani emmenmenti	I enjoyed wealth in cattle,

In the second example, it is essential to clench the throat ('ayin) at the start of 'ashani: the sound is that heard at the start of the Arabic words *'Arab* and *'Iraq*.

Guide to approximate sound of transliterated Egyptian with equivalents in Arabic

transliteration	note on pronunciation	equivalent in Arabic
ꜣ	glottal stop (as at start of English sentence in words with vowels)	آ
i	glottal stop at start of word, y in mid-word	إ or ى
y	y as in 'yes'	ى
ꜥ	clench deep in throat, Arabic 'ayin	ع
w	w as in 'way'	و
b	b as in 'bit'	ب
p	p as in 'pit'	
f	f as in 'fit'	ف
m	m as in 'man'	م
n	n as in 'man'	ن
r	rolled as in light Scots English, not weak as in southern English	ر
h	h as in 'hat'	ه
ḥ	strongly breathed h, Arabic 'Ha'	ح
ḫ	as ch in Scottish 'loch', Arabic 'kha'	خ
ẖ	softer than ch in Scottish 'loch' toward 'sh'	
z	z as in 'zap'	ز
s	s as in 'sap'	س
š	sh as in 'shine'	ش
ḳ	as if k deep in throat, Arabic 'qaf'	ق
k	k as in 'kitten'	ك
g	g as in 'girl'	Cairene ج
t	t as in 'top'	ت
ṯ	tj, as ch in 'church'	ج + ت
d	d as in 'dot'	د
ḏ	dj, as g in 'George'	classical Arabic ج

Part Two, Section One
more substantially preserved literary compositions of the Middle Kingdom

Tales

Compositions in which narrative is the dominant mode provide perhaps the most accessible branch of literatures, though the status allotted them in the hierarchy of language varies from culture to culture. The poetic narratives of Homer provide the foundations of classical Greek identity, whereas tales characterised as fables have not always been allowed into the literary sanctum (Allen 2000, 167-169 on the different Arab World and European reception of the *Thousand and One Nights*). The number and distribution of copies of the Tale of the Exile of Sanehat in Middle and New Kingdom might indicate the high regard in which the composition was held, though the sample is small. Its language and structure indicate a courtly context, as for the Tale of the Shipwrecked Official. By contrast, the language of the cycle of tales At the Court of King Khufu seems less refined; even this, though, would belong within the world of elite production, much as classical Arabic literary commentators allowed both types using fully inflected literary Arabic (*mu`rabah*) and types in a less grammarian-friendly style (*malhunah*) within a received set of seven types of poetry (Allen 2000, 81-83, on Safi al-din al-Hilli).

Three Middle Kingdom tales are substantially preserved: the Exile of Sanehat, the Shipwrecked Official, and a cycle of Tales of Wonder at the Court of King Khufu

The Exile of Sanehat

This is the tale of an Egyptian palace official called Sanehat. At the death of the old king, he fears strife and flees Egypt to build a new life in exile under a ruler in Syria. At the height of his powers he is challenged to a duel by a Syrian champion: Sanehat kills his opponent in the duel, and begins a period of peace. At the approach of old age, he feels driven to return home to end his days, and be buried, as an Egyptian. The reigning king of Egypt invites him back, and he returns to the palace he had left years earlier. He has learned what it means to be an Egyptian, and he has become an Egyptian again - but can he, or his audience, really be the same after this voyage of self-discovery?

The transliteration follows Koch 1990, using the two principal sources (Berlin 3022 for the bulk of the text, and Berlin 10499, for the first section, missing in 3022). The section divisions have been introduced here for convenience: after each section number are given the corresponding line-numbers in Berlin 10499 for the start, and Berlin 3022 from the point it is preserved.

1 (Berlin 10499, lines 1-2)

ꞽry pꜥt ḥꜣty-ꜥ *sꜣb ꜥḏ-mr*	**Nobleman and overlord**, governor and canal-cutter,
ꞽty m tꜣw styw	sovereign in the lands of the Syrians
rḫ nswt mꜣꜥ mry.f	One known to the king directly, his favourite,
šmsw sꜣ-nhꜣt	the Follower Sanehat
ḏd.f	He says:

2 (Berlin 10499, lines 2-5)

ꞽnk šmsw šms nb.f	I am a Follower who follows his lord,
bꜣk n ꞽpt nswt	a servant of the family-quarters of the king
ꞽrt pꜥt wrt ḥswt	Of the noblewoman, abounding in favour,
ḥmt nswt snwsrt m ẖnm-swt	King's Wife of Senusret in Khenemsut
sꜣt nswt ꞽmn-m-ḥꜣt m ḳꜣ-nfrw	King's Daughter of Amenemhat in Qaneferu,
nfrw nbt ꞽmꜣḫ	Neferu, lady of reverence

3 (Berlin 10499, lines 5-11)

rnpt-sp 30 ꜣbd 3 ꜣḫt sw 7	**Regnal year 30, month 3 of Flood, day 7**
ꜥr nṯr r ꜣḫt.f nswt-bꞽty sḥtp-ꞽb-rꜥ	The god ascended to his horizon, the dual king Sehetepibra
sḥr.f r pt ẖnm m ꞽtn	He fared up to the sky, joining with the sun-disk,
ḥꜥw-nṯr ꜣbḫ m ꞽr-sw	divine limbs merging with his creator
ꞽw ẖnw m sgr ꞽbw m gmw	The Residence was in silence, hearts in sorrow,
rwty wrty ḫtmw	The Double Gate sealed,
šnyt m tp-ḥr-mꜣst pꜥt m ꞽmw	The court with head on knees, the nobles in lament

4 (Berlin 10499, lines 12-16)

ist rf sb.n ḥm.f mšꜥ r tꜣ-timḥw	Now His Power had sent an army against the Land of the Timehu
sꜣ.f smsw m ḥry iry	With his eldest son as its commander,
nṯr nfr snwsrt	The good god Senusret
ti-sw hꜣb r ḥw ḫꜣswt	He was sent to strike the hill lands,
r sḳr imyw ṯḥnw	to smite the inhabitants of Tjehenu,
ti-sw ḥm iy.f	He was just on his return,
in.n.f sḳrw-ꜥnḫ n ṯḥnw	and had brought the captives of Tjehenu,
mnmnt nbt nn ḏrw.s	And all the limitless herds

5 (Berlin 10499, lines 17-22)

smrw nw stp-sꜣ hꜣb.sn r gs-imnty	The courtiers of the Palace despatched to the Western reaches,
r rdit rḫ sꜣ nswt sšm ḫpr m ꜥ-ẖnwty	To inform the King's Son of the turn of events in the Chamber
gm.n sw wpwtyw ḥr wꜣt	The envoys found him on the road,
pḥ.n.sn sw r tr n ḫꜣwy	And had reached him at the time of dusk
n sp sinn.f r-ssy	Not a slight moment did he delay,
bik ꜥḫm.f ḥnꜥ šmsw.f	The falcon, he flew off with his followers,
nn rdit rḫ st mšꜥ.f	Without letting his army know

6 (Berlin 10499, lines 22-25, second half corresponding to Berlin 3022, 1-2)

ist hꜣb r msw nswt	Now there was a despatch with regard to the King's children
wnw m-ḫt.f m mšꜥ pn	who were following him in this army
nis.n.tw n wꜥ im	One of them was summoned
ist wi ꜥḥꜥ.kwi sḏm.n.i ḫrw.f	Now I was up, and heard his voice
iw.f mdw.f iw.i m ꜥr wꜣ	When he was speaking - I was a short distance away

7 (Berlin 3022, 2-7)

psḫ ib.i sn ꜥwy.i	My heart stopped, my arms crossed,
sdꜣ ḥr m ꜥt.i nbt	trembling fell through my whole body
nfꜥ.n.i wi m nftft	I slipped back in starts
r ḥḥ n.i st dgꜣ	to seek out a hiding-place,
rdit wi imywt bꜣty	To place myself between the bushes,
r iwt wꜣt šm.s	to remove the way and its farer
irt.i šmt m ḫntyt	I made my way south
n kꜣ.i spr r ẖnw pn	without thinking of approaching this Residence.
ḫmt.n.i ḫpr ḥꜥꜥyt	I imagined there would be bloodshed,
n ḏd.i ꜥnḫ r-sꜣ nn	and I denied I could survive it

8 (Berlin 3022, 8-11)

nmi.n.i mꜣꜥty m hꜣw nhꜣt	I negotiated the Sea of Truth in the area of the Sycamore,
smꜣ.n.i m iw-snfrw	And I made it to the Island of Sneferu
wrš.n.i m ꜥḏ n sḫt	I rested on the curb of the marshes,
hḏ.n.i wn hrw	And moved on when it came to day.
ḫp.n.i s ꜥḥꜥ m r-wꜣt	I crossed a man standing at a fork in the road:
tr.n.f wi snd n.f	He hailed me, but I feared him

9 (Berlin 3022, 11-20)

ḫpr.n tr n msyt	Evening time fell
sꜣḫ.n.i r dmi ngꜣ	as I trod on to the mooring-point of the horned bull
dꜣ.n.i m wsḫt nn ḥmw.s	I ferried across in a cargo-boat without a rudder,
m swt n imnty	thanks to a breeze from the west
sn.n.i ḥr iꜣbtyw ikw	I crossed by the east of the quarry
m ḥryt nbt ḏw-dšr	in the ascent of the Goddess of the Red Mountain
rdit.i wꜣt n rdwy.i m ḫd	I forced my legs to move on northwards
dmi.n.i inbw-ḥḳꜣ	I reached the Walls of the Ruler,
iry r ḫsf styw r ptpt nmiw-šꜥ	made to repel the Syrians and trample on the nomads
šsp.n.i ksw.i m bꜣt	I took my shelter in the bush
m snd mꜣꜣ wršy tp inb imy hrw.f	From fear of being seen by the guard on the wall who was on duty
ir.i šmt tr n ḫꜣwy	And made my way at night

10 (Berlin 3022, 20-24)

ḥḏ.n tꜣ pḥ.n.i ptn	At daybreak I reached Peten
ẖn.kwi r iw n km-wr	And alighted at an island of the Great Black Water
ḫr.n ibt ꜣs.n.f wi	Thirst struck, it overwhelmed me
ntb.kwi ḫḫ.i ḫmw	I panted, my throat parched
ḏd.n.i dpt mwt nn	I said, this is the taste of death,
ṯst.i ib.i ḥʿw.i	Binding my heart and my body

11 (Berlin 3022, 24-28)

sḏm.n.i ḫrw nmi n mnmnt	I heard the sound of lowing of cattle
gmḥ.n.i styw	And sighted Syrians
siꜣ.n wi mtn im pꜣ wnn ḥr kmt	I was spied out by one of their scouts who had been in Egypt
ʿḥʿ.n rdi.n.f n.i mw ps n.i irtt	Then he gave me water, and milk was cooked for me
šm.n.i ḥnʿ.f n wḥyt.f nfr irt.n.sn	I went with him to his people. What they did was good.

12 (Berlin 3022, 28-31)

rdi.n wi ḫꜣst n ḫꜣst	Hill-land passed me to hill-land
fḫ.n.i r kpny ḥs.n.i r ḳdmi	I wound up in Byblos, and travelled up to Qedem
ir.n.i rnpt wʿ gs im in wi ʿmw-nnši	I had spent a year and a half there when Amunenshi fetched me,
ḥḳꜣ pw n rtnw ḥrt	He being a ruler of the hinterland of Syria

13 (Berlin 3022, 31-36)

ḏd.f n.i	He said to me
nfr tw ḥnʿ.i sḏm.k r n kmt	You would be well with me, you can hear Egyptian
ḏd.n.f nn rḫ.n.f ḳd.i sḏm.n.f šsꜣ.i	He said this because he knew my character, and had heard of my talent
mtr.n wi rmṯ kmt ntyw im ḥnʿ.f	The Egyptians who were there with him had given witness for me
ʿḥʿ.n ḏd.n.f n.i	Then he said to me
pḥ.n.k nn ḥr-sy išst	How is it that you have reached these parts,
in iw wn ḫprt m ẖnw	Has something happened in the Residence?

14 (Berlin 3022, 36-43)

ʿḥʿ.n ḏd.n.i n.f	Then I said to him,
nswt bity sḥtp-ib-rʿ wḏꜣ r ꜣḫt	The dual king Sehetepibra has gone to the horizon,
n rḫ.n.tw ḫprt ḥr.s	How it happened is not known.
ḏd n.i swt m iw-ms	But I was told indirectly.
ii.n.i m mšʿ n tꜣ-timḥi	I was coming with the Timehi-land army
wḥm.tw n.i	When it was reported to me
ib.i ꜣhd in.n.f wi ḥr wꜣt nt wʿrt	My heart failed, and brought me on the road of flight
n psg.tw.i	Though I had not been implicated
n wfꜣ.tw r ḥr.i	and no accusation had been made against me
n sḏm ṯs-ḥwr	(though no slander had been heard,
n sḏm.tw rn.i m r wḥmw	and my name had not been mentioned by the reporter -
n rḫ.i in wi r ḫꜣst tn	I do not know what brought me to this hill-land)
iw mi sḫr nṯr	It is as if a slight of the god,
mi mꜣꜣ sw idḥy m ꜣbw	As a Delta-man seeing himself in Abu
s n ẖꜣt m tꜣ sty	Or a marsh-man in the Land of the bow

15 (Berlin 3022, 43-45)

ʿḥʿ.n ḏd.n.f ḫft.i	Then he said before me
wnn irf tꜣ pf mi-m	How will that land be now,
m ḫmt.f nṯr pf mnḫ	without that effective god
wnnw snd.f ḫt ḫꜣswt	Whose fear permeated the hill-lands
mi sḫmt rnpt idw	like Sekhmet in a year of plague

16 (Berlin 3022, 45-51)

ḏd.kꜣ.i r.i n.f wšb.i n.f	Then I addressed myself to him in reply to him
nḥmn sꜣ.f ʿḳ r ʿḥ	Why, his son is entering the palace

i͗ṯ.n.f i͗wꜥt nt i͗t.f	And has taken up the inheritance of his father
nṯr pw grt nn snw.f	He is indeed a god without equal,
nn ky ḫpr r ḫr-ḥꜣt.f	with no other existing before him
nb sꜣt pw i͗ḳr sḫrw	He is a master of far-sightedness, excellent in planning,
mnḫ wḏwt prt hꜣt ḫft wḏ.f	effective in decrees, coming and going follow his decrees
ntf dꜣir ḫꜣswt i͗w i͗t.f m ḫnw ꜥḥ.f	He is the suppressor of the hill-lands when his father was in his palace
smi.f n.f šꜣt.f ḫpr	And reporting to him that whatever he ordained has come to pass

17 (Berlin 3022, 51-59)

nḫt pw grt i͗r m ḫpš.f	He is truly a strong man made by his strong arm,
pr-ꜥ nn twt.n.f	A man of action - noone comes close to him
mꜣꜣ.tw.f hꜣ.f r-pḏt	He is to be seen as he descends for archery,
ḫꜥm.f r-ḏꜥw	Joining the fray,
wꜥf ꜥb pw sgnn drwt	He is one who takes the horn, when (other) hands are weary,
n ṯs.n ḫrwy.f skw	- so his enemies cannot gather their forces
i͗ꜥ-ḥr pw tšb wpwt	He is one cleansed in sight, cleaving foreheads,
n ꜥḥꜥ.n.tw m hꜣw.f	None can stand in his way.
pd nmtwt pw sti.f bhꜣw	He is one who strides ahead to shoot down those in flight
nn pḥwy n dd-n.f-sꜣ	Giving no quarter to the man who turns tail.
ꜥḥꜥ-i͗b pw m ꜣt sꜣsꜣ	He is the stout-hearted in the moment of the charge
ꜥnw pw n rdi.n.f sꜣ.f	He is the returner who never turns tail
wmt-i͗b pw mꜣꜣ.f ꜥšꜣt	He is the broad-hearted one when he sees the multitude,
n rdi.n.f ḥms hꜣ i͗b.f	Who never places rest behind his heart

18 (Berlin 3022, 60-65)

wd-ḥr pw hꜣ.f i͗ꜣbtyw	He is the forward mover when he descends to the Easterners,
rš.f pw ḥꜣḳ r-pḏt	His delight is the plunder of archery,
ṯꜣ.f i͗km.f titi.f	He takes his shield, tramples underfoot,
n wḥm.n.f ꜥ r ḫdb	He never raises his arm twice for the kill
nn wn rwi ꜥhꜣw.f nn i͗tḥ pḏt.f	his arrow never strays, his bow never strains,
bhꜣ pḏt ḫr-ḥꜣt.f mi bꜣw n wrt	The nomads are routed before him as at the might of the Great Goddess
ꜥhꜣ.f ḫmt.f pḥwy	He fights and plans the outcome,
n sꜣ.n.f nn spt	He never guards, without event

19 (Berlin 3022, 65-70)

nb i͗ꜣmt pw ꜥꜣ bnit	He is a lord of mercy, full of kindness,
i͗ṯ.n.f m mrwt	He has conquered by love,
mr sw niwt.f r ḥꜥw.sn	his citizens love him more than themselves
ḥꜥ st i͗m.f r nṯr.sn	They rejoice over him more than over their god
swꜣ ṯꜣyw ḥmwt ḥr rnnwt i͗m.f	Men and women outdo (one another) in extolling him
i͗w.f m nswt i͗ṯ.n.f m swḥt	As he is king, and he had conquered still in the egg,
ḥr.f r.s ḏr ms.tw.f	His face was set to it from the moment he was born
sꜥšꜣ pw msyt ḥnꜥ.f	With him comes the increase in births
wꜥ pw n dd nṯr	He is the sole one of the gift of god,
rš-wy tꜣ pn ḥḳꜣ.n.f	How joyful is this land that he has come to rule –

20 (Berlin 3022, 71-75)

swsḫ tꜣšw pw	He is one who extends the borders
i͗w.f r i͗ṯt tꜣw rsw	He will seize the southern lands,
nn kꜣ.f ḫꜣswt mḥtt	Before considering the northern lands
i͗r.n.tw.f r ḥwt styw r ptpt nmiw-šꜥ	He has been made to smite the Syrians and trample the sandfarers
hꜣb n.f i͗mi rḫ.f rn.k	Send to him and let him know your name
m šn wꜣ r ḥm.f	Do not plot anything against His Power
[ḫt] nbt i͗r.f n.k [i͗rt i͗t.f]	He will do everything for you that his father did
nn tm.f i͗r bw nfr	He will not fail to do good
n ḫꜣst wnnty.sy ḥr mw.f	for the hill-land that will be loyal to him

21 (Berlin 3022, 75-81)

ḏd.in.f ḫft.i	Then he said before me:
ḥr ḥm kmt nfrt nts rḫt rwd.f	Then fair Egypt, she is indeed the land that knows his firmness.
mk tw ꜥꜣ wnn.k ḥnꜥ.i	You are here, though, and will be with me.
nfr irt.i n.k	What I do for you will be good
rdi.n.f wi m ḥꜣt ẖrdw.f	He placed me at the head of his children
mni.n.f wi m sꜣt.f wrt	He settled me with his eldest daughter
rdi.n.f stp.i n.i m ḫꜣst.f	And let me choose for myself from his hill-land,
m stpw n wnt ḥnꜥ.f ḥr tꜣš.f n kt ḫꜣst	From the choicest of his surrounds on his border to the next hill-land

22 (Berlin 3022, 81-85)

tꜣ pw nfr iꜣꜣ rn.f	It was a fair land, called Iaa
iw dꜣbw im.f ḥnꜥ iꜣrrt	There were figs there and grapes.
wr n.f irp r mw	It had wine more abundant than water
ꜥꜣ bit.f ꜥšꜣ bꜣḳ.f	Its honey was plentiful, its plant-oil innumerable
dḳr nb ḥr ḫtw.f	On its trees were all kinds of fruit
iw it im ḥnꜥ bdt	There was barley there and wheat,
nn ḏrw mnmnt nbt	And unlimited cattle of every kind

23 (Berlin 3022, 85-92)

ꜥꜣ grt dmit r.i m ii n mrt.i	Much also accrued to me as a result of the love of me
rdi.n.f wi m ḥḳꜣ wḥy m stp n ḫꜣst.f	He made me ruler of a clan from the most select of his hill-land
ir.n.i ꜥḳw m mint irp m ẖrt-hrw	I acquired food, jars and wine in the course of a day
iwf psw ꜣpd m ꜣšr ḥrw r ꜥwt ḫꜣst	Meat was cooked, ducks roasted, as well as the hill-land livestock
iw grg.tw n.i iw wꜣḥ.tw n.i	They laid snares for me, and laid down the catch for me,
ḥr r inw n ṯsmw.i	As well as the goods of my hounds
iw ir.tw n.i … ꜥšꜣw irtt m pst nbt	They made for me numerous [foods?] and milk in every kind of dish

24 (Berlin 3022, 92-99)

ir.n.i rnpwt ꜥšꜣt	I spent many years,
ẖrdw.i ḫpr m nḫtw	And my children had grown to adults.
s nb m dꜣir wḥyt.f	Each man of them in control of his own clan,
wpwty ḫd ḫnt r ẖnw ꜣb.f ḥr.i	Any envoy on his way to or from the Residence, he stopped by me
iw sꜣb.i rmṯ nbt iw.i di.i mw n ib	I sheltered everyone, I gave water to the thirsty,
rdi.n.i tnm ḥr wꜣt	I placed the man who went astray back on the road,
nḥm.n.i ꜥwꜣ	I rescued the afflicted,
styw wꜣ r štm	Any Syrians who fell to fomenting strife
r ḫsfꜥ ḥḳꜣw ḫꜣswt	and disturbing the rulers of hill-lands,
dꜣis.n.i šmwt.sn	I challenged their movements

25 (Berlin 3022, 99-109)

iw ḥḳꜣ pn n (r)tnw	This ruler of Syria
di.f iry.i rnpwt ꜥšꜣt m ṯsw n mšꜥ.f	made me spend many years as commander of his army
ḫꜣst nbt rwt.n.i r.s	Every hill-land I moved against,
iw ir.n.i hd.i im.s	I ensured I prevailed over it,
drt ḥr smw ẖnmwt.s	Removing down to the plants at its wells,
ḥꜣḳ.n.i mnmnt.s	I captured its cattle,
in.i ẖr.s nḥm wnmt.sn	brought away its servants, removed their food
smꜣ.n.i rmṯ im.s	And slew its inhabitants,
m ḫpš.i m pḏt.i	by my right arm, by my bow,
m nmtwt.i m sḫrw.i iḳrw	by my movements, by my excellent plans
ꜣḫ.n.i m ib.f mr.n.f wi	I became invaluable to him, and he loved me,
rḫ.n.f ḳnn.i	for he know how valiant I was
rdi.n.f wi m ḥꜣt ẖrdw.f	He placed me at the head of his children,
mꜣ.n.f rwd ꜥwy.i	For he saw the firmness of my arms

26 (Berlin 3022, 109-113)

iwt nḫt n rtnw	There came a hero of Syria
mtꜣ.n.f wi m ꜥfꜣ.i	who challenged me in my tent
pry pw nn snw.f	He was an unrivalled champion,

dr.n.f s r ḏr.s	Who had prevailed over the entire region
ḏd.n.f ꜥḥꜣ.f ḥnꜥ.i	He said he would fight me,
ḥmt.n.f ḥwt.f wi	He intended to smite me,
kꜣ.n.f ḥꜣḳ mnmnt.i ḫr sḥ n wḥyt.f	He planned to carry off my cattle before the council of his clan

27 (Berlin 3022, 113-127)

ḥkꜣ pf ndnḏ.f ḥnꜥ.i ḏd.kꜣ.i n rḫ.i sw	That ruler was consulting with me, so I said I did not know the man,
n ink tr smꜣ.f wstn.i m ꜥfꜣi.f	That it was not I who went to him and strode into his tent,
in nt pw wn.n.i sꜣ.f snb.n.i inbwt.f	Or was it I who opened his gate, and moved past his walls?
rḳt-ib pw ḥr mꜣꜣ.f wi ḥr irt wpwt.k	He must have been tempted to it, seeing me doing your missions
nḥmn wi mi kꜣ n ḥww	Well, I am like a bull of the strikers
m-ḫr-ib ky idr	amid another herd of cattle
hd sw kꜣ n ꜥwt ngꜣ ḥr ꜣm r.f	The bull of the herd smites him, the horned bull assails him
in iw wn twꜣ mrrw n šꜣ n tp-ḥr	Does a lowly man become loved when fate makes him a master?
nn pḏty smꜣ m idḥw	There is no desert-nomad who befriends a marshman
ptr smn idyt r ḏw	Does a marsh-reed flourish at the mountain
in iw kꜣ mr.f ꜥḥꜣ	Does a bull love to fight,
pry mr.f wḥm sꜣ m ḥr nt mḫꜣ.f sw	Should a herd-leader like to turn back in fear of being matched?
ir wnn ib.f r ꜥḥꜣ imi ḏd.f ḫrt-ib.f	If he wishes to fight, let him say his wish
in iw nṯr ḫm šꜣt.n.f	Does a god not know what he ordained?
rḫ nt pw mi-m	Or a man who knows how it will be?

28 (Berlin 3022, 127-134)

sḏr.n.i ḳꜣs.n.i pḏt.i wd.n.i ꜥḥꜣw.i	I went to rest, tied my bow, sharpened my arrows,
ꜥn.i sn n bꜣgsw.i sḫkr.n.i ḫꜥw.i	Whetting the blade of my dagger, arrayed my weapons
ḥḏ.n tꜣ rtnw iyt ḏdb.n.s wḥyt.s	At dawn Syria came, it roused its people,
sḥw.n.s ḫꜣswt nt gs-sy	It assembled the hill-lands on either side,
kꜣ.n.s ꜥḥꜣ pn	For it knew of this fight
iwt pw ir.n.f n.i ꜥḥꜥ.kwi	He came toward me as I stood
di.n.i wi m hꜣw.f	And I placed myself next to him
ḥꜣty nb mꜣḫ n.i	Every heart was burning for me
ḥmwt ṯꜣyw ḥr ꜥꜥi	Women and men pounding
ib nb mr n.i r ḏd	Every mind was aching for me, saying,
in iw wn ky nḫt ꜥḥꜣ r.f	'is there any hero that can fight against him?'

29 (Berlin 3022, 134-142)

ꜥḥꜥ.n ikm.f minb.f	And then his shield, his dagger,
ḥpt.f ns n nyswt ḫr	his armour, his holder of spears fell,
m-ḫt spr.n.i ḫꜥw.f	As I approached his weapons
rdi.n.i swꜣ ḥr.i	I made my face dodge
ꜥḥꜣw.f sp n iwtt	And his weapons were wasted as nothing
wꜥw ḥr ḫn m wꜥw	Each piled on the next
ꜥḥꜥ.n ir.n.f ꜣꜥr.f r.i	Then he made his charge against me
ḥmt.n.f ḥwt.f ꜥ.i	He imagined he would strike my arm
ḫꜥm.n.f wi sti.n.i sw	As he moved over me, I shot him,
ꜥḥꜣw.i mn m nḥbt.f	My arrow lodged in his neck,
sbḥ.n.f ḫr.n.f ḥr fnd.f	He cried out, and fell on his nose,
sḫr.n.i sw m minb.f	I felled him with his dagger
wd.n.i išnn ḥr iꜣt.f	I uttered my war-cry on his back,
ꜥꜣm nb ḥr nmi	Every Asiatic lowing
rdi.n.i ḥknw n mntw	I gave praise to Mont
mr.f ḥb n.f	As his servants mourned for him

30 (Berlin 3022, 142-149)

ḥkꜣ pn ꜥmw-nnši rdi.n.f wi r ḥpt.f	This ruler Amunenshi took me into his embrace,
ꜥḥꜥ.n in.n.i ḫt.f ḥꜣḳ.n.i mnmnt.f	Then I brought away his goods, I carried off his cattle,
kꜣt.n.f irt st r.i ir.n.i st r.f	What he had planned to do to me, I did to him,
iṯ.n.i ntt m imꜣ.f kfꜣ.n.i ꜥfꜣy.f	I seized what was in his camp, and uncovered his tent
ꜥꜣ n.i im wsḫ n.i m ꜥḥꜥw.i	There I was in greatness, I was broad in my standing,
ꜥšꜣ n.i m mnmnt.i	I enjoyed wealth in cattle,

ḫr irt nṯr r ḥtp n ṯs.n.f im.f	Thus the god acted to make peace for the one he had cursed,
th.n.f r kt ḫ3st	The one he had led away to another hill-land
iw min ib.f iʿ	Today his heart is appeased

31 (Berlin 3022, 149-156)
wʿr wʿr n h3w.f iw mtr.i m ẖnw
s33 s33y n ḥkr iw.i di.i t n gsy
rww s t3.f n ḥ3yt ink ḥdt p3ḳt
bt3 s n g3w h3b.f ink ʿš3 mrt
nfr pr.i wsḫ st.i sḫ3wy.i m ʿḥ

The fugitive flees from his surrounds, but my right place is in the Residence,
The deserter deserts from hunger, but I can give bread to my neighbour
A man abandons his land from nakedness, but I, I own white linen, finest cloth,
A man runs away for lack of one to send, but I, I own many servants
My estate is fine, my place is broad, my renown is in the palace

32 (Berlin 3022, 156-164)

nṯrw nb š3 wʿrt tn	Whichever god ordained this flight
ḥtp.k di.k wi r ẖnw	Be at peace, give me back to the Residence
smwn.k r rdit m3.i bw wrš ib.i im	Relent and let me see the place where my heart resides
ptr wrt r ʿbt ẖ3t.i m t3 ms.kwi im.f born	See how great it is to wrap my corpse in the land in which I was
mi m s3.i pw	Come in my defence, then,
ḫpr sp nfr di.n.i ḥtp nṯr	a good event has occurred, I have appeased the god
ir.f mi ḫt r smnḫ pḥwy n sfn.n.f	May he act so as to bring right the end for one he afflicted
ib.f mr n dḳr.n.f r ʿnḫ ḥr ḫ3st	May his heart ail for the one he excluded to live on the hill-land
in min rf ntf ḥtp	Today at last he is appeased
sḏm.f nḥ n w3	Let him hear the prayer of the exile,
wdb.fʿ r ḥw.n.f t3 im.f	May he bring back his arm for the one he forced over the land
r bw in.n.f sw im	Back to the place he brought him from

33 (Berlin 3022, 165-173)

ḥtp n.i nswt n kmt	May the king of Egypt be content with me,
ʿnḫ.i m ḥtpt.f	may I live in his pleasure
nḏ ḫrt ḥnwt t3 ntt m ʿḥ.f	Greeting the mistress of the land who is in his palace
sḏm.i wpwt nt ẖrdw.s	May I hear the missions of her children,
iḫ rnpy ḥʿw.i	that my body be young
nt rf i3w h3w	For now old age has descended
wgg 3s.n.f wi	Sloth has overwhelmed me
irty.i dns ʿwy.i nw	My eyes are heavy, my arms slack
rdwy.i fnḫ.sn šms ib wrd	My legs are unstable, my heart seeks rest
tkn wi n wḏ3	I am drawn close to departure,
sb.sn wi r niwt n nḥḥ	when they will bear me to the city of eternity
šms.i nbt-r-ḏr	May I follow the Lady of All
iḫ ḏd.s n.i nfr n msw.s	that she may tell me what is good for her children
sb.s nḥḥ ḥr.i	May she draw eternity over me

34 (Berlin 3022, 173-177)
ist rf ḏd n ḥm n nswt-bity ḫpr-k3-rʿ m3ʿ-ḫrw
ḥr sšm pn nty wi ḫr.f
wn.in ḥm.f h3b.f n.i ḫr 3wt-ʿ nt ḫr nswt
s3w.f ib n b3k im mi ḥk3 n ḫ3st nbt
msw nswt nty m ʿh.f hr rdit sḏm.i wpwt sn

Now report was made to the Person of the dual king Kheperkara justified
Concerning this condition I was suffering
Then His Power sent to me largesse of before the king
He extended his heart to this servant as to a ruler of any hill-land
And the king's children who were in his palace let me hear their commissions

35 (Berlin 3022, 178-187)

mity n wḏ iny n bꜣk im	**Copy of the decree brought to this servant**
ḥr int.f r kmt	**concerning bringing him to Egypt**
ḥr ꜥnḫ mswt nbty ꜥnḫ mswt	The Horus living of births, he of the Two Ladies living of births,
nswt-bity ḫpr-kꜣ-rꜥ	The dual king Kheperkara
sꜣ rꜥ imn-m-ḥꜣt ꜥnḫ ḏt r nḥḥ	son of Ra of Amenemhat living forever eternally
wḏ nswt n šmsw sꜣ-nhꜣt	Decree of the king to the follower Sanehat
mk in.tw n.k wḏ pn n nswt	See this decree of the king is brought to you
r rdit rḫ.k ntt pḫr.n.k ḫꜣswt	To inform you that you have travelled the hill-lands
prt m ḳdm rtnw	Going from Qedem of Syria
dd tw ḫꜣst n ḫꜣst	Hill-land gave you to hill-land
ḫr sḫ n ib.k n.k	following the counsel of your heart to yourself
ptr irt.n.k ir.tw r.k	What was it you had done, or had been done to you?
n wꜥꜣ.k ḫsf.tw mdw.k	You did not say wrong that your words be punished
n mdw.k m sḫ n srw itn.tw ṯsw.k	You did not speak in the council of officials that your phrases be bound
sḫr pn in.n.f ib.k	This matter, it carried off your heart -
nn rf m ib.i r.k	there was nothing in my heart against you
pt.k tn ntt m ꜥḥ mn.s rwd.s m-min	This your heaven who is in the palace, she is well and strong today
dp.tw.s tp.s m nsyt nt tꜣ	Her head is adorned with the kingship of the land
msw.s m ꜥḫnwty	Her children are in the inner palace

36 (Berlin 3022, 187-199)

wꜣḥ.k špss n dd.sn n.k	**May you add the riches of their gift to you,**
ꜥnḫ.k m ꜣwt.sn	that you may live by their offerings
ir n.k iwt r kmt	Prepare your return to Egypt,
mꜣ.k ḫnw ḫpr.n.k im.f	that you may see the Residence where you were born,
sn.k tꜣ r rwty wrty ḫnm.k m smrw	and kiss the ground at the Great Double Gate, and join the courtiers
iw min is šꜣꜥ.n.k tni	Today now you have begun to age
fḫ.n.k bꜣꜣt	You have unravelled virility
sḫꜣ n.k hrw n ḳrs sbt r imꜣḫ	You are reminded of the day of burial, of passing to reverence
wdꜥ.tw n.k ḫꜣwy m sft wtꜣw m-ꜥ tꜣyt	A night is cut for you with oils and wrappings from the Goddess Linen
ir.tw n.k šms wdꜣ hrw smꜣ-tꜣ	A procession of passing is made for you, on the day of burial
wi m nbw tp m ḫsbd	A case of gold, a mask of lapis lazuli,
pt ḥr.k di.ti m mstpt	the sky over you, placed in the bier
iḥw ḥr itḥ.k šmꜥw ḫr-ḥꜣt.k	The oxen drawing you, chanters in front of you
ir.tw ḫbb nnyw r r is.k	Dances are made by the sacred dancers at the door of your tomb
nis.tw n.k dbḥt-ḥtpw	Offerings are pronounced for you,
sft.tw r r ꜥbꜣw.k	meat is butchered at the door of your chapel
iwnw.k ḫws m inr ḥḏ	Your pillars are enriched with white stone
m ḳꜣb msw nswt	in the midst of (those of) the children of the king
nn wn mwt.k ḥr ḫꜣst nn bs tw ꜥꜣmw	Your death shall not be upon the hill-land, Asiatics will not inter you
nn dit.k m inm n sr ir.tw ḏr.k	You are not to be placed in a sheepskin as your enclosure is made
iw nꜣ ꜣw r ḥwt tꜣ mḥ ḥr ḫꜣt iwt.k	It is too long for wandering the land, think of the corpse and return

37 (Berlin 3022, 199-204)

spr.n wḏ pn r.i	**This decree reached me**
ꜥḥꜥ.kwi m ḥr-ib wḥt.i	**as I stood among my clan**
šd.n.tw.f n.i	It was read out to me
di.n.i wi ḥr ḫt.i	And I placed myself on my belly
dmi.n.i sꜣtw	I touched the ground
di.n.i sw sn ḥr šnby.i	And put it strewn over my chest
dbn.n.i n.i ꜥfꜣy.i ḥr nhm r ḏd	I went around my camp shouting aloud
ir.tw nn mi-m n bꜣk	How is this done for a servant
th.n ib.f r ḫꜣswt ḏrḏryt	whose heart led him astray to foreign lands
ḥr ḥm nfr wꜣḥ-ib nḥm wi m-ꜥ mwt	This is utter good, the mercy that rescues me from death
iw kꜣ.k r rdit	Your spirit will let
iry.i pḥwy ḥꜥw.i m ḫnw	me spend the end of my bodily days in the Residence

38 (Berlin 3022, 204-214)

mity n smi n wḏ pn	**Copy of the report to this decree**
bꜣk ꜥḥ sꜣ-nhꜣt *ḏd*	**The servant of the palace Sanehat** says
m ḥtp nfr wrt	In peace very greatly
rḫt wꜥrt tn ỉrt.n bꜣk ỉm m ḫm.f	Concerning this flight made by the humble servant in his ignorance
ỉn kꜣ.k nṯr nfr nb tꜣwy	It is your ka, good god, lord of the two lands,
mr rꜥ ḥs mntw nb wꜣst	Whom Ra loves, praised by Mont lord of Thebes
ỉmn nb nswt tꜣwy	and Amun lord of the thrones of the two lands,
sbk-rꜥ ḥr ḥwt-ḥr ỉtm ḥnꜥ psḏt.f	By Sobek-Ra, Horus, Hathor, Atum and his nine gods
spdw nfr bꜣw smsrw ḥr ỉꜣbty	Soped perfect of Might of Semseru, Horus the easterner
nbt ỉmḥt ẖnm.s tp.k	The lady of the cavern as she joins your brow,
ḏꜣḏꜣt tpt nw	the tribunal at the front of the flood,
mnw ḥr ḥr-ỉb ḫꜣswt	Min-Horus amid the hill-lands,
wrrt nbt pwnt nwt ḥr-wr-rꜥ	the great goddess, lady of Punt, Nut, Horwerra
nṯrw nbw tꜣ-mri	All the gods of Egypt,
ḫꜣst ỉww nw wꜣḏ-wr	of the hill-land, of the islands of the Great Green
di.sn ꜥnḫ wꜣs r šrt.k	May they give life and power to your nostrils
ẖnm.sn tw m ꜣwt-ꜥ.sn	May they join you in their giving
di.sn n.k nḥḥ nn ḏrw.f	May they grant you eternity without end
ḏt nn ḥnty.sy	and unbounded time
wḥm snd.k m tꜣw ḫꜣswt	Fear of you rebounds in lands and hill-lands,
wꜥf.n.k šnnt ỉtn	you grasp what the sun-disk circles
nḥ pw n bꜣk ỉm n nb.f	This is a prayer by the humble servant to his lord
šd m ỉmnt	for rescue from the west

39 (Berlin 3022, 214-223)

nb siꜣ siꜣ rḫyt	**Lord of insight, who perceives the populace,**
siꜣ.f *m ḥm n stp-sꜣ*	**whose insight** is the Person of the palace
wnn bꜣk ỉm snd ḏd st	This humble servant is in fear of saying it
ỉw mi ḫt ꜥꜣ wḥm st	It is like a matter too great to be repeated
nṯr ꜥꜣ mitw rꜥ	Great god, equal of Ra,
ḥr sšsꜣ bꜣk n.f ḏs.f	in informing the one who has worked for him himself
ỉw bꜣk ỉm m-ꜥ nḏ-r ḥr.f	This humble servant is in the hand of the one consulting about him
di.tw ꜣ ḫr sḫr.f	It has to be placed under his care
ỉw ḥm.k m ḥr ỉṯ	Your Person is Horus who seizes,
nḫt ꜥwy.ky r tꜣw nbw	your arms are stronger than all lands
wḏ grt ḥm.k rdit ỉnt.f	**Now your Majesty decrees that he be brought,**
mki m ḳdm ḫntyw-š m ḫnt kš	And Meki in Qedem, the mountain-men leading Kesh,
mnws m tꜣw fnḫw	Menus from the land of Fenkhu,
ḥkꜣw pw mtrw rnw	These are the rulers by their exact names
ḫprw m mrwt.k	who have come into your affection
nn sḫꜣ rtnw n.k ỉm.s mitt ṯsmw.k	Without mentioning Syria, as much yours as are your dogs

40 (Berlin 3022, 223-234)

ỉs wꜥrt tn ỉrt.n bꜣk	As for this flight made by this servant
n ḫmt.s nn s m ỉb.i n ḳmd.i s	It was not planned, it was not in my heart, I did not plot it
n rḫ.i ỉwd.i r st.i	I did not know how to separate myself from my place
ỉw mi sšm rswt	It is like the pattern of a dream
mi mꜣꜣ sw ***idḥy m ꜣbw***	It is as if a **Delta-man** saw himself **in Abu**,
s n ḫꜣt m tꜣ-sty	a marsh-man in the Land of Nubia
n snḏ.i n sḫwst m-sꜣ.i	I did not fear, I was not persecuted,
n sḏm.i ṯs-ḥwrw	I heard no accusation
n sḏm.tw rn.i m r wḥmw	My name was not heard in the mouth of the reporter
wpw-ḥr nf n ḏdf ḥꜥw.i	And yet my limbs went cold,
rdwy.i ḥr hwhw ỉb.i ḥr ḫrp.i	My legs panicked, my heart took hold of me
nṯr šꜣ wꜥrt tn ḥr stꜣ.i	The god who decreed this flight led me away:
n ỉnk ỉs kꜣ sꜣ ḫnt	I am not the arrogant, not I
snd s rḫ tꜣ.f	The man who knows his land, he fears,
di.n rꜥ snd.k ḫt tꜣ	Ra has set fear of you throughout the land,

ḥr.k m ḫ3st nbt	the dread of you in every hill-land
mi wi m ḫnw mi wi m st tn	Place me in the Residence or place me here,
ntk ḥbs 3ḫt tn	You are still the one who clothes this horizon
wbn itn n mrt.k	The disk shines for love of you,
mw m itrw swr.tw.f mr.k	water is in the river to be drunk at your desire
ṯ3w m pt ḫnm.tw.f dd.k	The air in the sky, it is breathed in when you say so

41 (Berlin 3022, 234-241)
iw b3k im r swḏt ***ṯ3t ir.n b3k im m st tn***
iwt pw iry r b3k im ir ḥm.k m mrr.f
ʿnḫ.tw m ṯ3w n dd.k mr rʿ ḥr ḥwt-ḥr fnd.k pw špss
mrrw Mntw nb w3st ʿnḫ.f ḏt
rdi.tw iry.i hrw m i33 ḥr swḏt ḫt.i n msw.i
s3.i smsw m-s3 wḥyt.i wḥyt.i ḫt.i nbt m-ʿ.f
ḏt.i mnmnt.i nbt dḳr.i ḫt.i nb bnri

This humble servant is to hand over **the staff acquired by this servant in this place**
Then this servant will be returned as your Person permits in his desire
We live by the breath of your gift, as Ra, Horus and Hathor love this your noble life
As Mont lord of Thebes wishes that it live forever
I was permitted a day in Iaa to hand over my things to my children
With my eldest son in charge of my clan, my clan and all my things in his hands,
My servants, all my cattle, my fruits, all my sweet trees

42 (Berlin 3022, 241-247)
iwt pw ir.n b3k im m ḫntyt
ḥdb.n.i ḥr w3wt ḥr
ṯsw im nty m-s3 pḫrt
h3b.f wpwt r ḫnw r rdit rḫ.tw
rdi.in ḥm.f iwt imy-r sḫtyw mnḫ n pr nswt
ʿḥʿw 3tpw m-ḫt.f ḥr 3wt-ʿ nt ḥr nswt
n styw iww m-s3.i ḥr sbt.i r w3wt ḥr
dm.n.i wʿ im nb m rn.f
iw wdpww nb ḥr irt.f
šsp.n.i 3tp n.i nfw
šbb ʿtḫ tp-m3ʿ.i r pḥt.i dmi n iṯt

This servant arrived south,
I touched on the ways of Horus,
And the commander there who was organising patrols
Sent a message to the Residence to inform them
Then his Power sent the good overseer of foragers of the King's House
Followed by ships laden with the gifts of before the king
For the Syrians who came along with me to bring me to the ways of Horus
I pronounced each of them by his name
All the cupbearers were busy at their tasks
I received and the captain loaded for me,
And there was kneading and straining beside me until I reached the landing of Itj(tawy)

43 (Berlin 3022, 248-256)

ḥḏ.n rf t3 dw3 dw3 iw iw 3š n.i	Very early at daybreak there came the summons for me
s mḏ m iwt s mḏ m šmt ḥr st3.i r ʿḥ	Ten men coming, ten men going to lead me to the palace
dhn.n.i t3 imywt sspw	I touched the ground between the dawn rays
msw nswt ʿḥʿ m wmtw ḥr irt ḥsfw.i	As the king's children stood on the walls of my approach
smrw st3w r w3ḫ	The courtiers were led to the audience hall
ḥr rdit.i ḥr w3t ʿḫnwty	as I was placed on the way to the inner palace
gm.n.i ḥm.f ḥr st wrt m wmt nt ḏʿm	I found His Power on the great throne on a podium of electrum
wn.kwi rf dwn.kwi ḥr ḫt.i	Then I was stretched out on my belly
ḫm.n.i wi m b3ḥ.f	I lost myself in his presence,
nṯr pn ḥr wšd.i ḫnms	This god addressed me friendlily

iw.i mi s it m ꜥḫḫw	As I was like a man seized in pitch black
bꜣ.i sbw ḥꜥw.i ꜣdw	My soul had gone, my body trembled
ḥꜣty.i n ntf m ḫt.i rḫ.i ꜥnḫ r mwt	My heart was no longer in my body - could I know life from death?

44 (Berlin 3022, 256-260)

ḏd.in ḥm.f n wꜥw m nn n smrw	**Then His Power said to one of those courtiers**
ṯs sw imi mdw.f n.i	Raise him and let him speak to me
ḏd.in ḥm.f	Then His Power said
mk tw iwt ḥw.n.k ḫꜣswt	Look at you, on return from travelling the hill-lands
ir.n wꜥrt hd im.k tni	The flight has worked its impact on you, you are grown old
pḥ.n.k iꜣwy	You have reached old age
nn šrr ꜥbt ḫꜣt.k	It is no trifle that your body will be purified,
nn bs.k in pḏtyw m ir.k sp sn gr	That you will not be interred by nomads - do not, do not be silent
n mdw.k dm.tw rn.k	You have not spoken, though your name is pronounced

45 (Berlin 3022, 260-263)

snd ꜣ n ḫsf	So fearful of punishment,
wšb.n.i st m wšb sndw	I answered with the answer of the fearful
ptr ḏdt n.i nb.i	What has my lord said to me
ir wšb.i st nn ḥr.i ꜥ n nṯr is pw	That I might answer it - there is no slight to the god in this
ḥr pw wnn.s m ḫt.i	It is terror that resides in my body
mi sḫpr wꜥrt šꜣꜣt	Just as the fated flight came to be
mk wi m-bꜣḥ.k	**See me before you -**
ntk ꜥnḫ ir ḥm.k m mrr.f	**you are life, may your Person do as he desires**

46 (Berlin 3022, 263-268)

***rdi.in** sb.tw msw nswt*	**Then** the king's children were brought in
ḏd.in ḥm.f n ḥmt nswt	And His Power said to the king's wife
mt sꜣ-nhꜣt iw m ꜥꜣm ḳmꜣ n styw	Here is Sanehat, returned as an Asiatic, remade as a Syrian
wd.s sbḥ ꜥꜣ wrt	She uttered a very great cry,
msw nswt m dnyt wꜥt	and the king's children in one outburst
ḏd.in.sn ḫft ḥm.f	They said before His Power
n ntf pw m mꜣꜥt ity nb.i	It cannot truly be him, sovereign my lord
ḏd.in ḥm.f ntf pw m mꜣꜥt	And His Power said, it is truly he.

47 (Berlin 3022, 268-279)

ist rf in.n.sn mnit.sn	At that they brought their counterpoises,
sḫmw.sn sššt.sn m-ꜥ.s	their images, their sistra in their hands
ms.in.sn st n ḥm.f	They waved them at His Power
ꜥwy.k r nfrt nswt wꜣḥ	Your arms are for the good, O king enduring
ḫkryt nt nbt pt	The adornments of the lady of heaven
di nbw ꜥnḫ r fnd.k	The goddess Gold gives life to your nose
ḫnm tw nbt sbꜣw	The lady of the stars unites with you
ḫd šmꜥ.s ḫnt mḥ.s	The south crown fares north, the northern south,
smꜣ twt m r n ḥm.k	united as one in the way of your Majesty
di.tw wꜣḏ m wpt.k	The cobra is set at your brow,
sḥr.n.k twꜣw m ḏwt	you have removed the weak from evil
ḥtp n.k rꜥ nb tꜣwy	Ra lord of the two lands is pleased with you,
hy n.k mi nbt-r-ḏr	praise to you as to the Lady of All
nft ꜥb.k sfḫ šsr.k	Rest your bow, untie your arrow,
imi ṯꜣw n nty m itmw	give breath to the one in lifelessness
imi n.n ḫnt tn nfrt	Allow us this good turn
m mtn pn sꜣ mḥyt	with this wayfarer, son of the north wind,
pḏty ms m tꜣ-mri	The nomad born in Egypt
ir.n.f wꜥrt n sndw.k	He took flight for fear of you,
rwi.n.f tꜣ n ḥr.k	he abandoned the land in dread of you
nn ꜣyt ḥr n mꜣ ḥr.k	There will be no destruction for the face that sees your face
nn snd irt dgꜣt n.k	There will be no fear for the eye that looks at you

48 (Berlin 3022, 279-290)

ḏd.in ḥm.f	Then His Power said
nn snd.f n di.f r ḥr	He shall not fear, nor be given over to terror
iw.f r smr m-m srw	He is to be a courtier among the officials,
rdi.tw.f m ḳꜣb šnyt	He may be placed in the midst of the court
wḏꜣ.tn r ꜥẖnwty	Proceed to the inner palace,
sbꜣt r irt ꜥḥꜥw.f	for instruction in appointing his standing
prt.i rf m-ẖnw ꜥẖnwty	So I went inside the inner palace
msw-nswt ḥr rdit n.i ꜥw.sn	The king's children giving me their arms
šm.n.i m-ḫt r rwty wrty	I went then to the Great Double Gate
rdi.kwi r pr sꜣ nswt špss im.f	I was installed at the house of a king's son, full of riches
sḳbby im.f ꜥẖmw nw ꜣḫt	With a bathroom, and images of the horizon
ḫtmt im.f nt pr-ḥḏ	With valuables from the treasury
ḥbsw nw šs-nswt ꜥntyw tpt	- clothing of royal linen and ointment of the first -
srw nswt mrr.f m ꜥt nbt	as for the king's officials whom he loves, in every room,
wdpw nb ḥr irt.f	Every cupbearer was busy at his task

49 (Berlin 3022, 290-300)

rdi swꜣ rnpwt ḥr ḥꜥw.i	Years were made to fall from my body,
ṯꜣ.kwi ꜥꜥb šnw.i	as I was shorn, my hair combed
iw rdi sbt n ḫꜣst ḥbsw nmiw-šꜥ	The load was returned to the hill-land, the garments to the nomads,
sd.kwi m pꜣḳt gs.kwi m tpt	I was arrayed in fine linen, and anointed with first quality oil
sḏr.kwi ḥr ḥnkyt di.n.i šꜥ n imyw.f	I lay down on a bed, and returned the sand to its dwellers
mrḥt n ḫt n wrḥ im.s	and the tree-oil to those who anoint themselves with it
iw rdi n.i pr n nb š	I was given the house of a lord of an estate,
m wn m-ꜥ smr	as a courtier should have,
iw ḥmwtyw ꜥšꜣw ḥr ḳd.f	Numerous craftsmen built it up,
ḫt.f nb srwd m mꜣwt	everything was strengthened anew
iw inn n.i šꜣbw m ꜥḥ	Foods were regularly delivered to me from the palace,
sp ḫmt sp fd n hrw	three times, four times a day
ḫrw-r ddt msw nswt	Besides the gifts of the king's children
nn ꜣt nt irt ꜣbw	without a moment of pausing

50 (Berlin 3022, 300-310)

iw ḫws n.i mr m inr m ḳꜣb mrw	A pyramid-chapel of stone was built for me amid the pyramids
imy-r mḏḥw (?) mr ḥr ššp sꜣtw.f	The overseer of scaffolders (?) of the pyramid procured its ground,
imy-r ḫtmtyw ḥr sš gnwtyw ḥr ḫtt	The overseer of sealers did the drawing, sculptors did the cutting,
imyw-r kꜣt ntyw ḥr ḥrt ḥr ḏꜣt tꜣ r.s	The overseers of works who were at the pyramid ferried for it.
ḫꜥw nb ddw r rwd ir ḫrt.f im	Every tool that is set to the temple-terrace, it found its task there.
rdi n.i ḥmw-kꜣ ir.n.i š ḥrt	I was given spirit-servants, and I made an estate for the cult,
ꜣḥwt im.f m ḫnt r dmi	Containing fields as endowment at the landing-stage
mi irt n smr tpy	as is done for the foremost official
iw twt.i sḫkr m nbw šndyt.f m ḏꜥm	My image was adorned with gold, its kilt in electrum,
in ḥm.f rdi irt.f	It is His Power who had it done.
nn šwꜣw iry n.f mitt	No vagabond ever received such treatment
iw.i ḥr ḥswt nt ḫr nswt	I am in the favour of before the king
r iwt hrw n mni	Until the coming of the day to moor

End note in Berlin 3022, line 311:
iw.f pw ḥꜣt.f r pḥwy.fy mi gmyt m sš
This is its completion from its start to its finish as found in writing

Sources for the Tale of the Exile of Sanehat

Two principal sources, Middle Kingdom papyri

1. Berlin 3022, preserving a copy of the Tale of Sanehat and an incomplete copy of a narrative known in Egyptology as the Tale of the Herdsman; Papyrus Amherst 4 comprises part of the start of the same manuscript (for other manuscripts found with it, see Question One, Group One)
2. Berlin 10499, found in a tomb beneath the Ramesseum precinct at Thebes, preserving copies of the Tale of Sanehat and the Tale of Khuninpu (for other manuscripts found with it, see Question One, Group Two)

Fragments from other late Middle Kingdom papyri

Buenos Aires

Papyrus Harageh 1 (UC 32773). This was found in a cemetery of that period at Harageh, at the mouth of the Fayum, and preserves part of the central portion of the Tale of Sanehat. It is not recorded in the publication exactly where it was found: Engelbach 1923: 32-33 refers only in general terms to the source of eight fragments of papyri, of which this was one: 'in the surface rubbish, and in the filling of some of the tombs, were found a small number of Middle Kingdom hieratic papyri, all more or less damaged'. At the end of the same volume, a summary record of contents of individual tombs is given, with mention of papyrus fragments for the Middle Kingdom tombs nos.265, 268, 269, 271 and 539. Of these, no.265 contained at least one skeleton of an adult woman, and no.271 two female and one male skeleton: all seem to have been robbed in antiquity.

Papyrus UC 32106C verso, from the Petrie excavations of the town-site at Lahun ('Kahun') in 1889: exact findspot not recorded. First identified by Mark Collier in 2002-3, so not in the edition Koch 1990.

New Kingdom sources

Papyri:

Moscow 4657, fragmentary papyrus of the late Eighteenth Dynasty

Turin 54015, Ramesside papyrus from Deir el-Medina

Ostraca used in Koch 1990

Cairo CG 25216 found in or at the tomb of Sennedjem (Daressy 1920, 154)

Ashmolean 1945.40 one of the largest Ramesside ostraca

Berlin 12341,12379, 12623 (found near the tomb of Sennedjem, Gardiner 1916, 119), 12624

Borchardt

British Museum EA 5629

Černý collection

Clère collection

Deir el-Medina 1011, 1045 (one side), 1174, 1437-8, 1439 (one side), 1440, 1609

Gardiner 354

Petrie Museum UC 31996-7, 34322-3

Senenmut 149 (one side) a limestone ostracon of, unusually, mid-18th Dynasty date

Varille collection

The Tale of the Shipwrecked Official

The tale is preserved on a single manuscript, Papyrus Hermitage 1115, probably acquired by a St Petersburg collector in the early nineteenth century, and 'discovered' in museum storage in the late nineteenth century. It is generally known in Egyptology as the Shipwrecked Sailor. It is debated whether the first words preserved on the papyrus are the beginning of the composition; a close parallel has recently been discovered by the expedition of Dieter Arnold at Dahshur, start of a fragmentary inscription from the tomb-superstructure of a high official (to be published by James Allen).
The tale is set within a tale. In the framing tale, an unnamed *ḥꜣty-ꜥ* 'Mayor' and *šmsw* 'Follower' arrive at the southern border of Egypt, on return from an expedition; the mayor is fearful following his failure, and the follower (not necessarily his follower - Middle Kingdom expedition inscriptions show that the two titles may be of equal social status) tells a tale of a previous expedition to reassure him. In the tale within this tale the Follower recalls how he was sole survivor of a shipwreck, washed up on an 'island of the ka' (the part of the person receiving sustenance; also the word for food to sustain the person) where a giant serpent ruled. The serpent tells the shipwrecked sailor how he was one of seventy-five serpents, but that a star fell and burnt the rest of his family: this further tale within a tale echoes in later religious writing, in the seventy-five addresses to the sun-god and his seventy-four forms (the Litany of Ra in tombs of New Kingdom kings). The shipwrecked sailor is rescued. The composition ends abruptly with the despairing reply of the mayor.
Points of comparison in classical Arabic literature might include the *ajaib* exotic tales of the imagination, and the motif of *al-faraj ba`d al-shiddah* or 'escape from hardship' in which the impact of calamity is softened by relating an earlier calamity with positive resolution (Allen 2000, 149, 161-162).
The section divisions here are those suggested by the red highlighting the original manuscript.
Standard transcription Blackman 1932, 41-48

1 (Papyrus Hermitage, lines 1 to 11)

ḏd.ꞽn šmsw *ꞽḳr*	**Then the** excellent **Follower said**
mk pḥ.n.n ḫnw	We have reached home!
wḏꜣ ꞽb.k ḥꜣty-ꜥ	May your heart prosper, O governor:
šsp ḫrpw ḥw mnꞽt	The mallet is taken, and the mooring-peg struck,
ḥꜣtt rdꞽt ḥr tꜣ	the tow-rope is laid on the ground.
rdꞽ ḥknw dwꜣ nṯr	Praise is given, god is thanked,
s nb ḥr ḥpt snw.f	every man embraces his fellow.
ꞽswt.tn ꞽꞽ.t(ꞽ) ꜥnd.t(ꞽ)	Your crew is returned safely,
nn nhw n mšꜥ.n	without a loss to our forces.
pḥ.n.n pḥwy wꜣwꜣt	We reached the ends of Nubia,
sn.n.n snmwt	and (now) we have crossed Senmut
mk r.f n ꞽꞽ.n m ḥtp	Look we are returned in peace,
tꜣ.n pḥ.n sw	we reach our own land

2 (Papyrus Hermitage, lines 11 to 21)

sḏm.k n.ꞽ *ḥꜣty-ꜥ*	**Listen to me** O governor
ꞽnk šw ḥꜣw	I am a man free from excess.
ꞽꜥ tw ꞽmꞽ mw ḥr ḏbꜥw.k	Wash yourself, place water on your fingers.
ꞽḫ wšb.k wšd.t(w).k	Just answer when you are asked,
mdw.k n nswt ꞽb.k m-ꜥ.k	and speak to the king with your heart in your control,
wšb.k nn nꞽtꞽt	reply without stammering,
ꞽw r n s nḥm.f sw	for the speech of a man can rescue him,
ꞽw mdw.f ṯꜣm n.f ḥr	his words can veil his face.
ꞽrr.k m ḫrt ꞽb.k	Do just as you please,
swrd pw ḏd n.k	it is tiresome to talk to you.

3 (Papyrus Hermitage, lines 21 to 30)

sḏd.ꞽ r.f *n.k mꞽtt ꞽry*	**Still, let me tell** you a similar tale
ḫpr m-ꜥ.ꞽ ḏs.ꞽ	that happened to me myself.
šm.kwꞽ r bꞽꜣ n ꞽty	I went to the mineral-hills of the sovereign,
hꜣ.kwꞽ r wꜣḏ-wr	I descended to the Great Sea
m dpt nt mḥ šnt mḏwty m ꜣw.s	in a boat a hundred and twenty cubits in length,
mḥ ḥm m wsḫ.s	twice twenty in its breadth,
sḳd šnt mḏwty ꞽm.s m stp n kmt	a hundred and twenty sailors in it of the best of Egypt.
mꜣ.sn pt mꜣ.sn tꜣ	In seeing the sky, in seeing the land,

mkꜣ ib.sn r mꜣw	their hearts were bolder than lions.

4 (Papyrus Hermitage, lines 30 to 46)

sr.sn *ḏꜥ n iyt*	**They could foretell** a storm before it hit,
nšny n ḫprt.f	tempest before it fell.
ḏꜥ pr iw.n m wꜣḏ-wr	A storm did happen, while we were in the Great Sea
tp-ꜥ sꜣḥ.n tꜣ	before we could touch land.
fꜣ.t(w) ṯꜣw ir.f wḥmyt	The sail was carried off, torn in two
nwyt im.f nt mḥ ḫmn	a wave over it of eight cubits.
in ḫt ḥḥ n.i s(y)	It was the mast that struck me down (though).
ꜥḥꜥ.n dpt mwt	Then the ship died.
ntyw im.s n sp wꜥ im	Of those on board, not one survived.
ꜥḥꜥ.n.i rdi.kwi r iw	Then I, I was borne to an island
in wꜣw n wꜣḏ-wr	by a wave of the Great Sea.
ir.n.i hrw ḫmt wꜥ.kwi	I spent three days there alone,
ib.i m snw.i	my heart my (only) companion,
sḏr.kwi m ẖnw n kꜣp n ḫt	sleeping inside a shelter of timbers.
ḳni.n.i šwyt	I hugged the dry lit land.
ꜥḥꜥ.n.i dwn.n.i rdwy.i	Then I stretched my legs,
r rḫ dit.i m r.i	to discover what I could put in my mouth.

5 (Papyrus Hermitage, lines 47 to 56)

gm.n.i *dꜣbw iꜣrrt im*	**I found** figs and grapes there,
iꜣḳt nbt špst	and every fine food-plant,
kꜣw im ḥnꜥ nḳwt	sycamore-figs there, fresh and dry,
šspt mi irt.s	and gourds as prepared (for eating),
rmw im ḥnꜥ ꜣpdw	fish there, and birds,
nn ntt nn st m ẖnw.f	there was nothing that was not within it.
ꜥḥꜥ.n ssꜣ.n(.i) wi	So I took my fill,
rdi.n.i r tꜣ n wr ḥr ꜥwy.i	and had to place on the ground, there was so much on my arms,
šdt.i ḏꜣ sḫpr.n.i ḫt	before taking a firestick and kindling a flame,
ir.n.i sb n sḏt n nṯrw	and I made a burnt offering to the gods.

6 (Papyrus Hermitage, lines 56 to 66)

ꜥḥꜥ.n sḏm.n.i *ḫrw ḳri*	**Then I heard** a cry so loud,
ib.kwi wꜣw pw n wꜣḏ-wr	I thought it was a wave of the Great Sea,
ḫtw ḥr gmgm	the trees splintered,
tꜣ ḥr mnmn	the earth shook.
kf.n.i ḥr.i	When I unveiled my face,
gm.n.i ḥfꜣw pw iw.f m iit	I found it was a serpent that was coming,
ny-sw mḥ mꜥbꜣ	it was thirty cubits,
ḫbswt.f wr.s r mḥ sn	(just) its beard was more than two cubits,
ḥꜥw.f sḫrw m nbw	its limbs were shot with gold,
inḥwy.fy m ḫsbd mꜣꜥ	its eyebrows with fast lapis-lazuli,
ꜥrḳ sw r ḫnt	rearing itself up ahead.

7 (Papyrus Hermitage, lines 67 to 80)

iw wp.n.f *r.f r.i*	**It opened** its mouth towards me,
iw.i ḥr ẖt.i m bꜣḥ.f	as I was on my belly in front of him,
ḏd.f n.i	saying to me:
n-m in tw n-m in tw nḏs	Who brought you, who brought you, fellow?
n-m in tw	Who brought you?
ir wdf.k m ḏd n.i in tw r iw pn	If you waste time telling me who brought you to this island,
rdi.i rḫ.k tw	then I shall let you know yourself,
iw.k m ss	as ash,
ḫpr.t(i) m nty n mꜣt.f	turned into someone never seen.
iw mdw.k n.i	You speak to me,
nn wi ḥr sḏm.i st	and I am not even hearing it,
iw.i m bꜣḥ.k	though I am in your presence.
ḫm.n(.i) wi	I have lost myself.

ꜥḥꜥ.n rdi.f wi m r.f	Then he took me in his mouth,
iṯ.f wi r st.f nt snḏm	carrying me off to his place of rest,
wꜣḥ.f wi nn dmit.i	and laying me down without touching me,
wḏꜣ.kwi nn iṯ im.i	I was whole, without a scrape on me.

8 (Papyrus Hermitage, lines 81 to 97)

***iw wp.n.f** r.f r.i*	**He opened** its mouth towards me,
iw.i ḥr ẖt.i m bꜣḥ.f	as I was on my belly in front of him,
ꜥḥꜥ.n ḏd.n.f n.i	and said to me:
n-m in tw n-m in tw nḏs	Who brought you, who brought you, fellow?
n-m in tw r iw pn n wꜣḏ-wr	Who brought you to this island of the Great Sea,
nty gswy.fy m nwy	whose both sides are of the waters?
ꜥḥꜥ.n wšb.n.i n.f st	Then I answered him his question,
ꜥwy.i ẖꜣm m bꜣḥ.f	my arms bent in his presence,
ḏd.i n.f	telling him:
ink pw hꜣ.kwi r biꜣ	I, I went down to go to the mineral-hills
m wpwty ity	as envoy of the sovereign,
m dpt nt mḥ šnt mḏwty m ꜣw.s	in a boat a hundred and twenty cubits in length,
mḥ ẖm m wsẖ.s	twice twenty in its breadth,
sḳd šnt mḏwty im.s m stpw n kmt	a hundred and twenty sailors in it of the best of Egypt.
mꜣ.sn pt mꜣ.sn tꜣ	In seeing the sky, in seeing the land,
mkꜣ ib.sn r mꜣw	their hearts were bolder than lions.

9 (Papyrus Hermitage, lines 97 to 108)

***sr.sn** ḏꜥ n iit.f*	**They could foretell** a storm before it hit,
nšny n ḫprt.f	tempest before it fell
wꜥ im nb mkꜣ ib.f	Every one of them was bold in his heart,
nḫt ꜥ.f r snnw.f	strong in his arm beside his fellow.
nn wḫꜣ m ḥr-ib.sn	There was no weakling among them.
ḏꜥ pr iw.n m wꜣḏ-wr	A storm did happen, while we were in the Great Sea
tp-ꜥ sꜣḥ.n tꜣ	before we could touch land.
fꜣ.t(w) ṯꜣw	The sail was carried off,
ir.f wḥmyt	torn in two
nwyt im.f nt mḥ ẖmn	a wave over it of eight cubits.
in ḫt ḥḥ n.i s(y)	It was the mast that struck me down (though).
ꜥḥꜥ.n dpt mwt.t(i)	Then the ship died.
ntyw im.s n sp wꜥ im	Of those on board, not one survived,
ḥr-ḫw.i mk wi r-gs.k	apart from me, and see I am beside you.

10 (Papyrus Hermitage, lines 109 to 123)

***ꜥḥꜥ.n in.kwi** r iw pn*	**Then I was borne** to this island
in wꜣw n wꜣḏ-wr	by a wave of the Great Sea.
ḏd.in.f n.i	Then he said to me:
m snd ꜣ m snd ꜣ nḏs	Do not fear then, do not fear then, little man,
m ꜣtw ḥr.k	do not guard your face.
pḥ.n.k wi	You have reached me,
mk nṯr rdi.n.f ꜥnḫ.k	because a god has made you live,
in.f tw r iw pn n kꜣ	and brought you to this island of the Double-spirit –
nn ntt nn st m ẖnw.f	there is nothing that is not within it,
iw.f mḥ ẖr nfrt nbt	it is filled with all good things.
mk tw r irt ꜣbd ḥr ꜣbd	Now you are to spend month upon month,
r kmt.k ꜣbd fd m ẖnw n iw pn	until you complete four months within this island.
iw dpt r iit m ẖnw	A ship will come from the Residence,
sḳdw im.s rḫ.n.k	with sailors aboard who are known to you,
šm.k ḥnꜥ.sn r ẖnw	so that you can go with them to the Residence,
mwt.k m niwt.k	and die in your city.

11 (Papyrus Hermitage, lines 124 to 129)

***rš-wy** sḏd dpt.n.f*	**What joy it is** for a man to tell the tale of what he has tasted
sn ḫt mr	at the passing of an evil thing.

sḏd.i r.f n.k mitt iry	So let me tell you the tale of an event like that,
ḫprw m iw pn	one that happened on this island.
wn.i im.f ḥnꜥ snw.i	I was there with my brothers,
ẖrdw m ḳꜣb.sn	and children, all together,
km.n.n ḥfꜣw sfḫ diw	we totalled some seventy-five serpents,
msw.i ḥnꜥ snw.i	my children with my brothers,
nn sḫꜣ.i n.k sꜣt ktt	without my mentioning to you the little daughter,
int.n.i m sšꜣ	whom I brought in wisdom.

12 (Papyrus Hermitage, lines 129 to 138)

ꜥḥꜥ.n sbꜣ *hꜣw*	**Then a star** fell down
pr.n nꜣ m ḫt m-ꜥ.f	and they went out in the flame from it.
ḫpr.n r.s nn wi ḥnꜥ ꜣm-ny	It happened, though, while I was not with the torching,
nn wi m ḥr-ib.sn	I was not in their midst.
ꜥḥꜥ.n.i mwt.kwi n.sn	And I died for them
gm.n.i st m ẖꜣyt wꜥt	when I found them as one pile of corpses.
ir ḳn n.k rwd ib.k	If you have valour, and your heart is strong,
mḥ.k ḳni.k m ẖrdw.k	Wrap your arms around your children,
sn.k ḥmt.k	kiss your wife,
mꜣ.k pr.k	savour your house,
nfr st r ḫt nbt	it is more beautiful than anything.
pḥ.k ẖnw wn.k im.f	When you reach the Residence, may you dwell there
m ḳꜣb n snw.k	in the throng of your brothers,
wn.k r.f	may you just be.
dmꜣ.kwi ḥr ẖt.i	I was moved in my body,
dmi.n.i sꜣtw m bꜣḥ.f	I touched the ground in his presence.

13 (Papyrus Hermitage, lines 138 to 144)

ḏd.i r.f n.k	**Then I may speak to you**
sḏd.i bꜣw.k n ity	May I report your powers to the sovereign,
di.i sšꜣ.f m ꜥꜣ.k	and let him appreciate your greatness,
di.i in.t(w) n.k ibi ḥknw	and have sent to you ibi-oil and oil of praise,
iwdnb ḥsꜣyt sntr	iudeneb-gum, resins and incense,
n gsw-prw sḥtp nṯr nb im.f	of the temple estates, on which every god feasts,
sḏd r.f ḫprt ḥr.i	to tell just what happened to me,
m mꜣt.n.i m bꜣw.f	with what I have seen of his powers.
dwꜣ.tw nṯr n.k m niwt	They will thank god for you in the city
ḫft-ḥr ḳnbt tꜣ r-ḏr.f	before the council of the entire land.

14 (Papyrus Hermitage, lines 144 to 148)

sft.i *n.k kꜣw m sb n ḫt*	**I shall slaughter** bulls for you as a burnt offering
wšn.n.i n.k ꜣpdw	after strangling the birds for you,
di.i in.t(w) n.k ḥꜥw ꜣtpw	and I shall send you ships laden
ḥr špss nb n kmt	with all the goods of Egypt
mi irrt n nṯr mrr rmṯ	as is one for a god whom people love
m tꜣ wꜣ n rḫ sw rmṯ	in a far land unknown to people.

15 (Papyrus Hermitage, lines 149 to 154)

ꜥḥꜥ.n sbt.n.f im.i m nn ḏd.n.i	**Then he laughed at me for the things I had said**
m nf m ib.f	as a folly on his heart,
ḏd.f n.i	and said to me:
n wr n.k ꜥntyw	you do not have enough myrrh
ḫprt nb sntr	in all that has come to be (?), or incense –
ink is ḥḳꜣ pwnt	no, I am the ruler of Punt,
ꜥntyw n.i im sw	and I have the myrrh from there, indeed
ḥknw pf ḏd.n.k in.t(w).f	That oil of praise you said would be brought
bw pw wr n iw pn	that is the greatness of this island.
ḫpr is iwd.k tw r st tn	But it will come to pass that when you leave this place,
n sp mꜣ.k iw pn	never again are you to see this island,
ḫpr m nwy	which is to become as waves.

16 (Papyrus Hermitage, lines 154 to 160)

ꜥḥꜥ.n dpt tf	**Then that ship**
ii.t(i) mi srt.n.f ẖnt	arrived as he had foretold before,
ꜥḥꜥ.n.i šm.kwi	and I went
rdi.n(.i) wi ḥr ẖt kꜣ	and climbed a tall tree,
siꜣ.n.i ntyw m ẖnw.s	and recognised the men who were aboard,
ꜥḥꜥ.n.i šm.kwi r smit st	and I went to report it,
gm.n.i sw rẖ st	but found that he knew it (already).
ꜥḥꜥ.n ḏd.n.f n.i	Then he said to me:
snb.t(i) snb.t(i) nḏs r pr.k	Fare well, fare well, little man, to your home.
imi rn.i nfr m niwt.k	Place my good name in your city.
mk ẖrt.i pw im.k	Here is my wealth with you.

17 (Papyrus Hermitage, lines 161 to 165)

***ꜥḥꜥ.n rdi.n(.i) wi** ḥr ẖt.i*	**Then I placed myself** on my belly,
ꜥwy.i ẖꜣm m-bꜣḥ.f	my arms stretched out before him,
ꜥḥꜥ.n rdi.n.f n.i sbt	and he presented to me a cargo
m ꜥntyw ḥknw iwdnb ẖsꜣyt	of myrrh, oil of praise, *iudeneb*-oil, gums,
tišps šꜣs msdmt	fine timber, *shas*, eyepaint,
sdw nw mm	tails of giraffes,
mrryt ꜥꜣt nt sntr	great clusters of incense,
nḏhyt nt ꜣbw	tusks of ivory,
ṯsmw gwfw kyw	hounds, baboons, apes,
špss nb nfr	and all fine wares.

18 (Papyrus Hermitage, lines 166 to 172)

***ꜥḥꜥ.n ꜣtp.n.i st** r dpt tn*	**Then I loaded it aboard** this ship
ḫpr.n rdi.tw.i ḥr ẖt.i	and I found myself on my belly
r dwꜣ nṯr n.f	to thank god for him.
ꜥḥꜥ.n ḏd.n.f n.i	Then he said to me:
mk tw r spr r ẖnw n ꜣbd sn	you are going to reach the Residence in two months,
mḥ.k ḳni.k m ẖrdw.k	and wrap your arms around your children,
rnpy.k m ẖnw ḳrst.k	and grow young within your burial.
ꜥḥꜥ.n hꜣ.kwi r mryt m hꜣw dpt tn	Then I went down to the shore near this ship,
ꜥḥꜥ.n.i ḥr iꜣš n mšꜥ nty m dpt tn	and called out to the forces aboard,
rdi.n.i ḥknw ḥr mryt n nb n iw pn	I gave praise on the shore to the lord of this island,
ntyw im.s r mitt iry	and those aboard followed my example.

19 (Papyrus Hermitage, lines 172 to 186)

***nꜥt pw ir.n** m ḫd*	**We sailed then** north
r ẖnw n ity	to the Residence of the sovereign,
spr.n.n r ẖnw ḥr ꜣbd sn	and reached the Residence in two months
mi ḏdt.n.f nbt	exactly as he had said.
ꜥḥꜥ.n ꜥḳ.kwi ḥr ity	Then I went in before the sovereign,
ms.n.i n.f inw pn	and brought him these supplies
in.n.i m ẖnw n iw pn	that I had brought from within this island.
ꜥḥꜥ.n dwꜣ nṯr n.f n.i	Then he thanked god for me
ḫft-ḥr ḳnbt tꜣ r ḏr.f	before the council of the entire land,
ꜥḥꜥ.n rdi.kwi r šmsw	and I was appointed Follower,
sꜣḥ.kwi m tpw.f	assigned its personnel.
mꜣ w(i) r sꜣ sꜣḥ.i tꜣ	See me after I touch land,
r-sꜣ mꜣ.i dpt.n.i	after I see what I have tasted.
sḏm r.k [n r].i	Listen then [to] my [speech]
mk nfr sḏm n rmṯ	for it is good to listen to people.
ꜥḥꜥ.n ḏd.n.f n.i	Then he said to me:
m ir iḳr ẖnms	do not be too excellent, friend.
in-m r dit mw [n] ꜣpd	Who is going to give water [to] a bird
hḏ-tꜣ n sft.f dwꜣ	on the dawn of its slaughtering in the morning?

20 (Papyrus Hermitage, lines 186 to 189)

***iw**.f pw ḥ3t.f r pḥwy.fy*	**Completed** from its start to its end
mi gmyt m sš	as found in writing
[*m*] *sš sš iḳr n ḏbˁw.f*	[as] a writing of the writer excellent in his fingers,
imny s3 imn-ˁ3 ˁnḫ wḏ3 snb	Ameny's son Amenaa may he live prosper and be well

Tales of Wonder at the Court of King Khufu

This literary composition in Middle Egyptian is set in the time of the Fourth Dynasty king Khufu, for whom the Great Pyramid was built (reigned about 2550 BC). From features such as the definite article, it is generally dated to the late Middle Kingdom or Second Intermediate Period (1800-1550 BC). Start and end are lost. The king is entertained by his sons, each of whom relate a tale of wonder in a previous reign, until Hordedef tells the king of a miracle-worker still alive, a man named Djedi. The king orders Hordedef to bring him to the palace, and Djedi performs miracles for the king, but also tells him that future kings are to be born to another family. The final preserved portion relates the birth of the kings-to-be, assisted by deities sent by the sun-god, and a domestic argument between their mother and a servant-girl, ending in tragedy. The names of the three kings are, with minor variants, those of the rulers at the start of the Fifth Dynasty: Userkaf, Sahura and Kakai. In the Old Kingdom sources the unique term 'mother of two kings' is attested for the mother of two of them, Khentkaues. Egyptologists have commented with fascination on the relation between the Middle Egyptian cycle of Tales of Wonder and the political history of the Fourth and Fifth Dynasties: unfortunately, the presently available Old Kingdom sources are insufficient to reconstruct the precise ties between kings and dynasties, and therefore it is difficult to reconstruct the path from 'reality' to the literary composition, and its effect on the contemporary audience.

The composition is preserved in a single copy on papyrus, dated by its handwriting to the Second Intermediate Period or early 18th Dynasty (Papyrus Berlin 3033, known after its first modern owner as Papyrus Westcar).

The transliteration follows Blackman 1988. The section divisions are introduced for convenience: in the original manuscript, the red passages marking a new section are at longer intervals.

1. (Papyrus Westcar, column 1, lines 12 to 17)

ḏd.in ḥm n nswt bity [ḫ]wfw mꜣꜥ [ḫrw]
[imi di.tw mꜣꜥ t ḫꜣ] ḥ[nkt] ds šnt iwꜣ [wꜥ sntr pꜣd sn n]
nswt bity ḏsr mꜣꜥ ḫrw
[ḥnꜥ rdit di.tw šns wꜥ ḥnkt ḏwiw] wꜥ iwf wri [sntr pꜣd wꜥ
n ḫry-ḥbt ḥry tp ... iw m]ꜣ.[n.i] sp.f n rḫ
ir[.in.tw] mi wdt [nbt ḥm.f]

Then the Power of the dual king [Kh]ufu true [of voice] said:
[Have offering made of a thousand loaves], a hundred jars of beer, [one] ox, [two balls of incense to] the dual king Djeser true of voice
[and have offering made of one broad loaf], one [jug of beer], a haunch of meat, [one ball of incense to the master lector ... for I have] seen his demonstration of knowledge.
[Then it] was done in accordance with [all] that [His Power] ordered.

2. (Papyrus Westcar, column 1, line 17 to column 2, line 2)

ꜥḥꜥ pw ir.n sꜣ nswt ḫꜥ.f-rꜥ [r mdt ḏd.f]
[di.i sḏm ḥm].k [b]iꜣyt ḫprt
m rk it[.k] nb-kꜣ mꜣꜥ ḫrw
w[ḏ]ꜣ.f r ḥwt-nṯr nt [ptḥ nb] ꜥnḫ tꜣwy
ist rf in [ḥm].f šm r [...]
in ḥm.f ir [..]nt nt [...]
[ḫry-ḥbt ḥry]-tp wbꜣ-inr ḥ[nꜥ ...] ḥmt wbꜣ-inr n[...]
[ꜥḥꜥ.n rdi.n.s? ..].tw n.f rd mḥ m ḥbsw [...]

Then the king's son Khafra stood to speak, and said:
[May I cause] your [Power to hear a mi]racle that happened
in the time of [your] forefather Nebka true of voice,
when he tra[vel]led to the temple of [Ptah lord] of Ankhtway.
Now His [Power] went to [...]
It is His Power that made [..].. of [...]
[the] mas[ter lector] Webainer wi[th ...] the wife of Webainer ..[...]
[and she had? ..] for him a chest filled with clothing [...]

3. (Papyrus Westcar, column 2, lines 2 to 14)

iwt pw ir.n.f
ḥnꜥ [tꜣ] wbꜣ[yt
ḫr-m-ḫt] hrw [swꜣ] ḥr [nn

is]t rf wn šsp[t m p3 š n w]b3-inr
ꜥḥꜥ.n [dd.n p]3 nds [n t3 ḥmt wb3]-inr
iw ms wn šspt [m p3 š n wb3-inr]
mtn ir.n 3t im.s
[ꜥḥꜥ.n h3b.n t3 ḥmt] wb3-inr
n ḥry-pr nty [m s3 p3 š r dd
i]mi sspd.tw t3 šspt [ntt m p3 š ...]
wrš.n.s im ḥr swr[i ...]ḥtp [...]
ḫr-m-ḫt [mšrw ḫpr
iwt pw ir.n].f
wn.in.f ḥr [h3t r p3 š
wn.in t3 w]b3yt [... wb3]-inr

Then he came with [the] servantwoman.
Days [passed] by, and then-
there was a pavilion [in the estate of We]bainer,
and the fellow [said to the wife of Weba]iner:
but there is a pavilion [in the estate of Webainer],
let us spend some time there.
[So the wife] of Webainer [sent a message]
to the house official who [was in charge of the estate, saying:]
have them fit out the pavilion [which is in the estate ...].
She spent the day there drink[ing ...] content [...]
After [evening fell],
he [made his return]
and was [going down to the estate,
and then the servant]woman [... Weba]iner

4. (Papyrus Westcar, column 2, line 15 to column 3, line 1)
[ḫr-m-ḫt t3-ḥḏ sn n hrw ḫpr
š3]s pw [ir.n p3 ḥry-pr ...] mdt tn
[...].k [...] s [...] p3 n[...] ir.n.f s.. [p3] š
[...] rdi.n.f sw n p3y.f [nb
...] ḥ3 [...] nt
ꜥḥꜥ[.n] ..f [...]
ꜥḥꜥ.n [dd.n wb3-inr] in n.i ꜥ [...
[...] n hbny [ḥr] ḏꜥm ms [...
[..h]3b (?) [...] wp[...]
di.n.f [ms]ḥ n [...] sfḫ
[wn.in].f [ḥr] šd [...] šd [...] ḥr [...]
iwt.f [r wꜥb m š.i ... n]ḏs [...]

[After two breaks of day had fallen,
the house official] hurried [...] this word,
[...] you [...] .. [...] the [...] he did .. [the] estate
[...] he gave it to his [master]
[...] .. [...] ..
Then he [...]
Then [Webainer said]: bring me a chest
[...] of ebony [and] silver-gold .. [...
... se]nding (?) [...] mess[age (?) ...]
he placed [a croco]dile of [...] seven [...
and then] he [was] reading [...] reading [...] on [...]
his arrival [to wash in my estate ... fe]llow [...]

5. (Papyrus Westcar, column 3, lines 1 to 10)
ꜥḥꜥ.n rdi.n.f sw n p3 [ḥry-]pr
ḏd.n.f n.f
i[r m]-ḫt h3w nḏs r p3 š
mi nt-ꜥ.f nt rꜥ nb
k3.k ḫ3ꜥ.k [p3 m]sḥ [...] r-s3.f

šꜣs pw ỉr.n pꜣ [ḥry-pr]
ỉṯ.n.f pꜣ msḥ n mnḥ m-ꜥ.f
ꜥḥꜥ.n [hꜣ]b.n tꜣ [ḥmt] wbꜣ-ỉnr
n pꜣ ḥry-pr nty m-sꜣ pꜣ [š] r ḏd
ỉmỉ sspd.tw tꜣ šspt ntt m pꜣ š
mk wi ỉỉ.kwi r ḥmst ỉm.s
ꜥḥꜥ.n [ss]pd tꜣ šspt [m] bw nb nfr
šꜣs pw ỉr.n[.sn]
wn.ỉn.s[n] ḥr hrw nfr ḥnꜥ pꜣ nḏs

Then he gave it to the house [official]
and said to him:
After the fellow has gone done to the estate
following his daily routine,
you are to cast [the croco]dile [...] behind him.
The [house official] hurried off,
and took the wax crocodile with him.
Then the [wife] of Webainer sen[t a message]
to the house official who was in charge of the estate, saying:
have the pavilion which is in the estate fitted out,
as I am coming to spend some time in it.
So the pavilion was [fit]ted out [in] full style.
Then [they] hurried off,
and made holiday with the fellow

6. (Papyrus Westcar, column 3, lines 10 to 17)
ḫr m-ḫt mšrw ḫpr
ỉwt pw ỉr.n pꜣ nḏs
mỉ nt-ꜥ.f nt rꜥ nb
ꜥḥꜥ.n ḫꜣꜥ.n pꜣ [ḥry-pr] pꜣ msḥ n mnḥ r-sꜣ.f r mw
ꜥḥꜥ.n [ḫpr.n].f m msḥ n mḥ sfḫ
ꜥḥꜥ.n mḥ.n.f m pꜣ nḏs
[...] st smnw wbꜣ-ỉnr
ḥnꜥ ḥm n nswt-bỉty nb-kꜣ [mꜣꜥ ḫrw]
n hrw sfḫ
pꜣ nḏs m ḏꜣt [...] snt

After night had fallen,
the fellow returned
following his daily routine.
Then the [house official] cast the wax crocodile behind him into the water,
and it [turned] into a crocodile of seven cubits,
and seized hold of the fellow
[...] ... Webainer
with the Power of the dual king Nebka [true of voice]
for seven days,
the fellow in crossing [...] savour (?) [...]

7. (Papyrus Westcar, column 3, lines 17 to 25)
[ḫr] m-ḫt pꜣ hrw sfḫ ḫpr
wḏꜣ pw ỉr.n nswt-bỉty nb-kꜣ mꜣꜥ ḫrw [...]
[ꜥḥꜥ.n] rdỉ.n sw ẖry-ḥbt ḥry-tp wbꜣ-ỉnr m bꜣḥ
ꜥḥꜥ.n ḏd.n [... s]ḏd.[n].ỉ
wḏꜣ [...] ḥm.k
mꜣn.k tꜣ [bỉꜣy]t ḫpr[t m] rk ḥm.k
[...]n[ḏ]s [...] s [...] wbꜣ-ỉnr
ꜥḥꜥ.n [... m]sḥ r ḏd
ỉnn.k [pꜣ] nḏs [...]
pr[t pw ỉr.n] pꜣ m[s]ḥ [...
ꜥḥꜥ.n] ḏd.n ẖry-ḥ[bt ḥry-tp wbꜣ-ỉnr [...] sw

[ꜥḥꜥ].n [...].n[.f] sw
ꜥḥꜥ.n [r]di.n.[f] [...] sw [...]

After the seventh day had come,
the dual king Nebka true of voice proceeded [...]
[then] the master lector Webainer placed himself in the presence,
and said [...] I [t]old,
may Your Power proceed [...]
and see the [mirac]le that happen[ed in] the time of Your Power,
[...] fe[ll]ow [...] .. [...] Webainer.
Then [...cr]ocodile saying:
bring on [the] fellow [...].
The cro[co]dile emerged [...
And] the master lec[tor Webainer] said: [...] him.
[...]ed [...he ...]ed him,
and [it] placed [...] him/it [...]

8. (Papyrus Westcar, column 3, line 25 to column 4, line 12)
ḏd.in ḥm n nswt [bity] nb-kꜣ mꜣꜥ ḫrw
smwn msḥ pn ḥꜣ
kst pw ir.n wbꜣ-inr
ꜥḥꜥ.n ṯꜣ.n.f sw
wn.in.f m drt.f msḥ n mnḥ
wn.in ḫry-ḥbt ḥry-tp wbꜣ-inr ḥr wḥm mdt tn
ir.n pꜣ nḏs m pr.f ḥnꜥ ṯꜣy.f ḥmt
n ḥm n nswt bity nb-kꜣ mꜣꜥ ḫrw
ꜥḥꜥ.n ḏd.n ḥm.f n pꜣ msḥ
inn.k pꜣy.k
hꜣt pw ir.n pꜣ msḥ r [..]t nt pꜣ š
n rḫ.tw bw šm.n.f im ḥr.f
ꜥḥꜥ.n rdi.n [ḥm n nswt] bity nb-kꜣ mꜣꜥ ḫrw
iṯ.tw tꜣ ḥmt wbꜣ-inr r šdw mḥty n ḫnw
ꜥḥꜥ.n rdi.n.f ḫt im.s [...]
ḳmꜣw.n itrw
mk biꜣyt ḫpr[t m] rk it nswt bity nb-kꜣ
m iryt ḫry-ḥbt ḥry-tp wbꜣ-inr

Then the Power of the [dual] king Nebka true of voice said:
Certainly this crocodile is the snatcher!
Webainer then bowed,
and he picked it up,
and it was in his hand, a crocodile of wax.
Then the master lector Webainer repeated this word
that the fellow had made in his house with his wife,
to the Power of the dual king Nebka true of voice.
And His Power said to the crocodile:
Bring on your own.
The crocodile moved down to [..].. of the estate,
the place where he went with it could not be seen.
Then the [Power of the dual] king Nebka true of voice had
them take the wife of Webainer to a well north of the Residence,
and he had them set fire to her [...]
created by the river.
That is the miracle that happen[ed in] the time of the forefather the dual king Nebka
as a deed of the master lector Webainer.

9. (Papyrus Westcar, column 4, lines 12 to 17)
ḏd.in ḥm n nswt bity ḫwfw mꜣꜥ ḫrw
imi di.tw mꜣꜥ t ḥꜣ ḥnḳt ds šnt iwꜣ wꜥ sntr pꜣd sn n
nswt bity nb-kꜣ mꜣꜥ ḫrw
ḥnꜥ rdit di.tw šns wꜥ ḥnḳt ḏwiw wꜥ iwf wri sntr pꜣd wꜥ

n ḫry-ḥbt ḥry tp wbꜣ-inr i[w mꜣ].n.i sp.f n rḫ
ir.in.tw mi wdt nbt ḥm.f

Then the Power of the dual king Khufu true of voice said:
Have offering made of a thousand loaves, a hundred jars of beer, one ox, two balls of incense to the dual king Nebka true of voice
and have offering made of one broad loaf, one jug of beer, a haunch of meat, one ball of incense to the master lector Webainer for I have [seen] his demonstration of knowledge.
Then it was done in accordance with all that His Power ordered.

10. (Papyrus Westcar, column 4, line 17 to column 5, line 7)
ꜥḥꜥ [pw] ir.[n] sꜣ nswt bꜣw.f-rꜥ r mdt ḏd.f
di.i sḏm ḥm.k biꜣyt ḫprt
m rk it.k snfrw mꜣꜥ [ḫrw
m iryt] ḫry-ḥbt ḥry-tp [ḏ]ꜣḏꜣ-m-ꜥnḫ[...] ... wꜣḏ [...] s
hrw nꜣ n iw tmmt ḫpr
[...] nbt nt pr nswt ꜥnḫ wḏꜣ snb
r ḥḥy n.f [st ḳbt n gm.n.f sy ḏd.in.f]
is in n.i [ḫry-ḥbt] ḥry-tp sš [mḏꜣt ḏꜣḏꜣ-m-ꜥnḫ]
in.in.tw.f n.f ḥr-[ꜥ]wy
ḏd.in n.f [ḥm.f
iw dbn.n.i ꜥt nbt nt] pr [nswt ꜥnḫ wḏꜣ snb]
r ḥḥy n.i st ḳbt n gm.n.i sy
ḏd.in n.f ḏꜣḏꜣ-m-ꜥnḫ
ḥwy ꜣ wḏꜣ ḥm.k r š n pr-ꜥꜣ ꜥnḫ wḏꜣ snb
ꜥpr n.k bꜣw m nfrt nbt nt ḫnw ꜥḥ.k
ib n ḥm.k r ḳbb n mꜣꜣ ḫnn.sn ḫnt m ḫd m ḫnt
iw.k ḥr mꜣꜣ sšw nfrw n š.k
iw.k ḥr mꜣꜣ sḫt.f ḫfꜣꜣt.f nfrw
iw ib.k r ḳbb ḫr.s

Then the king's son Baufra stood to speak, and said:
May I cause your Power to hear a mi]racle that happened
in the time of your forefather Sneferu true of [voice,
as a deed] of the master lector Djadjamankh [...] fresh [...] ..
[...] day of these, all had taken place,
[...] every [...] of the House of the King life! prosperity! health!
to hunt out for himself [a cool place, but he could not find it, and so he said:]
Go, bring me the master [lector], writer of [books Djadjamankh].
Then he was brought to him at once.
Then [His Power] said to him:
[I have gone round every room of the] House [of the King life! prosperity! health!]
to hunt out for myself a cool place, but I could not find it.
So Djadamankh said:
may it please Your Power to go to the lake of the Great House life! prosperity! health!
and a barge be equipped for you with every young girl who is within your palace.
The heart of Your Power will grow cool at seeing them rowing their way up and down,
as you look at the beautiful nests of your lake,
as you look at its marhes and its clusters of beauty,
your heart will grow cool under it.

11. (Papyrus Westcar, column 5, lines 7 to 13)

iw.i ḥm r irt ḫnt.i	Yes, I am going to make my sailing!
imi in.tw n.i wsrw mḏwty	Fetch me twenty oars
n hbny bꜣk m nbw	of ebony worked with gold,
ḥmꜥt iry m sbḳ bꜣk m ḏꜥm	their handles of shining-wood worked with silver-gold.
imi in.tw n.i st ḥmt mḏwty	Fetch me twenty women,
m nfrt nt ḥꜥw.sn m bnt ḥnskyt	beautiful in their bodies, in breasts and hair,
nty n wpt.sn m mst	who have not yet given birth,
ḥnꜥ rdit in.tw n.i iꜣdt mḏwty	and fetch me twenty nets,
ḥnꜥ rdit nn iꜣdt n nn ḥmt	and give the nets to the women,

wꜣḥ ḥbsw.sn	setting aside their clothes.
ʿḥʿ.n ir mi wḏt nbt ḥm.f	Then all was done as His Power ordered.

12. (Papyrus Westcar, column 5, lines 13 to 24)

wn.in.s[n] ḫr ẖnt m ḫd m ẖnt	**Then they rowed up and down,**
wn.in ib n ḥm.f nfr n mꜣꜣ ẖnn.sn	and the heart of His Power was glad at watching their rowing.
ʿḥʿ.n wʿt ntt r štyw ḥt.n.s m ḥnskt.s	Then the one who was at the steering-oar struck on her braid,
ʿḥʿ.n nḫꜣw n mfkꜣt mꜣt ḫr ḥr mw	the fish-pendant of new turquoise fell right into the water,
ʿḥʿ.n.s gr.ti nn ẖnt	and at once she stopped rowing,
wn.in pꜣy.s rmn gr nn ẖnt	and so her side stopped rowing.
ḏd.in ḥm.f in n ẖnn.n.tn	Then His Power said: what is this, that you don't row?
ʿḥʿ.n ḏd.n.sn tꜣy.n štyt gr.ti nn ẖnt	And they said: our steer stopped rowing.
ʿḥʿ.n ḏd.n n.s ḥm.f tm.t ẖn [ḥr-m	Then His Power said to her: [why] are you not rowing?
ʿḥ]ʿ.n ḏd.n.s	[And] she said:
nḫꜣw [pw n mfkꜣt] mꜣ[t ḫr] ḥr mw	it is because the fish pendant of new turquoise has fallen into the water.
ʿḥʿ.n [...] f s[...] n.s .. [...] f dbꜣ	Then he [...] ... to her (?) .. [...] from him in replacement (?).
ʿḥ[ʿ.n ḏd.n.s mr].i ḥnw[.i r snty.f]	And [she said] I [prefer my] object [to its copy].

13. (Papyrus Westcar, column 5, line 24 to column 6, 7)

ḏd.in ḥm.f
[is in n.i] ḫry-ḥbt [ḥry-tp ḏꜣḏꜣ-mʿ]n[ḫ]
[in.in.tw.f n.f ḥr ʿwy]
ḏd.in ḥm.f ḏꜣḏꜣ-m-ʿnḫ sn.i
iw ir.n.i mi nꜣ ḏd.n.k
wn.in ib n ḥm.f ḳb n mꜣꜣ ẖnn.sn
ʿḥʿ.n nḫꜣw n mfkꜣt mꜣt nt wʿt nt štyt ḫr ḥr mw
ʿḥʿ.n.s gr.ti nn ẖnt
ii.n ḥḏ.n.s pꜣy.s rmn
ʿḥʿ.n ḏd.n.i n.s tm.t ẖn ḥr-m
ʿḥʿ.n ḏd.n.s n.i nḫꜣw pw n mfkꜣt mꜣt ḫr ḥr mw
ʿḥʿ.n ḏd.n.i n.s ẖn mt ink dbꜣ.[i] sw
ʿḥʿ.n ḏd.n.s n.i mr.i ḥnw.i r snty.f

Then His Power said:
[Go, bring me the master] lector [Djadjama]n[kh].
[He was brought to him at once.]
Then [His Power] said to him:
Then His Power said: Djadjamankh my brother,
I did as you had said,
and the heart of His Power was cooled at seeing their rowing,
but the fish-pendant of new turquoise of one of the steers fell into the water,
and she stopped rowing,
and she ended up ruining her side.
I said to her: why are you not rowing?
And she said to me: it is because the fish pendant of new turquoise has fallen into the water.
And I said to her: row! I myself am to replace it.
And she said to me: I prefer my object to its copy.

14. (Papyrus Westcar, column 6, lines 7 to 17)

ʿḥʿ.n ḏd.n ḫry-ḥbt ḥry-tp ḏꜣḏꜣ-m-ʿnḫ ḏdt.f m ḥkꜣ
ʿḥʿ.n rdi.n.f rmn n mw n pꜣ š ḥr wʿ.sn
gm.n.f pꜣ nḫꜣw wꜣḥ ḥr pꜣḳyt
ʿḥʿ.n in.n.f sw rdi n ḥnwt.f
ist rf ir pꜣ mw iw.f m mḥ mdt-sn ḥr iꜣt.f
ḏr.in.f mḥ mḏwty-fd r-sꜣ wdb.f
ʿḥʿ.n ḏd.n.f ḏdt.f m ḥkꜣw
ʿḥʿ.n in.n.f nꜣ n mw n pꜣ š r ʿḥʿw.sn
wrš.n ḥm.f ḥr hrw nfr ḥnʿ pr nswt ʿnḫ wḏꜣ snb mi ḳi.f
pr.n fkꜣ.n.f ḫry-ḥbt ḥry-tp ḏꜣḏꜣ-m-ʿnḫ m bw nb nfr
mk biꜣyt ḫprt m rk it.k nswt bity snfrw mꜣʿ ḫrw

m iryt ẖry-ḥbt ḥry-tp sš mḏꜣt ḏꜣḏꜣ-m-ʿnḫ

Then the master lector Djadamankh spoke his speech of power,
and set one side of the waters of the lake on their back,
and found the fish-pendant lying on a pebble.
And he brought it back, to give to its owner.
At this moment the water lay twelve cubits on its back,
totalling twenty-four cubits after its redoubling.
Then he spoke his speech of power,
and returned the waters of the lake to their positions.
His Power spent the time in holiday
with the entire House of the King life! prosperity! health!
As a result he rewarded the master lector Djadjamankh with all good fare.
That is the miracle that happened in the time of your forefather the dual king Sneferu true of voice,
as a deed of the master lector, writer of books Djadjamankh.

15. (Papyrus Westcar, column 6, lines 17 to 22)

ḏd.in ḥm n nswt bity ḫwfw mꜣʿ ḫrw	Then the Power of the dual king Khufu true of voice said:
imi di.tw mꜣʿ t ḫꜣ ḥnḳt ds šnt	Have offering made of a thousand loaves, a hundred jars of beer,
iwꜣ wʿ sntr pꜣd sn n	one ox, two balls of incense to
ḥm n nswt bity snfrw mꜣʿ ḫrw	the Power of the dual king Sneferu true of voice
ḥnʿ rdit di.tw šns wʿ ḥnḳt ḏwiw wʿ	and have offering made of one broad loaf, one jug of beer,
sntr pꜣd	one ball of incense
n ẖry-ḥbt ḥry tp sš mḏꜣt ḏꜣḏꜣ-m-ʿnḫ	to the master lector and writer of books Djadjamankh
iw mꜣ.n.i sp.f n rḫ	for I have seen his demonstration of knowledge.
ir.in.tw mi wḏ[t] nbt ḥm.f	Then it was done in accordance with all that His Power ordered.

16. (Papyrus Westcar, column 6, line 22 to column 7, line 6)

ʿḥʿ p[w] ir.n sꜣ nswt ḥr-dd.f r mdt ḏd.f	**Then the king's son Hordedef stood to speak, and said:**
[…] n sp […] m rḫt.n ntyw swꜣ	[…] of instances […] of knowledge of those that have passed on,
n rḫ.n.tw mꜣʿ[t] r grg	and one cannot distinguish truth from falsehood.
[…] ḥm.k m hꜣw.k ḏs.k n rḫ.f […]	[…] Your Power in your own time, unknown […]
ḏd.in ḥm.f išst [pw] ḥr-[dd.f sꜣ.i	Then His Power said: what is [that? Hordedef my son?]
ḏd.in sꜣ nswt ḥr]-dd.f	[and the king's son Hor]dedef [said]:
iw wn nḏ[s] ḏdi rn.f	there is a fellow called Djedi
ḥms.f m ḏd-snfrw mꜣʿ ḫrw	living in Djed-Sneferu-true-of-voice.
iw.f m nḏs n rnpt šnt mdt	He is a fellow of one hundred and ten years,
iw.f ḥr wnm t šnt diw	and eats five hundred loaves
rmn n kꜣ m iwf	and the shoulder of a bull as meat,
ḥnʿ swri ḥnḳt ds šnt r mn m hrw pn	and drinks a hundred jars of beer down to today.
iw.f rḫ ṯs tp ḥsḳ	He can tie a severed head,
iw.f rḫ rdit šm mꜣi ḥr sꜣ.f	he can make a lion walk behind him,
wnḫ.f ḥr tꜣ	its leash on the ground,
iw.f rḫ tnw ipwt nt wnt nt ḏḥwty	he knows the whereabouts of the chambers of the sanctuary of Thoth.

17. (Papyrus Westcar, column 7, lines 6 to 16)

ist wrš ḥm n nswt bity ḫwfw mꜣʿ ḫrw
ḥr ḥhy n.f nꜣ n ipwt nt wnt nt ḏḥwty
r irt n.f mitt iry n ꜣḫt.f
ḏd.in ḥm.f
ḏs.k irf ḥr-dd.f sꜣ.i int.k n.i sw
ʿḥʿ.n sspd ʿḥʿw n sꜣ nswt ḥr-dd.f
šꜣs pw ir.n.f m ḫntḫtyt r ḏd-snfrw mꜣʿ ḫrw
ḫr m-ḫt nꜣ n ʿḥʿw mni r mryt
šꜣs pw ir.n.f m ḥry
snḏm.n.f m ḳni n hbny
nbꜣw m ssnḏm gnḫ rf m nbw
ḫr m-ḫt spr.f r ḏd ʿḥʿ.n wꜣḥ pꜣ ḳni
ʿḥʿ pw ir.n.f r wšd.f

gm.n.f sw sḏr ḥr [t]mꜣ m sš n [..].f
ḥmw ẖr tp.f ḥr ꜥmꜥm n.f
ky ḥr sin rdwy.fy

Now the Power of the dual king Khufu true of voice was occupied
in finding for himself the chambers of the sanctuary of Thoth,
to make for himself a copy of them for his horizon.
So His Power said:
yourself, off, Hordedef my son, to bring him to me.
Then the ships of the king's son Hordedef were made ready.
He hastened south to Djed-Sneferu-true-of-voice.
When the ships had moored at the riverbank,
he scrambled up,
and made himself comfortable in the ebony carrying-chair,
carrying-poles in hardwood, and the blade even in gold.
On arriving at Djed(i), the carrying-chair was set down.
He stood to address him,
on finding him lying on a [m]at in the porch of his [..],
a servant by his head massaging him, another oiling his legs.

18. (Papyrus Westcar, column 7, line 16 to column 8, line 5)

ꜥḥꜥ.n ḏd.n sꜣ nswt ḥr-dd.f	Then the king's son Hordedef said:
iw ẖrt.k mi ꜥnẖ tp m tni	Your condition is that of life before ageing,
ḥr iꜣwt st mni st ḳrs st smꜣ-tꜣ	for old age is the place of mooring, place of burial, place of funeral.
sḏr r šsp šw m ẖꜣt nn kḥkḥt nt sryt	O he who sleeps to dawn free from illness, without hacking cough.
nḏ ẖrt imꜣẖy pw	This is the greeting for one revered.
ii.n.i ꜥꜣ r nis r.k	I have come to summon you
m wpwt nt it.i ẖwfw mꜣꜥ ẖrw	on a mission of my father Khufu true of voice,
wnm.k špss n dd nswt	that you may eat the riches of the king's gift,
dfꜣw n imyw šmsw.f	the foods of those who are in his retinue,
sb.f tw m ꜥḥꜥw nfr	that he may lead you with a good lifespan
n ityw.k imyw ẖr(t)-nṯr	to your fathers who are in the cemetery.
ḏd.in ḏdi pn	Then this Djedi said:
m ḥtp m ḥtp	In peace, in peace
ḥr-dd.f sꜣ nswt [mr]y n it.f	Hordedef, son of the king, [belov]ed of his father.
ḥs tw it.k ẖwfw mꜣꜥ ẖrw	May your father Khufu true of voice favour you,
sẖnt.f [s]t.k m iꜣw	promoting your place among the elders,
šnt kꜣ.k ẖt r ẖftyw.k	may your spirit conjure defence against your enemies,
rẖ bꜣ.k wꜣwt ꜥfdt r sbẖt nt ḥbs bꜣg	your soul know the ways of the chest to the gate of the Veiled Weary.
nḏ ẖrt sꜣ nswt pw	This is the greeting for a son of a king.
ꜥḥꜥ.n ꜣw.n n.f sꜣ nswt ḥr-dd.f ꜥwy.fy	Then the king's son Hordedef extended his arms to him,
ꜥḥꜥ.n sꜥḥꜥ.n.f sw	and helped him to his feet.
wḏꜣ pw ir.n.f ḥnꜥ.f r mryt	He proceeded with him to the riverbank,
ḥr rdit n.f ꜥ.f	giving him his arm.
ꜥḥꜥ.n ḏd.n ḏdi	Then Djedi said:
imi di.tw n.i wꜥ n ḳꜣḳꜣw	have them give me a cargo-ship
in.tw.f n.i ẖrdw ḥr sšw.i	to bring me the children and my writings.
ꜥḥꜥ.n rdi ꜥḥꜥ n.f ḳꜣḳꜣ sn ḥnꜥ ist.sn	Then he was supplied with two cargo-ships and their crews.
iwt pw ir.n ḏdi m ḫd	Djedi came north
m wsẖ nty sꜣ nswt ḥr-dd.f im.f	in the barge on which was the king's son Hordedef.

19. (Papyrus Westcar, column 8, lines 5 to 22)

ẖr m-ẖt spr.f r ẖnw	**After arriving at the Residence,**
ꜥḳ pw ir.n sꜣ nswt ḥr-dd.f r smit	the king's son Hordedef went in, to report
n ḥm n nswt bity ẖwfw mꜣꜥ ẖrw	to the Power of the dual king Khufu true of voice.
ḏd.in sꜣ nswt ḥr-dd.f	The king's son Hordedef said:
ity ꜥnẖ wḏꜣ snb nb.i iw in.n.i ḏdi	sovereign life! prosperity! health! my lord, I have brought Djedi.
ḏd.in ḥm.f is in n.i sw	And His Power said: go and bring him to me
wḏꜣ pw ir.n ḥm.f	His Power proceeded

r wꜣḫy n pr-ꜥꜣ ꜥnḫ wḏꜣ snb	to the columned hall of the Great House life! prosperity! health!
sṯꜣ.in.tw n.f ḏdi	and Djedi was brought in to him.
ḏd.in ḥm.f pty st ḏdi tm rdi mꜣn.i tw	His Power said: what is this, Djedi, not letting me see you.
ḏd.in ḏdi	And Djedi said:
nisw pw iy ity ꜥnḫ wḏꜣ snb	the one come is one summoned, sovereign life! prosperity! health!
nis r.i mk wi ii.kwi	A summons on me, and see, here I am arrived.
ḏd.in ḥm.f in iw mꜣꜥt pw pꜣ ḏd	Then His Power said: is it true what they say,
iw.k rḫ.ti ṯs tp ḥsḳ	that you can tie a severed head?
ḏd.in ḏdi tiw iw.i rḫ.kwi	Djedi said: yes, I can,
ity ꜥnḫ wḏꜣ snb nb.i	sovereign life! prosperity! health! my lord.
ḏd.in ḥm.f	So His Power said:
imi in.tw n.i ḫnri nty m ḫnrt	have brought to me the captive who is in the camp,
wd nkn.f	and inflict the injury on him.
ḏd.in ḏdi n is n rmt	But Djedi said: not to people,
ity ꜥnḫ wḏꜣ snb nb.i	sovereign life! prosperity! health! my lord.
mk n wḏ.tw irt mnt iry n tꜣ ꜥwt špst	See it is not ordered that a fraction of that be done to the noble flock.
ꜥḥꜥ.n in n.f smn wḏꜥ tp.f	And a goose was brought to him, and its head cut off.
ꜥḥꜥ.n rdi pꜣ smn r gbꜣ imnty n wꜣḫy	And the goose was placed at the western wall of the hall,
ḏꜣḏꜣ.f r gbꜣ iꜣbty n wꜣḫy	and its head at the eastern wall of the hall.
ꜥḥꜥ.n ḏd.n ḏdi ḏdt.f m ḥkꜣ	Djedi spoke his speech of power,
wn.in pꜣ smn ꜥḥꜥ ḥr ḥbꜣbꜣ	and then the goose stood quivering,
ḏꜣḏꜣ.f m mitt	its head the same.

20. (Papyrus Westcar, column 8, line 22 to column 9, line 1)

ḫr m-ḫt spr.f wꜥ r wꜥ	**When one reached the other,**
ꜥḥꜥ.n pꜣ smn ꜥḥꜥ ḥr gꜣgꜣ	the goose stood up cackling.
ꜥḥꜥ.n rdi.n.f in.tw n.f ḫt-ꜣꜥ	Then he had a large goose brought to him,
ir.n.tw r.f m mitt	and the same was done to it.
ꜥḥꜥ.n rdi.n ḥm.f in.tw n.f kꜣ	Then His Power had a bull brought to him,
sḫr tp.f r tꜣ	its head brought down to the ground.
ꜥḥꜥ.n ḏd.n ḏdi ḏdt.f m ḥkꜣw	Then Djedi spoke his speech of power,
ꜥḥꜥ.n pꜣ kꜣ ꜥḥꜥ ḥr sꜣ.f	and the bull stood up behind him,
wnḫ.f ḫr r tꜣ	its leash down on the ground

21. (Papyrus Westcar, column 9, lines 1 to 12)

ꜥḥꜥ.n ḏd.n pꜣ nswt ḫwfw mꜣꜥ ḫrw	Then the king Khufu true of voice said:
pꜣ ir.f ḏd iw.k rḫ.ti tnw	now for that saying, that you are someone who knows whereabouts
nꜣ n ipt nt wnt nt ḏḥwty	of the chambers of the sanctuary of Thoth.
ḏd.in ḏdi ḥs.ti n rḫ.i tnw iry	Djedi said: be pleased, I do not know their whereabouts,
ity ꜥnḫ wḏꜣ snb nb.i	sovereign, life! prosperity! health! my lord
iw.i swt rḫ.kwi bw nty st im	but I know where the information is.
ḏd.in ḥm.f iw ir.f tn	Then His Power said: where then?
ḏd.in ḏdi pn iw ꜥfdt im nt ds	This Djedi said: there is a chest of flint
m ꜥt sipty rn.s m iwnw	in the chamber called Inventory in Iunu –
m tꜣ ꜥfdt	in that chest.
ḏd.in ḏdi ity ꜥnḫ wḏꜣ snb nb.i	Then Djedi said: sovereign, life! prosperity! health! my lord,
mk nn ink is in n.k sy	see, it is not I, though, who is to bring it to you.
ḏd.in ḥm.f in-m r.f in.f n.i sy	Then His Power said: who then is going to bring it to me?
ḏd.in ḏdi in smsw n pꜣ ḫrdw ḫmt	Djedi said: the eldest of the three children
nty m ḫt n rwd-ḏdt in.f n.k sy	who are in the belly of Ruddjedet is going to bring it to you.
ḏd.in ḥm.f mr.i is st nꜣ ḏdy.k	Then His Power said: I like what you say,
pty sy tꜣ rwd-ḏdt	but who is this Ruddjedet?
ḏd.in ḏdi ḥmt wꜥb pw n rꜥ nb sꜣḫbw	Djedi said: she is the wife of a pure-priest of Ra lord of Sakhebu,
iwr.ti m ḫrdw ḫmt n rꜥ nb sꜣḫbw	pregnant with three children of Ra lord of Sakhebu,
iw ḏd.n.f r.s	who has said of it:
iw.sn r irt iꜣt twy mnḫt	they are to exercise this effective office
m tꜣ pn r ḏr.f	in this entire land,
iw smsw n.sn-imy	and the eldest of them is
r irt wr mꜣw m iwnw	to be Greatest of Seers in Iunu

22. (Papyrus Westcar, column 9, lines 12 to 21)

wn.in ḥm.f ib.f wꜣ r ḏwt ḥr.s	Then His Power, his heart fell into sorrow over it.
ḏd.in ḏdi	Then Djedi said:
pty irf pꜣ ib ity ꜥnḫ wḏꜣ snb nb.i	what then, this mood, sovereign, life! prosperity! health! my lord.
in ir.tw ḥr pꜣ ẖrdw ḫmt ḏd.n.i	Is it over the three children I mentioned?
kꜣ sꜣ.k kꜣ sꜣ.f kꜣ wꜥ im.s(n)	Next is your son, next his son, and next one of them.
ḏd.in ḥm.f ms.s irf sy-nw rwd-ḏdt	Then His Power said: when then is she giving birth, Ruddjedet?
ms.s m ꜣbd wꜥ prt sw mdt diw	She is giving birth in month one of spring, day fifteen.
ḏd.in ḥm.f	Then His Power said:
iw sti ṯsw nw rmwy ḥsḳ	then the sandbanks of the Double Fish province are cut?
bꜣk.i ꜣ rd n st ḏs.i	otherwise I would hasten to her myself,
kꜣ mꜣn.i tꜣ ḥwt-nṯr nt rꜥ nb sꜣḫbw	to see the temple of Ra lord of Sakhebu.
ḏd.in ḏdi	Then Djedi said:
kꜣ rdi.i ḫpr mw nw mḥ fd	then I can place water of four cubits
ḥr ṯsw nw rmwy	on the sandbanks of the Double Fish province.
wḏꜣ pw ir.n ḥm.f r ꜥḥ.f	His Power proceeded to his palace.
ḏd.in ḥm.f	His Power said:
imi di.tw m ḥr n ḏdi	have Djedi assigned
r pr sꜣ nswt ḥr-dd.f	to the house of the king's son Hordedef,
ḥms.f ḥnꜥ.f ir ꜥḳw.f m	to dwell with him, and fix his daily food as
t ḫꜣ ḥnḳt ds šnt	a thousand loaves, a hundred jars of beer,
iwꜣ wꜥ iꜣḳt ḫrš šnt	one ox, a hundred bundles of leeks.
ir.in.tw mi wdt nbt ḥm.f	Then all was done as His Power ordered.

23. (Papyrus Westcar, column 9, line 21 to column 10, line 1)

wꜥ m nn hrw	**On one of these days,**
wn.in rwd-ḏdt ḥr šnt.s	**Ruddjedet was in her labour,**
ḳsn mss.s	and her birthing was hard.
ḏd.in ḥm n rꜥ nb sꜣḫbw	So the Power of Ra lord of Sakhebu said
n ist nbtḥwt msḫnt ḥḳt ẖnmw	to Isis, Nephthys, Meskhenet, Heqet and Khnum:
ḥwy ꜣ šꜣs.tn smsy.tn rwd-ḏdt	may it please you to rush to deliver for Ruddjedet
m pꜣ ẖrdw ḫmt nt m ẖt.s	the three children who are in her belly,
nty r irt iꜣt twy mnḫt m tꜣ pn r ḏr.f	who are to exercise this effective office in this entire land,
ḳd.sn rw-prw.tn	that they many build your temples,
sdfꜣy.sn ḫꜣwt.tn	cause your altars to be laden,
swꜣḏ.sn wdḥw.tn	cause your offering-tables to flourish,
sꜥꜣy.sn ḥtpw-nṯr.tn	cause your god's offerings to increase.
wḏꜣ pw ir.n nn nṯrw	These deities proceeded,
ir.n.sn ḫprw.sn m ḫnyt	after turning themselves into a musical troupe,
ẖnmw ḥnꜥ.sn ḥr ḳni	and Khnum with them as the bearer of the kit.

24. (Papyrus Westcar, column 10, lines 1 to 7)

spr pw ir.n.sn r pr rꜥ-wsr	They reached the house of Rauser,
gm.n.sn sw ꜥḥꜥ dꜣiw sḫd	and found him standing with his kilt reversed,
wn.in.sn ḥr ms n.f mnit.sn sḫmw	and so they shook their counterpoises and symbols at him,
ꜥḥꜥ.n ḏd.n.f n.sn	and he said to them:
ḥnwt.i mtn st pw ntt ḥr mn.s	my ladies, now is the moment the woman is in her labour,
ḳsn mss.s	for her birthing is hard.
ꜥḥꜥ.n ḏd.n.sn di.k mꜣ.n sy	They said: let us see her,
mk n rḫ.wyn smsy	for we are skilled in helping birth.
ꜥḥꜥ.n ḏd.n.f n.sn wḏꜣw	He said to them: go ahead.
ꜥḳ pw ir.n.sn tp m rwd-ḏdt	They went in before Ruddjedet,
ꜥḥꜥ.n ḫtm.n.sn ꜥt ḥr.s ḥnꜥ.s	and closed the room with just her and them (inside).

25. (Papyrus Westcar, column 10, lines 7 to 14)

ꜥḥꜥ.n rdi.n sy ist ḫft-ḥr.s	Isis placed herself facing her,
nbt-ḥwt ḥꜣ.s ḥḳt ḥr sḫꜣḫ mswt	Nephthys behind her, with Heqet speeding the births.
ꜥḥꜥ.n ḏd.n ist	Isis said:
im.k wsr m ẖt.s	Do not be mighty in her womb
m rn.k pwy n wsr r.f	in this your name of Mightier.

wꜥr.in ẖrd pn tp ꜥwy.sy	Then this child ran out on her arms
m ẖrd n mḥ wꜥ	as a child of one cubit,
rwd ḳsw.f nḫbt ꜥt.f m nbw	strong in its bones, its limbs shot with gold,
ꜥfnt.f m ḫsbd mꜣꜥ	its headcap of fast lapis lazuli.
iꜥ.in.sn sw šꜥd ḫpꜣ.f	Then they washed it, its umbilical cord cut,
rdi ḥr ifdy m ḏbt	to be placed upon a cloth on a brick.
ꜥḥꜥ.n ms.n sy msḫnt r.f	Then Meskhenet presented herself before it,
ꜥḥꜥ.n ḏd.n.s nswt	and said: a king
ir.ty.fy nsyt m tꜣ pn r ḏr.f	who shall exercise kingship in this entire land,
ḫnmw ḥr swḏꜣ ḥꜥw.f	while Khnum was making its body healthy.

26. (Papyrus Westcar, column 10, lines 14 to 22)

rdi.in sy ist ḫft-ḥr.s	Then Isis placed herself facing her,
nbt-ḥwt ḥꜣ.s ḥḳt ḥr sḫꜣḫ mswt	Nephthys behind her, with Heqet speeding the birth.
ḏd.in ist	Then Isis said:
im.k sꜣḥ m ẖt.s m rn.k pwy n sꜣḥ-rꜥ	Do not be treading in her womb in this your name of Tread-of-Ra.
wꜥr.in ẖrd pn tp ꜥwy.sy	Then this child ran out on her arms
m ẖrd n mḥ wꜥ	as a child of one cubit,
rwd ḳsw.f nḫbt ꜥt.f	strong in its bones, its limbs shot through,
ꜥfnt.f m ḫsbd mꜣꜥ	its headcap of fast lapis lazuli.
iꜥ.in.sn sw šꜥd ḫpꜣ.f	Then they washed it, its umbilical cord cut,
rdi ḥr ifdy m ḏbt	to be placed upon a cloth on a brick.
ꜥḥꜥ.n ms.n sy msḫnt r.f	Then Meskhenet presented herself before it,
ꜥḥꜥ.n ḏd.n.s nswt	and said: a king
ir.ty.fy nsyt m tꜣ pn r ḏr.f	who shall exercise kingship in this entire land.
wn.in ḫnmw ḥr swḏꜣ ḥꜥw.f	Then Khnum was making its body healthy.

27. (Papyrus Westcar, column 10, line 22 to column 11, line 3)

rdi.in sy ist ḫft-ḥr.s	Then Isis placed herself facing her,
nbt-ḥwt ḥꜣ.s ḥḳt ḥr sḫꜣḫ mswt	Nephthys behind her, with Heqet speeding the birth.
ḏd.in ist	Then Isis said:
im.k kkw m ẖt.s m rn.k pwy n kkw	Do not be dark in her womb in this your name of Dark.
wꜥr.in ẖrd pn tp ꜥwy.sy	Then this child ran out on her arms
m ẖrd n mḥ wꜥ	as a child of one cubit,
rwd ḳsw.f nḫbt ꜥt.f m nbw	strong in its bones, its limbs shot through with gold,
ꜥfnt.f m ḫsbd mꜣꜥ	its headcap of fast lapis lazuli.
ꜥḥꜥ.n ms.n sy msḫnt r.f	Then Meskhenet presented herself before it,
ꜥḥꜥ.n ḏd.n.s nswt	and said: a king
ir.ty.fy nsyt m tꜣ pn r ḏr.f	who shall exercise kingship in this entire land.
wn.in ḫnmw ḥr swḏꜣ ḥꜥw.f	Then Khnum was making its body healthy.
iꜥ.in.sn sw šꜥd ḫpꜣ.f	Then they washed it, its umbilical cord cut,
rdi ḥr ifdy m ḏbt	to be placed upon a cloth on a brick.

28. (Papyrus Westcar, column 11, lines 3 to 9)

prt pw ir.n nn nṯrw	Then these deities came out
sms.n.sn rwd-ḏdt m pꜣ ẖrdw ḫmt	after delivering for Ruddjedet the three children,
ꜥḥꜥ.n ḏd.n.sn	and said:
nḏm ib.k rꜥ-wsr	Rejoice, Rauser!
mk ms n.k ẖrdw ḫmt	Three children are born to you.
ꜥḥꜥ.n ḏd.n.f n.sn	And he said to them:
ḥnwt.i pty irt.i n.tn	my ladies, what can I do for you?
ḥꜣ di.tn pꜣ it n pꜣy.tn ḥr ḳni	Please give the grain to your porter,
iṯ.tn n.tn sw r swnt tnmw	take it instead of festive drink.
iwh.in sw ḫnmw m pꜣ it	So Khnum loaded himself up with the grain.

29. (Papyrus Westcar, column 11, lines 9 to 18)

wḏꜣ pw ir.n.sn r bw ii.n.sn im	Then they proceeded back to the place they had come from,
ꜥḥꜥ.n ḏd.in ist n nn nṯrw	but Isis said to these deities:
pty nꜣ ntt n ii.wyn r.s	What did we come for,
nn irt biꜣyt n nꜣ n ẖrdw	if not to work miracles for the children,

smi.n n pꜣy.sn it rdi iwt.n	and report to their father who sent us?
ꜥḥꜥ.n ms.n.sn	Then they fashioned
ḫꜥw ḫmt n nb ꜥnḫ wḏꜣ snb	three crowns of the Lord life! prosperity! health!
rdi.in.sn st m pꜣ it	and placed them in the grain.
ꜥḥꜥ.n rdi.n.sn iwt pt m ḏꜥ ḥr ḥyt	They made the sky come with a storm and rain,
ꜥḥꜥ.n ꜥnn.sn st r pꜣ pr	and made their way back to the house,
ꜥḥꜥ.n ḏd.n.sn	and said:
ḥꜣ dit.n pꜣ it ꜥꜣ m ꜥt ḫtm.ti	please may we place the grain here in a sealed room,
r iwt.n ḥr ḫnt mḥty	until we return from touring in the north.
ꜥḥꜥ.n rdi.n.sn pꜣ it m ꜥt ḫtm.ti	Then they placed the grain in a sealed room.

30. (Papyrus Westcar, column 11, lines 18 to 26)

ꜥḥꜥ.n rwd-ḏdt wꜥb n.s	Then Ruddjedet purified herself
m wꜥb n hrw mdt-ifd	in a purification of fourteen days.
ꜥḥꜥ.n ḏd.n.s n wbꜣt.s	Then she said to her servantwoman:
in iw pꜣ pr sspd	is the house ready?
ꜥḥꜥ.n ḏd.n.s	And she said:
iw.f sspd m bw nb nfr	it is ready with every goodness
wpw-ḥr hnw n in.tw	except for the drink, it hasn't been brought.
ḏd.n rwd-ḏdt	Rudjedet said:
tm.tw ms in hnw ḥr-m	so why hasn't it been brought?
ꜥḥꜥ.n ḏd.n tꜣ wbꜣt	And the servantwoman said:
nfr pw smnḫ ꜥꜣ	we have run out of ingredients here,
wpw ḥr pꜣ it n nn ḫnyt	except for the grain of those musicians,
iw.f m ꜥt ḥr ḫtm.sn	which is in a room under their seal.
ꜥḥꜥ.n ḏd.n rwd-ḏdt hꜣ in im.f	Ruddjedet said: go down and fetch some of it,
kꜣ.in rꜥ-wsr rdi.f n.sn ḏbꜣ iry	and Rauser can repay it to them
m-ḫt.f iw.f	when he returns.

31. (Papyrus Westcar, column 11, line 26 to column 12, line 8)

šꜣs pw ir.n tꜣ wbꜣt	The servantwoman hurried off,
wn.n.s tꜣ ꜥt	and opened the room,
ꜥḥꜥ.n sḏm.n.s ḫrw ḥsy šmꜥ ḫbt wꜣg	and heard the sound of chanting and singing, dancing and ullulating,
irrt nbt n nswt m tꜣ ꜥt	all that is done for a king, in the room.
šꜣs pw ir.n.s	She hurried off,
wn.in.s ḥr wḥm sḏmt.n.s nbt	and then was repeating all that she had heard
n rwd-ḏdt	to Ruddjedet.
wn.in.s ḥr dbn tꜣ ꜥt	So she walked around the room,
n gm.n.s bw irw st im	but did not find it being made anywhere,
ꜥḥꜥ.n rdi.n.s mꜣꜥ.s r pꜣ ḫꜣr	and she put her forehead to the sack,
gm.n.s ir.tw m ḫnw.f	and found it was being made inside it,
ꜥḥꜥ.n rdi.n.s r pds	which she then put in a chest,
rdi m ḫnw ky ḫtm istn m dḥr	placed inside another safe, bound with leather thongs,
rdi.n.s st r ꜥt wnnt ḫr ḫnw.s	and put it in a room containing her property,
ḫtm.n.s ḥr.f	and set a seal on it.
iwt pw ir.n rꜥ-wsr m ii m šꜣ	Rauser returned on his way from the field,
wn.in rwd-ḏdt ḥr wḥm n.f mdt tn	and so Ruddjedet repeated to him this tale.
wn.in ib.f nfr r ḫt nbt	Then his heart was happier than anything.
ḥmst pw ir.n.sn ḥr hrw nfr	They settled down to celebrate.

32. (Papyrus Westcar, column 12, lines 8 to 19)

ḫr m-ḫt hrw swꜣ ḥr nn	**After some days had passed by,**
ꜥḥꜥ.n šnt rwd-ḏdt n tꜣ wbꜣyt	Ruddjedet quarrelled with the servantwoman,
rdi.n.s ḫsf tw n.s m ḥwt	and had her punished with a beating.
ꜥḥꜥ.n ḏd.n tꜣ wbꜣyt	and the servantwoman said
n nꜣ n rmṯ nty m pꜣ pr	to the people who were in the house:
in ir.t(w) st nꜣ r.i	that is how they treat me,
iw ms.n.s nsyw ḫmt	though she has given birth to three kings.
iw.i r šmt ḏd st	I am going to go and tell
n ḥm n nswt bity ḫwfw mꜣꜥ ḫrw	the Power of the dual king Khufu true of voice.

š3s pw ir.n.s	She rushed off,
gm.n.s sn.s n mwt.s smsw	and found her eldest mother's-brother
ḥr mr mḥ nwt ḥr ẖtyw	tying flax in bundles on the terrace.
ꜥḥꜥ.n ḏd.n.f n.s ir.t r tn idyt šrt	He said to her: where are you off to, little girl?
wn.in.s ḥr wḥm n.f mdt t[n]	So she repeated this tale to him,
ꜥḥꜥ.n ḏd.n n.s p3y.s sn	and her brother said to her:
ir is irt.t p3y.t iit tp im.i	what a way to act, coming before me
iw.i ḥr snsn wṯst	to embroil me in gossip!
ꜥḥꜥ.n ṯ3.n.f mḥy š3i r.s	He took a stem of flax to her,
ꜥḥꜥ.n ir.n.f r.s sẖt bint	and gave her an evil thrashing.
š3s pw ir.n t3 wb3yt	The servantwoman rushed off,
r int n.s ikn n mw	to fetch herself a scoop of water,
ꜥḥꜥ.n iṯ.n sy msḥ	and a crocodile snatched her.

33. (Papyrus Westcar, column 12, lines 19 to 26)
š3s pw iry r ḏd st n rwd-ḏdt in p3y.s sn
gm.n.f rwd-ḏdt ḥms.ti tp.s ḥr m3st.s
ib.s ḏw r ḫt nbt
ꜥḥꜥ.n ḏd.n.f n.s
ḥnwt.i ir.t p3 ib ḥr-m
ꜥḥꜥ.n ḏd.n.s
t3 pw ktt ḫpr[t] m p3 pr
mk ms sy šm.ti r ḏd
iw.i r šmt wṯs.i
ꜥḥꜥ.n. rdi.n.f tp.f m ḫrw
ꜥḥꜥ.n ḏd.n.f
ḥnwt.i ḫn sy ii.ti r ḏd n.i [...]
iry.s 3 r gs.i
ꜥḥꜥ.n ir.n.i n.s sẖt bint
ꜥḥꜥ.n[*.s*] *šm.ti r* [*i*]*k*[*n*] *n.s nhw n mw*
ꜥḥꜥ.n iṯ.n sy msḥ

Off rushed her brother to tell Ruddjedet.
He found Rudjedet sitting with her head on her lap,
her mood more evil than anything.
He said to her:
my lady, why are you in this mood?
She said to him:
it is because of that girl who grew up in the house,
she has just gone off saying:
I am going to complain (?).
Then he said:
my lady, indeed she came to tell me [...]
she took a step to my side,
but I gave her an evil thrashing.
[She] had gone off to scoop up a little water for herself,
and a crocodile snatched her.

Teachings: didactic, dominated by the imperative

The category of teaching is marked by initial use of the Egyptian word *sbꜣyt*, and may be divided into those dominated by imperatives ('didactic teachings') and those dominated by descriptive assertions, usually of negative flavour ('reflective teachings', perhaps not separate from the 'laments' other than in their use of the initial word 'teaching'). In Arabic literature the didactic teachings find a parallel as *hikma* 'wisdom' literature in classics such as *adab al-katib* 'the etiquette manual of the bureuacrat' by Abd al-Hamid known as al-Katib 'the Secretary' or 'the Bureaucrat' (impossible to capture in English except with exclusively negative flavour, but German *Beamte*, French *fonctionnaire*, ancient Egyptian *sš*).
Three Middle Kingdom teachings are substantially preserved: the Teaching of Ptahhotep, the more fragmentary Teaching of a Man for his Son, and the Loyalist Teaching.

Teaching of Ptahhotep

The Teaching is set at court, with the highest official ('vizier' in Egyptological translation), a man named Ptahhotep, requesting retirement from the king. The official paints a bleak picture of old age, evidently to convince the king that retirement is necessary, and asks that he be replaced in office by his son as 'staff of old age', a term also found in a late Middle Kingdom legal document to denote a son taking the office of his father, presumably on condition that he continues to support the father (UC 32037: Collier and Quirke 2004). This term, the Middle Egyptian syntax and the late Middle Kingdom date of the two earliest surviving manuscript copies, point to a Twelfth Dynasty date of composition.
The king consents to the request of Ptahhotep, with the observation that the young cannot be born with wisdom - by implication they need the experience given by advanced age. In this way the introduction presents both a positive and the dramatised negative aspects of growing old in ancient Egyptian society.
The transliteration follows Jéquier 1911, using the copy on Papyrus Prisse as principal source: the other Middle Kingdom manuscript and all New Kingdom sources give a second version, with some phrases omitted, others added, others again shared but in different sequence, and with different wording within some phrases. Section divisions below follow the red highlighting in Papyrus Prisse: after each section number are given the corresponding line-numbers in Papyrus Prisse.

1 (Papyrus Prisse, column 4, line 1 to column 5, line 4)

sbꜣyt nt ỉmy-r nỉwt ṯꜣty ptḥ-ḥtp	**The teaching of the Overseer of the City and Vizier Ptahhotep**
ḫr ḥm n nswt bity issi ꜥnḫ ḏt r nḥḥ	before the power of the dual king Isesi living for ever and eternity.
ỉmy-r nỉwt ṯꜣty ptḥ-ḥtp ḏd.f	The Overseer of the City and Vizier Ptahhotep declares:
ity nb.i	O my sovereign,
tnỉ ḫpr ỉꜣw hꜣw	Old age has struck, age has descended,
wgg ỉw ỉḥw ḥr mꜣw	Feebleness has arrived, weakness is here again.
sḏr n.f ẖdr rꜥ nb	Sleep is upon him in discomfort all day.
ỉrty nḏsw ꜥnḫwy ỉmrw	Eyes are grown small, ears deaf,
pḥty ḥr ꜣḳ n wrd ỉb	Strength is being destroyed by weariness,
r gr n mdw n.f	Mouth silent, unable to speak,
ỉb tmw n sḫꜣ.n.f sf	Heart emptied, unable to recall yesterday.
ḳs mnn.f n ꜣww	Bones ache his whole length.
bw nfr ḫpr m bw bỉn	Goodness has turned to evil,
dpt nbt šmt	All taste is gone.
ỉrt ỉꜣw n rmṯ bỉn m ḫt nbt	What old age does to people is evil in every way.
fnd ḏbꜣ n ssn.n.f	Nose is blocked, unable to breathe,
n tnw ꜥḥꜥ ḥmst	how old (it feels) standing or sitting.
wḏ.t(w) n bꜣk ỉm ỉrt mdw ỉꜣw	Let a staff of old age be decreed to be made for this humble servant.
ỉḫ ḏd.ỉ n.f mdw sḏmyw	Let me tell him the speech of those who assess,
sḫrw ỉmyw-ḥꜣt pꜣw sḏm.n nṯrw	the advice of the ancestors once heard by the gods.
ỉḫ ỉr.t(w) n.k mitt	Then the same may be done for you,
dr.tw šnw m rḫyt	strife may be removed from the populace,
bꜣk n.k ỉdbwy	and the Two Shores may toil for you.

2 (Papyrus Prisse, column 5, lines 4-6)

ḏd.ỉn ḥm n nṯr pn	**Then the Power of this god said:**
sbꜣ r.k sw r mdt ẖr ḥꜣt	Teach him then the speech from the past
ỉḫ ỉr.f bỉꜣ n msw wrw	that he may provide the example for the children of the great.
ꜥḳ sḏm ỉm.f mtrt ỉb nb	May hearing enter into him, the measure of every heart.
ḏd n.f nn msy sꜣw	Speak to him. For noone can be born wise.

3 (Papyrus Prisse, column 5, lines 6-8)

ḥ3t-ᶜ m ṯsw n mdt nfrt	**Beginning of the phrasings of fine words**
ḏdt.n *iry-pᶜt ḥ3ty-ᶜ*	**Said by** the man of the elite, foremost of arm
it-nṯr mry nṯr	god's father and beloved of the god
s3 nswt smsw n ẖt.f	eldest son of the king of his body
imy-r niwt ṯ3ty ptḥ-ḥtp	overseer of the city, vizier Ptahhotep
m sb3 ḫmw r rḫ	in teaching the ignorant to be wise
r tp-ḥsb n mdt nfrt	according to the principles of fine words,
m 3ḫt n sḏm.ty.fy	something useful to whoever heeds,
m wggt n nty r tht st	and something harmful to whoever transgresses it.

4 (Papyrus Prisse, column 5, lines 8-10)

ḏd.in.f ḫr s3.f	Then he addressed his son:
m ᶜ3 ib.k ḥr rḫ.k	Do not be proud on account of your knowledge,
nḏnḏ r.k ḥnᶜ ḫm mi rḫ	but discuss with the ignorant as with the wise.
n in.tw ḏrw ḥmwt	The limits of art cannot be delivered;
nn ḥmww ᶜpr 3ḫw.f	there is no artist whose talent is fulfilled.
dg3 mdt nfrt r w3ḏ	Fine words are more sought after than greenstone,
iw gm st m-ᶜ ḥmwt ḥr bnwt	but can be found with the women at the grindstone.

5 (Papyrus Prisse, column 5, lines 10-13)

ir gm.k ḏ3isw m 3t.f	**If you meet an opponent in his moment**
ḫrp ib m iḳr r.k	A director of heart who is superior to you,
ḥ3m ᶜwy.k ḥms s3.k	bend your arms and bow your back;
mṯ3 ib.k r.f	take care over him,
nn mn.n.f n.k	for he will not be swayed for you.
sᶜnd.k ḏd bin	You can belittle bad speaking
m tm ḫsf sw m 3t.f	by not clashing with him in his moment;
nis.t(w).f m ḫm-ḫt pw	it will mean he is called a fool,
rmn.n d3ir ib.k ᶜḥᶜ.f	when your self-restraint has subdued his excess.

6 (Papyrus Prisse, column 5, lines 13-14)

ir gm.k ḏ3isw m 3t.f	**If you meet an opponent in his moment**
mitw.k nty m rmnwt.k	Your equal, a man from your levels,
dd.k ḫpr iḳr.k r.f m gr	silence is how you establish your superiority over him,
iw.f ḥr mdt bint	while he is bad mouthing,
wr wf3 in sḏmyw	greatly to the disgust of the assessors,
rn.k nfr m rḫ n srw	and your name is the good one in the mind of the officials.

7 (Papyrus Prisse column 6, lines 1-3)

ir gm.k ḏ3isw m 3t.f	**If you meet an opponent in his moment**
m ḥwrw n is mitw.k	Who is a poor man, and not your equal,
m 3d ib.k r.f ḫft ḫss.f	do not vent your hear on him by his wretchedness.
imi sw r t3 ḫsf.f n.f ḏs.f	Put him on land for him to oppose himself.
m wšd sw r isy ib.k	Do not answer him for the lightening of your heart
m iᶜ-ib n nty ḫft.k	Do not pour out your heart at the man facing you.
ḳsn pw ḥḏdw ḥwrw ib	The demolition of a wretched heart is a difficult matter.
tw r irt ntt m ib.k	What you wish will be done;
ḥw.k sw m ḫsf n srw	deflect him with the hostility of the officials.

8 (Papyrus Prisse column 6, lines 3-6)

ir wnn.k m sšmy	**If you are to be a leader**
ḥr wḏ n sḫr n ᶜš3t	at a command for the condition of the multitude,
ḥḥ n.k sp nb mnḫ	seek out for yourself every effective moment,
r wnt sḫr.k nn iw im.f	until your condition reaches faultlessness.
wr m3ᶜt w3ḥ spdt	What is Right is great, and (its) keenness enduring.
n ḫnn.t(w).s ḏr rk wsir	It has not been overturned since the time of Osiris.
iw ḫsf.tw n sw3 ḥr hpw	The one who overlooks laws is punished;
sw3t pw m ḥr n ᶜwn-ib	that is what is overlooked in the sight of the greedy.

in nḏyt iṯt ꜥḥꜥw	It is the small-minded that seize riches,
n pꜣ ḏꜣyt mni sp.s	but crime never managed to land its rewards.
iw.f ḏd.f sẖt.i r.i ḏs.i	Whoever says 'I snare for myself'
n ḏd.n.f sẖt.i ḥr ḥnt.i	does not say 'I snare for my needs'.
wn pḥwy mꜣꜥt wꜣḥ.s	The final part of what is Right is its endurance;
ḏdw s w it.i pw	of which a man says 'that is my father'

9 (Papyrus Prisse column 6, lines 8-10)

im.k ir ḥr m rmṯ	**Do not cause fear among people**
ẖsf nṯr m mitt	God punishes with the same.
iw s ḏd.f ꜥnḫ(.i) im	Anyone who says 'I can live by it'
iw.f šw.f m t n tp-r.f	lacks bread for his statement.
iw s ḏd.f wsr.i	Anyone who says 'I can be powerful'
iw.f ḏd.f sẖt.i r.i siꜣt.i	will have to say 'I snare against myself by my cleverness'.
iw s ḏd.f ḥwt.f ky	Anyone who says he will strike another,
iw.f pḥ.f rdi.t(w).f n ẖm.n.f	will end by being given to a stranger.
n pꜣ ḥr n rmṯ ḫpr	Terror has never happened by people,
wḏt nṯr pw ḫprt	what happens is what the god decrees,
kꜣ ꜥnḫ m ẖnw hrt	so live within harmony,
iy dd.sn ḏs iry	and their giving comes of its own accord.

10 (Papyrus Prisse column 6, line 11- column 7, line 3)

ir wnn.k m s n ḥmsw	**If you are a man at a sitting**
r st tt wr r.k	at thc table place of one greater than you,
šsp ddt.f diw r fnd.k	take whatever he causes to be set before you.
m gmḥ.k r ntt m-bꜣḥ.k	When you sight what is before you,
m sti sw m gmḥ ꜥšꜣ	do not pierce it with many glances
bwt kꜣ pw wdt im.f	Pressing it is an offence to the spirit.
m mdw n.f r iꜣšt.f	Do not speak to him until he has requested:
n rḫ.n.tw bint ḥr ib	you never know what may displease.
mdw.k ḫft wšd.f tw	Speak when he questions you,
iw ḏdt.k r nfr ḥr ib	and your speech will please.
ir wr wnn.f ḫꜣ t	A great man, when he is at a meal,
sẖr ḫft wḏ kꜣ.f	behaviour following the command of his spirit,
iw.f r rdit n ḥssy.f	he will give to the one he favours,
sẖr pw n grḥ ḫpr	that is the night-time behaviour that happens
in kꜣ dwn ꜥwy.f	It is the spirit that stretches out his arms
wr di.f n pḥ.n s	or a great man may cause a man not to advance;
iw wnm t ẖr sẖr nṯr	food is eaten under the plan of the god
in ẖm ꜥnꜥy.f ḥr.s	- only a fool complains about it.

11 (Papyrus Prisse column 7, lines 3-5)

ir wnn.k m s n ꜥḳ	**If you are a man of entry**
hꜣbw wr n wr	sent by official to official,
mty ḥr ḳd hꜣb.f tw	be precise in the form he sent you
ir n.f wpwt mi ḏd.f	carry out the mission for him as he says.
ꜥḥꜣ t(w) m sḏw m mdt	Guard against harming with words,
skn.ti wr n wr	embroiling official with official.
ndr mꜣꜥt m sn.s	Grasp what is right by its likeness;
n wḥm.tw is iꜥ n ib	an outburst of the heart is not repeated
m mdyw rmṯ nbt	from the speech of all people.

12 (Papyrus Prisse column 7, lines 5-7)

ir skꜣ.k rwd m sẖt	**If you plough for plants on the margins,**
di st nṯr wr m-ꜥ.k	the god grants it to be great by your hand
m sꜣ r.k r-gs hꜣw.k	Do not inflate your mouth beside your neighbours;
wr irt ḥryt nt gr	to inspire awe by being silent is greater.
ir nb ḳd m nb ḫt	A master of character who is master of wealth,

iṯ.f mi msḥ m ḳnbt	he seizes like a crocodile in the council.
m twꜣ n iwty msw.f	Do not scorn the childless man,
m ḥwr m ꜥbꜥ im	do not bemean by boasting over it.
iw wn wr it m ꜣhw	Even a father can have his plenty of grief;
mwt mst ḥtp kt r.s	a mother who has given birth may be less happy than a maid.
in wꜥ sḫprw nṯr	It is the lone man that the god fosters,
iw nb wḥyt nḥ sšms.f	while the lord of a clan may beg to be followed.

13 (Papyrus Prisse column 7, lines 7-9)

ir ẖs.k šms s iḳr	**If you are weak, follow a man of excellence**
nfr sšm.k nb ḫr nṯr	and all your conduct will be good before god.
m rḫ.n.k nḏsw ḫntw	When you have known lesser men before,
im.k ꜥꜣ ib.k r.f	do not be proud against him,
ḥr rḫt.n.k im.f ḫntw	from what you knew of him before.
snd n.f ḫft ḫprt.n.f	Respect him according to what he has become,
n iy is ḫt ḏs	for goods do not come of their own accord.
hp.sn pw n mrrw.sn	This is their law for their desire.
ir ṯtf iw sꜣḳ.n.f ḏs	An overflow - he has assembled it of himself.
in nṯr ir iḳr.f	It is the god who makes him excellent,
ḫsf.f ḥr.f iw.f sḏr	and protects him while he sleeps.

14 (Papyrus Prisse column 7, lines 9-10)

šms ib.k tr n wnn.k	**Follow your heart as long as you live.**
m ir ḥꜣw ḥr mddwt	Do not exceed what is said,
m ḫb tr n šms ib	do not subtract time from following the heart.
bwt kꜣ pw ḥḏt ꜣt.f	Harming its time is an offence to the ka.
m ngb sp ḫrt hrw	Do not deflect the moment of every day
m ḥꜣw n grg pr.k	beyond establishing your house.
ḫpr ḫt šms ib	As things happen, follow (your) heart.
nn km n ḫt iw sfꜣ.f	There is no profit in things if it is stifled.

15 (Papyrus Prisse column 7, line 10 to column 8, line 2)

ir wnn.k m s iḳr	**If you are a man of excellence**
ir.k sꜣ n simꜣ nṯr	and produce a son in the favour of god,
ir mty.f pḫr.f n ḳd.k	if he follows precisely the outline of your character,
nw.f ḫt.k r st iry	and ties your things to their proper place,
ir n.f bw nb nfr	do everything good for him,
sꜣ.k pw nsw sti kꜣ.k	he is your son, he belongs to the shooting of your ka
im.k iwd ib.k r.f	Do not separate your heart from him.
iw mtwt ir.s šnty	Seed may make a disputant;
ir nnm.f th.f sḫr.k	if he wanders, and breaks your advice,
btn.n.f ḏdt nbt	and has rebelled against all that is said,
šm r.f m mdt ḫst	and his mouth wanders into evil speech,
bꜣk.k sw r r.f mi ḳd.f	battle him in all his statements.
wd r.k m ḫbd.n.sn	He who attacks you is the one they have condemned.
wdd sdb n.f pw m ẖt	It means it was decreed from the womb that he be smitten
n nnm.n sšm.sn	Their guidance does not stray,
n gm.n iww.sn ḏꜣt	their stranded never find a ferry.

16 (Papyrus Prisse column 8, lines 2-6)

ir wnn.k m rwryt	**If you are in the approach hall**
***ꜥḥꜥ ḥms** r nmtt nbt*	**stand and sit** at every step
wdd n.k hrw tpy	as was ordered to you on the first day.
m swꜣ ḫpr šnꜥt.k	Do not waver - that causes your expulsion
spd ḥr n ꜥḳ smi	The sight of the one who enters to report is keen,
wsḫ st nt iꜣš.n.f	the space of the one he has summoned is broad.
iw rwryt r tp-ḥsb	The approach hall follows regulations,
sḫr nb ḫft ḫꜣy	every move according to the measure.
in nṯr sḫnt st	It is the god who promotes a place
n ir.tw rdiw ḳꜥḥ	Those who push forward are not made.

17 (Papyrus Prisse column 8, lines 6-11)

ỉr wnn.k ḥnʿ rmṯ	**If you are to be with people**
ỉr n.k mrt n kf3-ỉb	appoint for yourself people you can trust,
kf3 ỉb	and be trustworthy.
ỉwty pẖr.f ḏd m ẖt.f	The man without speech running through his body
ḫpr.f m ṯsw ḏs.f	is the one who becomes a commander himself.
nb ẖt m-m sẖr.f	A master of goods - what is he like?
rn.k nfr nn mdwy.k	Your good name is that you do not speak.
ḥʿw.k ḏf3w ḥr.k r h3w.k	Your body is fattened for you more than your contemporaries.
ʿb.tw n.k m ḫmt.n.k	You receive praise from those you do not know.
wnn ỉb sḏm n ẖt.f	When a heart heeds only its belly,
dỉ.f knt.f m st mrwt.f	it puts resentment of it in place of love of it.
ỉb.f 3kw ḥʿw.f ḫs3	His heart is afflicted, his body unkempt.
ỉw wr ỉb rdỉw nṯr	The great of heart is the gift of god,
ỉw sḏm n ẖt.f nsw ḫfty	the one who obeys his body belongs to the enemy.

18 (Papyrus Prisse column 8, lines 11-14)

smỉ sšm.k nn ʿm-ỉb	**Report your matters without hesitating**
dỉ sẖr.k m sḥ n nb.k	give your advice in the council of your master.
ỉr ṯṯf r.f ḫft ḏd.f	Anyone fully fluent in speaking,
nn ḳsn r wpwty smỉt	will find no difficulty in being a messenger in reporting.
nn wšb.tw m 3 rḫ st	Noone will contest 'but who can know it?'
ỉn wr r ḫt.f nnm	It is the one who exceeds his field who comes unstuck -
ỉr k3.f r ḫsf.f ḥr.s	if he intends to prevail by it,
ỉw.f gr.f ḥr ỉw ḏd.n.ỉ	he has to be silent at the words 'I said so'.

19 (Papyrus Prisse column 8, line 14 to column 9, line 3)

ỉr wnn.k m sšmy	**If you are a leader**
wstn sẖrw m wḏt n.k	with broad scope in what is commanded to you,
ỉrr.k ḫt tnw	you should do outstanding things,
sḫ3 n.f hrw ỉỉ ḥr-s3	so as to be remembered in days to come.
n ỉy mdt m ḳ3b ḥswt	A case would not arise out of the midst of praises.
bss k3pw ḫpr sf3t	The hidden beast intrudes - and then there is resistance.

20 (Papyrus Prisse column 9, lines 3-7)

ỉr wnn.k m sšmy	**If you are to be a leader**
hr sḏm.k mdw sprw	be patient in your hearing when the petitioner speaks,
m gnf sw r skt ẖt.f	do not interrupt him until his belly is emptied
m k3t.n.f ḏd.n.f st	of what he had planned to have said.
mr ẖr ỉw ỉʿt ỉb.f	The victim loves to sate his heart
r ỉrt ỉỉt.n.f ḥr.s	even more than accomplishing what he came for -
ỉr ỉr gnw sprt	if a petition is halted,
ỉw ḏd.tw ỉw tr r-m th.f st	people say 'but why did he break that rule?'.
nn sprt.n.f nbt ḥr.s m ḫprt.sn	Not everything for which he petitions can come to be,
snʿʿ ỉb pw sḏm nfr	but a good hearing is soothing for the heart.

21 (Papyrus Prisse column 9, lines 7-13)

ỉr mr.k *sw3ḥ ḫnms*	**If you wish** friendship to last
m ẖnw pr ʿḳ.k r.f	within a house you may enter,
m nb m sn m ḫnms r-pw	as master, as brother, or as friend,
r bw nb ʿḳ.k ỉm	anywhere you may enter,
ʿḥ3 tw m tkn m ḥmt	resist approaching the wife.
n nfr.n bw ỉrw st ỉm	The place where it is done is not happy,
n spd.n ḥr ḥr pḥ3 st	The face that opens it up is not sharp,
ỉw ngb.tw s ḫ3 r 3ḫt n.f	A thousand men are tied against what is good for them;
3t ktt mỉtt rswt	a little moment is like a dream,
ỉw pḥ.tw mwt ḥr rḫ st	but death is reached by knowing it.
ṯs pw ḥs stỉ ḫfty	It is a vile twist to shoot the enemy,
pr.tw ḥr ỉrt.f ỉb ḥr wỉn.f	it comes out on his doing, the heart restraining him.

ir whh m snk ḥr.s	The one who fails by lusting for her,
n mꜥr.n sẖr nb m-ꜥ.f	no plan succeeds by his hand.

22 (Papyrus Prisse column 9, line 13 to column 10, line 5)

ir mr.k *nfr sšm.k*	**If you wish** your conduct to be good
nḥm tw m-ꜥ ḏwt nbt	save yourself from all evil,
ꜥḥꜣ tw ḥr sp n ꜥwn ib	resist the opportunity of greed.
ẖꜣt pw mrt nt btw	It is a sore disease of the worm,
n ẖpr.n ꜥḳ im.s	no advance can come of it.
iw.s sibt itw mwtw	It embroils fathers and mothers,
ḥnꜥ snw ḥr mwt	along with mother's brothers.
iw nš.s ḥmt ṯꜣy	It entangles the wife and the man,
ṯꜣwt pw bint nbt	it is a levy of all evils,
ꜥrf pw n ẖbdt nbt	a bundle of all hatefulness.
wꜣḥ s ꜥkꜣ.f mꜣꜥt	The man endures whose guideline is what is Right,
šm r nmtt.f	who proceeds according to his paces.
iw.f ir.f imt-pr im	He can draw up a will by it.
nn wn is ꜥwn ib	There is no tomb for the greedy hearted.

23 (Papyrus Prisse column 10, lines 5-8)

m ꜥwn ib.k ḥr psšt	**Do not be greedy over a share,**
m ḥnt n is r ẖrt.k	do not be jealous of what is not your due,
m ꜥwn ib.k r hꜣw.k	do not be greedy against your kin.
wr twꜣ n sfꜣ r nḫt	The mild man receives more respect than the strong.
ꜥnd pw prr ẖr hꜣw.f	The one who goes out under his kin is a miserable man,
šw m int n mdt	deprived of the profit of speech.
in nhw n ꜥwnt ḥr.s	A fraction of the object of greed
sẖpr šnty m ḳb ẖt	creates a quarreler out of a cool temperament.

24 (Papyrus Prisse column 10, lines 8-12)

ir iḳr.k grg.k pr.k	**If you are excellent, found your household,**
mr.k ḥmt.k m-ẖn ḥsb	love your wife within reckoning.
mḥ ẖt.s ḥbs sꜣ.s	Fill her belly, clothe her back,
pẖrt pw nt ḥꜥw.s mrḥt	ointment is the remedy for her body.
sꜣw ib.s tr n wnnt.k	Gladden her heart as long as you live.
ꜣḫt pw ꜣḫt n nb.s	It is a field of benefit for its lord.
im.k wḏꜥ.s ryt	Do not impose her in affairs.
sḥr.s r sḫm dꜣir.s	Distance her from power, restrain her.
ḏꜥ.s pw irt.s mꜣꜣ.s	Her eye is her storm when it sees.
swꜣḥ.s pw m pr.k	This is what keeps her in your house:
šnꜥy.k s mw pw	Your quelling her, that is water.
kꜣt dit.s n ꜥwy.s	The womb puts her in her arms.
šnnt.s ir n.s mr	In her turmoil a canal is made for her.

25 (Papyrus Prisse column 11, lines 1-4)

sḥtp ꜥḳw.k m ẖprt n.k	**Make your staff happy with what has come to you,**
ẖpr n ḥssw nṯr	it has come to one whom the god favours.
ir whh m sḥtp ꜥḳw.f	Anyone neglecting the happiness of his staff
iw ḏd.tw kꜣ pw ꜥꜣb	is called a spirit of hoarding.
n rḫ.n.tw ẖprt siꜣ.f dwꜣ	Noone know what is coming, when planning tomorrow.
kꜣ pw kꜣ n mty ḥtpw im.f	The spirit of the correct man is the spirit that brings happiness.
ir ẖpr spw nw ḥswt	If moments of praising arise,
in ꜥḳ ḏd iywy	it is the staff who would cheer.
n in.tw ḥtpt r dmi	Food is not brought to town;
iw in.tw ꜥḳw wn ꜣḳ	staff are fetched when there is shortage.

26 (Papyrus Prisse column 11, lines 5-8)

im.k wḥm msk n mdt	**Do not repeat slander**
n sḏm.k sw	and do not listen to it.
prw pw n tꜣ-ẖt	It is the result of the hot-headed.

wḥm mdt m3	Repeat a word after seeing,
n sḏm.n st r-t3 m ḏd rsst	not heard entirely skewed in the saying.
mk ḫft ḥr.k rḫ iḳr	There before you is fine knowledge.
iw wḏ.tw ṯ3wt irt.s	When a levy is decreed to take place,
sḫprw r iṯt.s msdt mi hp	the one made to exact it is hated, by law.
mk sswn rswt pw	See what is the remedy for the dream -
ḥbs.tw ḥr.s	concealment.

27 (Papyrus Prisse column 11, lines 8-11)

ir wnn.k m s iḳr	**If you are as a man** of excellence,
ḥms m sḥ n nb.f	sitting in the council of his master,
s3ḳ ib nb r bw iḳr	rally every heart to excellence.
gr.k 3ḫ st r tftf	Your silence is more benefit than creeping talk.
mdy.k rḫ.n.k wḥʿ.k	You should say what you know how to explain.
in ḥmww mdw m sḥ	There are artists of words in the council,
ḳsn mdt r k3t nbt	speaking is more difficult than any labour.
in wḥʿ.s dd.s r ḫt	The one who can explain is the one who makes it work.

28 (Papyrus Prisse column 11, line 12 to column 12, line 6)

ir wsr.k dd.k snd.k	**If you are powerful in causing respect** for you,
m rḫ m hrt ḏd	by knowledge, in the calm of speech,
m wḏ tp n is r sšm	do not order people, except by the guidelines.
iw štm ʿḳ.f n iwt	The aggressive man ends up in trouble.
m k3 ib.k tm.f dḥi	Do not have your heart too high, or it will be brought down.
m gr s3w ḥn.k	Do not stay silent if it makes you stumble.
wšb.k mdt n nsr	When you answer the speech of a fiery man,
sḥr ḥr.k ḫn tw	distance your sight, restrain yourself.
iw nswt nt t3-ib sḫr.f	The spear of a hothead flies past,
ʿn ḫndw ḳd mtn.f	but a fine mover has his path smoothed.
mnš n hrw r 3w.f	A man who worries all day long
nn ir n.f 3t nfrt	will never be allowed a good moment.
wnf ib n hrw r 3w.f	A man who lazes all day long
nn grg n.f pr	will never have a solid house.
stw mḥ mi ḥmw sp r t3	A shot filled is like an oar abandoned on the ground,
ky nḏrw	when another is taken,
iw sḏm.n ib.f r ḫn 3	his heart has obeyed the wish 'if only I had...'

29 (Papyrus Prisse column 12, lines 6-9)

m ḫsf tw m 3t wr	**Do not block the moment of a great man**
m sḥnw ib n nty 3tpw	do not constrain the desire of one who is laden down.
ḫpr sdb.f r šnt sw	Barriers from him arise against the one who disputes with him,
sfḫ k3 m mrr sw	there is release for the ka with the one who shows love for him.
dd k3w pw ḥnʿ nṯr	This is the gift of sustenance, this with the god.
mrrt.f irt n.f	What he loves is action for him.
sḳd r.k ḥr m-ḫt nšn	When the face is turned back to you, after a storm,
iw ḥtp ḫr k3.f	there follows peace before his ka,
iw sdb ḫr ḫfty	and barriers before the enemy.
k3w pw srwd mrwt	Planting love brings sustenance.

30 (Papyrus Prisse column 12, lines 9-13)

sb3 wr r 3ḫt n.f	**Instruct the great in what is useful for him**
sḫpr ššp.f m ḥr rmṯ	Foster his image in the sight of people,
di.k ḫr s33.f ḫr nb.f	cause his wisdom to fall in front of his lord,
wnn ḏf3 n.k ḫr k3.f	and there may be rewards for you too before his ka.
iw ḫt nt mrwt r ḥtpw	The stomach of the loved will be content,
iw s3.k r ḥbs ḥr.s	your back will be clothed by it,
wn ššp.f ḥr.k r ʿnḫ n pr.k	his image will be over you for the life of your house,
ḫr sʿḥ.k mrr.k	Your noble, the one you love,
ʿnḫ sw ḥr.s	he is alive with it.

ir.f kꜥḥ nfr im.k gr	When he makes a good gesture, do not be silent.
wꜣḥ grt mrwt.k pw	This is indeed the guarantee of your love
m ẖt nt mrrwt tw	in the body of those who love you.
mk kꜣ pw mrr sḏm	See, it is the ka that loves to listen.

31 (Papyrus Prisse column 13, lines 1-4)

ir ir.k sꜣ s n ḳnbt	**If you play the son of a man of a council,**
wpwty n hrt ꜥšꜣt	a messenger for pleasing the multitude,
šd mꜣdw nw ꜥ	select the fringes of action.
mdy.k m rdi ḥr gs	In speaking do not take sides,
sꜣw ḏd.f sẖr.f	in case he speaks his opinion:
srw rdi.f mdt ḥr gs iry	'officials, he sets the case on that side',
wdb sp.k r wḏꜥt	and your mistake is turned into judgement.

32 (Papyrus Prisse column 13, lines 4-6)

ir sf.k ḥr sp ḫprw	**If you show mercy on a past failure,**
gsꜣ.k n s ḥr ꜥḳꜣ.f	incline to a man for his virtue.
swꜣ ḥr.f m sḫꜣ sw	Pass over him, do not recall it,
ḏr gr.f n.k hrw tpy	since he might stay silent for you on day one.

33 (Papyrus Prisse column 13, lines 6-9)

ir ꜥꜣ.k m-ḫt nḏsw.k	**If you are rich after your impoverishment,**
ir.k ḫt m-ḫt gꜣt tp im	and acquire property after lack of it,
m niwt rḫt.n.k	in the city that you have known,
m sšꜣw ḫprt n.k ḫntw	with awareness of what happened to you before,
m kfꜣ ib.k ḥr ꜥḥꜥw.k	do not place your trust in your wealth.
ḫpr n.k m rdiw nṯr	It came to you by the gifts of the god,
nn tw ḫꜣ ky mitw.k	so you will not be behind another like you,
ḫprw n.f mitt iry	but the same could happen to him

34 (Papyrus Prisse column 13, line 9 to column 14, line 4)

ḥms sꜣ.k n ḥry-tp.k	**Bend your back to your superior,**
imy-r.k n pr nswt	your overseer of the king's domain,
wnn pr.k mn ḥr ḫt.f	and your house will be fixed on its goods,
ḏbꜣw.k m st iry	your rewards in their place.
ḳsn pw itnw m ḥry-tp	The man who struggles with the superior is an irritant.
ꜥnḫ.tw tr n sft.f	You live as long as the superior is pleased with you.
n ḫꜣ.n kꜥḥ n kftf	The shoulder is not injured by being exposed.
m ṯꜣwy pr sꜣḫw	Do not seize the house of neighbours,
m dꜣir ḫt tkn im.k	do not suppress anything close to you,
nn st ꜣḫ n st	it gives no results in anything.
im.f siw r.k r sḏmt.k	Let him not speak ill of you before you have heard.
im pw n ib bḳbḳ	A troublemaker is a man with no mind.
ir rḫ st iw.f r šny	Whoever is known as a quarreller,
ḳsn pw n itnw m st tknt	there is trouble for the struggler in places near to him.

35 (Papyrus Prisse column 14, lines 4-6)

im.k nk ḥmt ẖrd	**Do not have sex with a child woman**
rḫ.n.k ḥsfwt r mw ḥr ḥꜣty.f	when you knew the approach to the water on its chest.
nn ḳb n ntt m ẖt.f	There is no cooling what is in his body.
im.f swḫꜣ r irt ḥsfwt	Do not go mad on making the approach.
ḳb.f m-ḫt ḥḏ.f ib.f	He is cool after damaging his heart.

36 (Papyrus Prisse column 14, lines 6-12)

ir ḏꜥr.k ḳd n ḫnms	**If you seek out** the character of a friend,
m šnn r.k tkn im.f	do not make your own enquiries, go direct to him,
ir sp ḥnꜥ.f wꜥw	make the case with him alone

r tmt.k mn ḫrt.f	to avoid suffering in his matter.
ḏ3is ḥnʿ.f m-ḫt ʿḥʿw	Debate with him after a period of time,
wšm ỉb.f m sp n mdt	and try his heart in the matter of the case.
ỉr pr m3t.n.f m-ʿ.f	If what he has seen comes out through him,
ỉr.f sp špt.k ḥr.f	and he does the matter that angers you about him,
ḫnms sw r-pw	or that makes him a friend,
m ỉṯw ḥr	do not seize the sight,
s3ḳ m wb3 n.f mdt	be collected, do not deluge him with words,
m wšb m sp n sh3	do not reply with a slight,
m wi tw r.f m hbw sw	do not react against him by destroying him.
n p3 sp.f tm iw	His moment cannot fail to come.
n wh.n.tw m š3 sw	Noone can escape from what is fated for him.

37 (Papyrus Prisse column 14, line 12 to column 15, line 2)

ḥḏ ḥr.k tr n wnn.k	**Let your face be bright as long as you live.**
ỉr pr m mḫr n ʿḳ.n	Whoever leaves the store cannot enter.
ỉn t n psšt ḫnty ḥr.f	It is the bread of sharing that causes envy.
srḫy pw šw m ẖt.f	A man with an empty stomach is a man to complain;
ḫpr ỉtnw m s3hhw	the opponent is born out of impoverishment.
m ỉr sw r tkn ỉm.k	Do not make him into someone to approach you.
sḫ3 pw s ỉ3mt	Favour is the memory of a man
n rnpwt ỉmt-ḫt w3s	in the years after ruin.

38 (Papyrus Prisse column 15, lines 2-5)

rḫ šwt.k *wnn ẖt.k*	**Know your plumage** and your property will last.
m ḫs bỉ3t.k r ḫnmsw.k	Do not be mean in your character towards your friends.
wdb.f pw mḥ.f wr sw r špssw.f	They are his river field when it floods, greater than his riches.
sw ẖt ky n ky	They are the property of one for another.
3ḫ bỉ3t nt s3 s n.f	The quality of a son of a someone is good for him;
ỉw ḳd nfr r sḫ3w	good character will be remembered.

39 (Papyrus Prisse column 15, lines 5-6)

ḥsf ḥr tp sb3 ḥr ḳd	**Punish from the head, teach by character.**
ỉw nḏrt ḫw r mnt bỉ3	The force against a criminal will be a model example.
ỉr sp n ỉs ḥr ỉyt	Any instance except for crime
rdi ḫpr ʿnʿy pw m ỉtnw	is what makes a moaner turn into an active opponent.

40 (Papyrus Prisse column 15, lines 6-8)

ỉr ỉr.k ḥmt m špnt	**If you marry a good-time girl**
wnft ỉb rḫt.n nỉwt.s	A joyful woman known to her town,
ỉw.s m hpwy	If she is wayward,
ʿn n.s nw	and revels in the moment,
m nš.s ỉmỉ r.k wnm.s	do not reject her, but instead let her enjoy;
ỉw wnft ỉb sip.s ʿḳ33	joyfulness is what marks calm water.

41 (Papyrus Prisse column 15, line 8 to column 16, line 2)

ỉr sḏm.k nn ḏd.n.ỉ n.k	**If you heed these things that I have told you**
wnn sḫr.k nb r ḥ3t	all your conduct will move forward.
ỉr sp n m3ʿt ỉry špss.sn pw	Their holding true, that is their wealth.
rwỉ sḫ3.sn m r n rmṯ	The memory of them moves in the mouth of people
m-ʿ nfr n ṯsw.sn	from the excellence of their phrasing.
ỉn.n.tw mdt nbt	When every saying has been brought,
n sk.n m t3 pn ḏt	it does not perish in this land ever.
ỉrt.s ššrt r nfr	Doing it is a matter for goodness,
mdw srw r.s	the words of the officials follow it.
sb3 s pw r ḏd n m-ḫt	This is the teaching of a man to speak to posterity,
sḏm.f st ḫpr m ḥmww sḏmw	hearing it he becomes an attentive craftsman.
nfr ḏd n m-ḫt ntf sḏm.f st	It is good to speak to posterity, for that is who will hear it.
ỉr ḫpr sp nfr m-ʿ wnn m ḥry-tp	If there good cases arise from the one who is the superior,
wnn.f mnḫ n nḥḥ	he will be eternally effective,

ỉw sꜣꜣ.f nb r ḏt	all his wisdom will last forever.
in rḫ sm bꜣ.f	The wise man nourishes his soul
m smnt nfr.f ỉm.f tp tꜣ	by establishing his goodness with it on earth.
sꜣ.tw rḫ ḥr rḫt.n.f	The wise man is famed for what he has learned,
in sr ḥr sp.f nfr	it is the official who is after his good conduct,
m-ꜥ n ib.f nst.f	from the action of his heart and his tongue,
ꜥḳꜣ spty.fy iw.f ḥr ḏd	his lips are reliable when he is speaking,
irty.fy ḥr mꜣꜣ	and his eyes in seeing,
ꜥnḫwy.f twt ḥr sḏm ꜣḫt n sꜣ.f	his ears intent in hearing what is useful for his son.
ỉr mꜣꜥt šw m grg	Who does what is right, is free from falsehood.

42 (Papyrus Prisse column 16, lines 3-13)

ꜣḫ sḏm n sꜣ sḏmw	**Hearing is good for a son who hears,**
ꜥḳ sḏm m sḏmw	**hearing enters into the hearer.**
ḫpr sḏmw m sḏmi	The hearer becomes one who is heard.
nfr sḏm nfr mdt	Hearing is good, as speech is good.
sḏmw nb ꜣḫt	The hearer is the master of what is useful.
ꜣḫ sḏm n sḏmw	Hearing is good for the hearer,
nfr sḏm r ntt nbt	hearing is better than any other thing;
ḫpr mrwt nfrt	love of good comes into being.
nfr-wy šsp sꜣ ḏd it.f	How beautiful it is when a son receives what his father says.
ḫpr n.f iꜣwt ḫr.s	Old age is achieved for him by it.
mrrw nṯr pw sḏm	The hearer is one whom the god loves.
n sḏm.n msddw nṯr	The one whom god hates does not hear.
in ib sḫpr nb.f	The heart is the creator of its master.
m sḏm m tm sḏm	Do not hear from the one who does not hear.
ꜥnḫ wḏꜣ snb n s ib.f	A man's heart is his life, prosperity and health.
in sḏmw sḏm ḏd	It is the hearer who hears the speaker,
mrr sḏm pw ir r ḏdt	he who acts according to what is said is the one who loves hearing.
nfr-wy sḏm sꜣ n it.f	How good when a son listens to his father.
rš-wy ḏddy n.f nn	How joyful is the one to whom this is said.
sꜣ ꜥn.f m nb sḏm	A son who is handsome is a hearing lord.
sḏmw ḏdw n.f st mnḫ.f m ẖt	The hearer to whom it is said is effective in the body,
imꜣḫy ḫr it.f	revered before his father,
iw sḫꜣ.f m r n ꜥnḫw	Memory of him is in the mouth of the people,
ntyw tp tꜣ wnnt.sn	Those who are on earth, and those who will be.

43 (Papyrus Prisse column 16, line 13 to column 17, line 4)

ỉr šsp sꜣ s ḏdt ỉt.f	**If the son of a someone receives what his father says,**
nn nm n sḫr.f nb	There can be no wavering for any of his plans.
sbꜣ.k m sꜣ.k sḏmw	Instruct your son to be a good hearer,
ỉḳr.ty.fy ḥr ib n srw	who will be excellent in the hearts of the officials,
sšm r.f r ḏddt n.f	guiding his mouth according to what he has been told,
mꜣw m sḏmw	seen as a hearer.
sꜣ ỉḳr.f nmtt.f tnw	The son who excels, his steps are distinguished,
nnm bs n tm sḏm	but there is no straight way in for the one who fails to hear.
dwꜣ rḫ r smnt.f	The morning of the wise man will be his security,
ỉw wḫꜣ mdd.f	while the fool is pressed down.

44 (Papyrus Prisse column 17, lines 4-9)

ỉr wḫꜣ ỉwty sḏm.f	**As for the fool unable to hear,**
nn ỉr n.f ḫt nbt	nothing can ever be done for him.
mꜣ.f rḫ m ḫm	He sees wisdom as ignorance,
ꜣḫt m mnt	and what is good as what is painful.
ỉr.f ḫbdt nbt	He commits every error,
r ṯsst ỉm.f rꜥ nb	to be accused of it each day.
ꜥnḫ.f m mwtt ḫr.s	He lives on what one dies of,
ꜥḳw.f pw ḫbn ḏd	corrupt speect is his food.
biꜣt.f im m rḫ n srw	His character in this is well-known to the officials,
ḥr mwt ꜥnḫ rꜥ nb	saying 'living death' each day.

sw3.t(w) ḥr spw.f	His faults are passed over
m-ˁ ˁš3 n iyt ḥr.f rˁ nb	from the sheer number of faults on him each day.

45 (Papyrus Prisse column 17, line 10 to column 18, line 12)

s3 sḏmw m šms ḥr	**A son who hears is a follower of** Horus
nfr n.f m-ḫt sḏm.f	It is good for him after he hears.
i3ww.f pḥ.f im3ḫ	In his old age he achieves revered status.
sḏd.f m mitt n ẖrdw.f	He can tell the same to his children,
m sm3w sb3w it.f	renewing the teaching of his father.
s nb sb3 mi ir.f	Every man teaches by his deeds.
sḏd.f ḫr msw	He tells on to the children,
iḫ ḏd.n.sn ẖrdw.sn	and they can tell their children.
ir bi3 m rdi ˁnḏt.k	Show character, do not pass on your weaknesses.
srwd m3ˁt ˁnḫ msw.k	Securing what is Right, is the life of your children
ir tpi iy ḥr isft	As for the principal who arrives with wrongdoing,
iḫ ḏd rmṯ m33t.sn	people say what they see
mitt is pf3 pw	'that is exactly how that man is'
ḏd n sḏm.ty.sn	to say to those who will hear
mitt is pf3 pw gr	'that is exactly how that man is' too.
m33 bw nb sn sgrḥ ˁš3t	Their everyone sees, and the multitude is pacified.
nn km.n špss m ḫmt.sn	There is no profit in riches without them.
m iṯ mdt m in.s	Do not remove a word, do not add it.
m rdi kt m st kt	Do not put one in place of another.
ˁḥ3 tw m wn ini im.k	Fight against opening up the bonds on you.
s3w tw r ḏd rḫ ḫt	Guard against a man of experience saying
sḏm r.k mr.k smnt.k	'listen up, if you wish to be secure
m r n sḏmyw	in the mouth of those who hear;
mdwy.k ˁḳ.n.k m sp n ḥmww	speak up when you have penetrated the case of the craftsman'.
mdw.k r sp n ḳn	You speak at the case of closure,
wnn sḫr.k nb r st.f	and all your plans will fall into place.

46 (Papyrus Prisse column 18, line 12 to column 19, line 3)

hrp ib.k ḫn r.k	**Flood your heart, restrain your mouth**
iḫ sḫr.k m-m srw	then your plans will be among the officials.
mtr ḥr ḳd ḫr nb.k	Be straight in character before your lord.
ir r ḏd.n.f s3 pf3 pw	Do as he has said, that is the son,
r ḏd n sḏm.ty.sn st	so those who hear it say
ḥs grt msy.n.f sw	'indeed favour gave birth to him'.
ḏd.k ḫt tnw	Say things of distinction,
iḫ ḏd srw sḏm.ty.sn	so the officials who hear may say
nfr wy prw n r.f	'how perfect is the issue of his mouth'.

47 (Papyrus Prisse column 19, lines 3-8)

ir r ḏdt nb.k r.k	**Do as your master has said for you.**
nfr wy sb3.n it.f	How good is one instructed by his father
pr.n.f im.f ḫnt ḥˁw.f	when he emerged from him out of his body,
ḏd.n.f n.f iw.f m ḫt r-3w	and he told him, while he was in the body, entirely,
wr irt.n.f r ḏddt n.f	May what he has done be greater than what he was told.
mk s3 nfr n dd nṯr	See, a good son, by the gift of the god,
rdi ḥ3w ḥr ḏddt n.f ḫr nb.f	surpassing what he was told before his lord.
ir.f m3ˁt	He does what is Right.
ir.n ib.f r nmtt.f	His heart has acted according to his set steps.
mi pḥ.k wi ḥˁw.k wḏ3	As you reach me, your body intact,
nswt ḥtp m ḫprt nbt	the king content with every happening,
iṯ.k rnpwt m ˁnḫ	take years of life.
nn šr irt.n.i tp t3	What I have done on earth is not little.
iṯ.n.i rnpt šnt mḏ m ˁnḫ	I took 110 years of life
n dd n.i nswt	by the grant of the king to me,
ḥswt ḫnt tpyw-ˁ	favour ahead of the ancestors,

m-ˁ irt mꜣˁt n nswt r st imꜣḫ	from doing what is Right for the king until the stage of revered status.

There follows an end-note confirming the unity of the composition (Papyrus Prisse, column 19, line 9):
iw.f pw ḥꜣt.f r pḥwy.fy mi gmyt m sš
'this is its completion, from beginning to end as found in writing'.

The Teaching of a Man for his Son

This didactic work is a literary composition in Middle Egyptian, of uncertain date. All surviving copies were written in the New Kingdom, but the style of language and echoes of other literary compositions date it to the Middle Kingdom (about 2025-1700 BC). No author is named on the surviving sources: the opening emphasises anonymity, either on the universalising principle 'everyman', or in the more elitist spirit of the stock phrase *sꜣ s* 'son of a man' meaning 'son of a somebody', so a man of higher social background.

The transliteration follows Fischer-Elfert 1999, retaining the section divisions proposed there, though the break from Introduction to Paragraph 1 seems contrary to the pattern in other Teachings: Fischer-Elfert also proposes a broader thematic division in his edition, with Part One covering sections 1-8, and Part Two the remaining passages, his sections 9-24.

Introduction

ḥꜣt-ꜥ m sbꜣyt ỉrt.n s n sꜣ.f	Beginning of the teaching made by a man for his son
ḏd.f sḏm ḫrw.ỉ m wn mdw.ỉ	He says: hear my voice, do not avoid my words,
m fḫ ỉb.k ḥr ḏdt.ỉ n.k	do not untie your heart from what I tell you.

1.

ỉr ḳd nn sn ỉm	Have character, without exaggerating it;
n ḫpr.n wsft nt sꜣꜣ	for a sensible man idleness does not happen.
mty gr ḫꜣm rmn	Silence is just, with arm inclined.
mnḫ ỉb ỉr ḏdt	The heart that does what is told is the effective one;
pnḳt mdt ẖr-ḥꜣt ḫpš	rejection of words leads to violence;
nn ḳn sꜥr r sḥ	there is no baggage-man raised to the audience-hall
ꜥḳ m mdt wbꜣ sḏm	Whoever enters into words, opens the way for hearing
nn ḳmꜣw nḏnḏ m-ꜥ.f	there is no winnower from whom one takes advice.
wḥꜥ mdt nn snm.f	Interpret words without humiliating;
ḫn ḥwr swḫꜣ.f ḏd sw	a mean phrase slights its sayer.

2.

m sṯn ỉb.k ḥr nṯr	Do not let your heart stray from god.
dwꜣ nswt mr.k sw m mrt	Praise the king, may you love him, as a servant
sbꜣḳ.f m dd bꜣw.f	He makes radiant by the giving of his powers
mh ḥr.f m šw r mnỉ	but whoever neglects him is deprived of a mooring.
wr sw r s ḥḥ n ḥs.n.f	He is greater than a million men for the one he has favoured,
dnỉt pw nt sḥtp sw	he is the shield for the one who makes him content.
ỉw pẖr.n.f r wr ẖr	Whoever has escorted will be great in wealth
dd.f ỉb.f n mr.n.f	It is to the one he has loved that he gives his heart;
sꜣw ḏd r.k r wḫꜣḫ sw	guard against speaking out and vexing him.

3.

ỉn ỉw hrw n rnnt ḥr thꜣt.f	Can the day of Renenet be varied?
ỉn ỉw wꜣḥ.tw hrw n ꜥḥꜥw	Can you add a day to a lifespan?
ỉn ỉw ḫbꜣ.tw ỉm.f r-pw	Can you subtract from it either?
msḫnt mỉ sp tpy	Meskhenet is like the time of creation,
nn ḥḏ šꜣꜥ.n.f	there is none who can destroy what he has ordained.
mk ỉst wr ḥst nt nṯr	See then, great is the favour of god,
ꜥꜣ ḫsf r-sy wr bꜣw.f	exceedingly great is his control, mighty his power.
mꜣꜣ.n.ỉ ḳfꜣw.f nn ḫpr m šꜣwt.f	I have seen his eminence, none can come into being against (?) him.

4.

ỉw.f sḫpr.f ḫm r rḫ	He can transform the ignorant into the wise,
msdd ḫpr m mrr	the hater become the loving,
ỉw.f dỉ.f sn ktkt wrw	he enables the least to be like the great,
ẖr pḥwy m tpy	the one in last place to become first,
šw ḫrt m nb ꜥḥꜥw	the man without property to be a lord of riches
ꜥndt m nb hny	the miserable to be a lord of jubilation.
ỉw.f dỉ.f mnỉ šw mnỉ	He enables the man without mooring-post to moor,
sswn m nb dmỉ	and the man who was traded to be lord of the docks.

ỉw.f sbꜣ.f ꜣbb r mdt	He teaches the love of speaking,
swbꜣ.f ꜥnḫwy ỉd	he opens the ears of the deaf

5.

ỉw nn r-ꜣw m ẖnw ꜥḥꜥw	All this is within a lifetime,
m rwty hrw n rnnt	beyond the day of Renenet,
nn smn msḫnt r.s	and Meskhenet can guarantee nothing for it,
wp-ḥr smn ṯꜣw r fnd	other than guaranteeing breath for the nose
wr n.k m-ꜥ.k	Greatness can be yours by your action,
ỉr.n.k ꜥḥꜥw.k m-ẖnw sḫrw nṯr.k	if you have spent your life within the frame of your god

6.

dwꜣ nswt swꜣš bỉty	Praise the king, adore the king
ỉꜣt pw ḫrt nṯr	that is the post that is before the god.
ỉmỉ bꜣw.f ḥꜥꜥw m wd.n.f	Spread his powers, rejoicing when he has decreed,
šnt ḫrt m mr.n.f	and devising plans (?) for what he has desired.
šw rn.f r ỉmꜣḫy	The nameless will become a revered man,
snm.f rdỉ n.f pḥwy	but he reduces whoever gives him the rear.
stk[n? ...] ẖt	... [...] body,
swbꜣ.n.f sw ỉw.f m-m ..-y	he has opened him/it up when he/it was among the ...
ỉr.n.f nmt ḫr .. tnw	He has made a slaughterhouse, and overthrown ... (?)

7.

wḏꜣ ḥꜥw pw šw m rn.f	He is the bodily health of the nameless
ỉw.f šnt.f n.f ẖt	he exorcises his body for him.
sw wnm nhw ꜥwy.fy	He is the right arm of the man whose arms are weak.
ḳrs.n.tw m pḫꜣ ỉm.f	A person is buried (only) as one cleansed by him,
sbꜣḳ.tw ḥn.tw ḥr rn.f	and is made radiant and secure at his name.
mḥy ḥtp ḥr mr.f	The anxious man finds peace at his pyramid,
nn ỉs n dm rn.f	but there is no tomb for the one who pronounces his name,
nn stỉ n šnt sw	there is no pouring of water for the one who plots against him.

8.

mꜣꜣ.n ḫꜣst nbt ẖr ḥryt.f	We see every foreign land in terror of him
ỉw wrw.sn ḥr ḳnb n.f st	and their leaders bowing down to him.
ḏꜣ bꜣw.f wꜣḏ-wr	His powers have crossed the great green water,
nbtyw ꜥnḫ ḥr snd.f	the islanders (?) alive in fear of him.
pwnt ỉdbw ḥꜣw-nbw	Punt and the shores of the farthest islands,
ỉw nṯr ḥr snwḥ n.f st	the god has roped them in for him(self).
tm wd ỉm.f pꜣ sꜣḥ tꜣ	Whoever does not attack him, has already touched land.
tm šnt sw ḥtp mr.f	Whoever does not plot against him, rests at his pyramid.

9.

m ḏd grg m-sꜣ ḳd mdt	Do not tell lies in the quest to build a speech -
ḳsn pw mtyw ḥr sḫwn	witnesses to a dispute make that difficult,
ỉw ṯn.tw s ḥr sp ḥwr	A man is tripped by a mean moment,
tm hꜣb.f m ky sp	and cannot send a second time.
ḫpr mnḫ m ꜥḳꜣ nst	Effectiveness arises from accuracy of tongue.
nn hꜣ mdt ꜥḏꜣ r tꜣ	Speech of malice cannot fall to the ground,
nn stwt ḥr swꜣḏ.n.f	and there is no building on what it has fostered.
nn mḥ-ỉb m wsf sp ḫn ḥwr	There is no peace of mind in delaying by a moment of evil.
ꜥrḳ mdt ỉṯ mnḫ[t] ḥr tmꜣ	Collect a speech, grasp what has effect on the mat,
ꜣḫ mꜣꜥt n ḏd st	What is Right works for the one who says it.

10.

[...] sḫr	[...] advice (?)
ỉmỉ mrt.n.k sdḥ rmn.k	Give what you have preferred, relax your shoulder
m ḳꜣ ḳꜥḥ.k wšd.k	Do not raise your arm at your asking,
ꜣms ỉb n mrwt	but nurture the heart in love -
nr.n.tw gr	it is the silent man one respects,

tr tri ḥr w3t	it is the courteous man who is treated well on the road.
wšd.tw ḳb r mdt	People ask for refreshment in speech,
rwi.tw r nb-r	and react against a 'mouth-master',
w3.tw ḥr ḳ3 ḫrw.f	avoiding one whose voice is too loud.

11.

iw ḳd ḳsn smḏd nb.f	The difficult character oppresses his master,
stkn sw nb ḏb3	and the master brings him to (his) return.
nn prt is pw nty [...]	There can be no fruit for the one who [...]
[...] *išst* (?)	[...] 'what?'
nn ḥkk n ḫrw n mry nst.f	There is no swallowing for the voice of a man who loves his tongue,
in ib ḳm3 bi3	it is the heart that creates talent.
ḫpr wpt m ḳbḥ srf	A mission should be the cooling of the inflamed.
ʿ3 mrt.f ḥr [.].*k*[..]	Love of him is greatest ...

12.

rhn.n.tw ḥr gr m sḥ	Assent is (secured) by silence in the hall.
ḫpp ʿš3 rw ḥr wʿ	A crowd of mouths collapses (?) at a lone (voice).
iṯ bnrit r msddt	What is sweet is seized upon rather than what is hateful,
w3ḏ pw sṯni ḳdw	choiceness of forms brings success.
ir ḫpr.k m sprw [*n.f*]	If you become one who [receives] petitioners,
wḏʿ.k s sn ḥr sẖwn	and are judging two men in a dispute,
sḏm st m iw n wʿ ky nmʿ	hear them at the arrival of one, the other to the side (?).
ir s sn wpp inw.sn	If there are two men whose characters are (both) under judgment,
pr.sn m ḥtpyw	they will leave content.

13.

[...] *n wʿ mry.k*	[...] for the one whom you love,
sm3w wḏʿ mdwt	that kills (?) the judgement
[...] *grg wrw ʿḥʿ ʿš3*	[...] falsehood of (?) leaders, the multitude stands (?)
[...] *ḫm sḏm*	[...] the ignorant to (?) a hearer.
mw pw dnit pw m3ʿt	Truth is both water and dam;
3s [...] *ḏdw grg*	the teller of lies is quick to [...] (?).
imi h3y mdw.k r t3	Let your words fall to earth;
wḫ3 [...]	a fool [...]
[*dnit?*] *pw sprw n.f*	He is a refuge for those who petition him (?)

14.

m sbi i[...]	Do not mock [...]
[*ʿ?*]*ḏ3 ḫpr* [...] *s nb*	Crime can befall (?) any man.
[*n?*] *snm.n.tw m nḥnw*	One should (?) not harm with gladness,
n in.tw ḫ3m [...]	or bring submission (?) [...]
in s sḥḏ ...	It is man who brightens grief (?)
[...] *mdw* [...] *smi*	[...] words [...] report,
wšb.f [...]	as he answers [...]
m fḫ ib.k 3ww gr.k	Do not unleash your heart; let your silence be long.
wšb [...]	Reply [...]
[...] *r ḏnr.f*	[...] to his need (?).
m [...]	Do not (?) [...]
[...] *ḥ*	[...] ...

15.

[...] *ir.f sẖ m ḫnms*	[...] he acts as scribe as a colleague,
[...] *ẖ33t ḏrḏrit*	[...] foreign corpses
ḏr nty wnn.f r.f [...].*f*	because he indeed is his [...]
ir rẖ.f wnwt (?) ...	If he knows the hour [...]
iw.f gr ẖr mdwt r.f	he is silent under the words against him,
r smi n nṯr niwt.f	to report to the god of his city,
ḏr nty wnn.f r.f m bt3w n sḥ	because he indeed is a fugitive of the hall.

16.

m wp s wsr r.k	Do not judge a man stronger than you,
wḏꜥ.k s sn ḥr sẖwn	in judging two men in dispute.
nmꜥ [...] r sp ḥwrw	Separate [...] for the evil moment (?)
mi prrt m r n wšbt	like that which comes from the mouth of the replies
ir wp.k s sn m ḳnbt	If you judge two men in council,
ḥms.k drt.k r r.k	you should sit with your hand on your mouth.
nn ḏwt r.k	There can be no evil against you;
mdwt.k psš.k ẖpr	your words and your share can take place.

17.

[...m]dwt m in st	[...] words from the one who delivers them,
m sḏm st ḏwt r.k	do not hear them - it is evil for you,
m hnn mdt [..]	do not agree with the words of [...]
wḏꜥ sw nṯr m ẖprw.f	- the god judges him in his forms.
[...]	[...]
nn dnit n.f [..]š[...]	there can be no refuge for him (?) [...]
[s]bꜣḳ.k ib.k r ẖr.k	Gladden your heart with what you have.

18.

ir ꜥḏꜣ m nb ꜥḥꜥ n ꜥwn	As for the criminal who is lord of wealth by seizure,
[...] m snḏ	[...] in fear
m nḥb n nty m rdit m btꜣw.f	Do not join someone who has been put to flight (?),
m ꜥḥꜥ [...] m mit[t]	do not stand [...] either,
mi pr[t] (?) m r n rš [...]	like coming (?) from the mouth of the joyful (?) [...]
[...] sḏr r ššp [...]	[...] sleeping to daybreak [...]
ꜥšꜣ-r r ꜥḥꜣ.k	Overtalking will fight against you.
dd.k ẖn[...]	May you give.. [...]

19.

ir mdt mitt ẖt pw	Speech - it is the echo of fire.
sdp pw wšb smẖ (?)	It is the scorching (?) that answers the ignorant (?),
ḥḏ (?) st r r n gr	it is bright in the mouth of the silent.
ir.s ḳbḥw m ꜥšꜣ ẖrw	It makes the cool man loudmouthed.
ꜣẖ hryt nfr wꜣḥ-ib	Harmony works - patience is good.
wšb n rẖ rwi n ẖm	Answer the wise man - avoid the ignorant.
nn ḥꜣẖ r šw m ḥnš	No hasty speech is free of stench,
wn n.f ẖt	or given an open heart.
ḳb srf tmm mryt	Be cool in fire, and complete in love.
m sḏm mdwt wṯst	Do not heed words that recruit,
m hnn ḏdt nbt (?)	do not agree to everything that is said.
ẖsf.k iw nḏnḏ.n.k	Resist when you have consulted;
ḳsn pw ḥꜣ-n-r-n.i	'I want I want' is painful.

20.

nn nb ktt pꜣ sꜣḥ tꜣ	There is no master of meanness who has managed to touch land.
sẖḥ tkn ib pḥy	The seeker who is near to the heart is the one who arrives.
nn ꜣs ib šw m ẖrwy.f	No light-hearted man can be free of his enemies;
nb imt pw ẖprt n.f mrt	it is the lord of favour to whom servants accrue.
nn kꜣ wšm.tw n.f mdwt	There is no-one who can plan to have words measured out to him (?)
ir gr.k ẖpr n.k pḥwy	If you are silent, the end will come to pass for you.
wšb.k m nfryt	Answer with nothing;
iw ẖn wꜥ ꜣbb ꜥšꜣt	a single utterance, that is the desire of most people.
[...] hrt ḥr.f	[...] at peace with it/him

21.

iw nḥ.tw ṯst nt wꜣḥ-ib (?)	People seek the phrase of the patient man (?);
[...] ꜣww nst stkn mhwt	[...] overextended of tongue is the one who draws in a clan.
nn hnw n ꜥšꜣ ẖrw	There are no supporters for the loudmouthed,

[..].f ḫrwy	his [...] hostility (?).
nn grg pr [...] mdwt	There is no founding a house for [the one who has excess of?] words;
nn smȝ.tw m ḥnyt	noone joins in with (a man of) envy,
wn.f mi ḥfȝw ḥr ȝt.f	he is like a snake on its strike.
iw ḳd bin smḏd.f nb.f	An evil character oppresses its owner;
nn šw n.f m dhn ẖr.f	he cannot escape the apportioning of what is his.

22.

[...] ẖr [...] ḫrwy	[...] under (?) [...] hostility
[...]tri	[...] respect (?)
ḫrp.k m btn sw	Control yourself, do not upset him.
ꜥḥȝ tw ḥr	Restrain yourself from [...]
[...].k m-sȝ ḏdt.k ḏs.k	You [...] after your own speech.
wȝḏ pw ḥs sw mwt.f	That is the man who flourishes – the one whose mother praises him.
ir.k mi šȝꜥt n.k	Do as you are ordered.
m [...] dd.k ḥr mn	Do not [...] your adding to suffering
ir s ḥs sw bw nb	Any man who is praised by everyone,
iw ḥr[.sn?] nb	all [their ?] faces
ḥr ȝbb [ḫnm]s (?) m-ḫt.f	desire [to be fri]ends (?) in his following.

23.

[...] nšny [...]	[...] raging [...]
[...] mi [...]	[...] like [...]
[...] gm (?) rmṯ nb	[...] finding (?) everyone
iw.f sḏr r šsp	He may sleep to daybreak
[...].f kywy	He [...] others
wȝḏ n.f gswy [...].f	Both halves (?) flourish for him in his [...]
ḫprt [...] n s mi ḳd.f	What happens [...] to a man according to his character,
gm.f [...] r.f	he finds [...] to him
r ḫt.tw (?) [...] biȝt.f	until [...] is cut (?) [...] his talent

24.

m hȝb ib.k r ꜥḥȝ	Do not lust after fighting.
snk.tw swȝ.k ḥr ȝbt	Your passing can be cut short (?) by the family.
m wp s sn m nšny.sn	Do not judge two men in their rage;
wḏb sḫwn r wḏꜥ sw	a dispute can turn against the one judging it.
iw.f ir [...] r	It makes [one (?) ...]-mouthed
ky ir.f m ḫfty	and the other acts as enemy
ḳb sḏ ḥr.f tm štm	He who remains deaf to it can rest, by not aggravating.
in s srwd ḫrwy.f	It is man who strengthens his enemy.
wȝḏ pw ḥnn m r.f	He who restrains his mouth is the one who flourishes;
ḫpr srḫy m ṯs ꜥḥȝ	complaints turn into declarations of war.

The end of section 24 survives on three sources, on each followed by a colophon (end-note) starting:

iw.s nfr m ḥtp	'its end, perfect, in peace'

Sources

Fragments of hieratic papyri of Dynasty 18:

- Papyrus Berlin 15733 b-f
- Papyrus Berlin 15738 a, c, f, g
- Papyrus (Pierpont Morgan) Amherst XV
- Papyrus Turin 54016
- Papyrus Turin 54017

Other papyrus fragments of the New Kingdom:

- Papyrus Berlin 15742
- Papyrus Clere I
- Papyrus Louvre N 3171

Hieratic on leather roll of Dynasty 18:

- British Museum EA 10258

Hieratic writing-board of the New Kingdom:

- Turin CG 58006

142 hieratic ostraca of the New Kingdom, full list in Fischer-Elfert 1999, vol. II, x-xxv

The Loyalist Teaching

This composition in Middle Egyptian is preserved on New Kingdom documents (Posener recorded it from 3 papyri, 1 wooden writing board, and 65 ostraca), and a slightly shorter version of the first part also on one late Middle Kingdom stela from Abydos (Cairo CG 20538, of a high official, the deputy treasurer Sehetepibra, reign of Amenemhat III). The first part celebrates kingship, in terms comparable to the eulogies presented below in Part Two, Section Three. The second half is dominated by a remarkable eulogy of the workers upon whom the elite depend (Berlev 1972, 30-32). The manuscript copies opened with a long sequence of titles before the name of the 'author' of the teaching: the name is lost on all extant copies, but the titles are attested for the treasurer Mentuhotep, who served king Senusret I, and whose monumental Abydos stela (Cairo CG 20539) served as model for another part of the Sehetepibra stela. However, the titles would have been appropriate to other high officials (other treasurers in particular?) from the central phase of the Middle Kingdom, after the founding of Itjtawy, and therefore the attribution of the Loyalist Teaching to that historical individual at Itjtawy under king Senusret I remains highly uncertain (Berlev 1972, 30). The final couple of lines appear on an Abydos stela belonging to Rehuankh, a leading official at the court of king Khaneferra Sobekhotep, mid-Thirteenth Dynasty (Berlin 7311: Grajetzki 2001, 43, pl.3): since these are the final words of the Teaching, it seems plausible that, on the stela, they are a conscious quotation from the Teaching, rather than being a wise saying in more general circulation.

The transliteration follows Posener 1976, with the section divisions proposed there.

Introduction

ḥꜣt-ꜥ m sbꜣyt	**Beginning of the teaching**
irt.n iry-pꜥt ḥꜣty-ꜥ	**made by the leader of nobility, foremost of action**
it nṯr mry nṯr	father of the god, beloved of the god,
ḥry-sštꜣ n pr nswt ꜥnḫ wḏꜣ snb	master of secrets of the house of the king, may he live, flourish, be well
ḥry-tp n tꜣ r-ḏr.f	overlord of the land to its limit
sm ḫrp šndyt [...]	sem-priest, controller of the kilted [...]
m sbꜣyt ḫr msw.f	as a teaching before his children.
ḏd.i wrt di.i sḏm.tn	Let me say what is great, may you listen,
di.i rḫ.tn sḫr n nḥḥ	as I cause you to know the manner of eternity,
sšr ꜥnḫ n mꜣꜥ	a matter of life in truth,
sbt r imꜣḫ	of proceeding to revered status.

2.

dwꜣ nswt *m ẖnw ẖt.tn*	**Praise the king** within your bodies
snsn ḥm.f m ib.tn	embrace His Power in your hearts.
imy nrw.f m ẖrt-hrw	Spread awe of him every day
ḳmꜣ n.f hnw r tr nb	Create rejoicing for him at every moment.
siꜣ pw imy ḥꜣtyw	He is the Insight into what is in hearts,
iw irty.fy dꜥr.sn ẖt nbt	his eyes probe every body.
rꜥ pw ꜥnḫ ḫr sšm.f	He is the sun in whose leadership (people) live.
iw nty ḫr šwt.f r wr ḫrw.f	Whoever is under his light will be great in wealth.
rꜥ pw mꜣꜣ stwt.f	He is the sun by whose rays (people) see.
sḥḏw sw tꜣwy r itn	He is the one who brightens the Two Lands, more than the sun-disk.

3.

wbd hh.f r ns n sḏt	**His heat scorches more than the tongue of the flame,**
snw sw ꜣt.f r ḫt	He is more devouring in his moment than fire.
swꜣḏ sw r ḥꜥp ꜥꜣ	He is more fertile than the great Flood,
mḥ.n.f tꜣwy m ḫtw n ꜥnḫ	he has filled the Two Lands with the trees of life.
ḏbb fndw wꜣww r nšny	Noses are blocked when he falls to raging,
ḥtpw.f tpi.tw ṯꜣw.f	when he is peaceful, people breathe his air.
dd.f ḏfꜣw n nty m šms.f	He grants provisions for anyone in his following,
sḏfꜣ.f mḏd mtn.f	and supplies the one who treads his path.
iw ḥsy.f r nb ꜥꜣbt	The one he favours will be a lord of offerings,
iw rḳy.f r iwty.f	the one he rejects will be a pauper.
iw mrt nswt r imꜣḫy	The servants of the king shall have revered status,
[...] *šnty.f*	[...] his opponents (?).

4.

in bꜣw.f ꜥḥꜣ ḥr.f
iw šꜥd .[f?] dd (?) šfyt.f
rs ḥr [...]
[...]*.tn* (?) *grg ḥr dwꜣw nfrw.f*
wbꜣ.f ḳmꜣ [...]
[...] *mr ib.f*
ꜥnẖ pw n dd n.f iꜣw
iw šnty.f r ẖry [...]
iw ẖꜣt [...]

It is his power that fights for him
[His?] slaughter (?) is what spreads (?) respect for him.
Watching over [...]
Your (?) [...] is founded upon the praise of his perfection.
He opens up the creation [...]
[...] that his heart desires (?),
It is the life (that comes) of giving him adoration.
His opponents will be beneath [...]
[Their] corpses [...]

5.

kꜣ pw *nswt* ***ḥw pw*** *r.f*
sẖpr.f pw m wnt.f
iwꜥt pw nt nṯr nb
nḏty ḳmꜣ sw
ḥww.sn n.f šnty.f
ist ḥm.f ꜥnẖ wḏꜣ snb
m ꜥḥ.f ꜥnẖ wḏꜣ snb
itm pw n ṯs wsrwt
iw sꜣ.f r ḥꜣ dd bꜣw.f
ẖnmw pw n ḥr nb
wttw sẖpr rẖyt
bꜣst pw ẖwt tꜣwy
iw dwꜣ sw r nhw.f
sẖmt pw r th m wḏt.n.f

iw sfꜣ.f r ẖr šmꜣw.f

The king is **Sustenance**, his word **Abundance**.
He is one who creates in his being.
He is the heir of every god,
the champion of the one who fashioned him.
They strike down his opponents for him.
Indeed His Power may he live, flourish and be well,
is in his palace of life, flourishing, health.
He is Atum at the tying of necks.
His protection is at the back of the giving of his powers.
He is Khnum for every body,
the begetter who brings the populace into being.
He is Bast, she who protects the Two Lands,
he is praised for his sheltering.
He is Sekhmet against the one who transgresses what he has ordered.
The one whom he humbles will be bearer of his travels.

6.

ꜥḥꜣ ḥr rn.f
twr ḥr ꜥnẖ.f
šw.tn m sp n bgsw
iw mrt n nswt r imꜣẖy
nn is n sbi ḥr ḥm.f
iw ẖꜣt.f m ḳmꜣ n mw
m itn ḥr fkꜣw n dd.f
mꜣt bit sns ḥdt.f
swꜣš wṯs sẖmty
ir.tn nn wḏꜣ ḥꜥw.tn
gm.tn st n ḏt
wn tp tꜣ nn šnw im.f
sbt ꜥḥꜥw m ḥtp

Fight on his name
cleanse in his life.
Avoid the instant of sloth.
The servants of the king shall have revered status,
but there can be no tomb for one who rebels against His Power
- his corpse will be something cast into the water.
Do not hold back from the presents of his giving,
revere the Bee, adore his White Crown,
worship the one who raises the Double Crown
As you do this, your bodies will be well,
you can find it (to be so) for eternity.
The one who remains on earth can have no grief from it,
to pass a lifetime in peace.

7.

ꜥḳ m tꜣ m dd nswt
ḥtp ḥr st n ḏt
ẖnmt tpḥt imy nḥḥ
iwnn msw.tn ẖr mrt.tn
iwꜥt.tn mn ḥr nst.tn
sn ḳd.i m wn mdwt.i
smnẖ tp-rd ir.n.i

Enter the earth by the gift of the king
content in the place of eternity
united with the cavern of the one within everlasting time,
with the home-shrine of your children bearing your love,
and your heirs established in your positions.
Copy my form, do not neglect my words.
Put into effect the rule I have drawn up.

8.

iẖ ḏd.tn n ẖrdw.tn
iw r sbꜣ ḏr rk rꜥ
ink sꜥḥ n sḏm n.f
ꜥḳ.n nb.f m sꜣrt.f

Speak then to your children
for the word has taught since the time of Ra.
I am a noble to be heard,
whose lord has entered his reflections.

m snn ḳd.ỉ m stn ḥr bỉ3t.ỉ
šw.tn m sp b3gw
ỉw s3 sḏm r ỉwty ḏwt.f
n mʿr.n sẖr nb ỉm.f

Do not pass by my form, do not stray from my talent.
Avoid the instant of sloth;
a son who hears will be without any evils.
Does not every plan succeed by it?

9.

ḥsy.tn nn m-ḫt rnpt
rwd ỉry m s3ḥ-t3
ky sp n sṯ3t ỉb.tn
m 3ḫ.tw ỉm.s ḫr ḥmw.tn
ḥn m rmṯ s3ḵ wnḏwt.tn
ṯ3r.tn ḥr ḥm n ỉryw
ỉn rmṯ sẖpr nty
ʿnḫ.tw ỉmy m ʿwy.sn
g3y.tw r.f sẖm m šw3w

You will be praising this after years -
Faithfulness to this assures success.
Another theme to guide your hearts,
as something to good effect before your workers:
be well-supplied with people, collect your staff together,
and fasten on the Agency of those who do.
It is people who bring what there is into being.
We live as men who have by their labour.
If there is a lack of it, poverty takes power.

10.

ỉ3t pw ỉrt ḏf3w
šw pr.f tf sntt.f
ỉw ḫrw.sn smn ỉnbw
nb ʿš3t pw sḏr r šsp
nn wn ḳd n wʿty
n h3b.n.tw m3ỉ m wpt
nn ỉdr ḏdḥ sw r ỉnbt
ỉw ḫrw.f mỉ ỉb ḫ3 šdyt
[..] r.f r wnmw

It is positions that produce supplies
The one whose house is empty, his foundation wavers
- their voices strengthen the walls.
The man who sleeps till dawn is the lord of a multitude;
there can be no sleep for the lone man.
A lion is not sent on a mission,
there is no cow that ties itself to the wall
- its voice would be like someone thirsty behind a well,
[...] more than fattened birds.

11.

***3bb.tw** ḥʿp gmm.tw st*
nn 3ḥt sk3t ḫpr sy ḏs.s
wrw wnn [...] ʿ
ỉn ḏdḥ ḥw wšbw
ỉn mnỉ [...]
[...] ʿwt ʿš3t nn ḏrw.sn
ỉ3wt [...] n nṯr
ỉr ʿpr ỉm st spd ḥr
m s3t ʿḥwty ḥr b3kw
ʿby.f gm.f n.k sw nrỉ
ỉr ʿnḫ.f ʿwy.fy
wš.k sw k3.f r šm3w

(People) desire the flood, and they find it,
but there is no field for ploughing that creates itself.
The herd is large when the herdsman (?) [...]
- it is the tethered bull that strikes the dueller.
It is ... [...]
[...] of many flocks without number,
the positions [...] of the god
Anyone who is experienced in it, is keen-sighted.
Do not overwhelm the field-labourer with work.
A man who complains, does he return to you next year?
If he is alive, there are (?) his arms,
but if you flay him, his thoughts turn to homelessness.

12.

***nḫb b3kw** r ḏ3wt šmʿ*
[...] pw ḥr ỉb n nṯr
nn sp n ʿḥʿ n ỉsfty
n gm.n mswt.f wḏ3t.f
ỉr sfn pḥwy ʿnḫ.f
nn wn msw.f tkn ỉb
ỉw mrt n sn ḥr.f
nn ỉwʿ n tff ḥ3ty
wr šfyt nt nb ḫrt
ʿš3 ḫrw ỉsft ḥr ỉb

Fix the produce-levy according to the grain harvest
A [...] man is [...] on the heart of the god.
There can be no opportunity for riches for an evil man;
His children do not find his residue.
The hard man causes the end of his life;
his children will not be devoted.
Affection will be for the one who passes him;
there can be no heir for the mean-spirited.
A master of manners is great in respect.
The loud-mouthed is an evil on the heart.

13.

***ỉn ḏw** ḫb3 ỉ3t.f*
grg niwt n mryty
mnw pw n s w3ḥ-ỉb
3ḫ gr [...]
[...] ḥmt n ỉyt
ʿnn sw sḫm sḥnn

It is the evil man who destroys his home ground,
and the loved man for whom a city is founded.
Patience is the monument of a man
- silence is good for (?) [...].
[...] foresee what has not come.
The man with power in a task turns about.

sfn ḳmꜣ.n.f idt	Does the cow reproduce for the hard man?
mniw ḏwt ꜥnd idr.f	A herdsman of evil – his cattle are few.

14.

ꜥḥꜣ ḥr rmt *m šs nb*	**Fight for people** in every way
ꜥwt pw ꜣḫt n nb.sn	- they are the flock that is good for their lord.
ntsn pw gmm ꜥnḫ.tw im.s	It is they who find what one lives on –
ꜣḫ st r-sy n smꜣyt tꜣ	it is good too for burial.
mꜣꜣ.tn n [...]w	See ... [...]
srs tp.tn ḥr ḥmw-kꜣ.tn	Watch over your ka-priests;
bꜣgsw sꜣ mnw n wꜥb	if the son is lazy, there is still the pure-priest.
iꜣm pw ḏdw n.f iwꜥ	The one called an heir is the one who does favour,
bs sꜥḥ nis ḥr rn.f	who initiates the noble, and recites on his name,
[...] ꜣḫ in šb [...]	[...] the blessed dead, and brings the food-offer[ings...]
ḥr-ntt ꜣḫ n irr r irw n.f	for doing is more useful to the doer than to the one for whom it is done;
in smw mkk ḥry tꜣ	it is the nourished dead who protect the one who is on earth.

A notice '[its end] in peace' after this final phrase in Papyrus Amherst XII+XIII indicates that this was the end of the composition.

Sources (Posener 1976, 3-11)
Abydos stela of deputy treasurer Sehetepibra, late Middle Kingdom (Cairo CG 20538)
Writing-board from Thebes, early Dynasty 18 (Cairo JE 43161+56802 = Tablet Carnarvon II)
Papyrus Louvre E4864, mid Dynasty 18
Papyrus Pierpont Morgan library Amherst XII+XIII two fragments from one roll, late Dynasty 18
Rifeh Papyrus UC 32781, early Dynasty 19
Pottery Ostracon Deir el Medina 1228
64 limestone ostraca from Thebes, Dynasty 19-20 (Posener 1976, 7-11 for full list)

Teachings: reflective, dominated by descriptive mode

Several Middle Egyptian literary compositions open with the phrase 'Teaching made by' with name, as for the didactic teachings, but their following contents seem more reflective than didactic, perhaps mainly because they incorporate more description than straightforward instruction using the imperative. Three are substantially preserved, though only on New Kingdom sources: the Teaching for King Merykara, the Teaching of Duau Khety (often called 'Satire of Trades' in Egyptology), and the Teaching of King Amenemhat I.

The Teaching for King Merykara

The Teaching for king Merykara is a literary composition in Middle Egyptian, the classical phase of the Egyptian language, probably of Middle Kingdom date (2025-1700 BC). In it, the author has a king of Egypt address his son, the future king Merykara, advising him how to be a good king, and to avoid evil deeds. Merykara is the name of a king of the Ninth or Tenth Dynasty, the line or lines of kings who ruled northern Egypt during a period of division, the First Intermediate Period (about 2150-2025 BC). Perhaps this setting would have allowed a Middle Kingdom author greater freedom in describing the limits of royal authority, than might have been possible in referring to kings of a unified Egypt; the Teaching for King Merykara is effectively a treatise on kingship, in which both good and evil aspects of government and military conflict are described. Here, in stark contrast to the continual recycling of architectural blocks, the king is instructed to quarry new stone, not reuse old monuments; the reality of reuse is acknowledged, but the ideal of new work is commended. Similarly, the destruction of a sacred territory at Abydos is recorded; the king expresses remorse, as if accepting responsibility for the unthinkable that must have recurred throughout history - sacrilege in the name of the ruling king. These contrasts of real and ideal make the composition a reflection on power unparalleled in ancient Egyptian writing.

The composition is preserved, not quite complete, across three mid- to late 18th Dynasty papyri (Hermitage 1116A verso; Moscow Pushkin 4658; Carlsberg VI). A small section of the composition has also been recognised on a Ramesside ostracon (Deir el Medina 1476).

The transliteration follows Quack 1992. Line numbers refer to Papyrus Hermitage 1116A , and the section divisions are those suggested by the red passages in that manuscript.

1. (Papyrus Hermitage 1116A, verso, lines 1-3)

[...]*y n sꜣ.f mry-kꜣ-rꜥ*	[... Khet?]y to his son Merykara
[...] *m sfn ḥr sp nḏr .. ḫsf.k*	[...] do not be merciful at a deed of violence .. May you punish
[...]*.sn ḥr mdt nbt*	[...] them for every case.
ḥꜣt [*pw nt* ...]	[it is] the start [of ...]

2. (Papyrus Hermitage 1116A, verso, lines 4 to 17)

[...] *sḫpr*	**[...] brought into existence**
sꜥšꜣ ẖꜣk[*w-ib* ...] *ḥnꜥ sḥw* [...]*.k* [...]	multiplying the disaffected [...] with counsel [...] you [...]
ỉr ḏd smỉ [...]	If a report is spoken [...]
ỉr r-sꜣ ḫpr mdt.k	If after your word is made,
r b[...] *ḥwt nm*[*ꜥ* ...]	at ..[...] bad, taking sides [...]
ỉrr.f gs.s (?) *m ꜥḥꜥ* [...] *kꜣ* [...]	he just makes its side (?) in a time (?) [...] then [...]
[...]*.f* [...] *psš* [...] *mr.ỉ*	[...] of him [...] dividing [...] my staff,
ḏꜣ [...] *ꜥšꜣ m ḥr*(?)*.k*	crossing (?) [...] numerous in your sight (?),
th.k ḥr wꜣt [...]	as you stray from the road [...]
smꜣ.k [...] *nkyw sw ḥr.s*	you slay [...] those who strike him for it.
rḫ.tỉ mrt.f mrr sw	Know his staff, love him.
ỉr gm [...*p*]*w n nỉwt*	if [...] find [...] it is [...] of the city-dwellers,
nb [*pw n*] *wḥyt*	[it is] the lord [of] the villagers.
ḥn n.k sw kꜣ tm.k [...] *ḥfꜣw ꜥšꜣ*	Order him to you, so that you do not [...] many snakes.
m ḥḏ s [*m tp*]*-rd n* [...]	Do not hurt a man [with instr]uction (?), not [...]
[*nt*]*f ḥry* (?) [... *ḥwt*] *wryt* [...] *t*	[h]e is the master (?) [...] great [estates] [...] bread
[...]*.f* [...]*.f* [...]*.f n wḥyt*	[...] he [...] he [...] he [...] for the villagers.
sꜣw tm [...]	Do not fail to [...]

3. (Papyrus Hermitage 1116A, verso, lines 18 to 24)

[...] *sꜣw n.n ꜥnḫw*	**[...] guard for us the living**
sn n ꜣbd [...]*.f ḥꜥw.f*	the passing of a month [...] he [...] his limbs,
ḏd.f mḥ.f sḫꜣ.f	he speaks his concern, he recalls:

[n]ḫt ꜣ ḥr tꜣ m ꜥt nt iwf	the strong is indeed in the land as a body of flesh,
[...] *rmṯ wꜣ*[... *ḥt*]*p n.f ib.k iꜥ*	[...] people ..[... be kind] to him when your heart is satisfied.
[...] *bw nb ḥr mst.f pw m wḥm*	[...] everyone says: that is his rebirth.
s[...]*.sn m ḥtpy* [...]*.k* [...] *mi nṯr*	They make [...] contented [...] you [...] like a god.
ir gm.k sw m iwty hnw.f [...]	If you find him to be someone with no supporters [...]
rḫ sw niwtyw.f mr.f ꜥšꜣ m dmdyt	whose city-dwellers know him, whose many servants are a unit,
sw [...] *ḫt.f* [...]*.tw rḫ.f*	he is [...] his goods [...] knowing him is [...].
ꜥḳ m [...] *m ibw*	He who enters into [...] in hearts,
ꜥn sw m ḥr ḏt.f	is perfect in the sight of his staff,
mn m itꜣḫ pw mdwty	(whereas) the man of speeches is entrenched in troublemaking.
dr sw smꜣ msw[*.f*]	Suppress him, kill [his] children],
sin rn.f [...] *hnw.f dr sḫꜣ.f*	erase his name [...] his supporters, suppress the memory of him.
mr.f mrr sw	Then will he be loved by his staff?

4. (Papyrus Hermitage 1116A, verso, lines 24 to 28)

sh*[...] *pw n niwt ḫnn ib	**The heart-troubler means chaos for city-dwellers**
iw.f sḫpr.f mrt sn m ḏꜣmw	He turns two sets of servants into troops.
ir grt gm.k ny-sw niwt	If you find someone mastering the city,
ḥꜣḫ sp.f swꜣ ḥr.k	one whose chance is fast, who passes you by,
sḫr sw m-bꜣḥ šnyt	fell him in front of the entourage.
dr sbi pw grw	Silence is the feller of the rebel;
tꜣḥ [*p*]*w n niwt mdwty*	a man of speeches is the troublemaker of the city.
kꜥh ꜥšꜣt dr tꜣ r.s	Bend the multitude, remove the heat from them,
nn ṯs id[*r*] *sbi m šwꜣw*	there is no levy that removes the rebel among the destitute,
ssbi.n it.f	made into a rebel by his father.

5. (Papyrus Hermitage 1116A, verso, lines 28 to 31)

[*i*]*n twꜣyw shꜣ* *mšꜥ* […]*.tw*	**It is beggars who rouse** an army […] ..
ir pḥwy.fy m šb	Make its ends as ..
šꜣy n.f ḳnd ꜥšꜣ di.tw ḥr šnꜥ	many .. are destined for it, they are given at the stores.
sfn […] *ḥsf.k*	Merciful […] you punish (?).
iw sšꜣ.k […] *m ḥꜥꜥwt*	you .. […]-people in rejoicing.
smꜣꜥ-ḫrw.k r-gs nṯr	You are justified beside the god,
iḫ ḏd rmṯ [*m ḫmt*]*.k*	so people say [even in] your [absence]
ḥsf.k r ḏꜣwt [..]*.k*	that you punish according the needs [..] of you.
pt pw nt s iwn nfr	Good character is the heaven of a man,
ksn pw sḥwri nd[..]*-ib*	belittling the ..-hearted is hard.

6. (Papyrus Hermitage 1116A, verso, lines 32 to 35)

ḥmww m mdt nḫt.k	**Skill in speaking is your strength**
ḫpš pw n nswt ns.f	the muscle of a king is his tongue.
ḳn mdt r ꜥḥꜣ nb	Speaking is more valiant than any fighting
n ii.n.tw ḥꜣ ḥmwy-ib	Noone prevails over one of skilled mind.
[…] *ḥr tmꜣ*	[…] upon the mat,
[…] *pw n srw sꜣꜣ*	wisdom is the [shelter?] of officials.
n tkk.n sw rḫw rḫ.f	Those who know his knowledge do not disturb him.
n ḫpr […] *m hꜣw.f*	No [wrongdoing] happens in his surrounds.
iw n.f mꜣꜥt ꜥtḫ.ti	What is Right comes to him ready brewed,
mi sḫrw n ḏdt.n tpyw-ꜥ	like the advice of what the ancestors told

7. (Papyrus Hermitage 1116A, verso, lines 35 to 38)

sn r ityw.k tpyw-ꜥ.k	**Surpass your forefathers, your ancestors**
bꜣk tw […] *m rḫ* […]	exert yourself […] in knowledge […]
mk mdt.sn mn m sšw	Their words are fixed in writings:
pgꜣ šd.k sn.k r rḫw	open to read and to surpass in knowing.
ḫpr ḥmww m sbbꜣyw	The expert is created out of constant learning.
m dw nfr wꜣḥ ib	Not evil, good is patience.
swꜣḥ mnw.k m mrwt.k	Make your monuments endure out of love of you.
sꜥšꜣ [...] *ḫnm n niwt*	Enrich […]-people, be joined to the city,
dwꜣ.tw nṯr ḥr fḳꜣ	so that the god is thanked for the rewards,

sb ḥr [...].k	processions for your […],
dwꜣw ḥr nfr.k	hymns for your goodness,
nḥb snb.k n nṯrw	and your health prayed for to the gods.

8. (Papyrus Hermitage 1116A, verso, lines 38 to 42)

[tr]i srw swḏꜣ rmṯ.k	**Respect the officials, make your people flourish**
srwd tꜣš.k pḫryt.k	Strengthen your border and your patrols
nfr irt n m-ḫt	It is good to act for posterity.
tri ʿnḫ n wbꜣ-ḥr	The life of the open-eyed is respected,
iw mḥ-ib r ꜣhw	a guarantee against the man of ruin (?).
imi sb.tw […] m iwn.k nfr	Cause people to come [to you?] by your good character.
ḫsy mr n.f tꜣ n [..].f	The one who desires for himself the land of his [..] is vile.
ḫm ḫt pw ḫnty iw n kwy	One who craves what belongs to others is an ignorant man.
swꜣ […] tp tꜣ nn ꜣw.f	The passing of […] on earth will not be long.
wꜣḏ pw sḫꜣ im.f	Whoever is remembered on it, he is the flourishing one.
n ʿkꜣ n s ḥḥ n nb tꜣwy	A million men do not match the lord of the two lands.
wnn […] ʿnḫ r nḥḥ	[…] living for eternity.
rwwi iw m-ʿ ir-sy	The one who comes with the Creator departs,
mi sfḫ nḏm-n.f	like the undoing of the indulger.

9. (Papyrus Hermitage 1116A, verso, lines 42 to 46)

sʿꜣ wrw.k ir.sn hpw.k	**Enrich your great men, so they enact your laws**
nn nmʿ n ḫwd m pr.f	A man rich in his house will not take sides.
nb ḫt pw tm gꜣw	The man who has no lack is the owner of goods.
n ḏd.n šwꜣw m mꜣʿt.f	Vagrants do not speak by his truth.
n ʿkꜣ.n ḏd ḥꜣ-n.i	One who says 'would that I had' is not just.
nmʿ.f n mry.f	He takes the side of his favourite.
gꜣs.f n nb ḏbꜣw	He sides with the lord of payments.
wr wrw.f wr	The Great One, his great men are great.
ḳn pw nswt nb šnyt	A king, lord of an entourage is a valiant (king).
špss pw ḫwd m srw	One rich in officials is the ennobled.
ḏd.k mꜣʿt m pr.k	May you say what is Right in your house,
snd n.k srw ntyw hr tꜣ	that the officials who are on earth fear you,
mty n nb ʿkꜣ ib	Straightness of heart is good for the lord.
in ḫnty dd snd n sꜣ	It is the Palace that causes fear in the stall.

10. (Papyrus Hermitage 1116A, verso, lines 46 to 53)

ir mꜣʿt wꜣḥ.k tp tꜣ	**Do what is Right, to endure on earth**
sgr rmw m ꜣir ḫꜣrt	Calm the weeper, do not oppress the widow,
m nš s ḥr ḫt it.f	Do not expel a man from the property of his father,
m ḥḏ srw ḥr nst.sn	Do not damage the officials on their seats of office.
sꜣ.ti ḥr ḫsf m nf	Beware punishing wrongfully,
m sḳri nn st ꜣḫ n.k	Do not kill: it is no use to you.
ḥsf.k m ḥwyw m sꜣwty	Punish with beatings, with imprisonment.
iw tꜣ pn r grg ḥr.s	This land will be well-founded by that
wp [ḥr] sbi gm sḫw.f	- except for the rebel whose plots are discovered.
iw nṯr rḫ ḫꜣkw-ib	The god is aware of the disaffected,
ḥw nṯr sdbw ḥr snf	and the god calls in the dues in blood.
in sfnw […] ʿḥʿw	The merciful […] lifetime.
m smꜣ s iw.k rḫ.ti ꜣhw.f	Do not kill a man if you are aware of his talents,
pꜣ.n.k ḥst sšw ḥnʿ.f	with whom you used to chant writings.
šd m sip […] ḥr nṯr	Read from the inven[tory? …] upon the god.
wstn rd m st štꜣt	Stride freely in the secret place.
iw bꜣ r st rḫw.n.f	The soul returns to the place it has known,
n tht.n.f wꜣwt.f nt sf	it does not stray from its ways of yesterday.
n ḫsf.n sw ḥkꜣ nb	No words of power can repel it,
spr r ddyw mw.f	arriving to those who supply its water.

11. (Papyrus Hermitage 1116A, verso, lines 53 to 57)

ḏ3ḏ3t wḏꜥ s3ryw	The tribunal that judges the wretch,
rḫ.n.k tm.sn sfn	you knew that they are not merciful,
hrw pf n wḏꜥ m3ir	that day of judging the miserable,
wnwt nt irt nt-ꜥ	the hour of carrying out the task.
ḳsn pw srḫy m s33	An accuser with knowledge is hard.
m mḥ ib.k m 3ww rnpwt	Do not rely on the length of years:
m33.sn ꜥḥꜥw m wnwt	they see a lifetime as an hour.
spp.sn m-ḫt mnit	they are the remainder after death;
rdiw spw.f r-gs.f m ꜥḥꜥw	his faults are placed beside him in heaps,
nḥḥ pw grt wn im	and being there is indeed eternity.
wḫ3 pw ir ṯs st	Anyone who makes complaint over it is a fool.
ir pḥ st nn irt iw	Anyone who reaches them without committing crimes,
wnn.f im mi nṯr	he will exist there like a god,
stnw mi nbw r nḥḥ	distinguished like the lords for eternity.

12. (Papyrus Hermitage 1116A, verso, lines 57 to 61)

ṯs ḏ3mw.k mry tw ḫnw	**Raise your troops, and the Residence loves you**
sꜥš3 mrt.k m šwt	Increase your staff from those available (?),
mk niwt.k mḥ.ti ḫr srwd m3w	Your city is filled with planted men, new men
rnpt mḏwty n3	Twenty years it is,
ḏ3mw nḏm ḥr šms ib.f	the troops indulge following his heart.
šwt ḥr [p]r[t] ḥr snnwt.s	The free-moving go [out] on its second (regiment?),
sꜥḳyw ḥr ꜥḳ n.f m ḫrdw ...	the registered enter for him as children ...
in isft ꜥḥ3y n.n	Is evil the one to fight for us?
ṯs.n.i im.s m sḫꜥt.i	I raised (troops) in it on my accession
sꜥ3 wrw.k sḫnt [...].k	Enrich your great men, promote your […],
imi ḥ3w ḥr ḏ3mw n [šm]sw.k	Make increase on the troops of your [fol]lowing,
ꜥpr m rḫt mniw m 3ḥt	equipped with staff-lists, fixed with fields,
s3ḥw m mnmnt	secured with livestock.

13. (Papyrus Hermitage 1116A, verso, lines 61 to 68)

m tnt s3 s r nḏs	**Do not prefer the son of a somebody to an ordinary man**
in n.k s ḥr ꜥwy.fy	Bring yourself a man for his ability.
ir.tw ḥmwt nbt r […] n nb ḫpš	Every art is accomplished according to […] of the Lord of Might
mk ḥr t3š.k ṯs mnw.k	Protect your border, command your fortresses,
3ḫ ṯst n nb.s	A battalion is good for its master.
ir mnw.k […] n nṯr	Make your monuments […] for the god.
sꜥnḫ rn pw n ir sy	That is giving life to the name, for the one who does it.
ir s 3ḫt n b3.f	A man should do what is good for his soul.
wꜥbt 3bd šsp ḥdty	Purification of the month, put on the white sandals,
ḫnm r-pr kf3 ḥr sšt3	join the sanctuary, unveil the secret face.
ꜥḳ ḥr ḫm wnm t m ḥwt-nṯr	Enter the shrine, eat bread in the temple.
sw3ḏ w3ḏw sꜥ3 ꜥkw	Make the victuals verdant, multiply the loaves,
imi ḥ3w ḥr mnyt	Increase the daily offerings,
3ḫ pw n ir sy	it is good for the one who does it.
srwd mnw.k ḫft wsr.k	Strengthen your monuments as you are mighty.
iw hrw wꜥ di.f n nḥḥ	Even one day adds to eternity,
wnwt smnḫ.s n m-ḫt	an hour embellishes posterity.
rḫ n nṯr m irw n.f	The one known to the god is one who acts for him.
sbtw.k r ḫ3st w3yt	Your prayers go to the distant hill-land,
iwty dd.sn sḫwy iry	without their gathering being given by them (?).
iw mr wšš ḫt ḫrwy	Feeble and shorn are the goods of the enemy.
n ḳbb.n ḫrwy m-ḫnw kmt	No enemy can be refreshed within Egypt.

14. (Papyrus Hermitage 1116A, verso, lines 68 to 75)

iw ḏꜣmw r ꜣir ḏꜣmw	**Troops will clash with troops**
mi sr.n tpyw-ʿ r.s	As had been foretold by the ancestors.
ʿḥꜣ r kmt m ẖrt-nṯr	The battle for Egypt was in the cemetery.
m ʿd iswt m ʿd spw	cutting up antiquity in the cutting of misdeeds.
iw ir.n.i mitt ḫpr mitt	I did just that, just that happens,
mi irt.n n tht n mitt m-ʿ nṯr	as done by one who would not stray that way by the hand of the god.
m bn ḥnʿ ʿ rsy	Do not be evil with the southern reach,
iw.k rḫ.ti sr n ẖnw r.s	for you know the prophecy of the Residence concerning it.
ḫpr.n n.f mi ḫpr nn	As that deed happened, so may that happen.
n tht.n.sn mi ḏd.sn	They do not err in their saying.
ḥss.i tn m ʿḳi [... t]ꜣš.s rsy r tꜣt	I am the praiser of Tjeni in ... [...] its southern border to Tat (?).
iṯ.n.i s mi gp n mw	I took it like a burst of water.
n ir st [...]-rʿ mꜣʿ-ḫrw	King [...]-ra true of voice had not achieved it.
sfn ḥr.s n ḥnn	Be merciful for that, in fixing terms.
s[...].s wḥm ḫtmw	[...] it, renew the treaties.
nn wʿb rdi sdgꜣ.f	there is no purity that lets itself be seen.
nfr irt n m-ḫt	It is good to act for posterity.

15. (Papyrus Hermitage 1116A, verso, lines 75 to 81)

nfr n.k ḥnʿ ʿ rsy	**May it be good for you with the southern reach**
iw n.k ḥry gwt ḥry inw	May there come to you those with levies, those with supplies.
iw ir.n.i mitt n tpyw-ʿ	I have done the same for the ancestors
nn it.f di.f sw	If he has no grain to give,
iꜣm n.k n gnn.sn n.k	show favour, so that they yield to you.
sꜣ tw m t.k ḥnḳt.k	Be satisfied with your bread and your beer.
iw n.k mꜣt nn šnʿ	Granite comes to you unopposed.
m ḥḏ mnw n ky	Do not harm the monument of another
wḥꜣ.k inr m r-ꜣw	You may quarry stone from Tura
m ḳd is.k m sẖnyt	Do not build your chapel out of ruins:
iryt r irt sy	that is done against the doing of it.
mk nswt nb ꜣwt ibw	The king is the lord of joyfulness.
sfnꜣ.k sḳd.k m ḫpš.k	You may rest, you may sleep by your might.
šms ib.k m irt.n.i	Follow your heart on what I have done.
nn ḫrwy m ḳꜣb tꜣš.k	There is no enemy in the circuit of your border.

16. (Papyrus Hermitage 1116A, verso, lines 81 to 85)

ʿḥʿ.n ʿḥʿ.i nb m niwt ib.f ḥḏ	**My standing arose as lord in the city, whose heart was hurt**
m-ʿ tꜣ mḥw ḥwt-šnw r smbꜣḳ	from the north land, Hutshenu to Sembaq
tꜣš.s rsy [r] rmwy	its southern border to Remwy
sḥtp.n.i imntt mi ḳd.s	I pacified the entire west,
r mn pdst nt š	as far as the foothills of the Lake
bꜣk.sn n.s dd.s mr[w]	they work for it, giving meru-wood,
mꜣꜣ.tw wʿn dd.sn n.n sw	and the juniper is seen, that they give it to us.
iꜣbtt m ḥwd pḏt	The east is plentiful in bowmen,
bꜣk.sn ḥr [...]	they work on [...]
ʿn.tw iww ḥryw-ib	the isles in the midst are turned back,
s nb m ḳꜣb.f	every man on his coil,
gsw-prw ḥr wr tri tw r.i	the regional estates say: how greater you are than I.

17. (Papyrus Hermitage 1116A, verso, lines 85 to 91)

mk [...] ḥḏ.n.st irw m spꜣwt	**[the land?] they had destroyed is now made into regions**
niwt *nbt wrt [...]*	**cities** of all kinds, of size [...]
ḥḳꜣt nt wʿty m-ʿ s md	the realm of the Sole One out of ten men
irw sr nḫb m bꜣkw	There is appointed the official fixed with revenues,
rḫt m ḥtr nb	staff-lists with all dues,
wn wʿb nḫb m ʿḥt	the pure-priest is fixed with land.
bꜣk n.k mi ṯst wʿt	Work is done for you as by one team.
nn ḫpr ẖꜣkw-ib pw m-m	It means there are no disaffected men rising among them,
nn mn n.k ḥʿpy tm.f iw	the Nile Flood does not fail you, by not arriving.

b3kw m-ʿ.k nt t3-mḥw	The produce is in your hand, from the north land.
mk ḥw mnit m w ir.n.i ḥr i3bt	The mooring-post is struck in the district I made in the east,
ḏrw ḥbnw r w3t ḥr	the flanks of Hebenu to the Way of Horus,
grg m niwt mḥ m rmṯ	established with city-dwellers, filled with people,
m stpw nt t3 r ḏr.f	with the best of the entire land,
r ḫsf ʿwy im.sn	to repel arms on them.
m33.i ḳn sn.f r.s	May I see a brave man who surpasses it,
ir.n.f ḥ3w ḥr irt.n.i	having exceeded what I have done.
3ft m-ʿ iwʿ ẖsy	Shame (?) would be from a vile heir.

18. (Papyrus Hermitage 1116A, verso, lines 91 to 94)

ḏd swt n3 gr n pḏt	**Say though this of the bowman:**
is ʿ3m ẖsy ḳsn pw n bw ntf im	the vile Asiatic, he is difficult because of the place where he is.
3hw mw št3 m ḫtw	lacking in water, scarce in wood,
ʿš3 w3wt iry ḳsn m-ʿ ḏww	many are its roads, hard because of mountains.
n ḥms.f m st wʿt	He has not settled in one place:
stšw ʿkw rdwy.fy	food forces his legs forward.
iw.f ḥr ʿḥ3 ḏr rk ḥr	He has been fighting since the time of Horus,
n ḳn.n.f n gr ḳn.tw.f	and is never conqueror, though nor has he ever been conquered.
n smi.n.f hrw m ʿḥ3	He does not announce a day in battle,
mi ṯ3 šnʿ n sm3yt	like a thief blocked by a band.

19. (Papyrus Hermitage 1116A, verso, lines 94 to 98)

ʿnḫ.i swt wnn.i wn.kwi	**As I, though, live, and exist in my existence**
wnn 3 pḏt.f m minbi m ḫtm	Its bowmen are indeed now as a blade in a safe.
swn ḏdḥ.i r.f	My emprisonment is open on it.
iw di.n.i ḥw st t3-mḥw	I made the north land smite them,
ḥ3ḳ.n.i ẖr.sn	I took their people as booty,
nḥm.n.i mnmnt.sn	I seized their cattle,
r bwyt ʿ3mw r kmt	until the Asiatics had tabu against Egypt.
m rdi ib.k m-s3.f	Do not let your heart concern him.
ʿ3mw pw msḥ ḥr mryt.f	A crocodile on its shore, that is the Asiatic:
ḥnp.f r w3t wʿt	he snatches on the lonely road,
n iṯ.n.f r dmi ʿš3t	but does not seize at the town of a multitude.

20. (Papyrus Hermitage 1116A, verso, lines 98 to 106)

šd mdnit *r w.s*	**Medinet is rescued** for its district,
smḥ gs.s kmwy	one of its sides waters Kemwer –
mk sy m ḫp n ḫ3styw	that is the focus of the desertmen.
inbw.s ʿḥ3 mšʿ.s ʿš3	Its walls are at war, its army numerous,
mr im.s rḫ šsp ḫt	the staff in it are able to bear arms
ḥr wʿb n ẖn w	as well as the pure-priest of the interior of the district.
ḏd-swt km.s ḏbʿ m nḏsw	Djedsut totals ten thousand men in regulars,
wʿb nn b3kw.f	the pure-priest has no labour-dues.
iw srw im.s ḏr rk r ẖnw	Officials are in it since the time of the Residence.
smn t3šw ḳn ḫnrtw.s	The borders are confirmed, its border-camps valiant.
mḥtyw ʿš3 smḥ st r-ʿ t3-mḥw	Numerous northerners irrigate it as far as the northern land.
b3kw m it m r-ʿ wʿb	Revenue in grain from the activity of the pure-priest
sw3t pw ḥr n ir st	that is the surpassing of the sight of the one who does it.
mk st ʿ3 n t3-mḥw	It is a gate to the northern land,
ir n.sn dnit r ḥnn-nswt	for them is made a dam at Hennesut.
mty ib pw niwt ʿš3	Numerous citydwellers are solace of the heart.
s3w pẖr m mr n ḫrwy	Beware being circled by the staff of the enemy:
iw s3wty snḫḫ rnpt	the guard is the one who prolongs years.

21. (Papyrus Hermitage 1116A, verso, lines 106 to 110)

sh3 t3š.k *r ʿ sy*	**If your border is attacked** at the southern reach
pḏt pw šsp ʿgsw	those putting on the battle-belt are (just) bowmen.
ḳd ḥwt m t3-mḥw	Build towns in the northern land.
nn šri rn n s m irt.n.f	The name of a man will not be weak by what he has done.

n ḥd.n.tw niwt.i grg.ti	My city, well-founded, is not destroyed.
ḳd ḥwt n twt.k	Build a town for your image.
iw ḫrwy mr.f ḥd-ib sp.f ḫs	The enemy loves despair, his chance for evil.
š3.n ḫty m3ᶜ ḫrw m sb3w	King Khety true of voice ordained in a teaching:
grw r sḫm-ib ḥḏḏ wdḥw	'one silent in the face of violent minds is the destroyer of offerings'.
tkk nṯr ᶜ sbi ḥr r-pr	The god always confronts a rebel's arm, for the sake of the temple.

22. (Papyrus Hermitage 1116A, verso, lines 110 to 116)

iwt pw ḥr.f mi irr.f *st*	**Consequences follow whatever the action** is
iw.f r s33 m š3t n.f sḫt r.f	Will he be satisfied just with what he is fated to snare?
n in.tw ḥry mw hrw pf n iwt	The loyal man (?) was not brought in on that day of reckoning.
sḫws wdḥw tr nṯr	Enrich the offering-tables, honour the god.
m ḏd ḫs pw ib	Do not say: despair.
m fḫ ᶜwy.ky	Do not relax your arms.
ir grt bšt.k	For the one who makes rebellion against you
ḥdty pt pw	is the destruction of heaven.
rnpt šnt mnw pw wḏ3 (?)	A sound monument is a hundred years.
ir rḫ ḫrwy nn ḥd.f st	If the enemy was aware, he would not destroy it,
m mrt smnḫ irt.n.f	for love of embellishing what he had done,
in ky iy m-s3.f	by the one to come after him:
nn wn šw m ḫrwy	for no-one is entirely without an enemy.
rḫ ḫt pw idbwy	The Two Shores god is the knower of matters,
nn wḫ3 n nswt nb šnyt	a king lord of an entourage will have no folly.
s33.f m pr.f nw ḫt	He is wise from his emergence from the womb,
stn.n sw ḫnty ḥḥw	and has been distinguished ahead of millions.

23. (Papyrus Hermitage 1116A, verso, lines 116 to 125)

i3t pw nfrt nsyt	**Kingship is the good office**
nn s3.s nn sn.s	It has no son, it has no brother
sw3ḥ mnw.s	to cause its monuments to endure:
in wᶜ smnḫ ky	one embellishes another,
ir s n nty ḫr-ḥ3t.f	a man acts for the one who was his predecessor,
m mryt smnḫ irt.n.f	from the wish that what he has made may be embellished
in ky iy ḫr s3.f	by another who comes after him.
mk sp ḫsy ḫpr m h3w.i	See a vile deed occurred in my time,
ᶜd.tw sp3wt nt tny	the districts of Teni were hacked up,
ḫpr.n is m irt.n.i	it happened even as something I did,
rḫ.n.i st r-s3 irt	though I learned of it after the deed.
mk ḏ3rw.i ḫnt irt.n.i	See the retribution on me, out of what I did.
ḫs pw grt nn 3ḫ n.i	It is too evil, it is no use to me
srwd swst.n.f	to restore what it laid waste,
sḫn kd.f	when its buildings lie demolished,
smnḫ sᶜn.n.f	to recreate what it overturned.
s33.ti r.s	Be on guard against it.
ḏb3.tw sḫ m mity.f	A blow is repaid with its like.
mḏd pw irt nbt	Every action may be returned (?).
snn ḫt r ḫt m rmṯ	Generation follows generation among humans
imn.n sw nṯr rḫ ḳdw	but the god who knows characters has hidden himself.
nn ḫsf ᶜ nb drt	There is no opposing the action of the lord of the hand,
tkk pw m m33t irty	he is the one who reaches in what the eyes can see.

24. (Papyrus Hermitage 1116A, verso, lines 125 to 131)

tr.tw *nṯr* ***ḥr w3t.f***	A god **may be honoured upon his way**,
irw m ᶜ3t msw m ḥmty	made out of precious stones, fashioned from copper,
mi nt ḏb3.ti m nt	as the floodwater exchanged with floodwater,
nn itrw rdi sdg3.f	there is no river that can make itself transparent.
fḫ ᶜ pw imn.n.f im.f	That is the breach of the channel in which it had hidden.
šm b3 r bw rḫ.n.f gr	So too the soul goes to the place it has known,
n th.n.f m w3t.f nt sf	and does not stray from its path of yesterday.
smnḫ st.k nt ḫrt-nṯr	Embellish your place of the cemetery,

sikr ḥwt.k nt imnt	Make excellent your chapel of the West,
m ꜥḳꜣ m irt mꜣꜥt	in being upright, in doing what is Right,
rhnt ib.sn pw ḥr.s	that is what their hearts rely upon.
šsp biꜣt nt ꜥḳꜣ ib	The quality of the upright of heart is preferred
r iwꜣ n ir isft	to the ox of the evildoer.
ir n nṯr ir.f n.k mitt	Act for the god so that he may do the same for you,
m ꜥꜣbt nt swꜣḏ ꜥb	with offerings for making the offering-stone flourish,
m ḫtt sšmt pw rn.k	with inscribed monuments, that is the guide of your name.
sšꜣ nṯr m irr n.f	The god is aware of the one who acts for him.

25. (Papyrus Hermitage 1116A, verso, lines 131 to 138)

ḥn rmṯ ꜥwt nṯr	Well-tended are people, the herd of the god,
ir.n.f pt tꜣ n ib.sn	he has made heaven and earth for their hearts,
dr.n.f snk n mw	he has driven off the crocodile of the waters
ir.n.f ṯꜣw ib ꜥnḫ sfn.sn	he has made the breath of the heart, that their nostrils might live.
snnw.f pw pr m ḥꜥw.f	They are his images who came from his body.
wbn.f m pt n ib.sn	He shines in the sky for their hearts.
ir.n.f n.sn smw ꜥwt	He has made for them plants and herds,
ꜣpdw rmw snmt st	birds and fish, to nourish them.
smꜣ.f ẖftyw.f	He kills his enemies,
ḥḏ.n.f msw.f	and he has damaged his children
ḥr kꜣt.sn m irt sbi	at their plotting to carry out rebellion.
irr.f šsp n ib.sn	He repeats daybreak for their hearts,
sḳdd.f r mꜣꜣ st	and sails by to see them.
ṯs.n.f kꜣri ḥꜣ.sn	He has raised a chapel behind them;
rmm.sn iw.f ḥr sḏm	when they weep he can hear.
ir.n.f n.sn ḥḳꜣw m swḥt	He has made for them rulers in the egg,
ṯsw r ṯst m psd sꜣ-ꜥ	commanders to command at the back of the vulnerable.
ir.n.f n.sn ḥkꜣw	He has made words of power for them,
r ꜥḥꜣw r ḫsf ꜥ n ḫpryt	as weapons to repel the blow of events,
rs ḥr.s grḥ mi hrw	watchful over them night and day.
smꜣ.n.f ẖꜣkw-ib m-m	He has killed the disaffected among them,
mi ḥw s sꜣ.f ḥr sn.f	as a man strikes his son for the sake of this brother.
iw nṯr rḫ rn nb	The god is aware of every name.

26. (Papyrus Hermitage 1116A, verso, lines 138 to 144)

im.k ir mnt nb r.i	**Do not make any failing on my words**
dd.s hpw nb ḥr nswt	they give all the laws for a king,
swn ḥr.k ṯs.k m s	to open well your eyes, to raise you as a man.
iḫ pḥ.k wi nn srḫy.k	Then you may reach me with no claimant on you.
m smꜣ wꜥ tkn im.k	Do not kill anyone who is close to you,
ḥs.n.k sw nṯr rḫ sw	whom you have favoured – the god is aware of him.
wꜥ im.sn pw wꜣḏ tp tꜣ	He is one of them, one flourishing on earth.
nṯrw pw šmsw nswt	They are the gods, the followers of the king.
imi mrwt.k n tꜣ-tmw	Inspire love of you in all people.
sḫꜣ pw ḳd nfr rnpt sbw im	A good character means memory, when years have passed on.
ḏd.tw.k ḥḏ rk n mn	May you be called the one who ended the time of pain,
in ntyw m pḥwy m pr ẖty	by those who are at the end in the House of King Khety,
m sšꜣ iwt.f min	by realising what is coming today.
mk ḏd.n.i n.k bw ꜣḫ n ẖt.i	Now I have told you the experience of my body.
irr.k m grg m ḥr.k	May you act in establishing in your sight.

Endnote of Papyrus Hermitage 1116A, at verso, lines 145 to 150

iw.s htpw	**Its end in harmony**
mi gmyt m sš mi gmyt m sš	as found in writing, as found in writing,
sš sš [ḫꜥ]-m-wꜣst n.f ḏs.f	a writing of the writer [Kha]mwaset of himself,
gr mꜣꜥ nfr biꜣt	silent and true, good of character,
wꜣḥ ib mr rmṯ	patient, loved of people,
tm ꜥḥꜥ m irt ky	who does not stand in the eye of another,
tm štm bꜣk n nb.f	who does not denounce a servant to his master,

sš nis ḥsb ṯs	writer of summons, calculator of levies,
sš3w ḥr m k3t ḏḥwty	wise in sight in the works of Thoth,
*sš ḫ*ʿ*-m-w3st*	the writer Khamwaset
n sn.f mry.f n st-ib	for his brother, his beloved and favourite,
*gr m3*ʿ *nfr bi3t*	silent and true, good of character,
sš3w ḥr m k3t ḏḥwty	wise in sight in the works of Thoth,
sš mḥ s3	the writer Meh son

The Teaching of Duau Khety - the 'Satire of Trades'

This composition contrasts the hardships of manual professions with the living standard of the writing man. It takes the literary form of a teaching from a father to his son, but effectively presents a treatise on class and labour in Ancient Egypt. The severity of the contrast between literate and manual lives has earned the composition the Egyptological name 'Satire of Trades', although the word 'satire' may not be appropriate for its stark realism. The composition is in the Middle Egyptian phase of the Egyptian language, and probably dates to the Middle Kingdom, perhaps specifically to early Dynasty 12, about 1950-1900 BC. A date earlier than the late Middle Kingdom may be indicated by the absence of a profession documented in late Middle Kingdom inscriptions, the faience-worker (*ṯḥnty*): although faience is a product attested already in the predynastic periods, mass-production of royal glazed steatite amulets begins at the end of Dynasty 12.
The transliteration follows Helck 1970a, using the copy on Papyrus Sallier II as principal source. The section divisions are those of Helck 1970a: after each section number are given the corresponding line-numbers in Papyrus Sallier II.

1 (Papyrus Sallier II, column III, line 9 to column IV, 1)

ḥꜣt-ꜥ m sbꜣyt irt.n	Beginning of the teaching made by
s n ṯꜣrw dwꜣw ẖty rn.f	the man of Tjaru (?) called Duau Khety
n sꜣ.f ppy rn.f	for his son called Pepy,
ist r.f m ẖntyt r ẖnw	while he was sailing south to the Residence
r rdit.f m ꜥt sbꜣ nt sšw	to place him in the writing school
m ḳꜣb msw srw imyw-ḥꜣt nt ẖnw	among the children of officials, of the foremost of the Residence

2 (Papyrus Sallier II, column IV, lines 1 to 4)

ꜥḥꜥ.n ḏd.n.f n.f	**He said to him**
mꜣꜣ.n.i ḳnḳnw	I have seen violent beatings:
dd.k ib.k m-sꜣ sšw	so direct your heart to writing.
dgꜣ.n.i nḥm ḥr bꜣkw.f	I have witnessed a man seized for his labour
mk nn wn m ḥꜣ sšw	Look, nothing excels writing
mitt ḥr mw pw	It is like a loyal man.
šd ir.k pḥwy kmyt	Read for yourself the end of the Compilation
gmy.k ṯs pn im.s m ḏd	and you can find this phrase in it saying
ir sš m st.f nbt nt ẖnw	'The scribe, whatever his place at the Residence
nn ḥwr.f im.f	He cannot be poor in it'

3 (Papyrus Sallier II, column IV, lines 4 to 6)

iw.f ir.f sꜣrt n ky	**He accomplishes the wish of another**
nn pr.f ḥtpw	when he is not succeeding
n mꜣꜣ.n.i iꜣt m mitt.s	I do not see a profession like it
m ḏdt ṯs pn im.s	that you could say that phrase for,
di.i mry.k sšw r mwt.k	so I would have you love writing more than your mother
di.i ꜥḳ nfrw.s m ḥr.k	and have you recognise its beauty
wr sw grt r iꜣt nbt	For it is greater than any profession,
nn wn mitt.s m tꜣ	there is none like it on earth
šꜣꜥ.n.f wꜣḏ iw.f m ẖrd	He has just begun growing, and is just a child,
tw r nḏ ẖrt.f	when people will greet him (already).
tw r hꜣb.f r irt wpwt	He will be sent to carry out a mission,
nn iy.f sw sd.f m dꜣiw	and before he returns, he is clothed in linen (like an adult man)

4. (Papyrus Sallier II, column IV, lines 6 to 8)

n mꜣꜣ.n.i gnwty m wpwt	**I do not see a sculptor on a mission**
nbwy n bꜣk (?) hꜣb.f	or a goldsmith on the task of being despatched (?)
iw mꜣꜣ.n.i ḥmtyw ḥr bꜣkw.f	but I see the coppersmith at his toil
r r n ḥryt.f	at the mouth of his furnace
ḏbꜥw.fy mi ẖrt msḥw	his fingers like crocodile skin
ẖnš sw r swḥt rmw	his stench worse than fish eggs

5. (Papyrus Sallier II, column IV, line 8 to column V, line 1)

ḥmww nb ṯ3y ʿnt	**Any craftsman using a chisel**
wrd sw r mny	is more exhausted than a labourer.
3ḥwt.f m ẖt	His fields are the timber,
ḥnw.f m ḥmt	his plough the metal.
m grḥ nḥm.f	No nightfall rescues him,
ir.n.f m ḥ3w nw ʿwy.fy ḥr irt	when he has done in excess of his arms in production;
m grḥ st3.f	In night he has to kindle a light

6. (Papyrus Sallier II, column V, lines 1 to 3)

ms-ʿ3t ḥr whb m mnḫ	**The jeweller drills in bead-making**
m ʿ3t nbt rwd	using all of the hardest hard stones.
ḳn.n.f mḥ nw 3ḫt	When he has completed the inlays
ʿwy.fy 3ḳw n wrd.f	his arms are destroyed by his exhaustion.
iw ḥms.f ḥr ʿḳw nw rʿ	He sits at the food of Ra
m3sty.fy 3t.f wʿf	with his knees and back hunched double.

7. (Papyrus Sallier II, column V, lines 3 to 5)

ẖʿkw ḥr ẖʿḳ m pḥwy mšrw	**The barber shaves into the end of the evening**
dd.f sw n ʿmyt dd.f sw ḥr ḳʿḥ.f	continually at the call, continually on his elbow,
dd.f sw m mrt r mrt	pushing himself continually from street to street
r wḫ3 r ẖʿḳ.f sw	looking for people to shave.
ḳnn.f ʿwy.fy r mḥ ẖt.f	He does violence to his arms to fill his belly,
mi bit wnmw r k3t.s	like bees that eat at their toil.

8. (Papyrus Sallier II, column V, lines 5 to 6)

bṯy ḫd.f r *idḥw*	**The reedcutter sails north to** the marshes
r iṯ n.f swnw	to take for himself the shafts (?).
ir.n.f m ḥ3w nw ʿwy.fy ḥr irt	When he has exceeded the power of his arms in action,
sm3.n sw ḫnmsw	When the mosquitoes have slaughtered him
ḫmyw sfd.n sw snny	and the gnats have cut him down too,
ḫr wnn.f wḏʿ	then he is the one broken in two.

9. (Papyrus Sallier II, column V, lines 5 to 6)

iḳd nḏs ẖr 3ḥwt.f	**The small potter is under his earth**
sʿḥʿ.f m ʿnḫw	even when he is stood among the living.
ḫm sw r š3wt r š3iw	He is muddier with clay than swine
r pst ẖr 3ḥwt.f	to burn under his earth.
ḥbsw.f nḫt m dbn	His clothes are solid as a block
ʿ3gsw.f m stp	and his headcloth is rags,
r ʿḳ ṯ3w r fnd.f	until the air enters his nose
pr m t3.f wḏ3	coming from his furnace direct.
ir.n.f ty m rdwy.fy	When he has made the pestle out of his legs,
sḥm im.f ḏs.f	the pounding is done with himself,
ḫmʿ hi n pr nb	smearing the fences of every house,
ḥw n iwyt.f	and beaten by his streets.

10. (Papyrus Sallier II, column VI, lines 1 to 3)

ḏd.i n.k mi ḳd inbw	**Let me tell you what it is like to be a bricklayer**
mr dpt	the bitterness of the taste.
ḫr wnn.f m rwty n sm3ʿt	He has to exist outside in the wind,
iḳd.f m d3iw	building in his kilt,
ʿ3gsw m sšny n3yt	his robes a cord from the weaving-house
r w3ww n pḥwy.fy	stretching round to his back.
ʿwy.fy 3ḳ m mnḫ	His arms are destroyed by hard labour.
šbn ḥsw.f nb	mixed in with all his filth.
wnm.f t dbʿw.f	He eats the bread with his fingers
iʿ.f sw ḥr tr wʿ	though he can only wash the once.

11. (Papyrus Sallier II, column VI, lines 3 to 5)

ẖs n mḏḥ n ḏri.f r-sy	**For the carpenter with his kit (life) is utterly vile**
snn šp m ꜥt	covering the roof in a chamber,
m ꜥt nt mḥ mḏ r mḥ siw	a chamber measuring ten cubits by six,
snn šp m ꜣbd	to cover the roof in a month
m-sꜣ wꜣḥ sbw m sšny nꜣyt	after laying the boards with cord of the weaving-house.
irw kꜣt.s nbt	All the work on it is done,
ir ꜥḳw dd.tw.f n.f	but the food given for it
nn pnḳ ẖrdw.f	couldn't stretch to his children.

12. (Papyrus Sallier II, column VI, lines 5 to 8)

kꜣry ḥr inn mꜣḫd	**The gardener has to carry a rod**
ḳꜥḥ.f nb ḥr tnw	and all his shoulder bones age,
ꜥt wrt ḥr nḥbt.f	and there is a great blister on his neck,
iw.s ḥr irt ꜥd	oozing puss.
sdwꜣ.f ḥr iwḥ iꜣḳt	He spends his morning drenching leeks,
mšrw.f ḥr šꜣwt	his evening in the mire.
ir.n.f ḥr hrw	He has spent over a day,
m-sꜣ ẖt.f bin	after his belly is feeling bad.
ḫpr ḫnw.f mwt.f ḥr rn.f	So it happens that he rests dead to his name
tnw r iꜣt nbt	aged more than any other profession.

13. (Papyrus Sallier II, column VI, line 8 to column VII, line 2)

ꜥḥwty ḥr ḥbt r nḥḥ	**The field labourer complains eternally**
kꜣ ḫrw.f r ꜥbw	his voice rises higher than the birds,
ḏbꜥw.fy irw m ꜥꜣwt	with his fingers turned into sores,
ḥr ḥꜣw nb n stnw	from carrying overloads of produce (?).
wrd sw r mtn r idḥw	He is too exhausted to report for marsh work,
ḥr wnn.f m stp	and has to exist in rags.
wḏꜣ.f wḏꜣ m mꜣiw	His health is the health on new lands;
mr r ḏbꜣw ir.f	sickness is his reward.
hꜣw.f im m ḫmt.n.sn	His labour-duty there is whatever they have forgotten.
prr.f im m-ꜥ r	If he can ever escape there from the order (?),
spr.f r pr.f ind	he reaches his home in utter poverty,
mḏd.n sw ḥr šmt	downtrodden too much to walk.

14. (Papyrus Sallier II, column VII, lines 2 to 4)

ḳny m-ẖnw nꜣyt	**The mat-weaver (lives) inside the weaving-house**
bin sw r st ḥmt	he is worse off than a woman,
mꜣsty.fy r r n ib.f	with his knees up to his stomach,
nn tpi n.f ṯꜣw	unable to breathe in any air.
ir ḫbꜣ.n.f hrw nn sḫt	If he wastes any daytime not weaving,
ḥw.tw.f m šsm diww	he is beaten with 50 lashes.
iw.f di.f ꜥḳw n iry-ꜥꜣ	He has to give a sum to the doorkeeper
r dit pr.f r ḥḏwt	to be allowed to go out to the light of day.

15. (Papyrus Sallier II, column VII, lines 4 to 6)

irw ꜥḥꜣw sfn.f *r-sy*	**The weapon-maker is humiliated** utterly
ḥr prt r ḫꜣst	going out to the hill-land.
iw wr dd.f n ꜥꜣt.f	What he give to his ass is greater
r kꜣt r-sꜣ iry	than the work that results,
iw wr dd.f n imy šꜣ	and great is his gift to the man in the country
ddy sw ḥr wꜣt	who puts him on the track.
spr.f r pr.f mšrw	He reaches his home in the evening,
wḏꜥ.n sw šmt	and the travelling has broken him in two.

16. (Papyrus Sallier II, column VII, lines 6 to 8)

sḫḫty ḥr prt r ḫꜣst	**The trader (?) goes out to the hill-land**
swḏ.n.f ꜣḫt.f n msw.f	after bequeathing his goods to his children,
snd ḥr mꜣiw ḥnꜥ ꜥꜣmw	fearful of lions and Asiatics.

rḫ.f sw r.f iw.f ḥr kmt	He recognises himself again, when he is in Egypt,
spr.f r pr.f mšrw	reaching his home in the evening,
wdꜥ.n sw šmt	and the travelling has broken him in two.
iw pr.f m d3iw m ḏbt	His house is of cloth for bricks,
nn iy snḏm-ib	without experiencing any pleasure.

17. (Papyrus Sallier II, column VII, line 9 to column VIII, line 1)

stny ḏbꜥw.fy hw3w	The leather-worker (?), his fingers are rotted,
sty iry m ḫ3wt	the smell of them is as corpses,
irty.fy wḥf m wr st3w	and his eyes are wasted by the mass of flame.
nn ḫsf.f stn.f	He can never be rid of his tannin (?),
wrš.f m šꜥd n ist	spending his day cut by the reed;
bwt.f pw ḥbsw.f	his own clothing is his horror.

18. (Papyrus Sallier II, column VIII, lines 1 to 2)

ṯbww bin sw r-sy	**The sandalmaker is utterly the worst off**
ḥr dbḥt.f r nḥḥ	with his stocks of more than oil.
wd3.f wd3 m ḫ3wt	His health is health as corpses,
psḥ.f m msk3w.f	as he bites into his skins.

19. (Papyrus Sallier II, column VIII, lines 2 to 6)

rḫty ḥr rḫt ḥr mryt	**The washerman does the laundry on the shore**
s3ḥ-t3 m ḫntyw	neighbour to the crocodiles.
pr it ḥr mw p3 ꜥd	'Father is going to the water of the canal (?)',
ḫr s3.f s3t.f	he says to his son and his daughter.
nn i3t ḥtp ḥr.s	Is this not a profession to be glad for,
tnw r i3t nbt	more choice than any other profession?
šbb šbnw ḥr st ḥsw	The food is mixed with places of filth,
nn ꜥt wꜥbt im.f	and there is no pure limb on him.
dd.f sw m d3iw n st ḥmt	He puts on the clothing of a woman
wnnt m ḥsmn.s	who was in her menstruation.
rmyt n.f wrš ḥr mk3nt	Weep for him, spending the day with the laundry-bat,
iw inr ḥr.f	with the cleaning-stone upon him.
ḏd.tw n.f š3m ms.tw r.i	He is told 'dirty washbowl, come here,
sḫr spty ir.k	the fringes are still to be done!'

20. (Papyrus Sallier II, column VIII, lines 6 to 7)

wḥꜥ 3pdw sfn r-sy	**The bird-catcher is the most utterly miserable**
ḥr gmḥ iryw pt	looking out for the keepers of the sky.
ir sw3 3pdw ḫnmw m ḥr.f	If the bird swarm passes over him,
ḫr.f ḏd.f ḥ3nr n.i m i3dt	he is left saying 'I wish I had the net'.
nn rdi.n nṯr ḫpr m-ꜥ.f	The god would not allow it to happen by him;
sfn.f ḥr sḫrw.f	he is made miserable by his condition.

21. (Papyrus Sallier II, column VIII, line 8 to column IX, line 2)

ḏd.i n.k mi wḥꜥ rmw	**Let me tell you what (the life of) the bird-catcher is like**
sfn.f r i3t nbt	he is more miserable than any other profession.
wn b3kw.f ḥr itrw	His toil is on the river,
šbnw ḥnꜥ msḥw	mixed in with the crocodiles.
ir ḫpr n.f dmdyt nt ipt.f	When the collection of his dues takes place,
ḫr wnn.f ḥr nhw	then he is always in lament.
nn ḏd n.f iw msḥw ꜥḥꜥ	He can never be told 'there are crocodiles surfacing':
šp.n sw sndw.f	his fear has blinded him.
ir pr.f ḥr mw pw p3 ꜥdw	If he goes out, it is on the water of the canal,
ḫr.f mi b3w nṯr	he is as at a miracle.
mk nn i3t šw m ḫrpw	Look, there is no profession free of directors,
wp-ḥr sš ntf pw ḫrp	except the scribe - he IS the director.

22. (Papyrus Sallier II, column IX, lines 2 to 5)

ir swt rḫ.k sšw	**If, though, you know how to write**
wn nfr n.k st r n3 n i3wt dd.i m ḥr.k	that is better life for you than these professions I show you;
mk iry ḥwrw.f iry	protector of the worker, or his wretch the worker?
nn ḏd n.f ˤḥwty s	The field labourer of a man cannot say to him
m s3w ir.k	'do not watch over (me)'.
mk ir st m ẖntyt r ẖnw	Look, the trouble of sailing south to the Residence,
mk ir st n mry.k	look, it is trouble for love of you.
3ḫ n.k hrw m ˤt sb3	A day in the school chamber is more useful for you
iw r nḥḥ k3t.s ḏww	than an eternity of its toil in the mountains.
iw.s 3s 3s di.i rḫ.k	It is the double-quick way, I show you.
di.i mry snhp btnw	Or should I inspire desire for being woken at dawn to be bruised?

23. (Papyrus Sallier II, column IX, lines 5 to 7)

ḏd.i n.k mi ktḫw mdwt	**Let me tell you in another manner**
r sb3.k rḫ.k	to teach you so that you know.
mi ˤḥˤ r bw ˤḥ3.tw.k	on how to rise at being fought.
m tkn ntyw dbt ḥr sḫrw.k (?)	Do not approach those who are a block to your plans (?)
ir ṯ3y.tw dbt ḥr 3s-ib	If the obstacle (?) were taken up at the hasty-hearted,
nn rḫ.tw bw ḫsf srf	none would know of suppression of the fiery.
mtr ḥr sḏmyw	Give witness before those hearing (the case);
ir n.f wšb wḏf3	and make a reply to him with (due) pause.

24. (Papyrus Sallier II, column IX, lines 7 to 9)

ir šm.k m pḥwy srw	**If you are walking behind officials**
m tkn w3w m ḥrt nfrt	do not come too close in good bearing.
ir ˤḳ.k iw nb pr m pr.f	If you enter when the lord of the house is at home,
iw bw ˤwy.fy n ky r ḥ3t.k	and his arms are extended to another before you,
iw ḥms.k drt.k m r.k	You are to be seated with your hand on your mouth.
m dbḥ 3ḫt r-gs.f	Do not request anything beside him,
ir n.f mi ḏdt im	but react to him when addressed,
m s3w ṯst r ṯt	and be careful at joining the table.

25. (Papyrus Sallier II, column IX, line 9 to column X, line 1)

dns im.k wr šfyt	**Be serious with anyone greater in dignity**
m ḏd mdt n ḥ3p	Do not speak matters of secrecy,
iw ḥ3p ẖt ir n.f ikm	for the secretive is the one who can shield himself
m ḏd mdt n pr-ib	Do not speak matters of boasting,
iw ḥms tw ḥnˤ ksm-ẖt	but take your seat with the restrained.

26. (Papyrus Sallier II, column X, lines 2 to 3)

ir pr.k m ˤt sb3	**If you come out from the school chamber**
m-ẖt smi.tw n.k mtrt	when you have been told the midday hour,
ḥr šmt iyt m iwyt	for coming and going in the streets
ḏ3is n.k pḥwy n bw n.k st	Debate for yourself the end of the place for you (?)

27. (Papyrus Sallier II, column X, lines 3 to 4)

ir h3b tw *sr m wpwt*	**If an official sends you** on a mission
ḏd.f mi ḏd.f sw	say it exactly as he says it,
m iṯ m rdit ḥr.s	without omission, without adding to it.
iw ḫ3ˤ.f h3nw	Whoever leaves out the declamation (?),
nn rn.f w3ḥ	his name shall not endure,
iw.f ˤrḳ m bi3t.f nbt	but whoever completes with all his talent,
nn wn imn r.f	nothing will be kept back from him;
nn tn.f r st.f nbt	he will not be parted from any of his places.

28. (Papyrus Sallier II, column X, lines 4 to 6)

m ḏd grg r mwt	**Do not tell lies against a mother**
3bw srw pw	- that is the extreme for the officials.
ir m-ẖt ḫpr ẖt	If the thing has happened,

ꜥwy.fy twt rdi ib sfn.f	his arms are mustered, and the heart has made him weak,
m rdi ḥr.s ḥnꜥ ksm	do not add to it with meekness.
iw ẖsy sw r ẖt sḏm.tw n.k	That is worse for the belly, when you have heard.
ir sꜣ tw t	If bread satisfies you,
sꜥm hnw sn n ḥnḳt	and drinking two jars of beer,
nn ḏr ẖt ꜥḥꜣ ḥr.s	there is no limit for the belly fighting for; it
ir sꜣ.tw n ky m ꜥḥꜥ	if another is satisfied standing up,
sꜣw ṯst r ṯt	be careful about joining the table.

29. (Papyrus Sallier II, column X, line 7 to column XI, line 1)

mk hꜣb.k ꜥšꜣt	**Look, you send out the throng,**
sḏm.k *mdt srw*	**you hear** the words of officials,
iẖ iry.k ḳi msw rmṯ	Behave then like the children of (important) people,
iw.k ḥr šmt m iṯ.s	when you are going to collect them.
mꜣꜣ.n.tw sš ḥr sḏm	The scribe is the one seen hearing (cases);
ḫpr sḏm pr-ꜥ	Would fighters be the ones to hear?
ꜥḥꜣ.k mdt nt r.s	Fight words that are contrary;
ꜣst rdwy.k iw.k ḥr šmt	move fast when you are proceeding -
nn kfꜣ ib.k	your heart should never trust.
smꜣ mtn r.s	Keep to the paths for it:
ẖnmsw s ḏꜣmw.k	the friends of a man are your troops.

30. (Papyrus Sallier II, column XI, lines 1-4)

mk rnnt ḥr wꜣt nṯr	**Look - Abundance is on the path of the god**
rnnt sš ḥr ḳꜥḥ.f	and Abundance is written on his shoulder
hrw n mst.f	on the day of his birth.
spr.f r ꜥryt	He reaches the palace portal,
tꜣ ḳnbt ir n.f rmṯ	and that court of officials is the one allotting people to him.
mk nn wn sš šw m wnm	Look, no scribe will ever be lacking in food or
ꜣḫt nt pr nswt ꜥnḫ wḏꜣ snb	the things of the House of the King, may he live, prosper, be well!
msḫnt wꜣḏt nt sš	Meskhenet is the prosperity of the scribe,
ddy ḥr-ḥꜣt ḳnbt	the one placed before the front of the court.
dwꜣ nṯr it mwt.k	Thank god for the father, and for your mother,
ddy ḥr wꜣt nt ꜥnḫw	you who are placed on the path of the living.
mk nn rdi.i m ḥr.k	See what I have set out before you,
msw n msw.k	and for the children of your children.

End note (Papyrus Sallier, column XI, line 5)

iw.s pw nfr m ḥtp	This is its end, perfect, in harmony

Principal sources used for Helck 1970a:

Dynasty 18:

- Papyrus Amherst (now in the Pierpont Morgan Library, New York), mid Dynasty 18
- Writing board Louvre 693, late Dynasty 18
- Ostraca 147-8 from the tomb of Senenmut, reign of Hatshepsut with Thutmose III

Ramesside Period:

- Papyrus Sallier II (in the British Museum), Papyrus Anastasi VII (in the British Museum), Papyrus Chester Beatty XIX (in the British Museum)

Late Third Intermediate Period, about 700 BC:

- Writing board Louvre E 8424

Other sources include a large number of Ramesside ostraca.

Not identified at the time of the Helck edition: Mid-18th Dynasty writing board UC 59421

The Teaching of King Amenemhat I

The composition presents the words of the king to his son Senusret I following an attack on his life, an unmentionable crime in a civilization where the ruler was son of the sun-god (on the ideology of kingship see Berlev 2003). The bitterness of the message gives this a bleak power without parallel even among the laments in Egyptian literature. One Ramesside source ascribes the composition to a *sš* writer/bureaucrat Khety (Part One, Question Three).
Transliteration following Helck 1969

1.

ḥꜣt-ꜥ m sbꜣyt irt.n	Beginning of the teaching made by
ḥm n nswt-bity sḥtp-ib-rꜥ	the Person of the Dual King Sehetepibra
sꜣ rꜥ imn-m-ḥꜣt mꜣꜥ-ẖrw	Son of Ra Amenemhat true of voice,
ḏd.f m wpt mꜣꜥt	Declaring in a revelation of truth
n sꜣ.f nb-r-ḏr	to his son the Lord of All,
ḏd.f ḫꜥ m nṯr	Saying, Rise as God
sḏm n ḏd.ti.i n.k	Listen to what I tell you
nsy.k tꜣ	That you may be king of earth
ḥkꜣy.k idbw	That you may rule the river-banks
ir.k ḥꜣw ḥr nfr	And achieve in excess of perfection

2.

sꜣḳ tw r smdt r.f tmt ḫpr	Gather yourself against dependants - nothing comes of it
tmmt rdi ib m-sꜣ ḥr.s	Every-one puts their heart in the direction of their fear.
m tkn im.sn m wꜥw.kwi	Never approach them alone.
m mḥ ib.k m sn m rḫ ẖnms	Trust none as brother. Make no friend.
m sẖprw n.k ꜥḳw nn km iry	Create no intimates - it is worthless

3.

sḏr.k sꜣw n.k ib.k ḏs.k	In sleep, guard your heart yourself
ḥr-ntt nn wnn mr n s	For a man has no servants
hrw n ḳsnt	On the day of woe.
iw di.n.i n šwꜣw sẖpr.n.i nmḥ	I gave to the destitute, and raised up the orphan.
di.n.i pḥ iwty-n.f mi nty-wn	I promoted the man with nothing as much as the man of means

4.

in wnm kꜣ.i ir ṯst	The very eater of my bread made the uprising.
rdi.n.i n.f ꜥwy.i ḥr sẖpr ḥr im	The one to whom I gave my arms, was creating fear from it,
wnḫw pꜥkt.i ḥr mꜣ n.i mi šwy	The one clothed in my fine linen was looking at me as if in rags,
wrḥw ꜥntyw stiw mw ẖry	The one anointed with myrrh was as one who poured lowly water.

5.

snnw ꜥnḫw psš.i m rmṯ	My living images, my own distinct from men,
irw n.i ḳꜣ mdt nty n sḏm.tw.f	Make for me lament as has not been heard.
bw-ꜥꜣ n ꜥḥꜣ n mꜣ.n.tw.f	The greatness of the fight too had not been seen.
ist ꜥḥꜣ.tw ḥr mtwn smḫ sf	See, if you fight in the arena, oblivious of yesterday,
nn km n bw-nfr n ḫm-rḫ.f	There is no good outcome for he who is unaware.

6.

r-sꜣ msyt pw ḫꜣw ḫpr	It was after the meal, night had fallen,
šsp.n.i wnwt nt nfr-ib	I took an hour of rest.
sḏr.kwi ḥr ḥnkyt.i bꜣg.n.i	I lay on my bed, for I had grown weary.
šꜣꜥ.n ḥꜣty.i šms ḳd.i	My heart began to follow sleep.
ist spẖr ḫꜥw nḏ r-ḥr.i	Suddenly weapons of counsel were turned against me.
ir.kwi mi sꜣ-tꜣ n smt	I was like a snake of the desert

7.

nhs.n.i n ꜥḥꜣw n ḫꜥw.i	I awoke to my bodyguard.
gm.n.i ḥwny-r-ḥr pw n mnf	I found it was a body blow by a soldier.
ir šsp.i ꜣst ḫꜥw m drt.i	If I had swiftly taken weapons in my hand,

iw di.n.i ẖt ḥmw m-ʿ b3b3[.tw]	I would have turned the wretch back in confusion,
nn swt ḳn grḥ nn ʿḥ3 wʿty	But there is no night champion, no-one who can fight alone.
nn ḫpr sp mʿr m-ḫmt n mkw	There can be no success without a protector.

8.

mk st3w ḫpr iw.i m ḫmt.k	See, the attack happened when I was without you,
n sḏmt šnyt sw3ḏ.i n.k	Before the court had heard I would hand over to you,
n ḥmst.i ḥnʿ.k iḫ iry.i sḫrw.k	Before I had sat with you, to make your position.
ḥr-ntt n ḥr.i st n ḫmt.i st	For I had not feared it, I had not envisaged it.
n in ib.i wsft nt b3kw	My hear had not borne the failure of servants.

9.

in iw p3.n ḥmwt ṯs skw	Had women ever raised troops?
in iw šd.tw ḫnnw m ḫnw pr	Had rebels ever been nurtured within the house?
in iw wb3.tw mw 3dd gbbw	Had water ever been opened up, while the canals were being dug,
swḫ3.tw ndsw ḥr iryt.sn	And with fellows at their tasks?
n iw iyt ḥ3.i ḏr mst.i	No disaster had come up behind me since my birth.
n ḫpr mitt sp.i m ir ḳnn	Never had the like happened - my moment was that of valiant doer

10.

iw h3b.n.i r 3bw ḫsy.n.i r idḥw	I ploughed south to Abu, fared north to the marshes.
ʿḥʿ.kwi ḥr ḏrw t3 m3.n.i ḳ3b.f	I stood at the limits of the land, and saw its contour.
in.n.i r ḏrw ḫpšwt	I reached the limits of the strongholds,
m ḫpš.i m ḫprw.i	by my strength and by my forms.

11.

ink ir it mr npri	I myself was maker of crops beloved of Nepri.
tr.n wi ḥʿpy ḥr pg3 nb	The Nile Flood honoured me at every embrace.
n ḥkr.tw m rnpwt.i n ib.tw im	None hungered in my years, none thirsted then.
iw ḥms.tw m irt.n.i ḥr sḏdt im.i	Men rested through what I had done, and told tales of me.
iw wḏ.n.i nb r st iry	All I had decreed was in its correct place.

12.

iw ḳnb.n.i m3iw in.n.i msḥw	I trapped lions and brought away crocodiles.
iw d3ir.n.i w3w3yw in.n.i mḏ3yw	I subdued the people of Nubia, and brought away the Medjay.
di.n.i iry.i styw ḥr šmt ṯsmw	I made the Asiatics do the dog walk.

13.

iw ir.n.i n.i pr sẖkrw m nbw	I made my house adorned with gold,
h3wt.f m ḫsbd	its ceilings in lapis-lazuli,
s3rwt m ḥḏ	its walls in silver,
s3tw m mnh3t	its floors in hard stone,
ʿ3w m ḥmt	its doors in copper,
ḳ3ryt m ḥsmn	its bolts of bronze,
ir n ḏt ḥryt ḥḥ ḥr.s	made for eternity, equipped for everlasting life.
iw.i rḫ.kwi m-ḏr ink nb iry r-ḏr	I know this, as it is I who am its Lord of All.

14.

iw ms msyt ʿš3t m mrrwt	Yet there are many lies in the streets,
iw rḫ ḥr tiw wḫ3 ḥr nfrw.f	The wise agree, the fool refutes it,
ḥr-ntt n rḫ.f st šw m ḥr.k	For whoever lacking your sight cannot know it.
s-n-wsrt ʿnḫ wḏ3 snb s3.i	O Senusret (Live! Prosper! Be well!), my son,
rdwy.i ḥr šmt ntk ib.i ḏs.i	My legs leave, but to you alone belongs my own heart,
irty.i ḥr gmḥ.k	Since my eyes saw you,
msy m wnwt nt nfr-ib	born in the hour of happiness,
r-gs ḥnmmt di.sn n.k i3wt	Beside the people of the Sun, as they pay you adoration.

15.

mk ir.n.i ḫr-ḥ3t ṯs.i n.k pḥw	See I have made the past, and ordered what is to come
ink mni n.k nty m ib.i	It is I who gathered together for you what is in my heart.

tw ḥr wꜣḥ ḥḏt n prt-nṯr	You are wearing the White Crown due to the offspring of the god.
ḫtm r st iry m šꜣꜥ.n.i n.k	The seal is in its place, as I ordained for you.
hꜣnw m wiꜣ n rꜥ	There is jubilation in the barque of Ra.
ꜥḥꜥ.n nsyt ḫpr ḫr-ḥꜣt	Kingship has risen, become what it was before.
…	…
sꜥḥꜥ mnw.k smnḫ rwd.k	Raise monuments, embellish your base.
ꜥḥꜣ …	Fight …
ḥr-ntt nn mr.n.f sw	For there is none to be loved
r-gs ḥm.f ꜥnḫ wḏꜣ snb	beside your (?) Agency (Live! Prosper! Be well!)

Sources for Helck 1969 edition:
Papyrus Millingen: this manuscript was seen and copied by A. Peyron in 1843, but since lost. It is dated by the handwriting to the second half of the Eighteenth Dynasty, and is the principal source for its length and clarity.
Early Eighteenth Dynasty writing-boards: Brooklyn I, Brooklyn II, Carnarvon 5
Mid-Eighteenth Dynasty ostraca: four limestone ostraca from the Theban tomb of Senenmut (Hayes 1942: nos. 142 to 145)
Late Eighteenth Dynasty ostraca: one from Malkata (Leahy1978: no. 180), one pottery vessel base from Amarna (Parkinson 1999a)
Late Nineteenth Dynasty manuscripts: British Museum EA 10185 Papyrus Sallier I, British Museum EA 10182 Papyrus Sallier II, Papyrus Berlin 3019; fragment from a Theban tomb (Gardiner 1935b: 140)
Ramesside Period: leather roll Louvre E 4920
Ramesside ostraca, large number, cited in the Helck 1969 edition, pages 1-5

Laments

Middle Kingdom literature includes several compositions dominated by negative descriptions of life. These find parallels in many literatures, including classical Arabic *zuhdiyya* in its more negative guises. In the eleventh century Abu al-Ala al-Maarri wrote:

> If only a child died at its hour of birth and never suckled from its mother in confinement

as if an echo of the pessimistic sentiment in the Lament of Ipuwer

> **No:** the little child (says) I wish I were dead

in the universal human language at a moment of despair over living (cited from Allen 2000, 122). Perhaps closer to Middle Kingdom laments, some expressions of the classical Arabic *ritha* 'elegy' extend beyond a named individual to wider society, as in the lament of Ibn al-Rumi for Basra after its destruction by the Zanj slave-army in the ninth-century (Allen 2000, 96).

Three Middle Kingdom 'laments' are substantially preserved: the dialogue of a Man with his Soul (beginning lost), the lament of Neferty (beginning in the form of a tale, also known in Egyptology as the Prophecy of Neferty), the lament of Ipuwer (beginning lost), and the cycle of laments of Khuninpu (beginning in the form of a tale, known in Egyptology by such 'titles' as the Tale of Khuninpu and, most often if socially misplaced, the Laments of the Eloquent Peasant).

Dialogue of a Man with his Soul

This is one of the most difficult and intriguing literary compositions surviving from Egypt: a man longing for death appears in mid-dialogue with his soul, in Egyptian ba, being the aspect of the person free to move to and from the body after death. The ba tries to persuade the man to enjoy life, and in the exchange the pair explore the meaning and value of life on this earth.

The literary composition in Middle Egyptian is preserved in a single copy on papyrus, dated by its handwriting to the late Middle Kingdom (Papyrus Berlin 3024, with fragments from the start of the roll now Papyrus Amherst III in the Pierpont Morgan Library, New York).

The transliteration of Berlin 3024 follows Barta 1969; the transliteration of Papyrus Amherst III follows Parkinson 2003. The section divisions are introduced for convenience: in the original manuscript, the only formally highlighted section is the red passage presenting the end statement of complete copying.

Fragments Papyrus Amherst III

Fragment H: parts of three lines, only one book-roll sign clear

Fragment I:

[…]*wt ꞽrt st* (?) […]	[…ev]il (?) to do it (?) […]

Fragment L:

[…].. *kꜣ* (?) […]	[…] then (?) […]
[…] *wnwt pw* […]	[…] it is the hour […]
[…] *sw ḥr stꜣ* […]	[…] him ..-ing […]
[…] *s* .. […]	[…] .. […]

Fragment J+K:

[…].. *sꜣt* […]	[…] .. beware (?) […]
[…*m*]*i r.k sbꜣ.i tw* […]	[…C]ome then, let me teach you […]
[…].*k iḫrw n imnt*[…]	[…] you […] adversity (?) of the west […]
[…] *ꞽw s* […]	[…] a man is […]

1. (Papyrus Berlin 3024, lines 1 to 3)

[…].*ṯn r ḏd* […]	[…] you saying […]
n nmʿ.n ns.sn […]*ꞽw ꞽr ẖꜣ*[…]	their tongue is not partial […] … […]
dbꜣw n nmʿ.n ns.sn	exchange, their tongue is not partial

2. (Papyrus Berlin 3024, lines 3 to 10)

ꞽw wp.n.ꞽ r.ꞽ n bꜣ.ꞽ	I opened my mouth to my soul
wšb.ꞽ ḏdt.n.f	to answer what it had said.
ꞽw nꜣ wr r.ꞽ m mꞽn	That is too much for me today.
n mdw bꜣ.ꞽ ḥnʿ.ꞽ	My soul has not spoken with me.
ꞽw grt wr r ʿbʿ	It is too much for exaggerating,
ꞽw mꞽ wsf.ꞽ ꞽm	like abandoning me there.
n šm bꜣ.ꞽ ʿḥʿ.f n.ꞽ ḥr.s	My soul has not travelled, but resists me for it.
[…] *nn* ʿ[…].*f* […].*f*	[…] no […] of it […] of it

m ẖt.i m šnw nwḥ	in my body, in a net of rope.
nn ḫpr m-ꜥ.f rwi.f hrw ḳsn[*t*]	On its own there shall be no escape for it on the day of pain.

3. (Papyrus Berlin 3024, lines 11 to 17)

mtn bꜣ.i ḥr tht.i	See all, my soul leads me astray,
n sḏm.n.i n.f ḥr stꜣs r mwt	I do not obey it, to hasten to death.
n iit(.i) n.f ḥr ḥꜣꜥ ḥr ẖt r smꜣt.i	before (I) have come to it, casting on the fire to burn me.
[…] *mnt.f* […].*f*	[…] its .. […] of it.
tk.f im.i hrw ḳsnt	It shadows me on the day of pain,
ꜥḥꜥ.f m pf gs mi ir nḥpw	stands on that side, as would the pot-turner.
pꜣ is pw prr in.f sw r.f	That is the one who comes out, bringing himself even.

4. (Papyrus Berlin 3024, lines 17 to 22)

bꜣ.i wḫꜣ r sdḥ ꜣh ḥr ꜥnḫ	My soul, too foolish to dull the pain over life,
ihm wi r mwt n iit.i n.f	leading me to death before I have reached it.
snḏm n.i imnt in iw ḳsnt pw	Sweeten the West for me, is that hard?
pẖrt pw ꜥnḫ	Life is a journey round,
iw ḫtw ḫr.sn	trees fall;
ḫndt r.k ḥr isft wꜣḥ mꜣir.i	tread then on evil, put down my misery.

5. (Papyrus Berlin 3024, lines 23 to 30)

wḏꜥ wi ḏḥwty ḥtp nṯrw	Judge me, Thoth, peace of the gods.
ḫsf ḫnsw ḥr.i sš m mꜣꜥt	Defend me, Khons, writer in truth,
sḏm rꜥ mdw.i sgr wiꜣ	Hear my word, Ra, silencer of the sacred boat,
ḫsf isds ḥr.i m ꜥt ḏsr[*t*]	Defend me, Isdes, in the holy chamber,
[*ḫr*]-*ntt sꜣr.i wdn* .. [...]	for my suffering is heavy .. […]
fꜣ.n.f n.i	it has carried to me.
nḏm ḫsf nṯrw štꜣ ẖt.i	Please may the gods repel the secrets of my body.

6. (Papyrus Berlin 3024, lines 30 to 33)

ḏdt.n n.i bꜣ.i	What my soul said to me:
n ntk is s iw.k tr ꜥnḫ	You are not a man, then: are you even alive?
ptr km.k mḥ.k ḥr ꜥnḫ	what do you gain from your care about living,
mi nb ꜥḥꜥw	like a lord of riches?

7. (Papyrus Berlin 3024, lines 33 to 39)

ḏd.i n šm.i iw nfꜣ r tꜣ	I say: I have not gone while this is on earth.
nḥmn tw ḥr tfyt nn nwt.k	Certainly you are fleeing, there will be no support for you.
ḫnri nb ḥr ḏd iw.i r iṯ.k	Every criminal says: I will take you.
iw grt.k mwt rn.k ꜥnḫ	Though you are dead, your name is alive.
st nfꜣ nt ḫnt ꜥfd nt ib	There is the place of resting, the treasure-chest of the heart.
dmi pw imnt ḫnt ḳs […] *ḥr*	The West is the touchpoint, the sailing .. […] ..

8. (Papyrus Berlin 3024, lines 39 to 55)

ir sḏm n.i bꜣ.i iwty btꜣ	If my soul listens to me, as one without hidden thoughts,
twt ib.f ḥnꜥ.i iw.f r mꜥr	and its heart is one with me, it shall be successful,
rdi.i pḥ.f imnt mi nty m mr.f	and I will cause it to reach the West like one who is in his tomb,
ꜥḥꜥ.n ḥry-tꜣ ḥr ḳrs.f	and a survivor stands over his burial.
iw.i r irt nꜣi [*ḥr*] *ḫꜣwt.k*	I will make a shelter (?) [at] your corpse,
sḏdm.k ky bꜣ m nnw	so that you make envious another soul in weariness,
iw.i r irt niꜣi iḫ tm.f ḫsw	I will make a shelter, it is not cold,
sḏdm.k ky bꜣ nt tꜣw	so that you make envious another soul of the heat.
swri.i mw ḥr bꜣbꜣt ṯsy.i šwt	I may drink water at the pool that I may raise the shade,
sḏdm.k ky bꜣ nty ḥkr	so that you make envious another soul which is hungry.
ir ihm.k wi r mwt m pꜣ ḳi	If you lead me to death in this form,
nn gm.k ḫnt.k ḥr.s m imnt	you will not find a place to rest in the West.
wꜣ[*ḥ*] *ib.k bꜣ.i sn*	Be patient, my soul, brother,
r ḫprt iwꜥw drp.ty.fy	until an heir comes who can make offerings,
ꜥḥꜥ.ty.fy ḥr ḫꜣt hrw ḳrs	who can stand at the tomb on the day of burial,
sꜣy.f ḫnkyt nt ḫrt-nṯr	when he tends the bed of the cemetery.

9. (Papyrus Berlin 3024, lines 55 to 68)

iw wp.n n.i b3.i r.f	My soul opened its mouth to me
wšb.f ḏdt.n.i	to answer what I had said:
ir sẖ3.k ḳrs nḥ3t ib pw	If you are recalling burial, it is loss of heart,
int rmyt pw m sind s	it is weeping at the reduction of man,
šdt s pw m pr.f	it is removing a man from his house,
ḫ3ᶜ ḥr ḳ33	casting on high ground.
n pr.n.k r ḥrw m3.k rᶜ	You do not go up to see the sun.
ḳdw m inr n m3ṯ	Those who built in stone, in granite,
ḫws m mrw nfrw m k3t nfrt	The builders of fine tombs in fine work,
ḫpr sḳdw m nṯrw	when the builders are become gods,
ᶜb3w iry wšw mi nnw	their offering-stones are desolate like the weary,
mwt ḥr mryt n g3w ḥry t3	the dead on the shore for lack of a survivor,
iṯ.n nwy pḥwy.fy	when the flood has taken its ends,
šw m mitt iry	the dry light the same.
mdw n.sn rmw spt	The fish at the water tips talk to them.
sḏm r.k n.i	Listen to me now.
mk nfr sḏm n rmṯ	For listening is good for people.
šms hrw nfr smḫ mḥ	Follow the good day, forget cares.

10. (Papyrus Berlin 3024, lines 55 to 85)

iw nḏs sk3.f šdw.f	A fellow ploughs his plot,
iw.f 3tp.f šmw.f r ḫnw dpt	and loads his harvest into the boat.
st3s.f sḳdwt ḥb.f tkn	He tows the sailing. As his feastday approaches,
m3.n.f prt wḫt nt mḥyt	he sees the darkness of the northwind emerge.
rs m dpt rᶜ ḥr ᶜḳ	Awake in the boat, as the sun goes in,
pr ḥnᶜ ḥmt.f msw.f	he goes out with his wife and his children,
3ḳ tp š šn m grḥ ḫr mryt	and is wrecked on the lake of crocodiles in a night infested.
ḏr.in.f ḥms psš.f m ḫrw ḥr ḏd	Then he manages to sit, and is split in a cry saying:
n rm.i n tf3 mswt	I did not weep for that mother-to-be,
nn n.s prt m imnt r kt ḥr t3	who cannot come from the West to another on earth;
mḥy.i ḥr msw.s sdw m swḥt	I think of her children smashed in the egg,
m3w ḥr n ḫnty n ᶜnḫt.sn	seeing the face of the Crocodile, before they have lived.
iw nḏs dbḥ.f mšrwt	A fellow asks for an evening meal,
iw ḥmt.f ḏd.s n.f iw r msyt	his wife tells him, it is for the late meal,
iw.f pr.f r ḫntw r ssṯ (?) r 3t	he goes outdoors to … for a while.
ᶜnn.f sw r pr.f iw.f mi ky	When he returns to his house, he is like another man,
ḥmt.f ḥr šs3 n.f n sḏm.n.f n.s	his wife pleads with him, he cannot hear her.
sṯ.n.f wš ib n wpwtyw	He has felt the heart-searing of the envoys.

11. (Papyrus Berlin 3024, lines 85 to 103)

iw wp.n.i r.i n b3.i	I opened my mouth to my soul
wšb.i ḏdt.n.f	to answer what it had said:
mk bᶜḥ rn.i m-ᶜ.k	See my name reeks with you,
r st 3sw m hrw šmw pt t3t	more than the smell of meat on a summer day of burning sky
mk bᶜḥ rn.i m-ᶜ.k	See my name reeks with you,
šsp sbnw m hrw r sf pt t3t	a haul of dead fish on trawling days of burning sky
mk bᶜḥ rn.i m-ᶜ.k	See my name reeks with you,
r sti 3psw r bw3t nt tri ḫr msyt	more than the smell of geese, more than reed lairs full of chicks
mk bᶜḥ rn.i m-ᶜ.k	See my name reeks with you,
r sti ḥ3mw r ḫ3sw nw sšw ḥ3m.n.sn	more than the smell of fishermen, more than nest pools where they fish
mk bᶜḥ rn.i m-ᶜ.k	See my name reeks with you,
r sti msḥw r ḥmst	more than the smell of crocodiles, more than a hut
ḫr sp3wt ḫr mrryt	by infested regions
mk bᶜḥ rn.i m-ᶜ.k	See my name reeks with you,
r st ḥmt ḏd grg r.s n ṯᶜy	more than a wife of whom lies are told to the husband
mk bᶜḥ rn.i m-ᶜ.k	See my name reeks with you,
r ḫrd ḳn ḏd r.f iw.f iw.f n msdw.f	more than a bold child told that he he is hated

mk bꜥḥ rn.i m-ꜥ.k	See my name reeks with you,
dmi n msḥ šnn bštw mꜣꜣ sꜣ.f	a quay of the crocodile, plotting attack on seeing his back

12. (Papyrus Berlin 3024, lines 103 to 130)

ḏd.i n-m min	Who do I speak to today?
snw bin ḫnmsw nw min n mr.ny	Brothers are evil, friends of today do not love.
ḏd.i n-m min	Who do I speak to today?
ꜥwn ibw s nb ḥr iṯt ḫt snw.fy	Hearts are greedy, every man robs the goods of his neighbour
iw sf ꜣḳ nḫt ḥr hꜣb n bw nb	Kindness is perished, the strong are sending (the orders) to everyone
ḏd.i n-m min	Who do I speak to today?
ḥtp ḥr bin	there is contentment with evil,
rdi r.f bw nfr r tꜣ m st nbt	goodness is cast to the ground everywhere
ḏd.i n-m min	Who do I speak to today?
sḫꜥr s m sp.f bin	he who should enrage a man with his deed,
ssbt.f bw nb iw.f ḏw	makes everyone laugh by his evil
ḏd.i n-m min	Who do I speak to today?
iw ḥꜥdꜣ.tw s nb ḥr iṯt snwy.f	people are violent, everyone is robbing his neighbour
ḏd.i n-m min	Who do I speak to today?
btꜣ m ꜥḳ ib sn irr ḥnꜥ.f ḫpr m ḫfty	the criminal is the intimate, the brother in action has become an enemy
ḏd.i n-m min	Who do I speak to today?
n sḫꜣ.t(w) sf n ir.t(w) n ir m tꜣ ꜣt	the past is not remembered, the helper is not helped in this moment
ḏd.i n-m min	Who do I speak to today?
snw bin inn.tw m ḏrḏrw r mtt nt ib	Brothers are evil, strangers have to be fetched for advising the heart
ḏd.i n-m min	Who do I speak to today?
ibw ḥtm s nb m ḥr m ḫrw r snw.f	hearts are laid waste, every man is downcast against his brothers
ḏd.i n-m min	Who do I speak to today?
ibw ꜥwn nn wn ib n s r hn.tw ḥr.f	hearts are greedy, no man has a heart that can be leaned on
ḏd.i n-m min	Who do I speak to today?
nn mꜣꜥtyw tꜣ sp n irw isft	there are no good people, the land is left to the evil doers
ḏd.i n-m min	Who do I speak to today?
iw šw m ꜥḳ ib	there is a lack of people to trust,
inn.tw m ḫmm r srḫt n.f	the unknown is brought in to be complained to
ḏd.i n-m min	Who do I speak to today?
nn hr ib pfꜣ šm ḥnꜥ.f nn sw wn	there is no-one glad at heart: that one I walked with, exists no more
ḏd.i n-m min	Who do I speak to today?
iw.i ꜣtp.kwi ḫr mꜣir n gꜣw ꜥḳ ib	I am burdened with misery, for lack of someone to trust
ḏd.i n-m min	Who do I speak to today?
nf ḥw tꜣ nn wn pḥwy.fy	Strife has struck the land, there is no end to it

12. (Papyrus Berlin 3024, lines 130 to 142)

iw mwt m ḥr.i m min	Death is in my sight today
snb mr	health to the sick,
mi prt r ḫntw r-sꜣ ihmt	like going out front after grieving
iw mwt m ḥr.i m min	Death is in my sight today
mi sti ꜥntyw	like the scent of myrrh,
mi ḥmst ḫr ḥtꜣw hrw ṯꜣw	like sitting under the sails on a windy day
iw mwt m ḥr.i m min	Death is in my sight today
mi sti sšnw	like the scent of lotus flowers,
mi ḥmst ḥr mryt nt tḫt	like sitting on the shore of drunkenness
iw mwt m ḥr.i m min	Death is in my sight today
mi wꜣt ḥwyt	like the path of rain,
mi iw s m mšꜥ r pr.sn	like the return of a man from the army to their home
iw mwt m ḥr.i m min	Death is in my sight today
mi kft pt	like the unveiling of the sky,
mi s sḫt im r ḫmt.n.f	like a man tracking down what he had forgotten
iw mwt m ḥr.i m min	Death is in my sight today
mi ꜣbb s mꜣꜣ pr.sn	like the desire of a man to see their home,
ir.n.f rnpt ꜥšꜣt iṯ m ndrt	after spending many years taken into captivity.

13. (Papyrus Berlin 3024, lines 142 to 147)

wnn ms nty im m nṯr ꜥnḫ	The one who is there, though, exists as a living god,
ḥr ḫsf iww n irr sw	avenging wrongdoing on the one who commits it;
wnn ms nty im ꜥḥꜥ m wiꜣ	the one who is there exists standing in the sun-boat,
ḥr rdit di.t(w) stpt im r rw-prw	having choice offerings made from there to the temples;
wnn ms nty im m rḫ ḫt	the one who is there exists as a man of knowledge,
n ḫsf.n.t(w).f ḥr spr n rꜥ ḫft mdw.f	who is not stopped at appeal to Ra as he speaks.

14. (Papyrus Berlin 3024, lines 147 to 154)

ḏdt.n n.i bꜣ	What the soul said to me:
imi r.k nḫwt ḥr ḫꜣꜣ	place your complaints on the pile,
ny-sw.i pn sn.i	my own, here, my brother.
wdn.k ḥr ꜥḫ	You may offer on the altar,
dmi-ꜥḥꜣ.k ḥr ꜥnḫ mi ḏd.k	and touch/fight over life as you say:
mr wi ꜥꜣ win n.k imnt	love me here, hold up the West for yourself;
mr ḥm pḥ.k imnt	love, still, to reach the West,
sꜣḥ ḫꜥw.k tꜣ	when your body may touch the earth,
ḫny.i r-sꜣ wrd.k	and I may alight after you rest weary.
iḫ ir.n dmi n sp	So may we make a dwelling together.

End note (Papyrus Berlin 3024, lines 154-155)
iw.f pw ḥꜣt.f r pḥwy.fy mi gmyt m sš
This is its completion, from start to finish, as found in writing.

The Lament of Neferty

This literary composition in Middle Egyptian, probably dating to the Middle Kingdom (about 2025-1700 BC), is set in the court of king Sneferu (reigned about 2650 BC). A lector-priest named Neferty is summoned to entertain the king with his fine language. Sneferu himself writes down the words of Neferty, who describes a future in which Egypt is overrun by foreigners and strife, until a king Ameny comes from the south to restore order. The historical setting is a literary device familiar from other Middle Egyptian works, such as the Tales at the court of king Khufu (preserved on one manuscript only, Papyrus Westcar). The dramatic juxtaposition of chaos and restored order is another literary device recurrent in Middle Egyptian literature, notably in the genre of Laments, such as the Lament of Ipuwer (also known from just one manuscript, see below). The composition emphasises the glory of king Ameny, possibly one or all of the four kings of the Twelfth Dynasty named Amenemhat, or a king of the Thirteenth Dynasty; most plausibly the reference is to king Amenemhat I, who seems to have consolidated the reunification of Egypt achieved under the Eleventh Dynasty. However, with this as with other compositions, it should be noted that the exact date and authorship were not recorded on any surviving sources.

The transliteration follows Helck 1970b, using the copy on Papyrus Hermitage 1116B as principal source. The section divisions are those of Helck 1970b: after each section number are given the corresponding line-numbers in Papyrus Hermitage 1116B.

1. (Papyrus Hermitage 1116B, lines 1 to 8)

ḫpr.n swt wnn *ḥm n nswt bity snfrw mꜣꜥ ḫrw m nswt mnḫ m tꜣ pn r-ḏr.f*
wꜥ m nn hrw ḫpr ꜥḳ pw ir.n ḳnbt nt ḫnw r pr-ꜥꜣ [ꜥnḫ wḏꜣ] snb r nḏ ḫrt
prt pw ir.n.sn nḏ.sn ḫrt mi nt-ꜥ.sn nt rꜥ nb
ḏd.in ḥm.f ꜥnḫ wḏꜣ snb n ḫtmw nty r-gs.f
isy in n.i ḳnbt nt ḫnw prt ꜥꜣ r nḏ ḫrt m hrw pn
stꜣ in.tw n.f ḥr-ꜥ
wn.in.sn ḥr ḫt.sn m-bꜣḥ ḥm.f ꜥnḫ wḏꜣ snb m wḥm-ꜥ
ḏd.in ḥm.f ꜥnḫ wḏꜣ snb n.sn
rḫw mtn rdi.n.i iꜣš.tw n.tn
r rdit ḏꜥr.tn n.i sꜣ.tn m sꜣꜣ sn.tn m iḳr
ḫnms.tn wd sp nfr ḏd.ty.fy n.i nhw n mdt nfrt
ṯsw stpw dꜣy ḥr n [ḥm].i n sḏm st
rdi.in.sn ḥr ḫt.sn m-bꜣḥ ḥm.f ꜥnḫ wḏꜣ snb m wḥm-ꜥ

It happened that the Person of the dual king Sneferu true of voice was the good king in this entire land.
One day it happened that the council of the Residence entered the Palace, [life, prosperity], health!, for the audience.
They emerged after they had made their audience in their regular daily manner.
Then His Power, may he live, prosper and be well, said to the sealer who was beside him
'Hurry and bring me the council of the Residence that went here for the audience today'
Back they were brought at once,
and they were on their stomachs in the presence of His Power, may he live, prosper, be well, a second time.
Then His Power, may he live, prosper and be well, said to them
'Comrades, look, I have had you summoned,
to have you seek out for me a son of yours who is wise, a brother of yours who is excellent,
a friend of yours who can strike the right chord, who will tell me some fine words ,
some choice phrases to entertain My [Power] at hearing them.'
Then they were placed on their stomachs in the presence of His Power, may he live, prosper, be well, a second time.

2. (Papyrus Hermitage 1116B, lines 8 to 17)

ḏd.in.sn ḫft *ḥm.f ꜥnḫ wḏꜣ snb*	**Then they said before** His Power, may he live, prosper and be well,
iw ḫry-ḥbt ꜥꜣ n bꜣst ity nb.n	There is a great lector of Bast, O sovereign our lord,
nfrty rn.f	called Neferty.
nds pw ḳn gꜣb.f sš pw iḳr n ḏbꜥw.f fingers,	he is a fellow valiant in his arm, he is a writer excellent in his
špss pw ꜥꜣ n.f ḫt r mity.f nb	he is a rich man, with more wealth than any of his equals,
ḥwy in.tw.f mꜣꜣ ḥm.f	let him be brought for His Power to see him.
ḏd.in ḥm.f ꜥnḫ wḏꜣ snb	Then His Power, may he live, prosper and be well, said

is in n.i sw	Go and bring him to me.
stꜣ.in.tw.f n.f ḥr-ꜥwy	Then he was brought to him at once.
wn.in.f ḥr ẖt.f	and he was on his stomach
m-bꜣḥ ḥm.f ꜥnḫ wḏꜣ snb	in the presence of His Power, may he live, prosper and be well.
ḏd.in ḥm.f ꜥnḫ wḏꜣ snb	Then His Power, may he live, prosper and be well, said
mi m nfrty ḫnms	Come then, Neferty, friend,
ḏd.k n.i nh n mdt nfrt ṯsw stpw	Tell me some fine words, choice phrases
ḏꜣy ḥr n ḥm.i n sdm st	to entertain My Power at hearing them.
ḏd.in ẖry-ḥbt nfrty	And the lector Neferty said,
in iw ḫprt in iw ḫprt.f sy	(on) what has happened, or what is to happen,
ity ꜥnḫ wḏꜣ snb nb.[i]	O sovereign, may he live, prosper and be well, my lord?
ḏd.in ḥm.f ꜥnḫ wḏꜣ snb	So His Power, may he live, prosper and be well, said
m ḫprt st swt min is ḫpr swꜣ.f	on what is to happen, for today is already happened and gone
ꜥḥꜥ.n dwn.n.f drt.f r hn n ẖrt-ꜥ	And he stretched out his hand to the chest of writing equipment
ꜥḥꜥ.n šd.n.f n.f šfdw ḥnꜥ gsti	and took out a papyrus roll and writing palette,
wn.in.f ḥr irt m sšw	and prepared to write down
ḏdt.n ẖry-ḥbt nfrty	what the lector Neferty would say,
rḫ ḫt pw n iꜣbt ny-sw bꜣst m wbn.s	as a man of knowledge of the East, belonging to Bast in her rising,
msw pw n ḥkꜣ-ꜥnḏ	as a child of the province Ruler-Anedj.

3. (Papyrus Hermitage 1116B, lines 17 to 21)

iw.f mḥ.f ḥr ḫprt m tꜣ	He gathered his thoughts on the events in the land,
iw.f sḫꜣ.f ḳni n iꜣbtt	he recalled the turmoil of the East,
ḫpw ꜥꜣmw m ḫpšw.sn	the rampage of Asiatics with their forces,
sh.sn ibw n ntyw ḥr šmw	disrupting the hearts of those at harvest,
nḥm.sn ḥtrw ḥr skꜣ	seizing those yoked in ploughing.
ḏd.f	He said:
ḫws ib.i rm.k tꜣ pn šꜣꜥ.n.k im.f	stir yourself, my heart, as you weep for this land where you started,
gr m iwḥ	silence would be refreshment.
mk wn ḏd.ti r.f m stryt	Look, what is said of it should (inspire) respect,
mk rf wn wr m ptḫ šꜣꜥ.n.k im tꜣ	look, now, the great is sent sprawling there where you started, the land.

4. (Papyrus Hermitage 1116B, lines 21 to 23)

***m wrd mk st** ḥft-ḥr.k*	**Do not tire: look at it** before you,
ꜥḥꜥ.k r ntt m-bꜣḥ.k	Stand up to what is in front of you,
mk rf wn wrw m sḫrw nw tꜣ	Look, now, the great are in the condition of the land,
iryt m tmt-ir šꜣꜥ rꜥ m grg	what was made is become unmade, Ra (must) begin his creation.
tꜣ ꜣḳw r-ꜣw n ḫpr ḏꜣt	The land is destroyed entirely, nothing is left over,
nn sp km n ꜥnt m šꜣt.f	there is not a trace of the fingernail in its fixed place.

5. (Papyrus Hermitage 1116B, lines 24 to 26)

***ḥḏ tꜣ pn** nn mḥ ḥr.f*	**This land is destroyed** without any to care for it,
nn ḏd nn ir rmw	any to speak up, any to make lament,
wnn tꜣ pn m-m	what will become of this land?
itn ḥbs	The sun disk is a being concealed,
nn psd.f mꜣꜣ rḫyt	and will not shine for the people to see,
nn ꜥnḫ.tw ḥbsw šnꜥ	and noone can live, when the clouds are covered.
wn.in.s ḥr-nb id m gꜣ.f	Then they are, every one, deafened in its absence.
iw.i r ḏd nty ḫft-ḥr.i	I am to say what is before me,
n sr.n.i ntt n iy	I am not prophesying what has not happened.

6. (Papyrus Hermitage 1116B, lines 26 to 30)

***itrw** šw nw kmt*	**The river** of Egypt is dry,
dꜣ.tw mw ḥr rdwy	the water is crossed on foot.
tw r ḥḥ mw n ꜥḥꜥw r sḳdw.f	Water is sought for boats for its sailings.
wꜣt.f ḫpr.ti m wḏb	Its course is turned into riverbank,
iw wḏb r nt	its riverbank into flood,
st mw r nty m st wḏb	the place of water into what should be the place of the shore.
iw rsw r ḫsf m mḥyt	The south wind does battle with the north wind,

nn pt m ṯꜣw wꜥ	there will be not one wind for the sky.
iw ꜣpdw ḏrḏri r mst	Alien birds will give birth
m ẖꜣt nt tꜣ-mḥw	in the pool of the Delta.
ir.n.f sš ḥr gswy	It has made a nest on the (Delta) fringes,
stkn sw rmṯ n gꜣw	and people approach it out of famine.

7 (Papyrus Hermitage 1116B, lines 30 to 35)

***ḥḏ nḥmn nfꜣ** n bw nfr*	**Utterly destroyed are those (times)** of happiness
nꜣ n šw ḳꜥhw	at those basin lakes,
wnyw ẖr wgs wbnw ẖr rmw ꜣpdw	with men set to slitting fish, overflowing with fish and fowl.
bw nfr nb rwi ptẖ m tꜣ n ḳsnt	All happiness has departed, flung down in the land of hardship,
m-ꜥ nfꜣ n ḏfꜣw styw ḫtyw tꜣ	from those supplies to the Asiatics who are throughout the land.
iw ḫrw ḫpr ḥr iꜣbtt	Men of violence have emerged in the East,
iw ꜥꜣmw hꜣt r kmt	Asiatics are coming down into Egypt,
gꜣ.tw ḫnrt ky r-gs nn sḏmm n.f	The confines are lost, another is beside, who will not be heard.
tw r isḳ mꜣḳt m grḥ	The ladder will be blocked in the night,
tw r ꜥḳ ḫnrtw	the camps will be entered,
tw r snbt ḳdd m irty	the bleary-eyed will be overpowered,
sḏr ḥr iw.i rs.kwi	as the sleeper says 'I am awake'.

8 (Papyrus Hermitage 1116B, lines 35 to 40)

***ꜥwt ḫꜣst r s**wri ḥr itrw nw kmt*	**Herds of foreign lands will d**rink from the rivers of Egypt
ḳbb.sn ḥr wḏbw.sn	They will be refreshed on their shores,
n gꜣ stri st	for want of any to drive them back.
iw tꜣ pn iṯ int	This land is to be taken and carried off,
n rḫ bs ḫpr.ty.fy imn m ḏd	unaware of the onset of what will happen, hidden in the saying:
ptr sḏm ḥr idw iw gr ḫft-ḥr	Look out, the hearer is going deaf, the silent one is before (us).
di.i n.k tꜣ m sny mn	I give you the land in the passing of evil -
tm ḫpr ḫpr	what should not happen, happens
tw r ššp ḫꜥw nw ꜥḥꜣ ꜥnḫ tꜣ m shꜣ	Weapons of war will be taken up, as the land lives in turmoil.

9 (Papyrus Hermitage 1116B, lines 40 to 45)

iw.tw r irt ꜥḥꜣw m ḥmt	**Weapons will be made of copper**
dbḥ.tw t snf	the bread they request will be blood,
sbt.tw m sbt n mr	they will burst into laughter at grief,
nn rm.tw n mwt	no-one will weep at death,
nn sḏr.tw ḫkr n mwt	no-one will sleep hungry for want for death,
ib n s m-sꜣ.f ḏs.f	and the heart of a man will only be after himself.
nn ir.tw sꜣmwt min	No mourning will be observed today -
ib stni n ḥr.s r-ꜣw	the heart is turned entirely to itself.
ḥms s r kꜥḥ.f sꜣ.f ky ḥr smꜣ ky	A man rests on his side - at his back one man kills another.
di.i n.k sꜣ m ḫrwy	I can show you the son as attacker,
sn m ḫfty s ḥr smꜣ it.f	the brother as enemy, man murdering his father.

10 (Papyrus Hermitage 1116B, lines 45 to 49)

r nb mḥ m mr wi	**Every mouth is filled with 'love me'**
***bw nfr** nb rwi*	**Happiness** is all gone
ꜣḳ tꜣ šꜣ.tw r.f hp	The land is laid waste, even though law is decreed for it,
ḥḏd m iryt wš.tw m gmyt	Destruction is a fact - ruin is reality.
iryt m tmmt ir.tw	What was done is undone.
nḥm ḫt s r.f rdi n nty m rwty	A man's property is taken from him, and given to the outsider.
di.i n.k nb m nhp rwty ḥtp	Let me show you the master in grief, the outsider in peace.
tm ir mḥ.n.f ir šw	The one who never received his fill, can now go and empty.
tw r rdit ḫt msdd r sgr r mdw	Goods are given out only hatefully, to silence the mouth of the speaker.
wšb.tw ṯs ꜥ pr ḥr ḫt	The phrase is answered at the arm raised with a stick,
mdw.tw m smꜣ sw	and people speak by murder.

11 (Papyrus Hermitage 1116B, lines 49 to 54)

***ẖn n mdt ḥr ib** mi ḫt*	**Speech alights on the heart** like fire
nn wḫd.n.tw pr n r	No-one can bear a word from the mouth.
ʿnd tꜣ ʿšꜣ ḫrpw.f	The land is poor, but rich in directors,
wš.f ʿꜣ bꜣkw.f	It lies ruined, but its labours are great
ktt it wr itp	The harvest is small, the grain-measure great,
ḫꜣʿ.tw.s m wbn	and must be measured out in daylight.
iw rʿ iwd.f sw rmṯ	Ra distances himself from mankind.
wbn.f wn wnwt	He rises and the hour is there,
nn rḫ.tw ḫpr mtrt	but no-one knows if midday will come.
nn tn.tw šwt	Shadows cannot be made out,
nn bꜣḳ ḥr dgꜣ.tw	sight cannot shine at being watched,
nn ibḥ irty m mw	eyes cannot brim with water,
wnn.f m pt mi iʿḥ	as he is there in the sky like the moon,
nn th nw.f nw šsꜣ	and his time for knowing cannot be impaired.
wn is stwt.f m ḥr	Yet his rays are in sight,
m sp m imyw-ḥꜣt	in the (same) moments as for the ancestors.

12 (Papyrus Hermitage 1116B, lines 54 to 57)

di.i n.k tꜣ m sny mny	**I give you the land in the passing of evil**
sꜣ ʿ m nb ʿ	the powerless is now powerful,
tw nḏ ḫrt nḏ ḫrt	the one who should greet receives the greeting,
di.i n.k ḫry r ḥry	I can show you the lower made the upper,
pḫr.ti m-sꜣ pḫr ḫt	stirred around after stirring around the body.
ʿnḫ.tw m ḫrt-nṯr	People live in a cemetery,
iw ḥwrw r irt ʿḥʿ wrt r .. r ḫpr	and the humble will acquire great wealth until [uproar] breaks out.
in šwꜣw wnm.sn t	It is the beggars who can eat bread,
bꜣkw bḥḳw	the labourers who enforce labour (?).
nn wn ḥḳꜣ-ʿnḏ r tꜣ msḫnt nt nṯr nb	The Sun-god Province can no longer be birth place of any god.

13 (Papyrus Hermitage 1116B, lines 57 to 61)

*nswt **pw r iyt n rsy***	There is a king **who will come from the south**
imny mꜣʿ ḫrw rn.f	Ameny true of voice is his name.
sꜣ ḥmt pw n tꜣ sty	He is the son of a woman of the Land of the Bow,
ms pw n ẖn nḫn	he is a child of the Heartland of Nekhen.
iw.f r šsp [ḥḏ]t	He will take up the [White] Crown,
iw.f r wṯs dšrt	he will raise up the Red Crown,
iw.f smꜣ sḫmty	he will unite the Two Mighty Goddesses,
iw.f r sḥtp nbwy	he will appease the Two Lord Gods,
m mrt.sn	with what they desire.
pḫr iḥy m ḫfʿ wsr m nwd	The field circuit is in his grasp, the oar in the jump.

14 (Papyrus Hermitage 1116B, lines 61 to 65)

***ršy** rmṯ nt hꜣw.f*	**Rejoice** O people of his time
sꜣ n s r irt rn.f	The son of a man will make his name
r nḥḥ ḥnʿ ḏt	for eternity and everlasting time.
wꜣyw r ḏwt kꜣyw sbiw	Those who fall into evil, or plan treason,
sḫr.n.sn r.sn n snd.f	they will be overthrown on themselves for fear of him,
iw ʿꜣmw r ḫr n šʿt.f	the Asiatics will fall at his slaughter,
timḥw r ḫr n nswt.f	the Libyans will fall at his fire,
iw sbiw nw nḏnḏ.f	the rebels at his force,
ḫꜣkw-ib n šfšft.f	the evil-hearted at his majesty.
iw ʿrʿt imt ḫnty	The rising cobra who is in the palace
ḥr shrt n.f ḫꜣkw ib	will overpower the evil-hearted for him.

15 (Papyrus Hermitage 1116B, lines 65 to 71)

***tw r ḳd inbw** ḥḳꜣ ʿnḫ wḏꜣ snb*	**They will build** the Walls of the Ruler life, prosperity, health!
nn rdit hꜣy ʿꜣmw r kmt	to prevent the Asiatics from coming down into Egypt
dbḥ.sn mw mi sḫrw šsꜣ	when they request water in skilled manner,
r rdit swri ʿwt.sn	to let their flocks drink.

ỉw mꜣꜥt r ỉyt r st.s	What is Right is returned to its place,
ỉsft dr.tỉ r rwty	and evil is expelled.
ršy gmḥ.ty.fy	Rejoice whoever will see,
wnn.ty.fy ḥr šms nswt	whoever will live in the following of the king.
ỉw rḫ ḫt r stỉ n.ỉ mw	The wise man will pour water for me,
mꜣꜣ.f ḏdt.n.ỉ ḫpr	when he sees what I have said come to pass.

Lament of Neferty: sources used in Helck 1970b

Principal sources (Dynasty 18):

- Papyrus Hermitage 1116B
- Writing board Cairo CG 25224
- Writing board British Museum EA 5647

Ramesside ostraca:

- Ashmolean Museum, Gardiner 326, 331, 371-2
- British Museum EA 5627
- Deir el-Medina 1074, 1182-9
- Liverpool 13624M
- Michaeilides 9
- Petrie 38, UC 39637
- Turin (number not cited)
- Vandier collection

The Lament of Ipuwer

A man named Ipuwer laments the condition of Egypt, prey to social disorder and reversal of classes, and to uncontrolled incursions by foreigners; he is speaking to the Lord of All (a term used for the king and for the creator god). Early Egyptological commentators interpreted the composition as a direct reflection of events in the First Intermediate Period, but such literal political reading has generally since been replaced by greater appreciation of the literary effect and intent of the contrast between ideal order and lamented chaos. The relation between literature and political history is almost impossible to assess, in the absence of precise datings for literary compositions, and this is highlighted by the Lament of Ipuwer: large foreign population built up along the eastern Delta fringe in the early to mid Thirteenth Dynasty, and therefore the Lament would have quite different impact on a reader in the late Twelfth and a reader in the late Thirteenth Dynasty - unfortunately, this does not help directly to date the composition.

The composition is in Middle Egyptian, preserved in a single copy on papyrus, dated by its handwriting to the early Nineteenth Dynasty (Papyrus Leiden I 344). The other side of the papyrus bears a copy of a long New Kingdom literary hymn to the god Amun. The Lament of Ipuwer is dated to the late Middle Kingdom by the name of the key speaker Ipuwer and by titles and institutions mentioned within it (notably *ẖnrt* and *ẖnrt wr*). The beginning and end of the composition are not preserved; of the surviving portion, pages one and eight to seventeen are incomplete, increasingly so towards the end of the roll.

The transliteration follows Gardiner 1909a. My section divisions have been introduced for convenience.

1. (Papyrus Leiden I 344, column 1, lines 1-9)

[… ỉryw]-ꜥꜣ ḥr šm n ḥꜣḳ n.n	[…] door[-keepers] are going to 'plunder for ourselves'
bnrytyw […]	confectioners […]
n ḏd rḫtyw fꜣt ꜣtpw.f n ꜥ[…	fullers refuse to carry his load …[…
… grg?]-ꜣpdw ṯs n.sn skw […	…] bird-[trappers] raise troops for themselves […]
… ỉ]dḥw ẖr ỉkmw	the Delta[-dwellers] bear shields,
ꜥtḫw […] *snm*	brewers […] nourishment,
mꜣꜣ s sꜣ.f m ḫrwy.f	a man sees his son as his enemy,
shꜣ […] *swt ky*	strife […] another though.
mi ḥr ḫpš wpwt […] *nꜣy*	Come with the strength of a mission […] those,
šꜣt n.tn m rk ḥr m hꜣw […]	what was ordained for you all in the reign of Horus, in the time […]
šm nb ḳd m ỉrtyw m-ꜥ ḫprt m tꜣ	The master of restraint walks in mourning from the events in the land.
ỉw šm […]	There went […],
ḫꜣstyw (?) *ḫpr m rmṯ m st nb*	foreigners (?) become people everywhere

2. (Papyrus Leiden I 344, column 1, line 9 to column 2, line 4)

ỉw ms *ḥr ꜥꜣdw* […]*.tw srt.n tpyw-ꜥ*	**No:** the face is pale […] what the ancestors foretold,
sprw r […]	arriving at […]
[***ỉw ms*** …] *rww* (?) […]	**No:** … moving (?) […]
[…] *tp tꜣ ẖr smꜣyw*	[…] upon earth under plotters,
šm s r skꜣ ỉn(?).f ỉkm.f	a man goes to plough and takes his shield
ỉw ms *sf ḥr ḏd sny* […]	**No:** the merciful says: pass (?) […]
[…] *ḥr.ỉ m nty wn*	[…] in my sight as one who exists
ỉw ms *ḥr ꜥꜣdw pḏt grg*	**No:** the face is pale, the bow ready,
ꜥḏꜣ m st nbt nn s n sf	violence is everywhere, with noone from yesterday.
ỉw ms *ḥꜣḳw* […] *m st nbt*	**No:** plunder […] everywhere,
bꜣk ẖry ỉṯ r gm.f	the lowly servant is stealing as much as he finds.
ỉw ms *ḥꜥpy ḥr ḥw n skꜣ.tw n.f*	**No:** the flood strikes, but there has been no ploughing for him,
s nb ḥr n rḫ.n ḫprt ḫt tꜣ	everyone says: we do not know what is happening throughout the land.
ỉw ms *ḥmwt wšr n ỉwr.n.tw*	**No:** women are barren, none conceive,
n ḳd.n ẖnmw m-ꜥ sḫrw tꜣ	Khnum does not create, from the condition of the land.

3. (Papyrus Leiden I 344, column 2, lines 4 to 9)

ỉw ms *šwꜣw ḫpr m nbw špss*	**No:** beggars have become lords of riches,
tm ỉrt n.f tbty m nb ꜥḥꜥw	one who did not even have sandals made for him is a lord of wealth.
ỉw ms *ḥmw ỉry ỉb.sn snm*	**No:** their servants, their hearts are fed,
n snsn.n srw rmṯ.sn nhm	officials do not mingle with their people in celebration.
ỉw ms .. *sḫm ỉꜣdt ḫt tꜣ snf m st nbt*	**No:** .. plague reigns throughout the land, blood is everywhere,

n ḳꜣn n mwt wnḫyt ḥr ḏd	death unlimited, the shroud is speaking
n tkn im.st	before it has been approached.
***iw ms** mwt ꜥšꜣ ḳrs m itrw*	**No:** death is multiplied, burials in the river,
nwy m ḫꜣt ḫpr is wꜥbt m nwy	the floodwater is the tomb, while the chapel has become a flood
***iw ms** špsw m nḫwt šwꜣw ḫr ršwt*	**No:** nobles are in grief, beggars in joy,
niwt nb ḥr imi dr.n ḳnw m-m.n	every town says: come let us drive out the brave among us.
***iw ms** rmṯ mi gmw sbw ḫt tꜣ*	**No:** people are like waterbirds, filth pervades the land,
nn ms ḥḏ ḥbsw n pꜣ n rk	there can now be no shining of cloth, in such a time.
***iw ms** tꜣ ḥr msnḥ mi nhp*	**No:** the land is turning like a potter's-wheel.
ꜥwꜣy m nb ꜥḥꜥw [...] m ḥꜣḳw	The weak is now lord of riches, […] is the plunderer.
***iw ms** kfꜣw ibw [..] iꜣ […]*	**No:** the trustworthy […] cry [out? …]
nḏs ḥrw iry.i m	the small man is terrified: what am I to do?

4. (Papyrus Leiden I 344, column 2, lines 9 to 14)

***iw ms** itrw m snf*	**No:** the river is now blood,
swri.tw im.f nyw.tw m rmṯ ib.tw mw	drinking from it, you recoil from people and thirst for water
***iw ms** sbḫt wḫꜣw ḏriwt ꜣmm*	**No:** gates, columns, walls are set on fire,
ḏrwt n pr nswt ꜥnḫ wḏꜣ snb mn rwd	the wall of the King's House life! prosperity! health! is firm, solid.
***iw ms** swḥꜣ dpt rsy*	**No:** the ship of the south is capsized,
ḫbꜣ šmꜥ ḫpr [..]yw šwy	Upper Egypt is hacked down, turned into dried ground.
***iw ms** msḥ[..]ꜣfy pꜣ rmw n iṯ.n.sn*	**No:** the crocodile[s?] are fat on fish, and do not snatch,
šm n.sn rmṯ ḏs iry ḥḏ pw n nn.tw	but people go to them of themselves. This is destruction! Or not!
ḏd.tw m dgꜣs ꜥꜣ mk sy šnw	People say: do not walk here, it is infested,
mk ḫnd.tw […] mi rmw	[…] tread as fish (?).
n tnw sw snd m-ꜥ ḥry ib	The fearful has not noticed it out of the terror of heart.
***iw ms** rmṯ ꜥnd*	**No:** people are too few
dd sn.f m tꜣ m st nbt	to place his brother in the ground, everywhere.
mdw rḫw ḫt […].f […].f ꜣw	The wise speaks […] of him, his/he […] ..
***iw ms** sꜣ s [..] g[ꜣ]w siꜣ.f*	**No:** the son of a man […], his insight is lacking (?),
ḫpr ms nbt.f m sꜣ ḥmt.f	the child of his lady has become son of his servantwoman

5. (Papyrus Leiden I 344, column 3, lines 1 to 6)

*[**iw**] **ms** dšrt ḫt tꜣ ḫꜣswt ḫbꜣ […]*	**No:** the desert covers the land, the desert-hills are hacking up […]
psḏt rwty iy.ti n kmt	the tribe from abroad has arrived in Egypt
***iw ms** sprt [...]*	**No:** […] are reached […]
nn ms wn rmṯ m st nb	but there are no longer any people anywhere.
***iw ms** nbw ḫsbd ḥḏ mfkꜣt*	**No:** gold and lapis, silver and turquoise,
ḥmgt ḥsmn ibht [...].n (?)	precious stone and bronze, .. […] ..
[…]ḫw r ḫḫw n ḥmt	[bed]eck the necks of servantwomen,
špsst ḫt tꜣ nbt-prw ḥr ḏd	while rich women roam the land, ladies of the house say:
ḥꜣ n.n wnm.ti n.n	had we but something to eat!
***iw ms** bw n [...] špst ḥꜥw.sn*	**No:** .. […] noblewomen […] their bodies,
snm m-ꜥ isyt	to eat on grass,
ib.sn btkw ḥr nḏ ḫrt […]	their hearts recoil (?) at greeting […]
***iw** [**ms**] gmgm hnw nw hbny*	**No:** the chests of ebony are smashed to splinters,
ssnḏm špst swꜣ.tw.f m ꜣtwt	precious hardwood is sawn to make beds
[…].sn	[…] of them

6. (Papyrus Leiden I 344, column 3, lines 6 to 10)

***iw ms** ḳdw [ḫp]r m ꜥḥwtyw*	**No:** the builders have be[come] farmhands,
wnw m dpt nṯr nḥb [..]	those on the boat of the god are now yoked [up].
n ms ḫd.tw r [kp]ny min	Today no-one sails north to [Kep]ny:
ptr ir.ti.n r ꜥš n sꜥḥw.n	what are we to do for cedarwood for our coffins?
ḳrs.tw wꜥb m inw.sn	The pure-priest is buried with their deliveries,
sdwḫ [..]w m sft iry r-mn m kftyw	[...] are embalmed with the resin from there, as far even as Keftiu.
n ii.n.sn ḥḏ nbw	They do not arrive: the gold is destroyed,
ḳn […] inyt nt kꜣt nb	[...] materials for every work are finished,
kfꜣw nt pr nswt ꜥnḫ wḏꜣ snb	the property of the King's House life! prosperity! health! is bared.
wr-wy iw wḥꜣtyw ḥr ḥbyt.sn	What a great event, the arrival of oasismen with their festive goods,
tmꜣyw […] m rdmt wꜣḏ	mats, [skins], with fresh herbs

[..]nw nw ꜣpdw	and bird-[…]!
ib irw [..]ꜣwt	the heart is made …

7. (Papyrus Leiden I 344, column 3, lines 10 to 13)

iw ms *ꜣbw tny […] šmꜥ*	**No:** Abu and Teny […] and Upper Egypt,
n bꜣk.n […]ꜥyt	there is no work done [for str]ife (?)
ḥd wḥꜥt dꜥbt irtyw mꜣꜥw nwt štꜣw	Destroyed are carob, charcoal, paint, posts, poles, firewood!
kꜣt ḥmw ḏꜣ[…] mit kmw ꜥḥ	The works of artists ..[…] .. stocks of the palace.
iw pr-ḥḏ r-m m-ḫmt bꜣkw.f	Why have a treasury without its produce?
nfr is ib n nswt	Why, the heart of a king is glad
iw n.f mꜣꜥt ḥr is [...]	when offerings come to him before .. […]
ḫꜣst nb mw.n pw wꜣḏ.n pw	that is when every land is our loyal subject, that is our flourishing.
ptr ir.tn r.s wꜣw r ꜣkw	What are you all to do about it, fallen into ruin?

8. (Papyrus Leiden I 344, column 3, line 13 to column 4, line 8)

iw ms *sbt ꜣkw […] ir.tw.f*	**No:** laughter is ruined […] is made,
imt pw ntt ḥt tꜣ šbn ḥr nḫwt	what covers the land is grief, mingled with pleas.
iw ms *mt (?) nb m nty wn*	**No:** every dead man (?) is now one in existence (?),
wnw m rmṯ kwy di.tw ḥr wꜣt	those who were people are now strangers cast onto the road.
iw ms *šny […] n ḥr nb*	**No:** everyone has dishevelled hair,
n tn.n.tw sꜣ s r iwty n.f sw	the son of a man cannot be distinguished from one without.
iw ms *[…] ḥr ḫrw*	**No:** […] at the voice,
n ꜥkꜣ ḫrw m rnpwt nt ḫrw	voices are not straight in the years of voices,
nn pḥwy ḫrw	there is no end to voices
iw ms *ẖrd šri mr.i mwt.i*	**No:** the little child – I wish I were dead,
ẖrdw kty [..] ḥr tmw sw r rdi ꜥnḫ	children of strangers (?) […] say: he ought not to have given life.
iw ms *mswt […] srw ḥw.tw r sꜣwt*	**No:** the babes [of?] officials are struck against the walls,
ẖrdw nw nḥbt diw ḥr kꜣnr	the children at the neck are cast on the pile.
iw ms *wn m wꜥbt [di].tw ḥr kꜣnr*	**No:** the one who was in the embalming-chapel is [cast] on the pile,
sštꜣw pw n wtw ḥr sḫr ḥr.f	and that means the secrets of embalmers are overturned with him.
iw ms *nfꜣy ꜣkw mꜣꜣ m sf*	**No:** those things are perished, that were seen just yesterday,
tꜣ spw n g[nwt].f	the land is left to its [weakness]
mi whꜣt mḥ m isw (?)	like the plucking of flax from the reeds (?).
iw ms *idḥw r ḏr.f nn dgꜣy.tw.f*	**No:** the entire Delta is not to be recognised,
mḥ ib n tꜣ mḥw m mtnw ḥw	the security of the northern land is now (just) well-trodden roads.
ptr nty tw r irt n ḫpr [..] m st nbt	What is going to be done? No […] happens anywhere,
ḥr.[t]w (?) ḏd.tw wꜣ r st štꜣw	and so it is said: woe to the place of secrets,
mk sw m ḫmw sw mi r[ḫ]w sw	it is with those ignorant of it as much as (with) those who know it.
ḫꜣstyw ḥmw m kꜣt i[d]ḥw	Foreigners are (now) skilled in the arts of the Delta

9. (Papyrus Leiden I 344, column 4, lines 8 to 13)

iw ms *di.tw ḫnmw ḥr bnwyt*	**No:** families are set to the grindstone,
ḥbsy pꜣkt ḥw.tw m ḏꜣwt	wearers of fine linen are beaten with sticks,
tmy mꜣ[ꜣ] hrw pr n if	those who never say the day go out unrestrained.
wnyw ḥr ḥnkyt nt hꜣi.sn	Those who were on the beds of their husbands –
imi sḏr.sn ḥr šdw [..]mtw	let them sleep on rafts [..]..
ḏd.i iw.f dns r.i r šdw	I say it is harder for me than timbers.
ḥry ꜥntyw iwh st ḥr ꜥndw	The wearer of scented oil is laden down with jars,
mḥ ḥr [..] rḫ st kniw	filled with […] she [no longer?] recognises a carrying-chair.
ḥr wbꜣw ḥd sw	For the servants are gone,
nfr pw pḫrt iry	so there is no remedy for it.
snni n.sn špswt mi bꜣkwt	Noblewomen are brought down like servantwomen.
ḥnyt m miꜥt m ḫnw nꜣt	Musicians are on the looms inside the weaving-factories,
ḥst.sn n mrt m irtyw.sy	their song is to the fringe with her lament,
ḏdw […] bnwyt	saying […] grindstones.

10. (Papyrus Leiden I 344, column 4, line 13 to column 5, line 2)

iw ms *ḥmwt nbt sḫm m rw.sn*	**No:** all servantwomen possess power in their retorts
mdw ḥnwt.sn	when their mistresses speak,
dns pw r bꜣkw	It is harder than forced labour.

iw ms *[nh?]wt sk gnw wnw*	**No:** the [sycamore?]s are chopped down, the branches stripped bare.
iwd.n.i sw ḥmw n pr.f	I have abandoned it – the servants to his house.
iw rmṯ r ḏd sḏm.sn st	People will say when they hear it.
ḥd fk3w n ḥ3w n ẖrdw	Gone are the rewards of abundant children
nn k3w n k[…]	There is no food for ..[…]
iw min dpt iry mi-m min	and today, how does it taste, today?

11. (Papyrus Leiden I 344, column 5, lines 2 to 9)

iw ms *srw ḥkrw ḥr swn*	**No:** the officials are starving and in pain,
šms.tw šmswt stk(?) […] *ḥr nḥwt*	followers are followed .. […] in pleas.
iw ms *t3w ḥr ḏd ir* […] *rḫ.n.i nṯr tn*	**No:** the hot-headed says if […] I knew where the god is,
k3 iry.i n.f	then I would act for him.
iw ms *[m3ʿt ḫt]ḫt t3 m rn.s pwy*	**No:** what is Right is spread through the land in this its name,
isft pw ir.sn ḥr grg ḥr.s	but it is Evil on which they are based in their actions.
iw ms *sḫsw ʿḥ3 ḥr n ḥn* […]	**No:** the fighter is running for the property […],
ʿw3yty (?) iṯ.tw ḫt.f nbt	the robbed, all his goods are taken.
iw ms *ʿwt nbt ibw.sn rmw*	**No:** all herds, their hearts weep,
mnmnt ḥr imt m-ʿ sḫrw t3	cattle groan from the condition of the earth.
iw ms *msw srw ḥw.tw r s3wt*	**No:** the babes of officials are struck against the walls,
ẖrdw nw nḥbt diw ḥr k3nr	the children at the neck are cast on the pile.
ẖnmw ḥr imt ḥr wrdw.f	Khnum groans in his weariness.
iw ms *šʿd sm3 st*	**No:** the massacre slaughters them.
snd ḥr ḫsf irw r ḫftyw.tn	The fearful man says: defend, act against your enemies,
iw grt ʿnd twt wḏ3w ḥr nty ktw	images and amulets are useless because of (?) the minor.
in iw m šms n ḫnty [..] *ḥnʿ wḏʿ.f*	Is it in the following of the foremost [..] with his slayer?
in iw m rḫ.sn m3iw 3šr n sḏt	Is it in the knowledge of them, a lion, the scorching of a flame?
in [...] *m iwḥ n ptḥ*	Is it […] in the watering of Ptah?
iṯ [..]*yt dd.tn n.f ḥr-m*	The […] is taken – why do you supply him?
n pḥ sw ind is pw dd.tn n.f	He is not touched: your supplying him is indeed feeble.

12. (Papyrus Leiden I 344, column 5, line 9 to column 6, line 1)

iw ms *ḥm (?)* […] *ḫt t3*	**No:** the servant (?) […] throughout the land,
nḫt ḥr h3b n bw nb	the strong man is sending (his message) to everyone,
ḥw s sn.f n mwt.f	a man strikes his mother's-brother.
iššy pw iryt ḏd […] *n 3kw*	What is the deed? says the […]-man to the perished man.
iw ms *w3wt* […]*w mtnw s3w*	**No:** the ways […] and the roads are watched,
ḥms.tw ḥr b3t r iit.tw ẖ3wy	they sit in the bush for the arrival of the nightfarer,
r iṯ 3tpw.f	to steal his load,
nḥmw nty ḥr.f ḥnmw m sḫt ḫt	what is on him is taken, he beaten with blows of the stick,
ẖdbw m nf	and criminally slain.
iw ms *nf3y 3kw m33 sf*	**No:** those things are perished, that were seen just yesterday,
t3 spw n gnwt.f	the land is left to its weakness
mi wḫ3w mḥw	like the plucking of flax.
ndsw pryw ḥr swn	The small go out in pain,
nbwy […] *nw* [..]	the goldsmith […] cords (?) [..]
h3 r.f grḥ pw m rmṯ n iwr n mst	If only this was the end of men, no pregnancy, no birth,
iḫ gr t3 m ḫrw nn ḫnw	then the land would be silent of voices, without tumult.

13. (Papyrus Leiden I 344, column 6, lines 1 to 5)

iw ms (blank space) *m smw*	**No:** (blank space) on plants,
sʿm.tw m mw	to be swallowed with water,
n gm.n.tw k3y smw 3pdw	fruit and plants of birds cannot be found,
nḥm […]*t m r n š3iw*	[…] is taken from the mouth of pigs
n ḥr ʿn n.k st r.i ḥr ḥkrw	The sight is not fairer for you more than me, say the hungry (?).
iw ms *it 3kw ḥr w3t nb*	**No:** the grain is perished on every path,
sḫ3w m ḥbsw ḫs3 m mrḥt	the one stripped of clothing is anointed with oil.
ḥr nb ḥr nn wn	Everyone says: there is nothing.
wḏ3 fk s3w.f pd r t3	The storeroom is bare, its guard stretched out on the ground,
m smw m-ʿ rwd pw n ib.i	with plants, that is from the growth for my heart.
iw.i ḏr r-sy	I am entirely estranged (?).

ḫ3 r.f ir.n.i ḫrw m t3y 3t	If only I had made a sound in that moment,
nḥm.f wi m-ᶜ wḫdt.i ir.tw im.st	so that he would save me from my pain inflicted there.

14. (Papyrus Leiden I 344, column 6, lines 5 to 14)

iw ms *ẖnrt ḏsr šd sšw.f*	**No:** the sacrosanct enclosure, its writings are removed,
sḫ3w st št3w wnt	the former place of secrets has been stripped.
iw ms *ḥk3w sḫ3w šmw sḫnw*	**No:** words of power are bared, pronouncements are gone,
snḥ3.tw ḥr sḫ3 st in rmṯ	they are vilified by being remembered by people.
iw ms *wn ḥ3 šd wpt.s*	**No:** the bureau is open, its lists removed,
ḫpr rmṯ ḏt nb [...]	servant people have become owners of [...]-men
iw ms [...] *sm3.tw šd sšw.sn*	**No:** [...] have been killed, their writings removed.
bin-wy n.i n indw m rk iry	How evil it is for me, for the loss in such a time.
iw ms *sšw nw tm3 dr sšw.sn*	**No:** the secretaries of the mat, their writings are forced out,
ᶜnḫt n kmt m h3y.i in.tw n.i	the grain of Egypt is now 'I'll go down and get'.
iw ms *hpw nw ẖnrt diw r ḫnty*	**No:** the laws of the enclosure are cast out,
šm.tw m ms ḥr.s m iwwyt	people walk in contravention of them in the city-quarters,
ḥwrw ḥr ng3t im m ẖnw mrt	the poor tear strips from them within the street.
iw ms *ḥwrw spr r ᶜ psḏt*	**No:** the poor have arrived at the terrain of the Nine Gods,
sḫ3w sšmw pf mᶜb3yt	and stripped bare is that guide of the Thirty
iw ms *ẖnrt wr m pr h3.f*	**No:** the great enclosure is now a place of free entry,
ḥwrw ḥr šmt iit m ḥwt wryt	the poor come and go in the Great Halls.
iw ms *msw srw ḫ3ᶜ m mrt*	**No:** the children of officials are cast onto the street,
rḫ ḥr tiw wḫ3 ḥr m bi3	the wise says yes, the fool says no,
nty n rḫ.f sy ᶜnw m ḥr.f	the man who, he did not know it, is bright in his face.
iw ms *wnw m wᶜbt di.tw ḥr ḳ3nr*	**No:** those who were in the embalming-chapel are cast on the pile,
sšt3 pw n wtw ḥr sẖr ḥr.f	and that means the secrets of embalmers are overturned with him.

15. (Papyrus Leiden I 344, column 7, lines 1 to 7)

mtn is *ḫt w3w.ti r ḳ3*	**See, all:** the flame has spread so high,
pr wbdt r ḫftyw t3	the scorching goes out against the enemies of the land.
mtn is *ir ḫt n p3 ḫpr w3w*	**See, all now:** things are done that could never have befallen before:
šd nswt in ḥwrw	the king is removed by the rabble.
mtn *ḳrs m bik m šfdt*	**See, all:** the one buried as Falcon is in wooden casing,
iw imnt.n mr w3 r šwt	what the pyramid concealed has ended emptied.
mtn is w3 r *sšw3w t3 m nsyt*	**See, all now:** the land **has ended** impoverished of kingship,
in nhw n rmṯ ḫmw sḫrw	by a few people who are ignorant of manners.
mtn is *w3 r sbiw ḥr iᶜrᶜt*	**See, all now:** it has ended with rebellion against the kingship-cobra,
[..] *nt rᶜ shr t3wy*	the [...] of Ra that pacifies the Two Lands.
mtn *sšt3w n t3 ḫmm drw.f*	**See, all:** the secrets of the land, its limits unknown,
sḫ3w ẖny hn.n.f n wnwt	the Residence is bared, and it has collapsed the same hour.
mtn *kmt w3.ti r stt mw*	**See, all:** Egypt is reduced to pouring water,
di mw r t3	the one who poured water onto the ground,
it.n.f nḫt ᶜ m m3irw	has seized the strong armed in misery
mtn *šd ḳrḥt m tpḥt.s*	**See, all:** the primeval serpent is removed from its lair,
sḫ3w sšt3w n nsyt bit	the secrets of the dual kings are laid bare.
mtn *ẖnw ḥr snd m-ᶜ g3wt*	**See, all:** the Residence is in fear from need,
nb .. r wd ḥ3ᶜyt nn ḫsf-ᶜ	the lord of .. shall project strife unopposed.

16. (Papyrus Leiden I 344, column 7, lines 7 to 14)

mtn *t3 ṯs n.f ḥr sm3yw*	**See, all:** the land it has been bound beneath plotters,
ḳn ḫsy ḥr nḥm [ḫt?].f	and the valiant, the wretch has seized his [goods].
mtn *ḳrḥt ḥr [...] nnyw*	**See, all:** the primeval serpent is [...]-ing the weary,
tm ir n.f ḏb3t m nb ḥ3t	he who could not make a tomb for himself is now lord of a chapel.
mtn *nbw wᶜbt dr ḥr ḳ3nr*	**See, all:** lords of the embalming-hall are pushed back onto the pile,
tm ir n.f ḳrs m pr-ḥḏ	he who could not make a burial for himself is in the treasury.
mtn *is n3 ḫprw rmṯ*	**See, all:** what people have become:
tmw ḳd n.f ᶜt m nb ḏrit	he who could not build a room for himself is now lord of columns.
mtn *ḳnbt nt t3 dr.ti r ḫt t3*	**See, all:** the council's land has been pushed back to roam the land,
dr m pryt nsyw	(they) are pushed back from the estates of kings.
mtn *špst ḥr šdw srw m šnᶜ*	**See, all:** the noblewomen are on rafts, the officials in the kitchens,

tm sḏr ḥr ḏrit m nb ḥnkyt	he who could not sleep even on boards is now owner of bedlinen.
***mtn** nb ḫt sḏr ib*	**See, all:** the lord of goods is gone to sleep thirsty,
dbḥ n.f tȝḥw.f m nb sḫrw	the one who begged his dregs for himself is now lord of beer-vats.
***mtn** nbw ḏȝywt m isywt*	**See, all:** the owners of robes are in rags,
tm sḫt n.f m nb pȝḳt	he who had did nothing woven for himself is owner of fine cloth.
***mtn** tm mḏḥ n.f imw*	**See, all:** one who could not have a boat built for himself
m nb ꜥḥꜥw	is now lord of a fleet,
nbt iry ḥr gmḥ st nn st m-ꜥ.f	their owner is gazing at them, they are no longer his.
***mtn** iwty šwyt.f m nb šwyt*	**See, all:** the man without his sun-shade is lord of shade,
nbw šwyt m wḫȝ n ḏꜥw	and the lords of shade are now the driven dust (?) of the storm
***mtn** ḫm ḏȝḏȝt m nb bnt*	**See, all:** the one who knew no lyre is now lord of the harp,
tm ḥsy n.f	he who could not have (anyone) sing for him
ḥr swḥȝ mrt	is now enhancing the Song Goddess.
***mtn** nbw wdḥw m ḥmty*	**See, all:** the owners of stands of copper,
n wnḫ hnw n wꜥ im	now not even flowers adorn the jars for any one of them.

17. (Papyrus Leiden I 344, column 7, line 14 to column 8, line 7)

***mtn** sḏr ḫȝry m gȝwt [g]m.f špss*	**See, all:** the widower sleeps failing to find riches,
tm n.f mȝȝ ꜥḥꜥ ḥr swdn	he who could not have a review (?) stands at the balance-block (?).
***mtn** iwty ḫt.f m nb ꜥḥꜥw*	**See, all:** the man without any goods is now the master of wealth,
sr ḥr ḥst.f	the official has to sing his praises.
***mtn** šwȝw nw tȝ ḫpr m ḥwdw*	**See, all:** the paupers of the land have turned into rich men,
ḫt m iwty n.f	the property man is now one without anything
***mtn** wdpww (?) ḫpr m nbw wbȝt*	**See, all:** the cupbearers have turned into lords of staff,
wn m wpwty ḥr hȝb ky	he who was an envoy is now sending another.
***mtn** iwty pꜥt.f m nb mḫr*	**See, all:** the one without his own bread is now the lord of a granary,
ḥnn šnꜥ.f m ḫt ky	while he who ordered his kitchens is now the property of another.
***mtn** wšw šny iwty mrḥt.f*	**See, all:** the man with dishevelled hair, the one without his own oil
ḫpr m nb ḫbbt ꜥntyw nḏm	has turned into a lord of great vats of sweet myrrh.
***mtn** iwtt m pds.s m nbt ȝtp*	**See, all:** the woman without her own box is now owner of furniture,
gmḥ ḥr.s m mw m nbt ꜥnḫ	one who looked at her face in the water is now owner of a mirror.
***mtn** isḫ*	**See, all:** in grief!
***mtn** nfr s ḥr wnm kȝw.f*	**See, all:** a man is happy eating his food.
snm ḫt.k m ȝw-ib	You, sire, eat your offerings in joy,
nn n.k ḥnḥn r.k	you do not have to hunt down for yourself.
ȝḫ pw n s wnm kȝw.f	Eating one's food is good for a man:
wḏ sw nṯr n ḥs.n.f	the god orders it for the one he has favoured.
(blank half-line)	(blank half-line)
n nṯr.f ḥr wdn n.f m sntr n ky	one who [did not know] his god offers him the incense of another,
n rḫ […]	the one who did not know […]

18. (Papyrus Leiden I 344, column 8, lines 7 to 14)

*[**m**]**tn** špst wryt nbt špssw*	**See, all:** great noblewomen, owners of riches,
ḥr rdi n msw.sn n ḥnkt	are giving of their children for cloth
***mtn is** s […] špst m ḥmt*	**See, all, indeed:** a man […] noblewoman as wife,
nḥw.n sw it.s iwty ḥr smȝ.f	her father has accused him, the pauper is out to kill him (?)
***mtn** msw ḳnbt m is[…]*	**See, all:** the children of the council are now ..[…]
kȝw nw idt.sn n ḥꜥkyw	bulls of their herds to the plunderers
***mtn** nsyw ḥr ḳnḳn m kȝw mȝi[…*	**See, all:** the cult-butchers are at work with starved (?) bulls
…]kyw	[…] …
***mtn** tm sft n.f*	**See, all:** the man for whom nothing was butchered
ḥr sft wnḏw	is butchering the temple cattle,
ḫm ḥntȝ ḥr mȝ[…] nb	the one who knew no .. is .. […] every […]
***mtn** nsyw ḥr ḳnḳn m rw*	**See, all:** the cult-butchers are at work just with geese,
dd.tw nṯrw r-ḏbȝ iwȝw	and the gods are sold for cattle
***mtn** ḥmwt […] ḥr wdn ȝpḥw*	**See, all:** servantwomen […] are offering ..,
špst iry (blank space)	their noblewomen (blank space)
***mtn** špst ḥr sḫs m rw […].sn*	**See, all:** noblewomen are running .. […] of them
ptḥ m snd n mwt	overturned in fear of death,
ḥryw nt tȝ ḥr sḫs	**mas**ters of the land are running,

nn ḥnt.n.sn m-ꜥ gꜣwt nb ḥs(?)[…]	without thought, from lack of a lord of .. […]

19. (Papyrus Leiden I 344, column 9, lines 1 to 8)

[***mtn***] *nbw ḥnkt ḥr sꜣtw*	[**See, all:**] owners of beds are on the ground,
sḏr btkw r.f m ꜣdt n.f šdw	while even the beggar sleeps after spreading a skin for himself.
mtn *špst wꜣww r ḥḳr*	**See, all:** noblewomen are reduced to starvation,
nsyw sꜣt m ỉrt.n.sn	while butchers are sated with what they have prepared
mtn *ỉꜣwt nbt nn st r st.s*	**See, all:** every office is out of its place,
mi idt tnbḫ nn mniw.f	like a herd that strays without its herdsman.
mtn *kꜣw m wdy nn nwy.s*	**See, all:** cattle are roaming without any watch,
s nb ḥr ỉnt n.f ꜣbw m rn.f	every man goes fetching for himself and branding with his name
mtn *smꜣ.tw s r-gs sn.f iw.f hꜣ*	**See, all:** a man is slain beside his brother, as he goes down,
iw.k sw r mkt ḥꜥw.f	though you are there to be the protection of his body.
mtn *iwty ḥtr.f m nb idr*	**See, all:** the man without his single pair is now owner of a herd,
tm gm n.f skꜣ m nb mnmnt	he who could not find ploughing-oxen for himself is owner of cattle.
mtn *iwty prt.f m nb šnwt*	**See, all:** the man without his crop-seed is now owner of granaries,
in n.f ṯꜣbt m dd pr st	he to whom issue-grain was brought is now he who has to give it out
mtn iwty *sꜣḥw.f m nb mrt*	**See, all: the man who had no** neighbours is now the owner of staff,
wn m irr.f wpt ḏs.f	while one who did is now one who has to make the errand himself
mtn *ḳnw nw tꜣ n smi* […]	**See, all:** the valiant of the land are not reported [to?],
[*s*]*ḫrw n rḫyt wꜣww r ꜣḳw*	[the con]dition (?) of the populace is reduced to ruin
mtn *ḥmw nb n bꜣkw.sn*	**See, all:** all craftsmen – they have not worked,
sšwꜣw ḫftyw tꜣ ḥmwt(yw).f	the enemies of the land have made vagabonds of its craftsmen
[…] *šmw n rḫ.f im*	[…] harvest, he has not known of it
tm […] .. […]	he who does not […] .. […]
[…] *ḥr ḫpr n smi.n.tw.f*	[…] is taking place, but it is not reported,
sš […] *ꜥwy.fy m-ḫnw.f*	the writer […] his hands inside it.

20. (Papyrus Leiden I 344, column 9, line 8 to column 10, line 3)

ḥḏ […]*.f m rk iry*	**Destruction:** […] of it in its time,
mꜣꜣ s […] *ḏꜣyw.f*	a man sees […] his enemies,
fn ḥr int ḳbḥ […]	the meek is bringing cool […]
[…]*yt sndw n* […]	[…]-room, the fearful, not […],
iw ḥwrw […] *ḥd hr.s*	the wretched […] light on it
ḥḏ […] *kꜣw iry m-ꜥ.sn*	**Destruction:** […] their food from them
[…] *snd n ḥryt.f*	[…] fearful for dread of him,
dbḥ nḏs […] *wpwty n is* […] *rk*	a fellow begs […] the envoy, not […] time
iṯ.tw.f ꜣtpw m ḫt.f	he is seized, laden with his goods,
nḥmw […] *swꜣ.tw ḥr sbꜣ.f*	taken […] his door is passed by
[…] *ḥꜣy ḏrit m ḫꜣ*	[… on?] the roof, the column in the hall,
ꜥwt ḥry bikw .. […]	the rooms filled with divine falcons .. […]
in nḏs rs.f tꜣ-ḥḏ ḥr.f nn ḥryt.f	it is the lad who wakes, dawn upon him, with no fear.
sḫs.tw ḥr mꜣꜥw	They run along the banks,
ḥnkw m wryt tꜣyt m ḫnw	marked by *wryt* -cloth woven (?) in the Residence,
iꜣmw pw ir.n.sn mi ḫꜣstyw	their products are tents, like foreigners
ḥḏt *irt hꜣb.tw ḥr.s in šmsw*	**Destroyed** is the delivery of messages by followers
m wpwt nbw.sn nn ḥryt.sn	on errands of their lords with no fear,
mk s diw pw ḏd.sn ḏd.sn	There is a man, of a group of five, and they say their saying:
šmw ḥr wꜣt rḫ.n.tn iw.n spr.wyn	go on the road, that you all know, for we have arrived

21. (Papyrus Leiden I 344, column 10, lines 3)

rmy r.f *tꜣ-mḥw*	**Weeping aloud** is Lower Egypt,
šnꜥ n nswt hꜣy.i in.tw n.i n bw nb	the storerooms of the king are I-go-I-get for everyone,
iw pr nswt ꜥnḫ wḏꜣ snb	the House of the King life! prosperity! health!
r ḏr.s ḫmt bꜣkw.f	in its entirety is without its revenue.
ntf it bty ꜣpdw rmw	To it belong barley, emmer, birds, fish,
ntf ḥḏt pꜣkt ḥmty mrḥt	to it belong white linen, fine linen, copper, oil,
ntf psš ḳn [*sšn*]*w*	to it belong baskets, bundles (?) of [lo]tus,
ḳniw bꜣkw nb nfr iy.f irw	matting, all good produce, to come as ready.
ir wdf skt st	If it delays, it is ruined

m pr nswt ꜥnḫ wḏꜣ snb	in the House of the King life! prosperity! health!
nn šw.tw [...] *nfꜣy*	without being emptied [...] those there

22. (Papyrus Leiden I 344, column 10, lines 6-12)

ḥd *ḫftyw nw ḫnw špsy*	**Destroy** the enemies of the noble Residence,
sbḳ ḳnbt	resplendent of council
[...] *im.f mi* [...]	[...] in it like [...]
šmw ms imy-r niwt nn sꜥšꜣ n.f	but the overseer of the city walks without an escort for him
ḥd [...] *sbḳ* [...] *ḫnw pf šps*	**Destroy** [...] resplendent [...] that noble Residence,
ꜥšꜣ hpw	plentiful in laws
[...] *s* [...]*.f nty* [...]	[...] .. [....] of it which [...]
[...] *pf šps* [...]*.f*	[...] that noble [...] of it
ḥd *ḫftyw nw ḫnw pf* [...]	**Destroy** the enemies of that Residence [...]
nn ꜥḥꜥ.n.tw	impossible to stand [against? ...]
[...] *nfꜣy šps*	[...] those noble [...]
ꜥšꜣ ḫꜣmw iw ms [...] ..	of many .., though [...] ..

23. (Papyrus Leiden I 344, column 10, line 12 to column 11, line 12)

sḫꜣw *tḫb* [...]	**Remember** the immersing [...]
wḫdyw r mnt.f ḥꜥw.f tri n ..	suffering for his pain, his body ...
[...]*w ḥr nṯr.f mk.f r* [...]	[...] .. upon his god to protect against (?) [...]
msw iry mty ḥr ḥw wḏnw	their children accurate in striking the intruders (?)
sḫꜣ[*w*] *d.. šnwt kꜣp m snṯr*	Remember .. the sanctuary, censing with incense,
ḫrpw mw m ḥst m nhpw	directing water in the jar in dawn-rites
sḫꜣw rw ḏdw trpw st	Remember the fattened geese, the ganders and ducks,
wdnw ḥtp-nṯr n nṯrw	offering god's offerings to the gods
sḫꜣw wšꜥ ḥsmn sspd t ḥḏ	Remember chewing natron, sharpening the white loaf
in s hrw iwḥ tp	by a man the day of moistening the head
sḫꜣw sꜥḥꜥ snw ḫt ꜥb	Remember setting up flagpoles, carving offering-stones,
wꜥb ḥr twry rw-prw	the pure-priest cleaning shrines,
ḥwt-nṯr skꜣḥ.ti mi irt	the temple plastered like milk,
snḏm sty ꜣḫt srwd pꜣwt	sweetening the scent of the horizon, confirming offerings
sḫꜣw nḏr tp-rd šbšb ssw	Remember binding rules, calculating dates,
šdt bs m wꜥbt r ḫst ḫt	removing entry into a sanctuary for villains
irt st pw m nf sswn-ib pw [...]	Doing it is a crime, it is appeasement [...]
hrw ḫnty ḥḥ ꜣbdt tn [...] *rnpwt rḫ*	the day before eternity, this monthly phase [...] years of knowing
sḫꜣw sft iwꜣw [...] *n.tn*	Remember the slaughter of oxen [...] .. of all of you
sḫꜣw pr wḫꜣ [...]	Remember the emergence of the evening(-offering?) (?) [...]
iꜣꜥš n.tn rdit rw ḥr ḫt [...]	calling on all of you to place geese on the fire [...]
[...] *wpwt ds dr* [...]	[...] mission, jar, removing [...]
mryt nt nwy [...]	riverbank of waves [...]
[...]*t nt ḥmt* [...] *mnḫt* [...]	[...] of .. [...] cloth [...]
rdit .. [...] *r sḥtp.tn*	placing .. [...] to make you all content
[...] *gꜣw rmṯ m-ꜥ i*[...] *n rꜥ wḏ* [...]	[...] lack of people from .. [...] of Ra, decreeing [...]
ḥr tri sw [...] *imntt* [...]	beseeching him [...] the west [...]
ꜥn[*d? ...*] *in* [...]	fe[w? ...] by [...]

24. (Papyrus Leiden I 344, column 11, line 12 to column 12, line 6)

mtn sw ḥr ḏꜥ [...]	All of you, why does he seek [...]
ḳd (blank space) *ḥr-m*	why fashion (blank space)
n tn snd r sḫm-ib	the fearful has not been distinguished from the strong-minded
iw inn.f ḳbḥ ḥr tꜣ[*w*]	If he would bring cool water on the he[at]
iw ḏd.tw mniw pw n bw nb	people would say: he is a shepherd for everyone,
nn bin m ib.f	there is no evil in his heart,
ꜥnd iꜣdr.f ir.n.f is hrw r nw st	his herd is reduced, but he has spent the day caring for it
ḫt n ib iry	Fire is in their hearts.
ḫꜣ ꜥd.f bit.sn m ḫt tpt	Had he only realised their nature in the first generation,
kꜣ ḥw.f sdbw dꜣ.f ꜥ r.s	he would have struck the stakes, stretching out an arm against it,
sky.f ꜥwt iry iwꜥt.sn	and destroyed its stock and their heirs.
ꜣbb mst r.s nhꜣt ḫpr	Instead birth was desired, and disaster has happened,

sꜣry ḥr wꜣt nbt	need is on every road
nfꜣ pw n wn.f wn nꜣ nṯrw ḥry-ib iry	That is it, it has not passed, as the gods are in its midst
prr styt m ḥmt rmṯ	Seed comes out only from human women,
n gm.n.tw ḥr wꜣt	it is not found on the road.
ḥw-ny r ḥry pr	Strife is on top, emergent,
dr n iw m sḫpr.n.sn	and the remover of evils is the one who made them happen
n iʿš n ḥꜣt m wnwt.sn	There is no announcer-on-the-deck in their hours.
in iw rf tny min	Where is he even, today?
in iw.f tri sḏr	Is he perhaps sleeping?
mtn n mꜣꜣ.n.tw bꜣw iry	All of you, his power is not being seen.

25. (Papyrus Leiden I 344, column 12, lines 6 to 12)

ir snm.n.tw.n n gm.n.i tw	If we had been fed I would not be finding you,
n iʿš.n.tw n.i m šw	I would not have been summoned from the void (?),
ꜣdy r sswn-ib pw ḫnt	.. is a fierce force for treatment (?)
[…] *grt ḥry r n bw nb*	[…] indeed master of the utterance of everyone,
mi n is snd st r s ḥḥw m rmṯ	as there is no fearing it for one man or a million
n mꜣꜣ […] *r* [*ḫ*]*ftyw*	There is not being seen […] against [en]emies
[…] *r ḫnty.f ʿḳ r ḥwt-nṯr* […]	[…] before him, entering the temple […]
[…]*.n.f ḫnt* […] *pfꜣ*	[…] (weeping) for him front […] that […].
ir swh[*ꜣ*] *ḏdt.f* .. […]	Confusion is made of his words (?) .. […]
n ḫr tꜣ […] *wbdt twtw*	The land has not fallen […] scorching images,
ʿd iswy iry nw […]	smashing their chapels (?), binding […]
mꜣꜣ.f hrw n i […] *nb*	He/it seeing the day of .. […] all […]
tm ir.n.f iwd pt r sꜣtw	He did not complete the separation of heaven from earth,
snd ḥr ḥr-nb i..	fear is on every face …
ir m ir.f st m pḥ.tin n …f r.s	If as he achieves it as we have arrived … of him for it,
m msdd.k nḥm	by your hatred of rescue (?)

26. (Papyrus Leiden I 344, column 12, line 12 to column 13, line 2)

ḥw siꜣ mꜣʿt ḥnʿ.k	Word, insight, right are with you,
shꜣ pw rdi.k ḫt tꜣ	but what you place throughout the land is chaos,
ḫnʿ ḫrw ḫnn	with the sound of strife.
mk ky ḥr wd r ky	One man is attacking another,
sni.tw r wḏ.n.k	and what you commanded is broken.
ir šmt s ḫmt ḥr wꜣt	If three men go on the road,
gmm.tw m s sn	they are found to be just two men,
in ʿšꜣt smꜣ ʿndt	for the greater number kills the lesser.
in iw mniw mr mwt	Is there a shepherd who loves death?
ḫr kꜣ wḏ.k ir.tw	Then you could order it to be done.
šb.n mrwt is pw wʿ msd ky	This is indeed the replacement of love: one is the hater of the other.
ʿnd ḫprw.sn pw ḥr wꜣt nbt	It means their forms are now few everywhere.
ir.n.k ist r sḫpr nfꜣ ḏd n.k grg	You are he who has made all that happen, you are being told lies

27. (Papyrus Leiden I 344, column 13, lines 2 to 8)

tꜣ m kꜣkꜣ sḫtm rmṯ	The land is a creeping plant that suffocates people,
n kꜣ.tw m ʿnḫ	noone thinks of living.
nn r ꜣw n rnpwt m ḥʿʿyt	These spans of years are strife.
ḫdb.tw s ḥr tp ḥwt.f	A man is killed on top of his farmstead (?),
iw.f rs.f m pr.f n tꜣš	as he watches in his border house.
in kn.f nḥm.f sw ʿnḫ.f pw	If he is bold, he may save himself: that is his life.
hꜣb.tw bꜣwt r nḏsw	Despatches are sent to (ordinary) fellows:
šm.f ḥr mtnw r mꜣꜣ.f wḏn	he goes on the road until he sees the flood:
itḥ.tw wꜣt ʿḥʿ.f snni	the road is withheld, he stops powerless,
nḥm nty ḥr.f ḫnm m sḫt nt ḫt	what is on him is seized, as he is beaten with blows of a stick,
ḫdb m nfꜣ	and murdered.
hꜣ dpt.k m nhy n mꜣirw iry	If only you could taste a little of the grief of it.
kꜣ ḏd.k m ḫt […] *bg.f m-m*	Then you would speak with .. […] how […] is he weary (?),

ky m inb m ḥ3w […]	another on the wall … […]
.. *šmm r ẖt* (?) *rnpwt ir mdt* [...]	.. scorched at the generation (?) of years, a matter is done [...].

28. (Papyrus Leiden I 344, column 13, line 9 to column 14, line 5)

[…] *nfr ꜥḥꜥw ḥr ẖnt*[…]	**[No, it is surely]** good when ships sail north […]
[…] *ḥr ꜥw3yt*	[…] on robbery.
iw irf ḥmw nfr […]	No, it is surely good […]
[*iw irf ḥ*]*mw nfr itḥw i3dt*	[No, it is su]rely good when the net is draw in,
mẖ3.tw 3pdw […]	when the catch is weighed […]
iw irf [*ḥ*]*mw nfr* […]	No, it is surely good […]
sꜥḥw.n.sn mtnw ḥr irt šmt	they have secured (?) the roads for making journeys.
iw irf ḥmw nfr ꜥwy rmṯ	No, it is surely good that the arms of people
sẖws.sn mrw	are building pyramids,
šd mrw irt mnw m nhwt n nṯrw	cutting canals, making monuments with trees for the gods.
iw irf ḥmw nfr rmṯ tẖw	No, it is surely good when people are drunken,
swri.sn myt ibw.sn nfr	as they drink the ferment, their hearts are happy.
iw irf ḥmw nfr nhm m rw	No, it is surely good when there is rejoicing in speech,
iw bw3w nw sp3wt ꜥḥꜥ	as the beggars of the districts are standing
ḥr m33 nhmw m špsw.sn	to see the rejoicing by their nobles,
ḥbsw m ḥ3tyw twryt r ḥ3t	clothed in finest linen, ointment on the brow,
srwdw m ḥry-ib	troops in the midst.
iw irf ḥmw nfr 3tiwt 3dt	No, it is surely good when the beds are spread,
wrsw n srw ṯ3r m wḏ3w	the officials have headrests, secure and sound,
s3rt nt s nb km.ti m ifd	the needs of every man are filled in a box,
ẖt m šwyt ẖtmw ḥr.f sḏr m b3y	wood in the dry place, sealed against him, sleeping in the bush.
iw irf ḥmw nfr pkt sš.ti	No, it is surely good when linen is spread out
hrw wp-rnpt	on the day of the New Year
[…] *ḥr* (?) *wdbw*	[…] on (?) the shore,
pkt m-ꜥ sš.ti ḥ3tyw ḥr stt	linen with (it?) spread out, fine linen on the ground,
imy-r ..[…]*w* […]	the overseer of .. […]-men […]
[…] *nhwt nḏsw ḥr* […]	[…] trees, fellows are […]

29. (Papyrus Leiden I 344, column 14, lines 6 to 9)
lost

30. (Papyrus Leiden I 344, column 14, line 10 to column 15, line 5)

[…] *sn sp ḥ3ḳ* (?) [...]	[…] of them time of plunder (?) […]
pẖr iry mi styw […]	its circuit like Syrians […]
[…]*n.f* (?) *iw.tw ḥr sẖrw iry*	[…] of him (?), they are on its conduct (?),
ḳn.sn n.sn	they finish for themselves,
nn gm.n.tw nty r ꜥḥꜥw ḥr m[*k?*] *st*	noone can be found to stand to pro[tect?] it.
[…*ḏ3?*]*mw*	[… tro]ops (?),
ꜥḥ3 s nb ḥr snt.f mk.f ḥꜥw.f	every man fights for his sister and protects himself.
in nḥsyw k3 ir.n mkt.n	Is it the Nubians? Then let us make our protection,
sꜥš3 ꜥḥ3wtyw r ẖsf psḏt	multiplying fighters to repel the bowmen.
in iw.s m timḥy k3 ir.n ꜥnw	Is it from the Libyans? Then let us make them turn back.
mḏ3yw nḏmw ḥnꜥ kmt	The Medjay are in harmony with Egypt.
mi-m irf s nb ḥr sm3 sn.f	How then can every man be killing his brother?
ḏ3mw ṯs.n n.n ẖpr m pḏt	Troops we raise for ourselves turn into a tribe of archers,
w3w r ḥb3	and end up plundering
ẖprt n.f im.f rdit rḫ styw sšmw n t3	The result has been to let the Syrians know the condition of the land.
iw grt ẖ3st nb ḥr sndw.f	Yet every foreign land lay under fear of it;
dpt n rḫyt ḥr	the taste of the populace was to say:
nn dit kmt šꜥy	there is no giving of Egypt (to) sand.
nẖt.s ḥr ḏrw [...]	It is strong on the borders […]
ḏd r.tn m-ẖt rnpwt [...]	to say of you all after years […]
[…]*3 sw ḏs.f in sp* ….*sn* […]	[…] destroy himself by the instant of their … […]
t3 (?) *im r sꜥnẖ msw.f wnn* [...]	the land (?) there to nourish its children, there will be […]
.. […] *ẖprt.tn* (?) […]	.. […] happened to you (?) […]
ḏd.in ḏ3mw […] *in* [...]	then the troops say […] .. [...]

31. (Papyrus Leiden I 344, column 15, lines 6 to 10)
lost

32. (Papyrus Leiden I 344, column 15, lines 11 to 13)

[...] ... [...]*w ir n.tn tbw* (*?*) [...]	[...] ... [...] .. retribution (?) is done for/by you all [...]
ḳmi inḥꜣst ꜥryt [...]	gum, lotus, seeds (?) [...]
[...] *m hꜣw n ꜥḳw* [...]	[...] in addition to the regular supplies (?) [...]

33. (Papyrus Leiden I 344, column 15, line 13 to column 16, line 1)

ḏdt.n *i.pw-wr*	**What was said by** Ipuwer
wšb.f n ḥm n nb r ḏr	in answer to the Person of the Lord of All
[...] *ꜥwt nb*	[...] every herd;
ḫm st pw m nḏmt ḥr ib	ignoring it is what pleases the heart.
iw ir.n.k nfr ḥr ibw.sn	You have made happiness on their hearts,
sꜥnḫ.n.k rmṯ im.sn	you have nourished people among them,
iw ḥbsw.sn ḫnty.sn	(yet) they cover their foreheads
n snd n dwꜣyt	for fear of tomorrow.

34. (Papyrus Leiden I 344, column 16, lines 1 to 3)

wn s pw tni tp-ꜥ sḏꜣ.f	[...] there was a man, ageing, just before his passing,
iw sꜣ.f m nḫn n sꜣrt.f	as his son was a child not yet trained (?)
šꜣꜥ.n.f ḫsf ḥr kꜣ[...]*pw ḥsb*(*t*)	He began to punish (?) .. [...] .. of a conscript woman (?)
n wpt.f r [..] *mdw*[*t?*]	he had not opened his mouth to speak (?),
ḫr.tn iṯ.tn sw m ḥsbw n ḫpw	and you all seize him as a conscript for death,
rmw [...] *šmt* [...]	weeping [...] walking [...]

35. (Papyrus Leiden I 344, column 16, lines 4 to 11)
lost

36. (Papyrus Leiden I 344, column 16, line 12 to column 17, line 23)

[...] *ḫt.tn wn tꜣ* [...]	[...] your following (?), the land was [...]
[...] *ḥr wꜣt nbt*	[...] everywhere.
ir iꜣꜥš.tw n ḥ[...]	If the [...] was called [...]
rmw r.f ms	weeping indeed (over) birth
[...]*.sn ꜥḳ r ḥwt-kꜣw*	[...] they [...] to enter the soul-chapels,
wbd twtw [...] *hꜣwt nt sꜥḥw*	burn the statues [...] corpses of the noble dead,
bi nty ḥꜣty-ꜥ (blank space)	the place which the mayor (blank space)
.. [..] *n ḫrp kꜣt* [...]	[...] to the director (?) of works [...]
.. [...]	.. [...]

The Tale and Laments of Khuninpu

This Middle Egyptian composition is known from four manuscripts apparently preserved in two Theban tombs (see Question One, Groups One and Two). A cycle of nine laments are framed by a dramatic narrative. The hero Khuninpu is an inhabitant of the desolate landscape of the Wadi Natrun, in the First Intermediate Period (perhaps one or two hundred years before the Tale was composed, though the date of composition remains debated). His Egyptian 'title' *sẖty* is often translated 'peasant', and the tale is often called in Egyptology 'the Eloquent Peasant', but the people of the Wadi were the diametrical social opposite of the Egyptian peasant farmer, in a fierce social division between the settled and the nomadic or semi-nomadic; that division exists today between farmer and bedouin, in Egypt, or between settled people and gypsy or traveller, in Europe. The Tale opens with a narrative episode in which Khuninpu is robbed by the servant of a high official, on his way to trade goods at the market in the Nile Valley. He petitions the high official, Rensi, so beautifully that Rensi tells the king of his eloquence, and the king orders him to be detained to extract more petitions from him; in increasing desperation, unaware that his wife is not starving at home but being supplied by the state, Khuninpu delivers nine petitions, culminating in the suicidal denunciation of power and the declaration of three principles at the heart of *mꜣꜥt* 'what is Right' (B2, 109-111):

> There can be no yesterday for the do-nothing
> There can be no friend for one deaf to Right
> There can be no festivity for the greedy hearted

The high official Rensi then had the petitions read out to Khuninpu, and then to the king. The fragmented end of the Tale seems to record the dispossession of the corrupt servant, and the giving of all his goods along with the stolen goods to Khuninpu.

In this tale the 'good man' suffers both from the servant who steals his goods, and from the king who effectively forces the fine petitions out of him. This is one of the most direct ancient Egyptian attacks on corrupt power; perhaps its setting in a period of political disunity allowed greater room for criticism of the corruption possible in the state (compare the Teaching for king Merykara, set in the same period).

Transliteration from Papyri Berlin 10499 (R) and 3023 (B1) and 3025 (B2) transcribed Parkinson 1991a, and with transliteration and translation into French Le Guilloux 2002

Journey and Theft

R1.1-1.4

s pw wn ẖw.n-inpw rn.f	There was a man called Khuninpu,
sẖty pw n sẖt ḥmꜣt	A marshdweller of the Salt Marshes,
ist wn ḥmt.f mrt rn.s	And he had a wife called Meret.
ḏd.in sẖty pn n ḥmt.f tn	This marshdweller said to this wife of his:
mt wi m hꜣt r kmt	Look, I am going down to Egypt
r int ꜥḳw im n ẖrdw.i	to buy food there for my children.
šm(.i) swt ẖꜣ.n.i nꜣ n it	I must go, then, when I have measured that grain
nty m pꜣ mẖr m wḏꜣt n sf	which is in the granary as the remnants from yesterday.
ꜥḥꜥ.n ẖꜣ.n.f n.s it ḥḳꜣt ẖmn (?)	Then he measured for her eight (?) barrels of grain.

R1.5-1.6

ḏd.in sẖty pn n ḥmt.f tn	Then this marshdweller said to this wife of his:
mt .. n.t it ḥḳꜣt sn	See, there are two barrels of grain for you,
r ꜥḳw ḥnꜥ ẖrdw.t	for food, with your children.
ir.t n.i swt it ḥḳꜣt siw	Make for me six barrels of grain, then,
m t ḥnḳt n hrw nb	into bread and beer for each day,
kꜣ ꜥnẖ.i im.f	So that I can live off it.

R1.7-6.1

hꜣt pw ir.n sẖty pn r kmt				This marshdweller went down to Egypt			
ꜣtp.n.f ꜥꜣw.f m				When he had laden his donkeys with			
iꜣꜣ	*rdmt*	*ḥsmn*	*ḥmꜣt*	reeds	herbs	natron	salt
ẖt [..]tyw		*ꜥwnt nt tꜣ-iḥw*		wood of [..]tyw-land		sticks of Farafra Oasis	
ẖnwt nt bꜣw		*ẖꜣwt nt wnšw*		skins of animals		furs of jackals	
nšꜣw	*ꜥnw*	*tnmw*	*ẖpr-wr*	*nšꜣ*-plants	*ꜥnw*-stones	*tnmw*-plants	*ẖpr-wr* plants
sꜣhwt	*sꜣkswt*	*miswt*		*sꜣhwt*	*sꜣkswt*-minerals	*miswt*-plants	
snt	*ꜥb[..]w*	*ibsꜣ*	*inbi*	*snt*-stones	*ꜥb[..]w*-stones	*ibsꜣ*-plants	*inbi*-plants

mnw	*nʿrw*	*wgs*	pigeons	*nʿrw*-birds	*wgs*-birds
wbn	*tbsw*	*gngnt*	*wbn*-plants	*tbsw*-plants	*gngnt*-minerals
šny-t3	*inst*		earth-hair plants	*inst*-minerals	
mḥ m inw nb nfr n sḫt ḥm3t			complete with all good produce of the Salt Marshes		

R6.2-6.7

šmt pw in sḫty pn	Then this marshdweller went
m ḫntyt r hnn-nswt	south to Henenesut.
spr pw ir.n.f r w n pr ffi	He arrived at the district of the House of Fefi
r mḥty mdnit	To the north of Medenit.
gm.n.f s im ʿḥʿ ḥr mryt	There he found a man standing on the shore;
nmty-nḫt rn.f s3 s pw isry rn.f	Nemtynakht was his name, the son of a man (of standing) called Isry,
ḏt pw nt imy-r pr wr mrw s3 rnsi	Estate-staff of the high steward Meru's son Rensi.

R6.7-7.6

ḏd.in nmty-nḫt pn	Then this Nemtynakht said,
m33.f ʿ3w n sḫty pn ʿ3byw ḥr ib.f	as his eyes fell on the donkeys of this marshdweller, tempting his heart
ḏd.f h3 n.i šsp nb mnḫ	To say if only I had some powerful figure,
ʿw3.i ḥnw n sḫty pn im.f	I could use it to steal the goods of this marshdweller.
ist rf pr nmty-nḫt pn	Now the house of this Nemtynakht
ḥr sm3-t3 n r-w3t	was at the junction of the byway;
ḫns pw	It was narrow,
n wsḫ is pw ḳnn.f r wsḫ n d3iw	indeed no broader in its span than the breadth of a cloth
iw w3t.f wʿt ẖr mw kt ẖr it	With its one end under water and the other under the crop.

R7.6-8.3

ḏd.in nmty-nḫt pn n šmsw.f	Then this Nemtynakht said to his guard:
is in n.i ifd m pr.i	Fetch me a sheet from my house.
in.in.tw.f n.f ḥr-ʿ	It was brought to him at once,
ʿḥʿ.n sš.n.f sw ḥr sm3-t3 n r-w3t	And he spread it over the junction of the byway,
wn.in ḥnn sdb.f ḥr mw	So its fringe rested on the water,
npnpt.f ḥr it	and its straight edge on the crop.

R8.3-8.6

šmt pw ir.n sḫty pn	This marshdweller proceeded
ḥr w3t nt rmṯ nbt	on the thoroughfare,
ḏd.in nmty-nḫt pn	And this Nemtynakht said:
ir hrw sḫty in ḫnd.k ḥr ḥbsw.i	have a care, marshman, not to tread on my clothing.
ḏd.in sḫty pn	Then this marshdweller said:
irw m ḏdt.k nfr mtn.i	May it be done as you say: my way is fair.
prt pw ir.n.f r ḥrw	He moved to go up.

R8.7-9.2

ḏd.in nmty-nḫt pn	And this Nemtynakht said:
in iw n.k it.i r w3t sḫty	Is my crop yours as a byway, marshman?
ḏd.in sḫty pn	Then this marshdweller said:
nfr mtn.i ʿḥmt k3t mtnw ẖr it	My way is fair. The bank is steep, and the road is under the crop.
ḥn.n.k r.f w3t r.n m ḥbsw.k	You have taken over the way, against us, with your clothing.
In nn r.f di.k sw3.n ḥr w3t	Can you not let us pass by on the road now?

B1.39-43

ʿḥʿ.n mḥ.n wʿ m n3 n ʿ3 r.f	Just then one of the donkeys filled its mouth
m b3t nt it-šmʿ	with a wisp of fine grain,
ḏd.in nmty-nḫt pn	And this Nemtynakht said:
mk wi r nḥm ʿ3.k sḫty	Now I am going to take your donkey, marshman,
ḥr wnm.f it-šmʿ.i	for eating my fine grain.
mk sw r hbt ḥr ḳn.f	It is going to plough for its brazenness.

B1.44-49

ḏd.in sẖty pn	Then this marshdweller said:
nfr mtn.i wꜥt ḥdt mḏ	My way is fair. One the destruction of ten!
in.n.i ꜥꜣ.i ḥr šnꜥ mḏ	I bought my donkey for ten ring-units,
iṯ.k sw ḥr mḥ.n.f r.f m bꜣt nt it-šmꜥ	and you seize it for having filled its mouth with a wisp of fine grain.
iw.i grt rẖ.kwi nb n spꜣt tn	But I know the master of this district:
n(y)-s(t) imy-r pr wr mrw sꜣ rnsy	It belongs to the high steward Meru's son Rensy.
ntf grt ẖsf ꜥwꜣ nb m tꜣ pn r ḏr.f	Now he is the punisher of every thief in this entire land:
in ꜥwꜣ.tw r.f m spꜣt.f	Is he going to have robbery in his district?

B1.49-55

ḏd.in nmty-nẖt pn	Then this Nemtynakht said:
in pꜣ pw ẖn n mdt ḏdw rmṯ	Is that the sense of the phrase that people say,
dm.tw rn n ḥwrw ḥr nb.f	"the name of the underling is pronounced for his master"?
ink pw mdw n.k	I am the one you are talking to,
imy-r pr wr pw sẖꜣy.k	and the high steward is the one you refer to!
ꜥḥꜥ.n tꜣ.n.f n.f iꜣꜣyt nt isr wꜣḏ r.f	Then he took up a branch of a green tamarisk against him,
ꜥḥꜥ.n ꜥꜣ.f ꜥt.f nb im.s	And was beating him all over his body with it.
nḥm ꜥꜣw.f sꜥḳ r spꜣt.f	His donkeys were taken and herded into his estate.

B1.55-58

wn.in sẖty pn ḥr rmyt ꜥꜣw wrt	Then this marshdweller cried aloud very greatly,
n mr n iryt r.f	At the ill that had been done to him,
ḏd.in nmty-nẖt pn	Until this Nemtynakht said:
m ḳꜣ ẖrw.k sẖty	Do not raise your voice, marshman.
mk tw r dmi n nb sgr	Look, you are at the town of the lord of silence.

B1.58-63

ḏd.in sẖty pn	Then this marshdweller said:
ẖw.k wi ꜥwꜣ.k ẖnw.i	You strike me, you rob my goods,
nḥm.k r.f nẖwt.i m r.i	you even take my cry from my mouth!
nb sgr di.k r.k n.i ẖt.i	O Lord of Silence, just give me my things,
iẖ tm.i sbḥ nrw.k	and then I can stop spiking your dreadfulness.
ir.in sẖty pn ꜥḥꜥw hrw md r hrw	And this marshdweller spent ten days to the day
ḥr spr n nmty-nẖt	Petitioning Nemtynakht,
n rdi.f mꜣꜥ.f r.s	But he paid no heed to it.

Turning to Rensy

B1.63-67

šmt pw ir.n sẖty pn r ḥnn-nswt	Then this marshdweller went to Henennesut
r spr n imy-r pr wr mrw sꜣ rnsy	To petition the high steward Meru's son Rensy.
gm.n.f sw ḥr prt m sbꜣ n pr.f	He found him leaving the gate of his house
r hꜣt r ḳꜣḳꜣw.f n ꜥryt	To board his palace barge.

B1.67-70

ḏd.in sẖty pn	Then this marshdweller said:
hꜣ rdi.t(w) swḏꜣ.i ib.k	Would that it be permitted that I communicate to you
ḥr pꜣ ẖn n mdt	over this matter of speech.
sp pw rdit iwt n.i šmsw.k n ẖrt-ib.k	It would be an opportunity to send me your preferred follower,
hꜣb.i n.k sw ḥr.s	That I might send him to you over it.

B1.70-73

rdi.in imy-r pr wr mrw sꜣ rnsy	And so the high steward Meru's son Rensy
šm šmsw.f n ẖrt-ib.f tp-im.f	Sent his preferred follower ahead of him
hꜣb sw sẖty pn ḥr mdt tn mi ḳi.s nb	For this marshdweller to send him on this matter in its every detail.

B1.73-80

wn.in imy-r pr wr mrw sꜣ rnsy	Then the high steward Meru's son Rensy
ḥr srẖt nmty-nẖt pn n srw nty r gs.f	Accused this Nemtynakht to the officials who were beside him,
ḏd.in.sn n.f	And then they said to him:

smwn sẖty.f pw iw n ky r gs.f	It is probably a marshman of his who went to someone else.
mk irt.sn pw r sẖtyw.sn	That is what they do to their marshmen
iww n kt-ẖt r-gs.sn	Who go to others beside them.
mk irt.sn pw	That is just what they do.
sp pw n ḥsf.tw n nmty-nḫt pn	What is the point of punishing this Nemtynakht
ḥr nhw n ḥsmn ḥnꜥ nhw n ḥmꜣt	For a bit of natron and a bit of salt?
wḏ.tw n.f dbꜣ st dbꜣ.f st	He can be ordered to repay it, and he repays it.

B1.80-82

gr pw ir.n imy-r pr wr mrw sꜣ rnsy	Then the high steward Meru's son Rensy fell silent,
n wšb.f n nn srw	And did not answer the officials
wšb.f n sẖty pn	how he would reply to this marshdweller.

The First Petition

B1.83-102

iw.in r.f sẖty pn r spr	Then this marshdweller came to petition
n imy-r pr wr mrw sꜣ rnsy	the high steward Meru's son Rensy,
ḏd.f	Saying:
imy-r pr wr nb.i wr n wrw	High steward, my lord! Great of the great!
sšmw n iwtt ntyw	Leader of what does not and what does exist!
ir hꜣ.k r š n mꜣꜥt	May you go down to the lake of Right,
sḳd.k im.f m mꜣꜥ	To sail on it with a fair wind,
nn kfꜣ ndbyt ḥtꜣ.k	Without the thread of your sails being unveiled,
nn ihm dpt.k nn iwt iyt m ẖt.k	Without your boat being wrecked, or harm befalling your mast,
nn swꜣ sgrgw.k	Without your fasteners being cut,
nn sḫm.k ḥꜣꜥꜥ.k ḥr tꜣ	Without your thrust hitting the shore,
nn iṯ tw nwt	Without the flood overpowering you,
nn dp.k ḏwt nt itrw	Without your tasting the evils of the river,
nn mꜣ.k ḥr snd	Without your sight of a fearful face.
iw n.k rmw šnꜥyw	Roe fish come to you
pḥ.k m ꜣpdw ḏdꜣ	You just pick up the fattened fowl,
ḥr-ntt ntk it n nmḥw	For you are the father of the orphan,
hi n ẖꜣrt sn n wḏꜥt	Husband of the widow, brother of the divorced woman,
šndyt nt iwtw mwt.f	Apron of the motherless.
imi iry.i rn.k m tꜣ pn r hp nb nfr	Let me create your name in this land by every good law:
sšmw šw m ꜥwn-ib	Leader free from greed,
wr šw m nḏyt	Great one free from grinding,
sḥtm grg sḫpr mꜣꜥt	Annihilator of falsehood, he who makes possible Right,
ii ḥr ḫrw dd r	Who comes at the voice of the one who gives a cry.
ḏd.i sḏm.k	I speak that you may hear:
ir mꜣꜥt ḥsy ḥs ḥsyw	Do what is Right, praised one praised by the praised.
dr sꜣirw	Remove affliction.
mk wi ꜣtp.kwi	See me, laden down,
ip wi mk wi m nhw	Judge me, for I am in loss.

Rensy tells the king

B1.102-108

ist rf ḏd.n sẖty pn mdt tn	Now this marshdweller delivered this speech
m rk ḥm n nswt bity	in the time of the dual king .
nb-kꜣw-rꜥ mꜣꜥ ḫrw	Nebkaura true of voice
šmt pw ir.n imy-r pr wr	The high steward Meru's son Rensy went
mrw sꜣ rnsy tp m ḥm.f	before His Power
ḏd.f	To say:
nb i gm.n.i wꜥ m nn n sẖty	My lord, I have come across one of those marshmen,
nfr mdw n wn-mꜣꜥ	Perfect in speech in all truth,
ꜥwꜣ ḥnw.f	Whose goods were stolen,
mk sw iw r spr n.i ḥr.s	And so he has come to petition me about it.

B1.109-115

ḏd.in ḥm.f
m mrr.k mꜣ.i snb.kwi
swdf.k sw ꜥꜣ
nn wšb r ḏdt.f nbt
in mrwt wn.f ḥr ḏd
gr iḫ in.t(w) n.n mdw.f m sš
sḏm.n st
ir swt ꜥnḫ ḥmt.f ḥnꜥ ẖrdw.f
mk iw wꜥ m nꜣ n sḫtyw
r šwt pr.f r tꜣ
ir grt ꜥnḫ sḫty pn m ḥꜥw.f
wnn.k ḥr rdit di.tw n.f ꜥḳw
nn rdit rḫ.f ntt ntk rdi n.f st

Then His Power said:
As you desire to see me well,
Delay him here,
Without answering anything he says,
In order to have him speaking.
Be silent, so that his speech may be brought to us in writing,
And we may hear it.
But ensure that his wife and his children live,
For one of these marshmen comes
Only when his house is bared to the ground.
And ensure that this marshman lives himself:
You are to have him given food,
Without letting him know that it is you who are giving it to him.

B1.115-118

wn.in.tw ḥr rdit n.f
t md ḥnḳt ds sn rꜥ nb
dd st imy-r pr wr mrw sꜣ rnsy
dd.f st n ḫnms.f ntf dd n.f st
ꜥḥꜥ.n hꜣb.n
imy-r pr wr mrw sꜣ rnsy
n ḥḳꜣ-ḥwt n sḫt ḥmꜣt
ḥr irt ꜥḳw n ḥmt sḫty pn
m it ḥḳꜣt ḫmt rꜥ nb

And so he was given
ten loaves and two jars of beer every day:
The high steward Meru's son Rensy was the one giving it –
He would give it to his colleague and he then gave it to him.
Then
the high steward Meru's son Rensy wrote
to the Domain Ruler of the Salt Marshes
About giving food to the wife of this marshdweller,
as three barrels of grain, every day

The Second Petition

B1.119-123

iw.in r.f sḫty pn r spr n.f sp sn
ḏd.f
imy-r pr wr nb.i wr n wrw
ḫwd n ḫwdw
nty wn wr n wrw.f
ḫwd n ḫwdw.f
ḥmw n pt sꜣw n tꜣ ḫꜣy fꜣ wdn
ḥmw m sbn sꜣw m gsꜣ
ḫꜣy m ir nwdw

Then this marshdweller came to petition him a second time,
Saying:
High steward, my lord! Great of the great!
Richest of the rich
Who is the greatest of his great men,
And richest of his rich men,
Rudder of heaven, pillar of earth, the scales carrying the weight:
O rudder, do not fail! O column, do not crash down!
O scales, do not waver!

B1.123-126

nb wr ḥr iṯt m iwtt nb.s
ḥr ꜥḏꜣ ḥr wꜥ
ḥrt.k m pr.k
ḥnḳt hnw ḥnꜥ t
ptr pnḳt.k m ssꜣt twꜣw.k
in mwt mwt ḥnꜥ ḥr.f
in iw.k r s n nḥḥ

Does a great lord go stealing from that without a lord
Or committing crimes against the lone man?
Your share is in your house,
Jars of beer, and bread:
What is your return to be sated on those begging from you?
Does the dead man die with his dependants?
Are you to be a man of eternity?

B1.126-130

n iw is pw iwsw gsꜣ tḫ nnm
mty mꜣꜥ ḫpr m tnbḫ
mk mꜣꜥt twḫ.s ḫr.k
nš.t(i) m st.s
srw ḥr irt iyt
tp-ḥsb n mdt ḥr rdit ḥr gs
sḏmyw ḥr ḥnp

Is it not an evil, a collapsed balance, a counterweight held back,
A right thinking man made into a hog?
See, what is Right is slipping away beneath you,
Dislodged from her place.
The officials are committing crimes,
Standards of speech are set aside,
The assessors are stealing.

B1.130-134

iṯ.f siꜣty pw n mdt m ꜥḳꜣ.s
ḥr irt r.f nwdw im.s
rdi ṯꜣw ḥr gꜣt ḥr tꜣ

Now the one to catch the violator of speech in its correctness
Is himself causing the flight from it.
The one who gives air is a rarity on earth,

srfw ḥr rdit n šnp.tw
psšw m ꜥwn
dr sꜣir m wḏ ir.t(w).f
dmi m wḏnw.f
ḫsf iw ḥr irt iyt

The one who brings breath is causing its stifling,
The sharer is now greedy,
The one to repel damage is now the one ordering it to be done.
The town is now its floodwaves.
The one to punish evil is committing crimes.

B1.134-135

ḏd.in imy-r pr wr mrw sꜣ rnsy
in ꜥꜣt pw n.k-imy ḥr ib.k
r iṯ tw šmsw

Then the high steward Meru's son Rensy said
Is it an important matter of yours, on your heart,
for a guard to seize you?

B1.135-139

ḏd.in sḫty pn
ḫꜣw n ꜥḥꜥw ḥr siꜣ n.f
mḥ n ky ḥr hḳs ḫꜣw.f
sšm r hpw ḥr wḏ ꜥwꜣt
n-m irf ḫsf.f bw-ḥwrw
dr nw ḥr irt nwdw
ꜥḳꜣ ky ḥr ḫꜣbb
wfꜣ ky ir iyt

Then this marshdweller said:
The measurer of heaps takes a cut for himself,
The man filling for another cheats on his amount,
The man guiding by the rules is ordering robbery.
Who then is there to fight off wretchedness?
The man to resist weakness is doing the wavering.
The uprightness of the other is bending,
The slander of the other is the cause of crime.

B1.139-142

itr gm.k r.k n.k
ḥwꜥ ḫsf ꜣw iyt
iw biꜣ r st.f nt sf
wḏ r.f pw
ir n irr r rdit ir.f
dwꜣ-nṯr n.f pw ḥr irt.f
nnit ḫt pw tp-ꜥ stit
wḏ ḫt pw n nb ḥnt

Are you to find for yourself then,
punishment passes fast, crime endures?
Character comes to its place of yesterday:
It is ordered indeed,
'Act for one who acts, to cause him to act'
That means he is thanked for his deeds,
That means things are deflected before the blow,
That means things are ordered for the lord of the task.

B1.142-154

ḥꜣ ꜣ ꜣt sḥtm.s
pnꜥ m rwi.k ꜥnd m ꜣpdw.k
ḫbꜣ m ḳbḥw.k
pr mꜣw špwt sḏmw sḫw
sšmw ḫpr m stnmw
ꜥnbrw in tr snb n.k
irr.k r.k irf r-m
mk tw nḫt wsr.t(i)
ꜥ.k pr ib.k ꜥwn
sf swꜣ ḥr.k
nḫ-wy mꜣir sky.k
twt.k n wpwty n ḫnty
mk tw swꜣ.t(i) ḥr nbt idw
nn n.k nn n.s nn.s nn r.k
n irr.k st n irr st
sf nb t nḫt n ḫnr
twt ṯꜣwt n iwtw ḫt.f
ḫnp ḫt in ḫni
sp bin iwty šwiw

Oh just for a moment that would destroy,
For chaos in your garden, decimation on your birds,
levelling off your waterfowl.
A sighted man can emerge blinded, a hearing man deaf,
A guide can turn into a stray.
Measure-man, does it go well for you?
But why act against yourself?
See you are powerful and strong,
Your arm is out, your heart is greedy,
Mercy has passed you by.
Woe to the wretch that you destroy!
You are like the envoy of the Crocodile-god,
You are set on the way of the Goddess of Plague:
Nothing for you, nothing for her, her no is no for you,
And if you have not been doing it, it has not been done.
As mercy is of the owner of bread, or strength of the enclosed man,
Theft is apiece with the man who owns nothing.
Removing goods by the enclosed
is an evil matter for one even without emptiness.

B1.155-7

nn r f ṯs.tw im.f
ḥḥ n.f pw
iw.k swt sꜣ.t(i) m t.k
tḫ.t(i) m ḥnḳt.k
iw.k ḫwd.t(i) m sšr nbw

Nothing could be raised from him,
For he is hunting for himself,
Whereas you are stuffed with your bread,
and drunk on your beer,
You are rich in every kind of cloth

B1.157-159

iw ḥr n ḥmy r ḥꜣt	The face of the pilot is to the front,
sbn dpt r mrr.s	But the boat wanders wherever it pleases:
iw nswt m ẖnty	The king is in the Palace,
iw ḥmw m-ꜥ.k	And the steer is in your hands,
rdi.tw iyt m hꜣw.k	But crime is permitted in your setting.

B1.159-161

ꜣw sprw.i wdn fdḳ	My plea is long, for the case is heavy.
išst pw nty im	What is going on in there,
kꜣ.tw	People must think.
ir ibw snb mryt.k	Be a refuge! May your shore be safe.
mk dmi.k šnw	Right now your landing-stage is infested.

B.162-170

ꜥḳꜣ ns.k im.k tnmw	May your tongue be straight, do not waver;
tꜣmw pw n s ꜥt im.f	The organ within is a serpent for a man.
m ḏd grg sꜣw srw	Do not tell lies, and watch the officials;
mnḏm pw ꜥḏyw sḏmyw	The assessors are a basket of harm,
smw.sn pw ḏd grg	For their pasture is the telling of lies,
wn.f is ḥr ib.sn	That is light on their hearts.
rḫ ḫt n rmṯ nbt	Oh knower of all people,
in ẖm.k m hꜣw.i	Can you not know of my case?
dr sꜣir n mw nb	Oh remover of need for all waters,
mk wi ḥr mtnw iw	See me on the road, boatless.
mni mḥ nb	Oh moorer of every drowning man,
šd bgꜣw	Rescue the shipwrecked,
ẖdr.k wi m hꜣw ir ḏr.k	Defend me in a case at your door.

The Third Petition

B1.170-174

iw.in r.f sḫty pn	Then this marshdweller came
r spr n.f ḫmt-nw sp	to petition him a third time,
ḏd.f	Saying:
imy-r pr wr nb.i	High steward, my lord!
ntk rꜥ nb pt ḥnꜥ šnwt.k	You are the Sun-god lord of heaven with your entourage,
iw ḫrt bw nb im.k mi nwy	And the affairs of all people are with you like the waves.
ntk ḥꜥpy swꜣḏ šꜣw	You are the Flood-god making the lands green,
grg iꜣwt ẖbꜣt	establishing the dry high ground.

B1.174-179

ẖsf ꜥwꜣ nḏ ḥr mꜣir	Punish the robber, champion the afflicted
m ḫpr m wḏnw r sprw	Do not become a wave against the plaintiff
sꜣw tkn nḥḥ	Beware the approach of eternity.
mr wꜣḥ mi ḏd	Desire enduring, following the saying:
ṯꜣw pw n fnd irt mꜣꜥt	'doing what is Right is the air for breathing'.
ir ẖsft r ẖsfw n.f	Punish the one who should be punished
nn sn.tw r tp-ḥsb.k	And none can compare you against your measure

B1.179-182

in iw iwsw nnm.f	Can the scales err?
in iw mḫꜣt hr rdit ḥr gs	Can the balance be partial
in iw r.f ḏhwty sfn.f	Can Thoth be corrupted?
iḫ r ir.k iyt	Then it is for you to commit evil,
rdi.k tw snw n ḫmt pn	You can make yourself second to these three.
ir sfn ḫmt ḥr sfn.k	If three are corrupt, then you are corrupted.

B1.182-186

m wšb nfrt m bint	Do not answer good with evil,
m rdi kt m st kt	Do not put one thing in the place of another.

rwd mdt r snmyt	Words grow more than weeds
r dmi n ẖnm m wšb.s	At the touch of smell in their reply;
ntf iyt r rdit rwd ḥbsw	An arrival is flooded to cause cloth to grow.

B1.186-190

spw ẖmt pw r rdit ir.f	This makes three times to have him act!
ir.k ḥmw r ndbyt	Act as steer against the fringe,
šd wḏnw r irt mꜣꜥt	Rescue the flooded to apply what is Right!
sꜣw ḥꜣ.k r.k ḥr nfryt	Avoid flowing against yourself by the towrope:
ꜥḳꜣyt nt tꜣ irt mꜣꜥt	The straight of the land is to do what is Right.

B1.190-196

m ḏd grg iw.k wr.t(i)	Do not tell lies while you are great.
m is iw.k dns.t(i)	Do not be light while you have stature
m ḏd grg ntk iwsw	Do not tell lies – you are the balance
m tnbẖ ntk tp-ḥsb	Do not be a hog – you are the measure
mk tw m tp-wꜥ ḥnꜥ iwsw	You are as one with the balance:
ir gꜣs.f ḥr.k gsꜣ	If it collapses, you collapse too.
m sbn ir.k ḥmw	Do not err when you are acting as steer;
šd ḥr nfryt	Keep hold of the towrope.
m iṯ ir.k r iṯw	Do not take, but act against the taker.
n wr is pw	There is no greatness
wr im ꜥwn-ib	in the great there – (if) he is greedy .

B1.197-202

tẖ pw ns.k	Your tongue is the balance,
dbn pw ib.k	Your heart is the weight,
rmnw.f pw spty.ky	Your lips are its arms.
ir ḥbs.k ḥr.k r nẖt-ḥr	If you veil your face at the strong-minded,
n-m irf ẖsf.f bw-ḥwrw	Who is going to punish a wretched case?
mk tw m ḥwrw n rẖty	You are as a wretch to a washerman,
ꜥwn-ib ḥr ḥdt ẖnmw	The selfish man who destroys friendship,
btn mḥnk.f n twꜣ.f	The quarreller who embroils his pacifier,
sn.f pw iy in n.f	Whose brother then has to come to deliver for him.

B1.202-209

mk tw m ẖnty ḏꜣ nb ḥmt	You are the ferryman who ferries the briber,
ꜥḳꜣy ꜥḳꜣ.f fdḳ	The straightener whose straightness is warped.
mk tw m ḥry šnꜥ	You are the store master
n rdi.n.f swꜣ šw ḥr-ꜥ	Who does not allow the empty-handed to pass at once.
mk tw ṯnẖr n rẖyt	Look at you, the boar of the lapwings,
ꜥnẖ m ḥwrw nw ꜣpdw	Living off the most miserable of birds.
mk tw wdpw rš.f pw rḥs	Look at you, the cupbearer whose joy is slaughter,
nn iꜣtyw iry r.f	Without any of its injuries affecting him.
mk tw m mniw n ḏw.s is r.i	You are the herdsman – it is no evil on me,
n ip.n.k	You cannot count.

B1.209-215

iḫ ir.k nhw m msḥ skn	Then you can suffer loss from the crocodile, the voracious,
ibw tš r dmi n tꜣ r ḏr.f	For the shelters are vanished at the landing-point throughout the land.
sḏmw n ꜣ sḏm.n.k	Oh hearer, but no, you do not hear!
tm.k tr sḏm ḥr-m	Why though do you fail to hear?
iw min ꜣ ḫsf n.i ꜣdw	Today, right now, punish the aggressor for me;
iw msḥ ḥt.f	There is the crocodile in pursuit.
ptr r.f km iry n.k	What gain can it possibly bring you?
gm.tw imnw mꜣꜥt	The hidden, what is Right, is (always) found,
rdi.t(w) sꜣ grg r tꜣ	And falsehood (always) rejected.
m grg sbꜣ n iit.f	Do not build on tomorrow before it has come,
n rḫ.n.tw iyt im.f	For none can know the evil within it.

B1.215-218	
ỉst r.f ḏd.n sḫty pn mdt tn	Now this marshdweller had delivered this speech,
ỉmy-r pr wr mrw sꜣ rnsy	While the high steward Meru's son Rensy
r pgꜣ n ꜥrryt	Was at the porch of the palace gateway.
ꜥḥꜥ.n rdỉ.n.f ꜥḥꜥ ỉmy-sꜣ sn r.f	Then he set two bodyguards on him
ẖr smỉw	With lashes,
ꜥḥꜥ.n ꜥꜣg.sn ꜥt.f nbt ỉm	And they thrashed every limb of his body with them.
B.218-224	
ḏd.ỉn sḫty pn	So this marshdweller said:
sꜣ mrw tnm ḫr.f	The son of Meru is a man astray,
ḥr.f šp r mꜣꜣt.f sḫ r sḏmt.f	His face blind to what he should see, deaf to what he should hear,
th-ỉb ḥr sḫꜣyt n.f	Without care for what he should remember.
mk tw m nỉwt nn ḥḳꜣ-ḥwt.s	You are a city without its governor,
mỉ ẖt nn wr.s	Like a clan without its master,
mỉ dpt nn sḫry ỉm.s	Like a boat without a pilot on board,
smꜣyt nn sšmw.s	A gang without its guide.
mk tw m šntw ỉṯꜣ	You are the policeman who steals,
ḥḳꜣ-ḥwt šspw	The city governor who takes bribes,
ỉmy-r w ḫsf ḥꜥḏꜣ	The district official to repel violence
ḫpr m ỉmy-ḥꜣt n ỉr	Turned into the model for the criminal.

The Fourth Petition

B1.225-231	
ỉw.ỉn r.f sḫty pn r spr n.f fd-nw sp	Then this marshdweller came to petition him a fourth time,
gm.n sw ḥr prt m sbꜣ	having found him leaving the gate
n ḥwt-nṯr nt ḥry-š.f	of the temple of Heryshef,
ḏd.f	Saying:
ḥsw ḥs tw ḥry-š.f	Favoured one, may Heryshef favour you
ỉỉ.n.k m pr.f	As you have come from his house.
ḥḏ bw nfr nn ꜥbt.f	Happiness is destroyed, it has no following.
ptḫ sꜣ n grg r tꜣ	Backs are turned to falsehood against the land.
ỉn ỉw tꜣ mẖnt sꜥḳt.s	Is that ferry its enterer?
ḏꜣ.t(w) ỉr.f m-ꜥ.s	Or are crossings to be done then with that?
ḫpr sp m msdd	An opportunity turns to hatefulness.
ḏꜣt ỉtrw m sꜣ tbwty	Crossing the river on the back of sandals,
ḏꜣt nfr nn	Is a crossing good? No!
B1.232-236	
n-m tr sḏr r šsp ḥḏ	Who then can sleep till dawn breaks?
šmt m grḥ sby m hrw	Or is it walking by night and marching on by day?
rdỉt ꜥḥꜥ s r sp.f	Allowing a man to rise to his moment
nfr n wn-mꜣꜥt	Is good in truth indeed.
mk nn km n ḏd n.k st	But there is no point in telling that to you.
sf swꜣ ḥr.k	Mercy has passed you by.
nḫ-wy mꜣỉr sky.k	How plaintive is the wretch you ruin.
B1.236-242	
mk tw mḥw ỉꜥ ỉb.f	You are a harpooner who satisfies his heart,
wdd r ỉrt mrt.f	Who shoots to achieve his desire,
ḫꜣꜥ dbw stỉ smꜣw	Hunter of hippopotami, shooter of wild cattle,
pḥ rmw sḫt ꜣpdw	Catching fish and snaring birds.
nn ḫꜣḫ r šw m wꜥrw	The hasty speaker is never free of stumbling,
nn ỉs ỉb dns sḫr-ẖt	The light-hearted is never heavy in pulse.
wꜣḥ ỉb.k rḫ.k mꜣꜥt	Calm your heart to know what is Right,
dꜣỉr stpt.k r nfr bss grw	Control your choice for the good of drawing in the quiet man.

B1.242-248

nn sẖmw mḏd bw iḳr	No overarcher can tread excellence
nn wn ẖꜣẖ ib in.tw ꜥ	No hasty-hearted man is given a hand.
sgmḥ irty swḏꜣ.tw ib	Eyes are to be opened, and the heart made to swell;
m kꜣhsw ẖft wsr.k	Do not terrorise by your power,
tm spr bw ḏw r.k	To avoid the complaints of evil against you.
swꜣ ḥr sp iw.f r sn-nw	Bypass a matter and it only redoubles.
in wnm dp	Only the eater can taste.
iw wšd wšb.f	and only the asked answer.
in sḏr mꜣꜣ rswt	Only the sleeper can see a dream.

B1.248-256

ir wḏꜥ rwt m ḥsfw n.f	If judgement on one to be punished
iw.f m imy-ḥꜥt n ir	Is a model for the criminal,
wẖꜣ mk tw pḥ.t(i)	Fool, you are caught!
ẖm ẖt mk tw wšd.t(i)	Ignoramus, you are under enquiry,
pnḳ mwy mk tw ꜥḳ.t(i)	Water-scooper, you are sunk!
ḥmy m sbn dpwt.k	Pilot, do not deviate your boat,
sꜥnẖw m rdi mwt.tw	Life-giver, do not cause death,
sḥtmw m rdi ḥtm.tw	Destroyer, do not cause destruction,
šwyt m ir m šw	Shadow, do not turn into hot air,
ibw m rdi iṯt msḥ	Shelter, do not let the crocodile catch!
fd-nw sp ꜣ m spr n.k	But this is the fourth time of pleading to you –
in r.f wrš i r f	Am I to spend my life doing this?

The Fifth Petition

B1.256-262

iw.in r.f sḫty pn r spr n.f diw-nw sp	Then this marshdweller came to petition him a fifth time,
ḏd.f	Saying:
imy-r pr wr nb.i	High steward, my lord!
iw ẖwdw ḥr [...]	The trapper is [...]-fish,
nyw ḥr smꜣ iy	The spearer is killing the *iy*-fish,
sti rmw ḥr ẖꜣẖ ꜥwbbw	The fisherman is hunting down *ꜥwbbw*-fish,
ḏꜣbḥw r pꜣḳrw	The netter is after the *pꜣḳrw*-fish.
iw wḥꜥ rmw ẖbꜣ.f itrw	The fish catcher is devastating the river.
mk tw m mnt iry	You are just the same.

B1.262-270

m ꜥwn ḥwrw ḥr ẖt.f	Do not rob the poor of his goods
fn rḫ.n.k sw	The weak, you recognised.
ṯꜣw pw n mꜣir ẖt.f	The air for a wretch is his goods.
dbb fnd.f pw nḥm st	Taking them means blocking his breathing.
rdi.n.tw.k r sḏm mdt	You were appointed to hear cases,
r wḏꜥ sn-nw r ḥsf ꜥwꜣ-ir.f	To judge the second, to punish violent crime.
mk fꜣ pw n iṯꜣ iry.k	But your action is to sustain the thief.
iw mḥ.tw ib im.k	Trust is placed in you,
iw.k ẖpr.t(i) m thw	And you have turned into a lawbreaker.
rdi.n.t(w).k r dnit n mꜣir	You were appointed as a refuge for the wretch,
sꜣw mḥ.f	So stop him drowning –
mk tw m š.f stꜣw	You are his lake of loss.

The Sixth Petition

B1.270-278

iw.in r f sḫty pn r spr n.f si-nw sp	Then this marshdweller came to petition him a sixth time,
ḏd.f	Saying:
imy-r pr wr nb.i	High steward, my lord!
nb sis.f grg sḫpr mꜣꜥt	The lord who brings wrongs low is he who makes Right possible;
sḫpr bw nb nfr sḥtm bw	One who makes possible all goodness is the destroyer of emptiness,
mi iw sꜣw ḏr.f hḳr	Just as the arrival of fullness removes hunger,
ḥbsw ḏr.f ḥꜣwt	Or of clothing removes nakedness,

mi ḥtp pt r sꜣ dꜥ ḳꜣ	As the sky is calm after a violent storm,
sšmm sḥsw nb	Warming all who were shivering,
mi ḫt pst wꜣḏwt	Like a fire heating what was raw,
mi mw ꜥḫm ibt	Like water quenching thirst.

B1.278-287

mꜣꜣ m ḥr.k	See from your face!
psšw m ꜥwnw	The sharer is now greedy,
shrr m ir ꜣhw	The peacemaker is a cause of destruction,
stwt m ir mnwt	The healer is a cause of pain.
iw siꜣty sšrr mꜣꜥt	The cutter is belittling what is Right.
mḥ nfr n hḳs n wbn mꜣꜥt	A good filling neither empties nor overfills what is Right.
ir in.k imi n snw.k	If you gain, give to your fellow.
wgyt šwt m ꜥḳꜣ	Jaw without any straightness!
iw ꜣhw sšm.f r iwdt	The man of destruction may guide to exile,
iw sḫry inn.f rwwt	The judgemental may cause flight,
n rḫ.n.tw wnnt m ib	None can know what resides in the heart.

B1.288-296

m wsf ir.k r smit fdḳ.k	Do not delay your action against the reporting of your corruption!
n-m ṯs.f ꜥḥꜣ-mw m ꜥ.k	Who would raise a mooring-post in your hand,
mi ḫt wn sp n mwy ḫpr	Like a door that opens at the moment of a flood happening?
ir ꜥḳ dpt iw šdt.s ꜣḳw	If a boat is holed, its delivery is loss,
ꜣtpw.s n tꜣ ḥr mryt nbt	Its cargo grounded along the whole shore.
iw.k sbꜣ.t(i) iw.k ḥmw.t(i) iw.k twt	You are trained, expert, fit
n is n ꜥwn	If only for grasping.
iw.k ir.k twtw bw nb	You are acting the image of everyone,
iw hꜣw.k m nwdw ꜥḳꜣ	Your affairs are as straight loops,
siꜣty n tꜣ r ḏr.f	Butcher of the entire land!
kꜣny n bw-ḥwrw	Gardener of misery,
ḥr ntf ḥsp.f m iwyt	Busy watering his garden with evil,
r sḫpr ḥsp.f m grg	To turn his garden into falsehood,
r ntf iyt n ḏt	To water it with crimes for the place of eternity.

The Seventh Petition

B1.297-304

iw.in r.f sḫty pn r spr n.f sfḫ-nw sp	Then this marshdweller came to petition him a seventh time,
ḏd.f	Saying:
imy-r pr wr nb.i	High steward, my lord!
ntk ḥmw n tꜣ r ḏr.f	You are the steer of the entire land,
sḳdd tꜣ ḫft wḏ.k	The land sails according to your command.
ntk sn-nw n ḏḥwty	You are the second to Thoth,
wḏꜥ nn rdit ḥr gs nb	Who judges without taking any side.
wꜣḥ.k nis tw s r sp.f n wn-mꜣꜥ	Be patient, when a man calls you over his case of true need.
m šnt ib.k nnk st	Do not bridle in your heart because it is not yours.
ḫpr ꜣw-ḥr m ḥwꜥ-ib	A joyful man is become downcast.
m wꜣ n ntt n iyt	Do not fail at what has not come,
m ḥꜥw n ntt n ḫprt	Do not rejoice over what has not happened.
iw wḫd sꜣw.f m ḫnms	A man in pain may be enhanced as a friend,
sḥtm sp ḫpr	And a case that is settled may be undone.
n rḫ.n.tw wnnt m ib	None can know what resides in the heart.

B1.305-310

ḫbꜣ hp ḥḏ tp-ḥsb	The rules are laid waste, the standards are destroyed.
nn mꜣir ꜥnḫ ḥꜥḏꜣ.f	No wretch can live on his humiliation.
n wšd sw mꜣꜥt	Right has not questioned him.
iw grt ẖt.i mḥ.t(i)	My belly is filled, true,
ib.i fꜣ pr is m ẖt.i	But my heart is carried away, right out of my body,
n ꜥ iry	By its effort.
ngt pw m dnit mw.s ꜣsw	This is a breach in a dam, its waters cascading through,

wn r.i r mdt	Opening my mouth to speak.
ꜥḥꜥ ꜣ ꜥḥꜣ.n.i mri.i	Stop now, I have fought my weapon away,
pnḳ.n.i mwy.i	I have used up my last saliva,
snf.n.i ntt m ẖt.i	I have puffed out what was in my body,
iꜥ.n.i šꜣmw.i	I have washed out my rags.

B1.311-319

ẖn.i ḫpr	My speech is done,
mꜣirw.i ḏr ẖft-ḥr.k	My woes are strewn before you.
ptr ḏꜣrw.k	What do you need?
iw wsf.k r tht.k	Your inaction will be your downfall,
iw ꜥwn ib.k r swẖꜣ.k	Your greed will make you ridiculous,
iw snm.k r sẖpr ẖrwyw.k	Your food will prosper your enemies.
in iw.k swt r gmt ky sẖty mitw.i	Or are you going to find another marshdweller like me?
in iw wsfw spry r ꜥḥꜥ r r n pr.f	Is a leisured man, a plaintiff to stand at the entrance of his house?
nn gr rdi.n.k mdw.f	There is no silent man - you have made him speak,
nn sḏr rdi.n.k rs.f	No sleeper - you have made him wake,
nn ẖbꜣ ḥrw sspd.n.k	No sight-damaged - you have equipped,
nn tm-r wn.n.k	No closed-mouthed - you have opened,
nn ẖm rdi.n.k rẖ.f	No innocent - you have made him experienced,
nn wẖꜣ sbꜣ.n.k	No fool - you have taught.
ẖsrw ḏwt pw srw	Officials are the ones there to remove evil,
nbw bw nfr pw	They are the masters of happiness,
ḥmwt pw nt sẖpr ntt	They are the experts for making things possible,
ṯs tp ḥsḳ	And solving the severed head.

The Eighth Petition

B1.320-324

iw.in r.f sẖty pn r spr n.f ẖmn-nw sp	Then this marshdweller came to petition him an eighth time,
ḏd.f	Saying:
imy-r pr wr nb.i	High steward, my lord!
iw ẖr.tw n ẖnt wꜣ	The plunge into avarice is deep.
iw ꜥwn-ib šw.f m sp	The greedy man is deprived of any chance,
iw wn sp.f n wht	And his chance is bound to fail.
iw ꜥwn-ib.k nn n.k st	Your greed, there is nothing in it for you;
iw ꜥwꜣ.k nn ꜣẖ n.k	Your theft, there is no profit in it for you.

B1.324-331

rdi ꜣ ꜥḥꜥ s r sp.f	Instead, let a man rise to his moment,
nfr n wn-mꜣꜥ	Good in all truth,
ẖrt.k pw m pr.k	For your share is in your house,
ẖt.k mḥ.t(i)	Your belly filled.
wbn it ttf.s	Any more grain and it would spill out,
ꜣḳ prw.s n tꜣ	Its surplus perished on the ground.
iṯ ꜥwꜣ nḥmw	Robber! Thief! Grabber!
srw ir.n.tw r ẖsf r iyt	Officials are appointed to punish crime,
ibw pw n ꜣdw	But are now a shelter for the attacker!
srw ir.n.tw r ẖsf r grg	Officials are appointed to punish Wrong,
n rdi.n snd.k spr n.k	But fear of you stops anyone pleading to you.
n siꜣ.n.k ib.i	You cannot penetrate my heart;
gr ꜥnn sw r irt ṯst n.k	A silent man who turns back to raise concerns, to you,
n snd.n.f n twꜣ n.f st	He would not be afraid of putting them to him,
n in sn.f r.k m ẖnw mrrt	if (?) his brother had not been brought against you from inside the street.

B1.331-334

iw šdw.k m sẖt	Your pools are in the marshes,
iw fḳꜣ.k m spꜣt	Your rewards are in the province,
iw ꜥḳw.k m šnꜥ	Your food is in the stores,
iw srw ḥr rdit n.k	The officials are supplying you,

iw.k ḥr iṯt	And you go stealing!
in iw.k m ꜥwꜣy	Are you a robber?
iw stꜣ.tw n.k skw ḥnꜥ.k	Are troops brought along for you, together with you,
r psšt šdwt	To share out the plots?

B1.334-344

ir mꜣꜥt n nb mꜣꜥt	Do what is Right for the lord of Right,
nty wn mꜣꜥt nt mꜣꜥt.f	The one whose Right is the true Right.
ꜥr šfdw gsti ḏḥwty	Reed, paper, palette of Thoth!
ḥr.t(i) r irt iyt	Avoid the committing of crime.
nfr nfrt nfr r.f	What is good is good, even better,
iw swt mꜣꜥt r nḥḥ	Indeed what is Right is for eternity.
hꜣꜣ.s m-ꜥ ir.s r ẖrt-nṯr	Descending with its maker into the cemetery,
iw ḳrs.t(w).f smꜣ tꜣ im.f	Where he is buried and laid to rest,
n sin.tw rn.f tp tꜣ	And his name has not been erased upon earth.
iw.f iw sḫꜣ.tw.f ḥr bw nfr	He, he is remembered for goodness.
tp-ḥsb pw n mdw nṯr	That is the measure of the words of god.
in iwsw pw n gsꜣ.n.f	Is that a scale that could crash down,
in mḫꜣt pw n rdi.n.s ḥr gs	Is that a balance that would be partial?

B1.344-353

mk wi r iwt mk ky r iwt wšd.k	I am to return, but another is to come to question you.
m wšb m wšd grw	Do not answer, do not question the silent.
m pḥ nty n pḥ.n.tw.f	Do not catch the one who cannot be caught.
n sf.n.k n mn.n.k	You cannot feel mercy, you cannot feel pain,
n bhꜣ.n.k n sksk.n.k	You cannot escape, you cannot destroy.
n rdi.n.k n.i dbꜣw n mdt tn nfrt	You cannot give me an exchange for this fine word
prt m r n rꜥ ḏs.f	That comes from the mouth of the Sun-god himself:
ḏd mꜣꜥt ir mꜣꜥt	Say what is Right, do what is Right,
ḏr-ntt wr.s ꜥꜣ.s wꜣḥ.s	For it is great, it is grand, it endures.
gmw.tw kft.s	If its secret can be found out,
sbw.s r imꜣḫ	Its route is to the status of revered spirit.

B1.353-357

in gsꜣ iwsw	Does a balance collapse?
ḥnkw.f pw fꜣyw ḫt	Then its supports will bear the matter.
n ḫpr.n prw n tp-ḥsb	There is no escape from the measure.
n spr.n sp ḫs r dmi	No vile deed can reach safe shore.
ẖr sꜣ r sꜣḥ-tꜣ	The oppressed will be the neighbour.

The Ninth Petition

B2.91-97

iw.in r.f sḫty pn r spr n.f psd-nw sp	Then this marshdweller came to petition him a ninth time,
ḏd.f	Saying:
imy-r pr wr nb.i	High steward, my lord!
mḫꜣt pw nt rmṯ ns.sn	Tongues are the balance of people;
in iwsw ḏꜥr wḏꜣt	The scales are the quest for settling accounts,
ir ḫsft r ḫsfw n.f	For punishing the one who is to be punished.
sn.tw tp-ḥsb r.k	The measure is applied against you;
[...] *grg ḫpr*	[...] a wrong has happened.
ḥrt.f ꜥnn.s mꜣꜥt r ꜥḳꜣ.f	His share has turned Right back against his line,
ḫt pw nt grg mꜣꜥt	And what is Right is now the thing of wrong.
swꜣḏ.f pw n nw.tw.f	It means he flourishes, he has not been bound.

B2.98-103

ir šm grg iw.f tnm.f	If wrong proceeds, erring on,
n ḏꜣ.n.f m mḫnt	It cannot cross on the ferry,
n sšꜣ	Cannot hasten.
ir ḫwd ḫr ḫr.f	Whoever grows rich from under him,

nn msw.f nn ꞽwꜥw.f tp tꜣ — Can have no children, no heirs upon earth.
ꞽr sḳdd ẖr.f — Whoever sails with him,
n sꜣḥ.n.f tꜣ — Cannot touch land,
n mnꞽ.n dpwt.f r dmꞽ.s — His boat cannot moor at its quay.

B2.103-109
m dns n ꞽs.k — Do not be heavy, not that you have been light.
m ꞽhm n ḫꜣḫ.k — Do not lag, not that you have been hasty.
m nmꜥ m sḏm n ꞽb — Do not show bias, in hearing the heart.
m ḥbs ḥr.k r rḫ.n.k — Do not veil your face after you have knowledge.
m šp ḥr.k r dgꜣ.n.k — Do not blind your sight after you have sighted.
m nꞽ twꜣ tw — Do not push away the one pleading with you.
hꜣ.k m pꜣ wsf — May you descend from this sluggishness,
smꞽ ṯs.k — May your judgement be delivered.
ꞽr n ꞽrr n.k — Act for one who would act for you.
m sḏm n bw nb r.f — Do not listen to everyone around,
nꞽs s r sp.f n wn-mꜣꜥ — Summon the man to his case in deed.

B2.109-115
nn sf n wsf — There is no yesterday for the sluggard,
nn ḫnms n sẖ mꜣꜥt — There is no friend for one deaf to Right,
nn hrw nfr n ꜥwn-ꞽb — There is no celebration for the grasping.
ḫpr wṯsw m mꜣꞽry — The fine speaker becomes a wretch,
mꜣꞽry r sprw — And the wretch is ever a plaintiff.
ḫpr ḫfty m smꜣw — The enemy becomes someone to kill.
mk wꞽ ḥr spr n.k — Look at me, pleading to you,
n sḏm.n.k st — And you do not hear it.
ꞽw.ꞽ r šmt — I am going to go
spr.ꞽ ḥr.k n ꞽnpw — And plead over you to Anubis.

The Judgement
B2.115-122
rdꞽ.ꞽn ꞽmy-r pr wr mrw sꜣ rnsy — Then the high steward Meru's son Rensy
šm ꞽmy-sꜣ sn r ꜥn n.f — Sent two bodyguards to bring him back.
wn.ꞽn sḫty pn snd — So this marshdweller was afraid,
ꞽb.f ꞽrrt r ḫsf n.f — Thinking it was done to punish him
ḥr mdt tn ḏdt.n.f — For this speech he had delivered.
ḏd.ꞽn sḫty pn — So this marshdweller said:
ḫsfw n ꞽb m mw — An approach to the thirsting man with water,
ḏꜣt r n ẖrd n sbnt m ꞽrtt — A feed for the suckling child with milk?
ntf mwt n nḥy — His is death for one yearning,
mꜣ.f n ꞽy.f — Who sees at his coming,
ꞽꞽ wdf mwt.f r.f — His death is coming, slowly, against him.

B2.122-129
ḏd.ꞽn ꞽmy-r pr wr mrw sꜣ rnsy — Then the high steward Meru's son Rensy said:
m snd sḫty — Do not be afraid, marshman.
mk ꞽrr.k r ꞽrt ḥnꜥ.ꞽ — You are just being made to be with me.
rdꞽ.ꞽn sḫty pn ꜥnḫ ḥr — Then this marshdweller swore aloud:
wnm.ꞽ ꜣ m t.k — Am I to eat on your bread,
swrꞽ.ꞽ ꜣ [ḥnḳt].k r nḥḥ — And drink your [beer] to eternity?
ḏd.n ꞽmy-r pr wr mrw sꜣ rnsy — The high steward Meru's son Rensy said:
sꜣw grt ꜥꜣ — Just wait here,
sḏm.k nꜣy.k n sprt — To hear your pleas.
rdꞽ.ꞽn.f šdt ḥr ꜥrt mꜣt — And he had read out from a fresh scroll
sprt nbt r ẖrt[...] — Every plea in [its] details (?).

B2.130-133
sꜥḳ.ꞽn s(t) ꞽmy-r pr wr mrw sꜣ rnsꞽ — Then the high steward Meru's son Rensy delivered
n ḥm n nswt-bꞽty nb-kꜣw-rꜥ mꜣꜥ-ḫrw — To the Person of the dual king Nebkaura true of voice,

wn.in nfr st ḥr ib.f	And they were excellent on his heart
r ḫt nbt ntt m tꜣ pn r ḏr.f	More than anything in this entire land.
ḏd.in ḥm.f	Then His Power said:
wḏʿ tw ḏs.k sꜣ mrw	Make the judgement yourself, son of Meru!
B2.133-B2.141	
rdi.in imy-r pr wr mrw sꜣ rnsi	So the high steward Meru's son Rensy
šm imy-sꜣ sn r […]	Sent two bodyguards to […]
ʿḥʿ.n.f in ir wpwt m […]	And he was brought, and an inventory made of [...]
ʿḥʿ.n gm n.f tp siw ḥr r [...]	And he was found to have six servants as well as […]
r it-šmʿ.f r bty.f	And his barley and his wheat,
r ʿꜣw.f r šꜣw.f r ʿwt […]	His donkeys, his swine, the herds […]
nmty-nḫt pn n sḫty pn […]	of this Nemtynakht to this marshman […]
[…]*t.f nbt ḏ*[…]	[…] all his […] .. [...]
n nmty-nḫt pn […]	of/to this Nemtynakht […]
B2.142	
iw.f pw […]	This is its end […]

Part Two, Section Two
Middle Kingdom literary compositions preserved in fragments

The fragments in this section have been assigned tentatively to those categories indicated by the more substantially preserved compositions of Part Two, Section One. Clearly the shorter the fragment, the more speculative must be its categorisation, and the less certain even its original independent existence. Two fragments from otherwise unidentified compositions might come from one and the same composition, even where they seem in different modes, for example narrative and imperative, because the better preserved compositions demonstrate the combination of generic modes within a single composition. In consequence, the number of extant fragments cannot be used to calculate directly the total of extant literary compositions. For example, the 'tale of the fowler' might be the central portion of the composition starting with the fragment the 'lament of Neferpesdjet'. Only the identifiably separate compositions can be used to calculate a total of extant compositions. The total number of 'starts of compositions', including the better-preserved compositions above, offers one secure starting-point for such a calculation. In order to reinforce this point as clearly as possible, in this section of translations, the compositions are grouped into those with start preserved, those with end preserved, and those with neither start nor end preserved. Within each of those three sets the fragments are in the sequence of the categories suggested by the better-preserved compositions above – tales, teachings and laments.

Different assessment of fragments has led to differences among recent listings of literary compositions. In order to clarify the principles behind this listing, note is needed of the items omitted, particularly with reference to the most comprehensive listing with exhaustive bibliography, that by Richard Parkinson, to which the reader is referred (Parkinson 2002). I have excluded items on the following grounds:

1. date of composition: Moscow Mythological Tale, as Eighteenth Dynasty, following Korostovtsev 1960a (as Parkinson notes, other items have been removed by some commentators to the New Kingdom, notably the Teaching of Amenemhat I, the Hymn to the Nile Flood, the cycle of tales at the Court of king Khufu; if Middle Kingdom literature ends at 1700 BC with renewed political disunity then, it is possible that the cycle of tales at the Court of king Khufu, the Tale at the Palace, and the Eulogy of the King may belong to the Second Intermediate Period instead)
2. content category: Cairo CG 58040 Mythological Tale, as part of an incantation against snake bite (the composition on the other side was identified by Alan Gardiner as 'philosophical', but I agree with Parkinson that it is more probaby an incantation for good health); Lahun fragments formerly considered of possible literary content may now be assigned to other categories, UC 32095D, 32107B, 32110D, 32116A, 32149A, 32217G (Collier and Quirke 2004)

I would also consider the Abydos ostracon Simpson 1995 A4 as a Ramesside practice opening to a Teaching, as a writing exercise or a doodle, rather than a Middle Kingdom wisdom text (Parkinson 2002, 307, see his comments for similar difficulty with many Ramesside ostraca p.293). As noted in Part One, the Hymn to the Nile Flood and Eulogies of the King are borderline cases, and I have placed them at the end of the sequence as Section Three.

Part Two, Section Two
Middle Kingdom literary compositions preserved in fragments
List

2a. start preserved
Tales
King Neferkara and General Sasenet
Teachings
Hordedef
Laments
Khakheperraseneb Ankhu
Neferpesdjet (assigned to this category by parallel of start of Tale of Khuninpu)
Two literary titles on a papyrus sheet: Papyrus Pushkin) 1695

2b. end preserved
Tale or Lament
Tale of Hay
Teachings
For Kagemni

2c. without start or end
Tales
The king and the spirit
Tale of a herdsman
Horus and Seth: Lahun fragments UC 32158 etc
One or two tales of travel, Lisht fragment 'Papyrus Lythgoe' MMA 09.180.535
At the palace, fragments Papyrus British Museum EA 10475
Khenemsu and Nemay: Lahun fragment UC 32105B
Cloth, Turquoise and a King: Lahun fragment UC 32105A
Nakhti: Lahun fragment UC 32107A
Lotus eaters: Lahun fragment UC 32271B
Teachings
Ashmolean Writing Board
Papyrus Ramesseum II
Lahun fragment UC 32106C recto, 32117C
Laments
Sasobek
Lament of a fowler?

2d. sets of small fragments identified as separate and literary
Forty fragments from the Theban West Bank (Austrian Institute excavations)
Papyrus Ramesseum fragment
Lahun fragments

2a. Fragments preserving the beginning of a composition

The Tale of King Neferkara and General Sasenet

The composition is in Middle Egyptian, and dated to the Twelfth Dynasty by the titles of high officials mentioned in one part: one part, probably the start of the tale, is preserved in a single copy on a late Eighteenth or early Nineteenth Dynasty plastered writing-board (Oriental Institute of Chicago 13539) and another part is preserved in a single copy on a Twenty-sixth Dynasty papyrus (Papyrus Chassinat I = Louvre E 25351). The first editor Georges Posener noted a third possible source, a stone writing-tablet of the early Twentieth Dynasty (Institut Français d'Archéologie Orientale au Caire, ostracon Deir el-Medina 1214), giving starts of lines at the start of a narrative composition; as not certainly from the Neferkara and Sasenet tale, it is presented here separately after the other two sources, although Posener demonstrated how it might fit in with the apparent opening-lines of the tale on writing-board OIC 13539.

Published Posener 1957.

Writing-tablet OIC 13539

[... *kꜣ*]-[*rꜥ*] *sꜣ rꜥ* [...] *mꜣꜥ ẖrw m nswt* [...]	[...-]ka[ra] son of Ra [...] true of voice as king [...]
isk r.f iry p[*ꜥt* ...] *ḥm.f* [..]*ity rn.f* [...]	Now a leader of no[bles ...] His Power [..] called Ity [...]
mrwt [...] *ḏ* [...] *imy-r mšꜥ sꜣ-snt*	love [...] .. [...] the general Sasenet,
iw nn wnw st ḥmt m [...]	who did not [have] a wife [...]
[...] *ir.n imy-r mšꜥ sꜣ-snt r sẖt r sḏꜣ ib* [...]	[...] .. general Sasenet to the marsh for leisure [...]
[...] *tti m mꜣꜥ-ẖrw* [...]	[...] King Teti as true of voice [...]

Papyrus Chassinat I, page 1

[...]..	[...] ..
[... *p*]*r* (?)	[go]ing out (?)
[...]*.f*	[...] of him/it
[...]*s*	[...] of her/it (?)
[...]*y*	[...] .. (-foreigner?)
[...]*nt*	[...] ..
[...] ..	[...] ..

Papyrus Chassinat I, page 2, lines 1-7

[...] *wn* [...]
[...] *imy-r mšꜥ sꜣ*-[*snt wn*]*.in.f mtmt i*[...]
[...] *nfr-kꜣ*-[*rꜥ*] *šm* [...] *imy-r mšꜥ*(?) *sꜣ-snt*
[...] *nswt imy-r ẖnrt* (?) *imy-r pr wr imy-r ꜥẖnwty*
[...] *sš nswt ṯꜣw sš ꜥn n* [*nswt*] *imy-r ꜣḥwt*
[...]*y nt ẖnw* [...] *nt mn-nfr nn* [...]
[...] *mn-nfr*

[...] was (?) [...]
[...] general Sa[senet.] Then he investigated (?) .. [...]
[...] Neferka[ra. Then] general Sasenet went
[...] (official of?) the king, overseer of the enclosure (?), high steward, overseer of the inner palace,
[...] secretary of the king, equipment-bearer of secretary of documents of [the king], overseer of fields,
[...]-men of the Residence, [...]-men of Mennefer, without
[...] of Mennefer

Papyrus Chassinat I, page 2, lines 7-14

[...] *is* [*r.f sprw*] *n mn-nfr spr r* [...]
[...]*.f m ḥs ḥs*[*w m šmꜥ*] *šmꜥw m tiꜣ t*[*iꜣw m g*]*ꜣwꜣ gꜣwꜣ*[*w r*] *pr sprw n mn-nfr* [...]*.sn ḳnw*
[...] *ir r.f iw sprw n mn-*[*nfr*] *r* [...] *ḫft imy-r rwryt*
[...]*.f ḥs ḥsw šmꜥ šmꜥw tiꜣ tiꜣw m gꜣwꜣ gꜣwꜣw r pr sprw n mn-nfr nn sḏm.sn*
ḳnw.sn [...] *ḥr swnḫ r.f pr.n sprw n mn-nfr ḥr rmt r ꜥꜣ wrt šnw.f m* .. [...]

[...] Now the [petitioner] of Mennefer arrived to [...]
[...] of him by the singing of the singer[s, by the chanting] of the chanters, by the clapping of the per[cussionists, by the flute]-playing of the flautist[s until] the departure of the petitioner of Mennefer,
[...] them [...] finishing off

[…] Then petitioner of Men[nefer] arrived to […] before the overseer of the palace-approach […] of him, the singing of the singer[s, by the chanting] of the chanters, by the clapping of the percussionists, by the flute-playing of the flautists until the departure of the petitioner of Mennefer without them hearing, finishing off […] by overpowering him,
and the petitioner of Mennefer left weeping very greatly, his hair in .. […]

Papyrus Chassinat I, page 3, lines 1-11
[…].f […].f ḥr […].f r […]
ꜥḥꜥ.n […] ḥm n nswt bity nfr-kꜣ-rꜥ ḥr šm m grḥ
m ḳdyt wꜥt nn rmt nb ḥnꜥ.f
ꜥḥꜥ.n rwi.n.f sw r.f nn rdit mꜣꜣ.f sw
ꜥḥꜥ.n pw irt.n ḥn-t sꜣ ṯti ḥr mḥ ḥr ḏd
ir is nty pw mꜣꜥt pw pꜣ ḏd sw pr m grḥ
šm pw irt.n ḥn-t sꜣ ṯti ẖr pḥ n nṯr pn nn rdit tꜣ ib.f r.f
r mꜣꜣ iry.f nb
spr pw ir.n.f r pr imy-r mšꜥ sꜣ-[snt]
ꜥḥꜥ.n ẖꜣꜥ.f dbt hꜣb.n.f m rd.f
kꜣ rdi.t(w) hꜣ n.f […]
pr pw irt.n.f r ḥry
is r.f ḥn-t sꜣ ṯti ꜥḥꜥ r wḏꜣ ḥm.f
ḥr m-ḫt irt ḥm.f mr.n.f ẖr.f wḏꜣ.f r ꜥḥ.f
šm.n ṯti m-sꜣ.f
ir m-ḫt wḏꜣ ḥm.f r pr-ꜥꜣ ꜥnḫ wḏꜣ snb
šm.n ṯti r pr.f

[…] he […] he […] upon […] he […] to [..]-house
Then […] the Person of the dual king Neferkara went by night
on his own (?), noone with him,
and he moved off then without letting himself be seen.
Hente's son Tjeti stood up in thought, saying:
So that is it, that statement that he goes out at night, it is the truth.
Hente's son Tjeti went hard behind this god without letting him realise it,
to see all that he would do.
Then he arrived at the house of the general Sa[senet],
and he threw a stone he had struck with his foot,
to have them let down for him [a ladder],
and he climbed up.
Then Hente's son Tjeti stood until His Power proceeded.
After His Power had done what he desired, he then proceeded to his palace,
and Tjeti went after him.
After His Power had proceeded to the Great House life! prosperity! health!
Tjeti went to his house.

Papyrus Chassinat I, page 3, lines 11-14
isk wḏꜣ in ḥm.f r pr n imy-r mšꜥ (?) sꜣ-snt
iw wnwt fd pẖr m grḥ
ir.n.f kt wnwt fd m pr n imy-r mšꜥ (?) sꜣ-snt
ꜥḳ.f r pr-ꜥꜣ iw wnwt fd wnw r ḥḏ-tꜣ
wn.in ḥn-t sꜣ ṯti šm ḥr […].f tnw grḥ
nn rdit tꜣ ib.f r.f
ir sꜣ ꜥḳ ḥm […]

Now His Power went to the house of the general (?) Sasenet
as four hours had rolled by in the night,
and he spent another four hours in the house of the general (?) Sasenet,
going into the Great House with four hours left till daybreak.
Then Hente's son Tjeti went on his […] each night,
without letting him realise it.
After the entry of the Person […]

Writing-tablet IFAO oDeM 1214

Side One

ḫpr swt wn ḥm n nswt bi͗ty [...]	There was a time when the dual king [...]
r swt r sḏꜣ [...]	to wander for leisure [...]
gmyt wꜥ [...]	discovery of a lone [...]
ḥr ḏd i͗[...]	saying: O [...]
wn [...]	.. [...]

Side Two

.. [...]	.. [...]
šꜣwꜣb[...]	stick (-figure?) [...]
ḥry ḏww št[...]	..upper, evils .. [...]
nḏm sw ꜥꜣ wr i͗w.sn [...]	he was extremely pleasing, as they [...]
r nty gm sw i.i͗[...]	..that Ii[...] found him/it [...]
šmt r swt[...]	going wandering [...]

The Teaching of Hordedef

Hordedef son of king Khufu of the Fourth Dynasty figures among the key characters in the cycle of Tales at the Court of King Khufu, dating to the late Middle Kingdom or Second Intermediate Period (above, Part Two, Section One). His name also figures throughout the later, mainly Ramesside, sources for reverence of great men and great writers of the past. The Teaching ascribed to him, but in Middle Egyptian, has survived only in part, on Ramesside ostraca and a Late Period writing-board. The division into sections below follows Helck 1984.

1.

ḥꜣt-ꜥ m sbꜣyt irt.n	Beginning of the teaching made by
iry pꜥt ḥꜣty-ꜥ sꜣ nswt ḥr-ḏd.f	the leader of nobles, foremost of action, king's son Hordedef
n sꜣ.f mnꜥt.f ꜣw-ib-rꜥ rn.f	to his son, whom he nursed, called Auibra.
ḏd.f	He says:
ꜥb tw ḫft-ḥr irty.ky	Gather yourself facing your eyes,
sꜣw ꜥb tw ky	do not let another gather you.
ir iḳr.k grg.k pr.k	If you are to excel, establish your house,
irr n.k ḥmt m nbt pr	take to yourself a wife as lady of the house,
ms.tw n.k sꜣ ṯꜣy	so that a male child may be born to you.

2.

ḳd.k pr.k n sꜣ.k	You are to build your house for your son,
iw ir.n.k bw wn.k im	you have made a place where you can live.
smnḫ pr.k n ẖrt nṯr	Adorn your house of the cemetery,
siḳr st.k nt imntt	so that your place of the West may be made excellent.
šsp dḥꜣw n.n mwt	Poor return for us is death,
šsp ḳꜣ n.n ꜥnḫw	a high return for us, the living.
iw pr mwt n ꜥnḫ	The house of the dead belongs to the living.

3.

ḥḥy n.k šꜣꜥt r n ꜣḥwt	Seek out for yourself a tied land, a corner of fields,
m iwḥ.n [...] *r sšw*	watered by [...], according to documents,
r skꜣ r ḥꜣmw grg	for ploughing, for fishing and trapping
m-sꜣ ḫpr rnpt nt šwꜣw	as a guard when there happens a year of wandering.
[*wnm*]*.n.f irr.f m ꜥwy.fy*	One who has [eaten] can act with his hands.

4.

ir.k n.k r wꜣḥt	Make for yourself for the offerings,
rwḏw pn ḥm-kꜣ n iswt	a manager here, and a soul-priest for the chapel,
stt [*sn n.k*] *ḳbḥ*	[that they may] pour cool water for you,
mi s iḳr imt-pr.f	as does a man excellent in his testament.
stp n.k šꜣꜥt ḫntt ꜣḥwt.k	Select for yourself a tied land from the best of your fields,
m iwḥ tnw rnpt	from the land watered every year.
ꜣḫ sw n.k r iwꜥt	It is more useful to you than an heir,
sḫnt.k sw r [...]	so promote it beyond [...]
[...] *n* [..] *rmṯ*	[...] .. [..] people.

5.

***s*[*ḫꜣ n*]*.k** mi ḏdt sw*	**Re[call to] yourself** according as is said:
mk nn wn iwꜥt sḫꜣ n ḏt	see, there is no inheritance for the memory of eternity
[...]	[...]
[...] *r ḫry.k di.ti r ḏꜣnr.k*	[...] more than your dependants, given according to your needs.
stp n.k [...]	Select for yourself [...]
[...] *bꜣ.k r nṯr*	[...] your soul to divinity.

6.

dmit pw n bw nb im.f	It is a settlement for everyone within it,
mwt [...]*r*	dying [...] ..
ir thꜣ.tw [...] *irr.f*	if one breaches [...] he does.

ỉr mwt m s tkn ỉm.f	If the death in a man approaches him,
hrw th.f dmdy [..]	the day of his breaching the endpoint (?) [...]
nt ỉrr n.f sft	of the one doing the butchery for him,
ỉw ḳrs[*.tw.f*] *m ẖbdt m ẖrt-nṯr*	[he is] buried as criminal in the cemetery,
ẖprw sꜣ[..] *n sꜣmt m ḏwt*	the grief-lock will turn to dirt,
ẖsf.f pw nt nṯr ḥtpw.f	his peace is his punishment from the god,
sḥḏ ḥr ẖwt.f	illuminating his wrongdoing,
ỉw mꜣỉrw	the needy <...?>

7.

stp n.k ẖnit m rmṯ	Select for yourself a joyful band of people
ỉmi snd.k ẖpr [...]	Let the fear of you fall [...]
wdn n.k ẖt	that offerings be made to you
mi wꜥb rꜥ n ḏbꜣt	as by a pure-priest of Ra (?) of the robing-chamber.
wnm rmw ḥr ꜥnb n nmt	Eat fish at the edge of the meat-block (?)
ṯꜣ [...] *m dd.k hrw.k n.sn*	.. [...] as your giving of your day to them
wnn ib.k pẖꜣ [...] *s* [...] *ḥtpw*	Your heart will be glad [...] .. [...] content,
n gm.[*n.tw*] *ḏdt.f r.k*	and [none] can find it said of you
m ḏwt nt nṯr m ḥꜣn[*r*]	that there is an evil of the god in the wish (?).

8.

nḥm [...] *ỉr* [...]*.tw r.s*	Rescue (?) [...] doing [...] for it,
smnẖ[*.k pr.k*] *si*[*ḳr.k st.k*]	embellish [your house], make [your place] excel (?)
[...]*w.s tpy mꜣꜥ*	its [...] of the first to be offered (?),
[...] *n ỉrr n.f st*	[...] for the one who does it for him.
wẖꜣ pw mꜣꜥ n rmṯ	the good of people is to be sought out,
[...]*.f m smꜣy*	[...] of him as confederate,
[...] *nty wnn m* [*s*]*ẖ*[*wn*]	[...] who is to be an op[ponent]

9.

[...] *pw* [...]*.f* [...] *m nm*[...]	[...] it is [...] of him [...] ... [...]
[...] *ẖry.k* [...] *ḥr r* [...]	[...] your goods (?) [...] face (?) to (?) [...]

Sources

Ramesside ostraca: Munich 3400, Berlin 12383, Chicago, Deir el-Medina 1205-8, 1229-30, 1396, 1604, Gardiner 12, 62, 337, Petrie 53, Turin 57416, Vienna 14

Late Period wood writing-board: Brooklyn 37.1394E

The Lament of Khakheperraseneb Ankhu

This Middle Egyptian composition is dated to the late Middle Kingdom by the first name of the person to whom the Lament is ascribed: Khakheperraseneb means 'may Khakheperra be well', Khakheperra being the throne name of King Senusret II of the mid Twelfth Dynasty, and Khakheperraseneb was a popular late Middle Kingdom name. The surviving portion of the composition is preserved in a single copy on a mid Eighteenth Dynasty plastered writing-board (British Museum EA 5645) with the title 'compilation': it is not known whether the title presents the original Middle Kingdom start of the composition, or whether it describes the copy on the writing-board, perhaps a New Kingdom selection of sayings drawn from different parts of the late Middle Kingdom original. The short lines 4 and 9 of Side One of the writing-board are taken here as ends of sections, and the first phrase on Side Two would be appropriate to the start of another section. Each section might represent a separate 'quotation', if the compilation presents an Eighteenth Dynasty selection. However, the reasons for the short lines and the copying date in line 9 might be connected with the occasion of the copying (time available, choice of copyist), rather than with the formal structure of the composition 'as composed'.

The composition is celebrated in Egyptology for its opening section on the problem of literary innovation. Classical Arabic literature provides both a parallel from the pre-Islamic poet Antara, and a tradition of commentary on it going back a thousand years, to Ibn Rashiq in the eleventh century AD (Kilito 1985, 17-20). Kilito cites the parallel in the poem of Antara as follows:

> Les poètes ont-ils encore laissé quelque chose à dire?
> Et as-tu enfin reconnu l'endroit où séjournait l'aimée?

The lament that nothing has been left to say occurs at the very start of that literary tradition, a temporal context that strengthens the surprise for modern readers at finding in ancient sources ideas that might be thought exclusively modern. The ancient poets undermine an arrogance of our modernity.

Published Gardiner 1909a.

Side One, lines 1 to 4

sḥwy mdt ḳd ṯsw	Compilation of sayings, construction of phrasings,
ḏʿr ḫnw m ḥḥy n ỉb	exploration of expressions in a quest of the heart
ỉr.n wʿb n ỉwnw	made by the pure-priest of Iunu
snt sꜣ ḫʿ-ḫpr-rʿ-snb ḏdw n.f ʿnḫw	Senet's son Khakheperraseneb called Ankhu
ḏd.f	He says
ḥꜣ n.ỉ ḫnw ḫmm	If only I had expressions unknown,
ṯsw ḫppy	phrasings of adventure,
m mdt mꜣt tmt swꜣ	of new words, not used ones,
šwt m wḥmyt	free from repetition,
nn ṯs.n sbt r ḫrw	not expressed by oral tradition,
ḏdt.n tpyw-ʿ	of what the ancestors have said:
ẖꜣk.ỉ ẖt.ỉ ḥr ntt ỉm.s	I wring out my body for what is within it,
m fḫ n ḏd.ỉ nb	in a release of all my speaking,
ḥr ntt r.f wḥmw ḏdt	for what was said would be just repeated,
ỉw ḏddt ḏd	what is always said is there to say.
nn ʿbw mdt ỉmyw-ḥꜣt	There is no claim on the sayings of forefathers,
gm ỉs ỉmyw-ḫt	those who follow always find it out.

Side One, lines 5 to 9

n ḏd ḏd ḏd ḏd.ty.fy	A speaker has not spoken; one who would speak is speaking.
gmy ky ḏdtỉ.f	Let another find what he would speak.
n mdt.n mdt ḥr sꜣ ỉry	A word does not express afterwards,
ỉr.n.sn ḏr-ʿ	they have done (that) since before.
nn mdt ntt kꜣ sḏd.s (?)	There are no words that can be devised to tell it.
ḥḥy pw r ꜣḳt	It is a quest to ruin,
grg pw nn sḫꜣ.ty.fy	it is lies, there is noone who will recall
rn.f n ktḫy	his name to others.
ḏd.n.ỉ nn ḫft mꜣ.n.ỉ	I have said this from what I have seen:
šꜣʿ r ẖt tpt nfryt r ỉw ḥr-sꜣ	from the first generation to those who come after,
sny.sn r swꜣt	they imitate what has gone.
ḥꜣ ꜣ rḫ.ỉ ḫm.ny kywy	If only I knew what others do not,
m tmmt wḥmt ḏd.ỉ st	in the escape from repetition, that I might speak it
wšb n.ỉ ỉb.ỉ	and my heart might respond to me,
sḥḏ.ỉ n.f r mn.ỉ	I might illuminate my pain for it,

win.i n.f ȝtpw nty ḥr psd.i
ẖnw m sfn.n wi
sšr.i n.f mnt.i m-ᶜ.f
ḏd.i iḥ ḥr srf.i

I might offload on it the burden that is on my back,
the matters that have brought me down,
that I might pour out to it how I suffer,
saying grief to soothe myself.

Side One, lines 10 to 14

ink pw ḥr nkȝy m ẖprt
sẖrw ẖpr ẖt tȝ
ẖprw ḥr ẖpr nn mi sf
dns rnpt r snnwt.s
shȝ tȝ ẖpr m ḥḏ.ny
irw m […]
rdi.tw mȝᶜt rwty
isft m ẖn sḥ
ẖnn.tw sẖrw nṯrw
wn.tw m-ᶜ ẖrw.sn
wnn tȝ sny mn
i[r]tyw m st nbt
niwt spȝwt m iᶜnw
ḥr nb twtw ẖr iw
šfyt rdiw sȝ r.s
tkw nbw sgri
nhpw ḥr ẖpr rᶜ nb
ḥr tnbh r
ẖprt di.i r ḥr.sn ȝtp ᶜt.i
snni wi ḥr ib.i
wẖd sw ḥȝp ẖt.i ḥr.f
ks pw ky ib
ir ib ḳn m st ḳsnt
snnw pw n nb.f
ḥȝ n.i ib m rḫ ẖwdw
kȝ iry.i sẖny ḥr.f
ȝtpw sw m mdwt nt mȝi
dr.i n.f mn.i

It is I who is thinking over what has happened,
the conduct that has come to pervade the land,
the forms forming, (but) not like yesterday,
the year weighs heavier than its pair.
The land collapses, turns into waste,
made into […]
What is Right is cast out,
evil is inside the council-hall.
The norms of the gods are in strife,
people run off with their provisions.
The land is passing in pain,
there is lamentation everywhere.
Towns and districts are in mourning.
Everyone is united under crime.
Dignity – it is expelled.
The silent lords are assailed.
As the turn of dawn comes every day,
faces are scattered from
what happens. I give voice to them, my limbs weighed down,
I am saddened in my heart,
it is painful to conceal my inside over it,
it would be the bowing of another heart.
The heart bold in the place of hardship,
that is a mate to its master.
If only I had a heart with knowledge of suffering,
Then I could manage to alight on it,
to weigh it down with words of misery,
so that I might remove through it my pain.

Side Two, lines 1 to 3

ḏd.f n ib.f
mi m-ᶜ ib.i mdw.i n.k
wšb.k n.i ṯsw.i
wḥᶜ.k n.i nȝ nty ẖt tȝ
ntyw ḥḏ ptḥ
ink pw ḥr nkȝy m ẖprt
ihw bs m min
nhpw n swȝ ḏrḏrw
ḥr-nb gr ḥr.f
tȝ r ḏr.f m sẖrw ᶜȝ
nn ẖt.i šwt m iw
bw-nb twtw ḥr irt st
ḥȝtyw snmw
dd ḥr m ddw n.f ḥr
ib n sny hr
dwȝ.tw r.s m ẖrw hrw
n win.n st ibw
hrt sf im mi pȝ hrw
ḥr sn r.s n ᶜšȝ
ḥr ḏri nn ᶜrḳ šsȝ.f

He says to his heart:
come along, my heart, that I may speak to you,
that you may reply to my turns,
that you may explain for me these things that pervade the land.
Those who are of light, are trampled upon.
It is I, the one who is thinking over what has happened.
Affliction is ushered in today.
At daybreak the strangers have not passed,
everyone is silent over it,
(though) the entire land is in great crisis.
There is no man of the generation who is free from crime:
everyone is united in doing it.
Hearts are grasping.
The order-giver is now the man-given-orders;
the heart of both of them gives consent.
People wake to it as the course of the day.
Hearts have not resisted it.
The course of yesterday on it is as this day.
Sight is modelled on it for the multitudes (?),
Sight estranged, there is none to bind his wisdom.

Side Two, lines 4 to 6

nn ḏnw	There is noone enraged
di.f r	enough to give voice.
dwꜣ.tw r wḫd rꜥ nb	People wake to pain every day.
ꜣww wdn mn	The weight of the sufferer is prolonged.
nn pḥty n mꜣirw m-ꜥ r.f	There is not strength for the wretched from, even,
m-ꜥ wsr r.f	from one more powerful than him
ḫꜣt pw gr r sḏmt	Silence over what has been heard is a disease.
ih pw wšb n ḫm	Replying to the ignorant is torment.
ḫsf ḫn ḥr sḫpr rḳw	Suppression of speech is creating hostility.
n šsp.n ib mꜣꜥw	The heart does not take the smooth path,
n wḫd.tw smi n mdt	a report of a matter cannot be suffered.
mr nb s ṯs.f	A master of a man loves his turn of phrase.
bw-nb grg ḥr ḫꜣbb	Everyone is fixed on falsehoods.
bṯ mty mdt	Precision in speech escapes.
ḏd.i n.k ib.i wšb.k n.i	I speak to you, my heart, so that you may answer me.
n gr.n ib pḥ	A conjured heart cannot be silent.
mk ẖrw bꜣk mi nb	The condition of the servant is that of the master.
ꜥšꜣ wdn ḥr.k	Much is weighing upon you.

The Lament or Tale of Neferpesdjet
Petrie Museum UC 32156A
From the town-site at Lahun, fragments of a papyrus roll with hieratic on the recto the start of a literary composition, opening with the same phrase as that in the Tale of Khuninpu, with the name deciphered by Paul Smither as Neferpesdjet (unpublished notebook): it is written in vertical lines, the first in red. The verso bears part of an accountancy table. The spacing between the two main fragments is uncertain.
Published Collier and Quirke 2004

Smaller fragment	
s pw wn nfr-psḏt rn.f	**There was a man called Neferpesdjet,**
nḏs pw ḳn [...]	who was a bold fellow [...]
Larger fragment	
[...*n.f?*]*ỉ*[*m?*]*y ..-ỉ rn.f*	[...] belonging to (?) [him], called ..-i
ṯsw pw (?) [..] *kꜣwtyw*	who was the commander, [who directed?] the porters.
ḏd.ỉn n.f nꜣ n kꜣwtyw[...]	Then those porters said to him [...]
nfr ỉrt n.k t nḏm ỉrt n.k ḥnḳt (?) ...	It is good to make bread for you, sweet to make beer (?) for you and
nbt ptr ꜣ rdỉ.k ỉrt n.n [...]	all ..., but what are you going to have made for us [in return for?]
s	it?

Two Literary Titles on a papyrus sheet
Papyrus Pushkin 1695 is a sheet 29 x 21 cm bearing on each side a literary title in Middle Kingdom handwriting. These may be the opening lines of two otherwise lost literary compositions, or the exercises of a creative hand, for works that almost, but never quite came into existence. The size of the sheet is that of late Middle Kingdom letters, as if it had been prepared for that purpose, but then put instead to another use.
Published Posener 1969

Recto:
ḥꜣt-ꜥ m mdt ḏdt.n *wꜥb sḫmt rn-snb*
[...]*.f ḥr rṯnw ḥr pḥwy ỉmy-r ḫtmtyw snb.t*(*y*)*.fy*
[...] *m ḥm n stp-sꜣ* (?) [...] *m mꜣw* (?) *ḥr*

Beginning of the speech delivered by the pure-priest of Sekhmet Renseneb
[returning] from lower Retjenu in the rearguard of the overseer of sealers Senebtyfy
[...] in the Person of the palace (?) [...] as a revelation (?)

Verso
ḥꜣt-ꜥ m mdt ḏdt.n sꜣ ḥrỉ ḥꜣmw pw n nỉwt rst ỉwrw rn.f ỉꜣšw
m-ḫt wn.f m ḫnt n ỉ[..]*.f ḥr sḫr*(?)*.f n p*[...]
nn sp ḫpr m-ꜥ.f ḫtm [...] *ḏd.tw n rmṯ nbt*
[...] *nḏst* (?)

Beginning of the speech delivered by the son of Hori, a fisherman of the Southern City, called Iuru, when summoned
after he was in the Outer Palace for his [..] on account of his condition of ..[...]
Never had closure (?) happened by his hand [...] All are told
[...] small (?)

In the publication of the sheet, George Posener noted the possible connection between the title of the verso ‘hero’ and the content of the unidentified literary composition ‘tale of a fowler’ on the verso of Papyrus Butler (British Museum EA 10274) ‘sans insister sur ce rapprochement’ (Posener 1969, 106).

2b. Fragments preserving the end of a composition

The Tale of Hay
From Lahun, Petrie Museum UC 32157 (lot LV.1) verso
First edition Griffith 1898, 4, pl.4; re-edition Collier and Quirke 2004

Column 1
[...] *n.f ḏd mdt tn ir.n.sn ḫt r.f rdi.in.sn sw m*
[...] *mrrt p3ḳt r 3ḥt.f sty ir.n ḥr.f*
[...] *inst n wdnt ḫr m-ḫt ḏd.n*
[...] *.s s3 ḫ3t.i sḏ3.n.f 3tp.f sw r s3w*
[...] *ḥdb.n.f sw ḥr s3tw ḏd.f i.yhy*
[...] *m 3ḥt tn n ḫnms pḥ.n.f wi*
[... ... ...]
[... ...] *in rmṯ*
[... ...] *mk nn wi*
[... ...] *ḫsf.i*
[... ...] *nn smit.f*
[... ...] *nb ḫpš pf n*
[... ...] *m33 iry ..*
[... ...] *iry bin pn im.f*
[... ...] *ḏ3ḏ3.f wn.in.f ḥr*

[...] he [...] to say this matter, and they pursued him. Then they put him in
[...] the street, fine linen at his field, the shooting which the sight of him caused (?)
[...] red linen of the offering pile (?). Then there said
[...] its [...] back (from?) my front (?). He died, and he left (?) him to prevent
[...] he felled him to the ground, saying 'Hey'
[...] in this field for Khenmes. He reached me
[... ... ...]
[... ...] by people
[... ...] punish me
[... ...] without reporting it
[... ...] that lord of strenght for
[... ...] seeing ...
[... ...] did this evil with him
[... ...] his head. Then he

Column 2
sm3 [...] *nkn (?)* [...]
mi šwt [..] *3pdw ꜥḥꜥ.n sm3.n.f* [...]
ir.n.f [...] *ḳr*[*s* ...] *h3y sꜥḳ.n.f ḫnms* [...]
ir.f ... rdi.n.f sw r ḳrswt nt h3y
[...] *r t3-mḥw .. w3rt.n.f rdi.in.f sw ḥr tp*
[...] *mr n nfr-k3-rꜥ m3ꜥ-ḫrw ḏd.f snbt ḫnms r .. n*
[...] ... *r sp3t nt ḏt wnn mniw sšm (?) ...*
[...]*m.f šm tw (?) ḥnꜥ.k sḫ3w.tw irt imy-r w*
[...] *snb n ḫnmsw šm.n št.n.f špt*
iw.f pw

killed [...] injury (?) [...]
like the plumage [of?] birds. Then he killed [...]
he caused [...] bur[y ...] Hay, and made Khenmes enter [...]
causing (?) ... He gave it for the burial of Hay
[...] to the Delta .. what he had tied. Then he placed him/it on the top
[...] pyramid of Neferkara true of voice saying, may it please Khenmes for the .. of
[...] ... for the personal estates, and the herdsman will be guide (?) ...
[...]he [...] go then (?) with you, that the deeds of the Overseer of the District be remembered
[...] health of Khenmesu when the one whom he wrapped (?) had gone, in suffering (?)
This is its end

The Teaching for Kagemni

The end of this composition is preserved at the start of the great Middle Kingdom literary manuscript Papyrus Prisse, before the copy of the Teaching of Ptahhotep.
The following translation follows the transcription in Gardiner 1946.

[...]	[...]
wḏꜣ sndw ḥs mt	The respectful man flourishes, the precise man is praised,
wn ẖn n grw wsḫ st nt hr	The tent is open to the silent, the place of the quiet man is broad.
m mdw spd dsw r th mtn	Do not speak up: knives are sharp against one straying from a road
nn ḥn n is ḥr sp.f	There is no progress except at its moment.
ir ḥms.k ḥnꜥ ꜥšꜣt	If you sit down with a multitude,
msd t mrr.k	avoid the food you love.
ꜣt pw ktt dꜣir ib	Self restraint is a minor moment,
ḫw pw ꜣfꜥ iw ḏbꜥ.t(w) im	but gluttony is an evil, people point it out.
iw ikn n mw ꜥḫm.f ibt	A scoop of water quenches thirst,
iw mḥt r m šww smn.f ib	a mouthful of herbs fortifies the heart.
iw nfrt idn bw nfr	A good thing is the substitute for good being.
iw nh n ktt idn wr	A little of a small thing is the substitute for a large.
ẖs pw ḥnt n ẖt.f	Someone grabbing for his belly is a vile man.
swꜣ tr smḫ.n.f wstn ẖt m pr.sn	Time passes, he has forgotten the stride of the belly in their house.
ir ḥms.k ḥnꜥ ꜣfꜥ	If you sit down with a glutton,
wnm.k ꜣḫf.f swꜣ	eat when his gorging is past.
ir swri.k ḥnꜥ tḫw	If you drink with a drunkard,
šsp.k iw ib.f ḥtpw	accept only when his heart is satisfied.
m ꜣtw r iwf r-gs skn	Do not seethe over meat beside the voracious man.
šsp di.f n.k	Accept as he gives you.
m win st kꜣ ssft pw	Do not reject it. That is the way to calming.
ir šww m srḫ n t	One who is free from accusations over food,
n sḫm.n mdt nbt im.f	No word can have power over him.
ḫrr n ḥr r dfꜣ ib	.. (?) (is) for/to the face at feeding the heart (?).
iꜣm n.f kꜣh r mwt.f	Even one spiteful to his mother is kind to him.
mrt.f pw bw nb	All people are his subjects.
imi pr rn.k iw gr.k m r.k	Let your name go forth while you are silent with your mouth,
nis.t(w).k	so that you may be summoned.
m ꜥꜣ ib.k ḥr ḫpš m ḥr-ib ḏꜣmw	Do not boast over strength among the troops,
sꜣw itn.k	in case you are contested.
n rḫ.n.tw ḫprt	None know what might happen,
irrt nṯr ḫft ḫsf.f	what the god might do in punishing him.
rdi.in ṯꜣty nis.t(w) n nꜣy.f n ẖrdw	Then the vizier had his children summoned
m-ḫt ꜥrḳ.f sḫr rmṯ	after encompassing the ways of people,
bit.sn ḥr iit ḥr.f	their character coming before him
ḏr.n ḏd.n.f n.sn	He ended by saying to them:
ir ntt nbt m sš ḥr pꜣ šfdw	Everything that is in writing on this book-roll,
sḏm st mi ḏd.i st	Hear it as I say it.
m sn ḥꜣ ḥr šꜣꜣt	Do not pass beyond what has been ordained.
wn.in.sn ḥr rdit st ḥr ẖt.sn	Then they placed themselves on their bellies.
wn.in.sn ḥr šdt st mi ntt m sš	Then they read it exactly as in writing.
wn.in nfr st ḥr ib.sn	Then it was beautiful on their hearts
r ḫt nbt nty m tꜣ pn r ḏr.f	more than anything that is in this entire land.
wn.in ꜥḥꜥ.sn ḥms.sn ḫft	Then their conduct and dwelling was accordingly so.
ꜥḥꜥ.n ḥm n nswt bity ḥwny mni.n.f	Then the dual king Huny passed away.
ꜥḥꜥ.n sꜥḥꜥ ḥm n nswt bity snfrw	Then the dual king Sneferu was made to arise
m nswt mnḫ m tꜣ pn r ḏr.f	as the good king in this entire land.
ꜥḥꜥ.n rdi kꜣ-gm.n.i r imy-r niwt ṯꜣty	Then Kagemni was appointed as overseer of the city and vizier.
iw.f pw	This is its end.

2c. compositions without beginning or end preserved

Tales

The king and the spirit of Khentika son of Snefer

The composition is known from one fragmentary late Third Intermediate Period or Late Period papyrus (Papyrus Chassinat II, Louvre E 25352). Enough survives to indicate that it was a narrative involving a king, a cupbearer, a 'sealer' (official in the reception- and living-rooms) and a spirit who identifies himself as Khentika son of Snefer. The composition is in Middle Egyptian, and is very tentatively dated to the late Middle Kingdom by parallels for certain phrases: the longest is that pointed out to me by Wolfram Grajetzki for *ḏd.ỉn ḥm.f n ḫtmw nty r-gs.f* in *rdỉ.ỉn ḥm.f nỉs.tw n.f rḫ nswt nty r-gs.f ḏd.ỉn n.f ḥm.f* at line 12 of the great Abydos stela of the mid-Thirteenth Dynasty king Khasekhemra Neferhotep (Helck 1983, 23). The fragments were assigned letters in descending order of size; the original relative positions are not known, but the suggestions of the first editor, Georges Posener, are followed here, with Fragments D and C coming before A+B.

Published Posener 1960.

Fragment D	
[...] *n.f* [...]	[...] to/by him [...]
[...] *n* (?) *n pꜣ* [...]	[...] .. to the [...]
Fragment C	
[...]*w rdỉ n.f wꜣwt* [...]	[...] .. made ways for him [...]
[...] *wnḫ n ḥb*[*sw?* ...]	[...] wrapped in clo[th? ...]
[...].*tw wdpw pt*[...]	[...] .. cupbearer .. [...]
[...] *pꜣ wdpw wn*[...]	[...] the cupbearer .. [...]
[...] .. [...]	[...] .. [...]

Fragments A+B	
[...].*n sꜣ* [...]	[...] of us after [...]
[...] *rdỉ.n.k* [...]*ỉ m s*[...]	[...] you have given [...] ... [...]
[...] *r sḫm.tn* [...].*n*	[...] until you all forget [...] of us.
ꜥḥꜥ.n [...].*f n.f ꜥ.f ḳꜥ.f n.f* [...]	Then [...] he [...] to him his arm, spitting at him [...]
[... *ꜣ*]*ḫ r bw* [...]	[... spi]rit to the place [...]
ḏ[*d*].*ỉn ḥm.f n ḫtmw nty r-gs.f*	Then His Power said to the sealer who was beside him:
ḥs.tn [...] *gmgm* [...]	you are all to praise (?) [...] ruined [...]
šsp pꜣ nḏs m wnḫ n ḥb[*sw?* ...]	receive the fellow in a wrapping of clo[th? ...]
[...].*f wꜥb twrỉ m drt* [...].*f*	[...] of him pure and cleansed from the hand [...] of him
[*wnḫ*] *wḥs n mꜣwt*	[a wrapping] of ..-cloth anew.
wn.ỉn.f rdỉt wꜣḥ.f ḥtpt ḥr ꜥ[...]	Then he had him place offering upon the ..[...]
[...] *ꜥḫ ḥr sṯs šw* [...]	[...] rising to the pillars of Shu [...]
nn sw m pt nn sw m tꜣ	he was not in the sky, he was not on earth,
wꜣw rdwy.f r sꜣtw [...]	his feet were raised off the ground [...]
[... *ḥwt?*]-*ḥr nn sp rm.k* [...].*f n.ỉ*	[... Hat]-hor (?), never are you to weep [...] of him to me.
ḏd.ỉn ꜣḫ pn ỉnk ḫnt-kꜣ sꜣ s[*n*]*fr*	Then this spirit said: I am Khentika son of S[n]efer,
ỉty nb.ỉ [...]	sovereign, my lord. [...]

The Tale of a Herdsman

This literary composition survives as 25 lines and remnants of further washed-out signs preceding and following, at the end of a papyrus containing another literary composition (Papyrus Berlin 3022). It presents a mixture of dialogue, narrative and description. Initially a man relates to a group his encounter with an inhumanly beautiful woman in the marshes, rounding off his tale with a charm recited against the perils of the water (generally crocodiles rather than women); the next day, his fears are realised as the woman appears to him. Since the first edition, though, Richard Parkinson has succeeded in deciphering erased traces from the washed-out portions. Pending a final reedition, the translation below follows the published photographs (Gardiner 1909b).

mtn wi hꜣ.kwi [r] sš	See, all of you, I went down [to] a pool
iw.f tkn m mẖr pn	which is close to this lowland,
iw mꜣ.n.i st ḥmt im.f	I saw a woman there,
nn s m ḥmw rmṯ	whose physique is not that of (ordinary) humans;
šnwy.i ḏdf mꜣꜣ.i stw.s	my hair went on end as I stared at her locks (?),
n nꜥꜥ n iwn.s	for the smoothness of her skin
nn sp iry.i ḏdt.n.s	I would never do what she had said (otherwise)
šfšft.s ẖt ḥꜥw.i	(but) awe of her pervaded my body.
ḏd.i n.tn	**Let me say for you:**
iẖ kꜣw ḥꜣ.n iẖ ḏꜣ bḥsw	So bulls, let us ferry ahead, and the calves cross over,
sḏr ꜥwt r ꜥ n mꜣḥ	for the night-rest of the herd at the terrain of the flax-fields (?),
mniw m sꜣ iry	the herdsman at their back,
smḥ.n n ḥꜣ kꜣw m-ꜥ ḳbw rdi r pḥwy.fy	our skiff for moving the bulls with the heffers put on its ends,
rḫw ẖt nw mniw ḥr šdt ḥsw	the wise men of the herdsman reading the water-chant
m ḏd rf pn	**by just this saying:**
ḥꜥ kꜣw.i mniw ṯꜣyw	My spirits rejoice, herdsmen, men,
nn wn srwy m šꜣ pn	there will be no disturber in this field,
rnpt ḥꜥpy ꜥꜣ	in a year of the great Nile-flood,
wḏ wḏt n sꜣw tꜣ	decreeing the decrees to the stalls (?) of the land,
n tn š r itrw	(when) lake cannot be distinguished from river.
wḏꜣ rk r ẖnw n pr.k	Go then to the yard of your house,
iw idt (?) mn m st.sn	the herds (?) are firmly in their places.
iy iw snd.k ꜣḳ šfšft.k rwt r ꜣḳt	Arrival, fear of you is ruined, awe of you has gone to ruin,
nšny n wsrt	the raging of the Mighty Goddess,
sndw n nbt tꜣwy	the fears of the Lady of the Two Lands.
ḥḏ.n rf tꜣ *dwꜣ sp sn*	**The day broke then** the next morning (?)
iw ir mi ḏd.f	and it was done as he said:
ẖp rf sw ntrt tn iw.f di.f ḥꜣt n š	this goddess did meet him when he went forward to the lake,
ii.n sḥꜣ.s m ḥbsw.s	and she did strip off her clothing
tḥtḥ.s šnw.s	and shake her hair loose.

The water charm survives in somewhat different form among the formulae to procure eternal life written on the coffin of Buau Mentuhotep (Cairo CG 28027, T9C, from Thebes, early Middle Kingdom); incantations recited against dangerous creatures often appear in funerary literature, to protect the deceased in the afterlife. The charm has been allotted the number 'Coffin Text 836' in the standard Egyptological edition of Middle Kingdom funerary literature. Its opening section contains the parallels to the Tale of the herdsman:

ḥḏ.n rf tꜣ ḏꜣ.n.f smꜣ ḥꜣ m smꜣ	Day broke. He crossed the ford, the herd in the ford,
šfwt.k rwt.ti r ꜣḳt	Awe of you has gone to ruin,
nšn n wsrt snd n nbt tꜣ	rage of the Might Goddess, fear of the Lady of the Land.
iw kꜣ.k m st n bꜣ.k iw snd.k ꜣḳ	Your ka is in the place of your ba, fear of you is ruined.
wḏꜣ r ir.f n.n ḥsw-m-mw	The utterance is well, it has made us the water chant.
wḏꜣ r.k imy .. n pr ..	Your utterance is well, that is in .. of the house of ..

On its relation to the Tale, see Parkinson 2002, 300 with n.9.

The Tale of Horus and Seth: the seduction of Horus by Seth
Lahun Papyrus UC 32158 with related fragments UC 32148B and UC 32150A

The 'core literariness' of this composition remains a subject of debate between those who interpret it as a religious narrative for recitation in healing and those who accept it as literary. On formal grounds of style of handwriting and presentation, in comparison with the other Lahun papyri, I consider it literary, though, from another site and perhaps slightly later, the Ramesseum Papyri manuscripts with incantations for good health might be taken to show the same style and presentation in that 'functional' (so 'not core-literary') category. For the references to previous discussions on the basis of the main segment preserved, UC 32158, see Parkinson 2002, 294.

UC 32158

One main fragment with one small piece detached from the right edge at column 1 lines 5-6, mounted in a single frame, bearing parts of two 'pages' of horizontal lines, probably each with nine lines, followed by parts of two vertical lines.

column 1 (horizontal lines)

[...] (trace)	[...] (trace)
[...] *sw*	[...] him
[...]*ꜣ.f*	[...] his ..
[...]*n ỉry r.f*	[...] which he did to him
[...]*.ỉ pn ỉw.ỉ grt r rdỉt*	[...] this my .. Now I shall give
[...] *n.k r ẖt mk tw*	[...] to you at the body. See you/one (?)
[...] *kfꜣ* (?) *nn n.f rdỉ.ỉ*	[...] conceal (?) It is not to him that I give
[...] *ẖt ỉw.k ḥr mw rdỉ* ..	[...] the body. You are on the water, there is given (?) ..
[...] *ḏd.ỉn ḥm n* [*stẖ*]	[...] Then the Person of [Seth] said

column 2 (horizontal lines)

n ḥm n ḥr nfr-wy pḥwy.ky wsḫ rdwy [...]
ḏd.ỉn ḥm n ḥr sꜣ r.k ḏd.ỉ [...]
r ꜥḥ.sn ḏd.ỉn ḥr n mwt.f ỉst [...]*.n*
stẖ rḫ m-ꜥ.ỉ ḏd.ỉn.s n.f ꜥḥꜣ tw m ꜥḳ.n.f r.s m-ḫt ḏd.f n.k sy
k[*y*] *sp ḫr.k ḏd.k n.f ỉw ḳsn r.ỉ ḥr ḳd ḥr-ntt dns tw r.ỉ*
nn rmn (?) *pḥty.ỉ pḥty.ky kꜣ.k n.f ỉr-m-ḫt rdỉ.n.f n.k pḥty*
ḫr.k ḫꜥꜣ.k ḏbꜥw.k ỉmt-ny ḫpdw.k mk rdỉ [...] *n.f s mỉ*
[...]*y mk wnn nḏm sy ḥr ỉb.f r ḳꜣt* [...]
nw [*mt*]*wt pr m ḥnn.f nn rdỉt mꜣ st rꜥ* [...]

to the Person of Horus, how beautiful your buttocks are, broad of legs [...]
Then the Person of Horus said, be careful in case I tell [...]
to their residence. Then the Person of Horus said to his mother Isis [...] ..
Seth to have sex with me. Then she said to him, resist when he has entered it; after he tells you it again, then you should tell him, it is much too difficult for me because you are heavier than I am,
my strength cannot shoulder your strength – that is what you should say to him; after he has placed his strength on you,
then you should push your fingers between your buttocks, see there is given [...] he has [...] it like
[...].. see it will be sweet on his heart more than the height [...]
that [se]ed that comes from his phallus without letting Ra see it [...]

vertical lines after column 2:

[...] *mỉ r.k m ... n.ỉ*	[...] come on, do not ... to me
[...] .. *ḳmꜣw* (?)	[...] .. winnower (?)

UC 32150 A

Ten fragments, with several smaller items mounted in same frame perhaps related; the original relation of fragments is uncertain.

Fragment 1

[...] *ỉb wꜥ wn* [...]	[...] heart one being [...]
[...] *smꜣyw n* [...]	[...] confederates of [...]
[...] *wnm.f ḫt ḥnꜥ.k rꜥ* [*nb?* ...]	[...] he eats meals with you [every?] day [...]
[...] .. *wꜥ dd.k mꜣst.k* (?) [...]	[...] .. one, with you placing your thigh (?) [...]

[...] *ỉn* (?) ...*f r.k r rdỉt dbḥ* (?) [...]	[...] bring (?) his ... against you to cause to be requested (?)
[...]	

Fragment 2

[...] *n ḥm n ḥr* .. [...]	[...] of the Agency of Horus .. [...]
[...] .. *nmyt* [...]	[...] (goddess?) travelling (?) [...]
[...] *ḥr ḥr* (?) [...]	[...] Horus on (?) [...]

Fragment 3

[...] *rdỉt* [...]	[...] to give [...]
[...] *rꜥ nb* [...]	[...] every day [...]
[...] *ḥnꜥ.k* [...]	[...] with you [...]

Fragment 4, column 1 (ends of horizontal lines)

[...] *rd.f* (?)	[...] his leg (?)

Fragment 4, column 2 (vertical line)

[...]*.f wnn nfr*..	[...] his [...] there will be perfect ..

Fragment 5

[...] ... *ỉb* (?) [...]	[...] heart (?) [...]
[...] .. *n.k ṯbw* (?) .. *ỉrt* ...*f* ... [...]	[...] .. to you (?) sandal (?) .. do ... he/it ... [...]
[...]*.k mk ꜥḥꜥ ꜥꜣy sꜣ ỉst* (?) [...]	[...] of you (?). See, stand here, son of Isis (?) [...]
[...] ... *mỉ* ... *ỉ* .. [...]	[...] ... [...]

Fragment 6

[...] ... [...]	[...] ... [...]
[...] *ẖr tbwty.k dꜣỉr*	[...] under your sandals, push away
[...] *ỉs* (?) *snt.k* .. [....]	[...] indeed (?) your sister .. [...]
[...] ... *n.f-ỉmy* [...]	[...] ... belonging to him/it [...]
[...] ... [...]	[...] ... [...]

Fragment 7

[...] ...*f*	[...] he/it ...
[...] *nḥḥ*	[...] eternity

Fragment 8

[...] *ỉ* [...]	[...] .. [...]
[...] *ḏw* [...]	[...] evil (?) [...]

UC 32148B

Two fragments, rotted to a threadbare condition. The phrase *ḥm n nswt bity* may indicate that the narrative on the manuscript continued to the point where Osiris as king makes a pronouncement, or where Horus has been proclaimed king at the end of this struggle with Seth. Note though that the fragments UC 32148B have been identified as part of the same manuscript as UC 32150A+32158 only on the basis of the handwriting and comparison of the condition with the margins of UC 32158.

Larger fragment:

[...] *dỉ n* ... [...]	[...] given to ... [...]
[...] .. *rꜥ* .. [...]	[...] .. Ra .. [...]
[...] ... [...]	[...] ... [...]
[...] *s* (?) ... *nṯr* .. [...]	[...] ... god ... [...]

Smaller fragment

[...] ... *pn s* (?) [...]	[...] this ... [...]
[...] *n ḥm n nswt bity* [...]	[...] for the Agency of the dual king [...]
[...] ... [...]	[...] ... [...]
[...] *n.f* (?) ... [...]	[...] to him (?) ... [...]
[...] ... [...]	[...] ... [...]

Four other fragments possibly but not certainly from this manuscript are part of UC 32308.

One or two tales of travel

Lisht fragment Papyrus Lythgoe, MMA 09.180.535

The surviving section is 11.7 cm high, 19.6 cm in length, estimated by its first editor as originally about 16 cm in height. Excavation records indicate that it was found in the cemetery southwest of the Amenemhat I pyramid, ‘in front of pit 526 and near pit 524’. It seems then to be a stray find like the fragment of the Tale of Sanehat and other, non-literary papyrus fragments found among the late Middle Kingdom tombs at Harageh.

Both sides of the fragment bear vertical columns with narrative, one refers to a ship, the other to water, and both sides seem to record a rare word *ḥꜣwyt* with wood-determinative, and on these grounds it seems plausible that the two segments of writing come from a single literary composition dominated by narrative. However, in this fragmentary condition, it cannot be excluded that the two sides bore originally two tales rather than one.

Published Simpson 1960.

Recto:

[...] *ḏ..* **[..]*wt* [..] *n* [..]** *ṯꜣty ḏfꜣ sꜣ n*[...]	[...] ... **[...] .. [..] .. [..]** vizier Djefa’s son N[...]
r tꜣ sẖt nt ṯꜣty wḥꜥw [*ntt*]	[...] to that marsh of the vizier Hunter [which]
wnn.s ḥr i͗ꜣbtt nt ẖnw [*ꜣ*]	used to be on the east of the Residence
ṯp.n.f kpnt nt pr nswt ꜥnẖ wḏꜣ snb [*m*]	he loaded a Kepny-ship of the House of the King life! prosperity! health! [with]
bw nb nfr m ꜥḥꜥw (?) *n ꜣṯpt*[*.n?*]	all good things in heaps (?) of what he [had?] loaded
.f m pr.f wrš.n.sn sꜣ.f ḥr [*i͗rt h*]	from his house, while they spent time as his son
cel[ebrated]	
-rw nfr ẖr-m-ẖt m[*š*]	- now after evening
-rw ẖpr ꜥḥꜥ.n rdi.n[...]	fell, [...] gave [...]
[*ḥꜣw*]*yt rdi tꜣ šdt* ..[...]	[...]-block, the .. in place [...]
[...]*nw ms ẖft s* ..[...]	[...] ... though according to (?) .. [...]
[...].. *wr ḥn*[...]	[...] .. great .. [...]

Verso:

[...]..[...]	[...] .. [...]
[...]*.f tꜣ ḥꜣwy*[*t...*]	[...] of him that ..-block [...]
[...].. *ḥmst m ẖn*[*w...*]	[...]-woman seated inside [...]
ḏd.n.f n.s n-m tr tn [...]	he said to her: who are you? [...]
pr.i pw ꜥḳ.n sw smꜣyt [...]	it is my house, the plotters entered it [...]
n.sn wi ḥr mw wnn.in.sn ḥnꜥ p[...]	they had [...] me on the water; then they were with ..[...]
sꜣḥ.i ir n.f in.f sꜣt.f prt sḥ[...]	my neighbour (?) done for him by him, his daughter gone
..[...]	
ꜣbdw ꜥšꜣ swꜣ ꜥḥꜥ.n nswt [...]	many months had gone by, then the king [...]
[...] *st* [...]*w nn* ...[...]	[...] place [...] .. not ... [...]
[...]..[...]	[...] .. [...]

A tale at the palace Papyrus British Museum EA 10475 verso

This composition survives on the back of a highly fragmentary manuscript dated by its handwriting to the Second Intermediate Period, and reassembled by Richard Parkinson with Bridget Leach (Papyrus British Museum EA 10475: Parkinson 1999b). There are red points ('verse-points') at intervals. Roughly the upper quarter of this composition seems to be preserved; for the other side of the manuscript, and comments on provenance, see below, Hymns in praise of the king, Part Two, Section 3b. The papyrus has not yet been fully published, but Richard Parkinson provides a comprehensive account in the article cited; this transliteration and translation follow his preliminary edition there of the more connected portions on the surviving fragments.

Column 1 fragmentary

Column 2, lines 1-2	
[...] *mꜣꜣ i͗nbw*	[...] seeing the walls.
n rḫ.i ni͗wtyw i͗pn	I did not know those city-dwellers
[...] .. *n ꜥḥ dns*[...] *rd ꜥꜣ šfyt*	[...] .. of the palace, heavy [...] step, great in dignity
Column 3, lines 1-4	
di͗.n.f n.s ḥḏwt mrḥt šspt nt bi͗t	He gave her white cloth, oil, a comb (?) of honey
di͗.n.f n.s hnw ẖr msdmt	He gave her jars bearing eye-paint,
ḫbbt ẖr ꜥntyw	vessels bearing resins,
di͗.n.f n.s tpt	He gave her first quality oils,
ḥsw ḥr ḥsyt […] *ḫbꜣw ḫbꜣ*[…]	the singers in song […] the dancers (?) danc[ing? …]
Column 4	
nnm mi͗ s mꜣꜣ ḫt	weary, like a man seeing things.
sṯꜣ n.f pr-ꜥnḫ mi͗-ḳd.f	The entire House of Life is brought to him.
Column 5, lines 1-4	
[…] *ẖr st-ḥr.s*	[…] under her supervision,
i͗pt nswt r ḏr.s ẖr drt.s	the entire private apartments of the king under her hand.
ḥtr.n.f ꜥḳw.s mi͗ nswt	He fixed her regular revenue at the level of a king,
ḥwt-nṯr mi͗ […]	the temple as […].
i͗r.i͗n.tw ꜥḥꜥw r hrw ḥm	Then a whole forty days was spent
m ḥb nfr n [...]	in celebration of [...]
i͗w.tw ḥr swri͗ .. […] *ḫbt ḫn*[…]*m*	people drinking, .. […] dancing, performing (?) […] ..

This was the final column of writing on this side of the manuscript, the next space for a column being preserved but blank.

Lahun Fragments possibly of Tales
Published Collier and Quirke 2004

A Tale of Khenemsu and Nemay?
Lahun fragments UC 32105B and part of UC 32105E
UC 32105B is a fragment with horizontal lines of hieratic, possibly from the same manuscript as UC 32105 A (see the next item below). The personal name Khenemsu is found in UC 32157 verso (Griffith 'story of Hay'), but the handwriting seems different.

[...] *nꜣ n (?)* [...] *m-ꜥ (?)*	[...] these (?) [...] from (?)
[...*ḥ*]*nꜥ.k (?) i͗nk b*[...] *r ḫḫw n* [...]	[...w]ith you (?) I am the ..[...] at the neck of [...]
[...] *i͗rn s* [...] *i͗n (?) m nꜣ n* [...]	[...] done for/by a man [...] bring (?) from these [...]
[... *nm*]*ꜥy ḫnmsw ꜥḥꜥ.n ḏd.n nm*[*ꜥy* ...]	[... Nem]ay and (?) Khenemsu. Then Nem[ay] said [...]
[... *ꜥḥ?*]*ꜥ.n ḏd.n nmꜥy pn ꜣbw* [...]	[... Then ?] this Nemay said '[I?] wish [...]
[...] *m bẖsw ḥr ḥḏw ꜥḥꜥ.n ḏd.n ḫn*[*msw?* ...]	[...] with a loaf and onions. Then Khe[nemsu?] said [...]

UC 32105 E
Among the smaller fragments in the same frame, catalogued as UC 32105E, two mounted below UC 32105B probably belong with it, from the handwriting and content: one bears the title *imy-r st* 'overseer of the stores', and another seems to preserve part of the phrase [*ꜥḥ*]*ꜥ.n ḏd.n nm*[*ꜥy*] , possibly even the start of UC 32105B line 4, though the fibres do not seem distinctive enough to confirm or refute this.

A Tale of Cloth, Turquoise and a King?
Lahun fragment UC 32105A (perhaps part of UC 32105B?)
UC 32105A comprises three fragments with vertical lines of hieratic, from perhaps one manuscript, relative positions uncertain. Other fragments from the same manuscript may be among the small items numbered UC 32105E. It is possible that fragment UC 32105B, written in horizontal lines, is also from the same manuscript as UC 32105A: it is listed as the preceding item 'Tale of Khenemsu and Nemay'.

Transliteration and translation
UC 32105 A Fragment 1: h. 13 cm, w. 15.3 cm

[...]*r.s* [...]	[...] her [...]
[...]*.f pw n* [...]	this is its/his [...] of/for [...]
[...]*rt i͗.* [...]	[...] ... [...]
m ḫꜣ n pr mnḫt (?) [...]	in the bureau of the House of Cloth (?) [...]
tpw ẖkr m mf[*kꜣt*]	of first quality decorated with tur[quoise]
mꜣt wnḫ.n.s šmꜥw [...]	that is new. She donned fine linen [...]

UC 32105 A Fragment 2: h. 7.0 cm, w. 9.8 cm

[... *ḥ*]*nꜥ* [...]	[...] and (?) [...]
rḫyt mdw [...]	the people, speaking (?) [...]
wḥꜥt ṯssy [...]	solving what is tied [...]
nfr i͗b ḥnꜥ i͗nt n[...]	good for the heart, and bring to [...]
[...]*.n (?)* [..] *hrw* [...]	our (?) [..] day [...]

UC 32105 A Fragment 3: h. 6.0 cm, w. 10.5 cm

[...] *i͗b.f ḥr mꜣ (?)* [...]	[...] his heart at seeing (?) [...]
[...] .. *ḫt.f (?) bnri͗* [...]	[...] .. his things (?) sweet [...]
[...] *ḏd.i͗n ḥm.f* [...]	[...] then His Power said [...]
ḥs w[*i͗?* ...]	Favour m[e? ...]

A Tale of Nakhti, or a lament in a petition against Nakhti?
Lahun fragment UC 32107A
Recto:
[...] .. *rn n sbꜣw* .. [...] *.s*
mk mꞽn ꞽb.k ḥr ḏd ḫprrw (?) *mdw* [... *ꜣ*]*s sp sn*
[...]*.f ḫft-ḥr.f ꞽnk* [...] *ḫnt.k(wꞽ) ḥs.n.ꞽ r*
[..] *ḏd ḥw.ꞽ n* (?) *sꜣw wg*[*s*](?)*.n.ꞽ mw nw mwt*
[...] *ꜥḳ r bw nty ꞽb.k ḫb.k* [*ꜣt*]*pw rḥwy sꜣ nḫtꞽ*
[...]*.f ḥr ḏd mꜣ.n.f wꞽ ꜣs.kwꞽ r bw ẖr ḥm.k ḥr*
[...] *mwt.kwꞽ mꞽn ꞽḫ tm.ꞽ mꜣꜣ ḫpr.t(y).sy*
[...] *ꞽs ꞽn n.ꞽ rḥwy sꜣ nḫtꞽ ꞽn.tw.f n.f ḥr-ꜥ sp sn*

[...] .. name of gates .. [...] its [...]
See today your heart is saying the one who comes into being (?) speaking [... qu]ickly (twice)
[...]he [...] before him: 'I [...] going north, and returned to
[..] saying I strike for (?) the guard (?) I have savoured (?) the waters of death
[...] enter the place where you wish to assess [the car]go of Rehwy's son Nakhti
[...] he [...] saying that he saw me hastening to the place where Your Person is, to
[...] I am dead today, rather than see what may happen'
[...] 'Bring me Rehwy's son Nakhti' and he was brought to him right away.

A Fragment from Lahun with mention of Lotus Eaters
UC 32271B verso
Fragments of a papyrus roll with hieratic on both sides. One main fragment pair, almost joining, and one small; fourteen minor fragments with traces of writing may come from this or one of the other three items mounted in the same frame. The reference to lotus-eaters seems unparalleled within Egyptian literature.

Main fragment pair:	
wꜣḫ (?) [...]*.ꞽ mr.kwꞽ*	inundated [...] I, being loved
dꞽw n.ꞽ ḫt (?) *rdꞽ n.ꞽ bnꞽt rdꞽ n(.ꞽ?)*	I am given things (?). Let me be given sweetness, be given
mrwt ꞽn wnw pr ꞽn	love, by the openers of the house, by
ꜥmw sšnw sš r.f	the consumers of lotus-plants. Indeed surpasses (?)
[*m*]*r*[*wt?*]*.ꞽ m ẖt nt ḥr nb wnwt* (?)	[love?] of me in the body of everyone, hour (?)
[...]..[...]	[...] .. [...]
Small fragment:	
[...*ps*]*š* (?) *nw* (?) [...]	[di]vide (?) wa[ters/these (?)]

Teachings

Papyrus Ramesseum II
One in a group of late Middle Kingdom manuscripts, this papyrus survives as two sections, one 46 cm long and 12.5 cm high, the other 54 cm long and 10.5 cm high. The original position of the sections relative to one another is not known. Both bear sequences of phrases in the tradition of teachings and laments.
Published Barns 1956

Section One, column 1
[... *h3b?*]*.tw b3k sikr n mrwt ir.f m3ʿ*[*t* ...]
wsf.f m mḥ wsf.f bw nb [...]
snm.n sikr sw n nb.f ir.n.f [...
... *ḫtm.ti r rwty k*[...] *h3b sw*
[*ḥd?*] *is ḥdt ḥdw wsfw* [...]
[...] *snmw iwty di mḥ wsf.f iḳrw.f*
[...] *sb3 irr ir h*[*3*]*b.k m3ʿt*
[...]*.k m psš r mdw sh ḥ3* (?) *di.f* [...]
[...] *nṯr ḥry nšn.f r pḥty*[*.f* ...] *m ḥwyt*
[...] *ḏb3* [..]*f nḫwt* (?) [...]*.s*
iw nhw sšmw [...] *sn ʿnḫ*
[...] *hn.f in iw ir.f* [...] *rdi di* (?) *hrw* [...]
[...]*t sḏm mtrw sp.f wḫ3 iw* (?) [...]
[...] *hrw* [...]*k* [...]

[...] a servant who is advanced is [sent?] in order that he may do what is Righ[t ...]
He fails the drowning man, he fails everyone
[...] the one who advanced him before his master has been saddened when he did [...]
... locked outside .. [...] the one who sends him
Destruction indeed [destroys?] the destroyer, failings [...]
[...] the sorrows of the pauper (?) cause him to fail his talents (?)
[...] teach the one who does, so that the one you send does what is Right
[...] of you as a mouth-splitter, a word that subverts ... it causes [...]
[...] the supreme (?) god [...], raging to [his] (full) strength [...] with tempest
[...] .. [..] .. pleas (?) [...] of it (?)
a few leaders (?) [...] the passing of life
[...] he agrees, does he do [...] ... [...]
[...] .. the careful man hears his deed of folly .. [...]
[...] day [...] .. [...]

Section One, column 2

[...] *wḏ3w ḥr ḥ*[...]	[...] the dead are [...]-ing [...]
[...] *ir pḥwy mdw* [...]	[...] making the end of speech [...]
[...] *rdi m b3ḥ sḏm* [...]	[...] placed in the presence, hearing [...]
[...] *sšw imyw* [...]	[...] the writings that are in [...]
[...] *sm3 sw m bw nb* [...]	[...] joining him in every place [...]
[...] *ḥr pds* (?) [...]	[...] dread, box (?) [...]
[...] *sšr.f pḥ* (?) [...]	[...] as he shoots (?), reaching (?) [...]
[...] *m ḏd* [...]	[...] in saying [...]

Section One, verso

[…] *m* […]
[…] *ỉrt ḫpr b*[*n*]*rỉ* […] *ḫrt m* [..]*š*[…] *sp sn nr n rdỉ* (?) […]
[…].*f n wḫꜣ ỉr.f ns wʿ n* […] *r wšb* […].*f ky n ḫm rḳy.f*
[… *ỉ*]*nm ḥḏ ḫr sn ỉwnw ỉr ḳmꜣw* (?) *ḥn*[…]
[…] *ỉb.s ʿšꜣ ḳdw sbꜣ ḳn r mst bỉꜣt* […] *ỉwnw ḫprt*
[…] *ḏd.n tp-r n wnt ʿnḫ n ḫm nṯr* […] *d*[*d*] *ṯꜣw m fnd.f* [*s*]*fḫ sw*
[…] *nn šn sw snd tn* [*n*] *nṯr pw m* […]
[…] *mỉtt nbt pw sʿr.s hrw r ḥḥ* […] *ṯꜣm ḥr m-ḫt swꜣ ḏn*[*d*].*f*
ỉmn ḫpr m sbꜣ ḫʿry ỉw.f ỉr.f sbꜣw dd sꜣw m ỉb.f
šw […]

[…] … […]
[…] deeds, sweetness (?) happens […] … [..] .. […] twice fear of [what] was given […]
[…] his […] of folly, as he makes one tongue to […] to answer […] he […] another to the ignorant so that he complies
[… tr]aits that are destroyed, then characters pass, creatures do .. […]
[…] her/its desire, numerous of forms, a bold teacher shall produce talent […] characters events
[…] pronouncement has said, there is not life for one who does not know the god […] one who gives breath in his nose to release him
[…] fear shall not envelop him, he is the one whom the god chosen from […]
[…] the like, she is the mistress who raises a day to eternity […] veiling his face after his anger has passed,
hidden one who takes form as a raging star, he makes instruction, one who places experience in his heart,
free [from …]

Section Two, column 1

r r pf n rwty	At that outer gate
sšsꜣwy n wḫrw ḫprw m ỉb	Treatment for the ills that arise in the heart
dd ṯꜣw ḫpr ḥr sbꜣ m wḥʿ ỉb	Giving breath arises in teaching with unleashing the heart
ẖr-ʿ ptr.f sbꜣw	The apprentice watches the teacher
dr sꜣw m ỉwty sꜣw.f	The remover of protection is a man without protection
sỉꜣt n sỉꜣt .. […]	Injury on injury (?) .. […]
[…]*t ḥr pgꜣ* [...]	[…]-store (?) unrolling […]

Section Two, column 2

ḫpr m dmỉ ỉm (?)	Arising from its touch (?)
pḫꜣ pḥ n ỉrr.f ỉs ḥmwy wḫꜣ sw	A proven expert cannot achieve skill – folly of Seth (?)
dd nṯr ʿḳꜣ.f btꜣ mỉ sbꜣ […]	the god causes him to be straight in crookedness like a teacher (?)
ỉrr s ỉrrt.f n rḫ.f ỉrw st r.f […]	A man always does his deed unaware of one doing it against him
[…]	
ỉm.tn tnỉ ḥr ỉrrt	Do not resist what is being done.
m mdwy n ỉʿ-ỉb.f	Do not speak to the man in midflow.
ỉrw n.tn mỉ ḳd šmsw ỉb.tn	Act for yourselves entirely as follows your hearts.
ḏd [...]	Say […]

Section Two, verso

[…] r ỉtn […]
ỉ[…]m [..].f pw ỉb h[n ḥr].f ḫpr n […]
sm [..] m bw […] ỉb n wḫꜣ ỉtn nm[…]
ỉwtw (?) ḥr .. ḫpr nṯrt ḥr sḏw km.n wḫꜣ […] sḥwy bỉnt
šw […].f ḥr [..] m [..] ḫt m-ꜥ ḥr n wḫꜣ ḥḏ […]
[…] ḏw ḳd ḥr sršt ẖt grḥ ḏw ḳd srwd.f […]
mtn hmw n ḫm n rḫ tnw.f gmm.f ḫt mỉtw.f mỉ ḫpr bỉꜣt
tnỉ.n.ỉ ṯs.tw ḫt ꜣtp m […]
[…].f smỉw (?) ḫr.tw r rḫ ꜥšꜣ-r ḫr.tw r mdww
rn n grw ỉr m th n sỉꜣ.n rḫ ḫt ỉwn.f
rḫ ḫt ḥr sḫt mỉ ḫm ꜥm.f ꜣḫw.f
sẖ.n ỉb ꜣḫ rḫt.n.f
rḫ ḥr ḏd.ỉ n-m
[...].f [..] r n grgy ṯꜣm ḥr n mnḫw
n ḥtm.n mdt r sꜣ.s (?) n pḫꜣ.n nšnnw ḥḏ
ỉw smw nb ꜣḳ.f mỉ ḫpr.f n ỉs ṯꜣw n r
n gꜣꜣ.n ḥḏw r ḥḏt km.f p[…]

[…] a mouth restraining […]
.. […] .. […] it is his […] a heart that can be re[lied up]on when [trouble?] happens […]
plants […] in [every?] place […] the heart of the fool, restraining .. […] the pauper …, the goddess is maligning, when the fool has completed […] a collection of eviles,
void […] of him on [..].. [..] … the face of the fool is bright […]
[…] the evil character gratifies the belly, the evil character sows […]
The fare of the ignorant, its number is not known, he finds things of his equal as if a miracle has happened.
I have aged, the things are raised, the ..[..] are loaded […]
[…] of him/it. Tattler, they call the wise; chatterer, they call the speaker.
The name of the silent is made into misery (?),
the experienced man cannot recognise his character.
The experienced says the trapper is like the ignorant, swallowing his talents,
the talented heart is deaf to what it once knew.
The wise man says: to whom can I speak?
[…] of him/it [..] the mouth of the liar is the veil on excellence,
a dispute does not end after (?) it, the rage does not break the destroyer,
every plant perishes as it sprouts, without even a breath of speaking,
the destroyer does not want for what to destroy, as he completes ..[…]

Fragments of one or two teachings on a writing-board (Ashmolean Museum 1964.489a, b)
The early twentieth century AD notes relating to this plastered wood writing-board indicate that it was from Thebes, perhaps from the same excavations, by Lord Carnarvon, that yielded two similar writing-boards with copies of the Teaching of Ptahhotep and a celebratory inscription of King Kamose. All three date to the very late Seventeenth or very early Eighteenth Dynasty, the sixteenth century BC.
There are red verse-points marking rhythmic intervals of the composition on both sides of the board: where preserved, these have guided the line-divisions below.
Published Barns 1968.

Fragments of better-preserved side (1964.489a)

[...s]mnḫ.n nṯr smnḫ sw	[...] the god has embellished the one who embellishes himself,
rs.ti ḥr.f tn.n.f tw ir.k n.f	watching over him, he selected you, to act for him.
[...] *tn.f wꜥ*	[...] he selects alone
tn irr.k n stn tw	select, may you act for the god who selects you
pꜣt.n.k irt m ḫt [...]	what you had once done is a matter [...]
[...] *ḥtp r.k nṯr.k*	[...] may your god be content over you
m šꜣ.f ꜥwy wnḏwt.f	in his share of action of (?) his flock
rdi.n.f n.k st ẖr st ḥr.k	he gave them to you under your personal charge
sẖrw.k [...] *mꜣꜥt*	your condition [...] what is Right
irr.k m wpwt nṯr	may you act on the mission of the god
nn ḥr.f rdi tw ḥr sẖrw.f	is it not the sight of him that sets you on his model?
hꜣb.n.f ir m wpwt.f	he has sent a man to act on his mission
[...]	[...]
ir wp.f gm.f m mꜣꜥt	if he judges, he finds by what is Right
nṯr pf rdi ẖr st ḥr.k	that god who places under them your charge
spr r.k ḥswt [...]	so that praise reaches against you [...]
[...] *wḏꜣ.k is ḫft.s tp tꜣ*	[...] then may you prosper by it on earth
mnḫ.k im [...] *n ḥs*[...]	may you be effective there [...] there does/did not praise
[...]	
[...*i*]*m*[*.k?*] *sn r ir m ḏwt* [...]	[... do] not model yourself on acting in evil
Small fragment:	
[*bꜣ*]*ḳ m* [...]*prr r* [...]	[...resplen]dent in [...] who always goes out at [...]
Small fragment:	
[...] .. *ḥr.ti r* [...]	[...] .. far from [...]

Fragments of less well preserved side (1964.489b)

[...]*w m* .. [...] *ir n* [...] ..	[...] ... [...] act for (?) [...] ..
[...] *r irt ḫft rḫ* [...] ..	[...] to act by knowledge [...] ..
[...] *ẖrw.s hpw ḫbd btnw ḥst* [...] ..	[...] its dependants the laws, the rebel hates praise (?) [...] ..
tn.tw iḳr m sẖrw.f	the excellent man is distinguished by his behaviour
iw snd n rḫ [...]	the fearful man does (?) not know [...]
[...] *ẖms ꜣ m sẖrw*	[...] bow down then in behaviour
ḥr-wy btn wꜣḏt [...]	how distant is the rebel from (?) flourishing [...]
[...]*.s n.k st*	[...] it/she [...] it for you
ḥhy.tw ꜣḫt n rmṯ	how highly prized is what is good for people
bṯt wggt n [...]	escape from sloth and (?) .. [...]
[...] .. *ir ny* (?)	[...] .. act for it (?)
smnḫ.sn m smnḫ.sn	their embellishers are their embellishment (?)
nn [...]*.f*	there is no [...] of him
dns wḏꜣ [...]*ty*	heavy is the prospering (?) [...] ..
in [...]	it is [...]

Two Lahun fragments, perhaps teachings

UC 32106C recto

Red points occur by the right lower side of each phrase of writing at regular and remarkably short intervals, as in line 5 for the phrase *m bw ktt* alone. Below line 6 is preserved part of a sign, interpreted here as a writing of the number 6; line-numbering is rare in Middle Kingdom paratext, and this may be the only instance of a line-number in the lower margin. In 2003 Mark Collier identified the traces on the verso as part of the opening passages of the Tale of Sinuhe, corresponding to B1-8 = Koch 1990, 11-13

[...] *ỉmn* [...] *rḫ.tw rn.f* ·	[...] hide [...] the man whose name is known. ·
[...] *ỉb wr* · *n ỉrr rwi.i* · *n ḥr ꜥ*	[...] great heart. · My move cannot be forced. · There cannot be violence
[...]*.f ꜥḥꜥw* ·	[...] he (?) [...] a lifetime. ·
[...] *pw*	[...] it means [...]
[...] *pw* · *m bw ktt* ·	[...] it means [...]· – in small matters (?).·
[...] *m ꜥnḫ* *6(?)*	[...] in life. (Line) 6(?)

UC 32117C

Recto

[...] ... [...]	[...] ...[...]
[...] *ỉn mỉn nn n ꜣpdw ỉnt (?) ꜥḥꜥ.n nn* [...] [...]	[...] it is today these birds are brought (?), and then these
[...]*r (?) n ỉw kꜣ.k (?) m ḥtp snfrw ỉšs* [...]	[...] ... your ka (?) is content, Sneferu. What [...]

Verso

[...] *r tꜣ pn* [...]	[...] to this land [...]
[...] *prr ḫpy ḥr-ꜥwy wn.ḫr* [...]	[...] who go out, dead at once (?). Then [...]
[...]*n ṯsm n nb.f* .. [...] ...*f* [...]	[...] as a dog [circles?] its master .. [...] his ... [...]

Laments

Lament of Sasobek

An opening narrative episode introduces a dancer and a man named Sasobek, who is imprisoned in a dungeon, and gives voice to laments. A similar prison setting recurs over a thousand years later, in the demotic Teaching of Ankhsheshonqy; in that, the opening narrative episode records how Ankhsheshonqy is imprisoned at the border fortress Defenna, for not telling the king about a plot against his life by the chief physician (Smith 1980).

This composition seems to be preserved only on Papyrus Ramesseum I, originally a fine book-roll 23 cm in height, found reduced to fragments among other late Middle Kingdom manuscripts (see Question One, Group Two). The first editor, John Barns, was able to reconstruct one set of fragments from near the beginning of the roll (set A): the remainder he could group into several sets, but was not able to determine their original sequence, and so assigned them letters simply in order of size (fragment groups B to G). The literary composition was written on one side only of the roll (recto): the back of the book-roll bears just one short note, an administrative account.

Published Barns 1956, 1-10, hieroglyphic transcriptions pl.1-6.

Fragments A, lines 1-16

[...] im.i iḫ di.i smꜣ.tw.f	[...] with me, then I am to have him killed.
nwꜣ pw [...]	Then [...] caught sight of [...].
ꜥḥꜥ.n ḏd.n.f n sꜣ-sbk pn	He told this Sasobek:
mk ḥꜣty-ꜥ nfr [sꜣ inni ...] nhwt	the mayor Nefer'[s son Ineni ...] plea.
ꜥḥꜥ.n sti.n.f nšw	Then he poured a cup (?)
[...] n nty m mnw tp tꜣ	[...] for the one who is in grief on earth,
n mꜣ.n.k sw [...]fn	you do not see him [...] feebly.
ꜥḥꜥ.n šm r.f [...] im.i	Then [...] went off [...] with me,
ḏd.tw r.f mdt tn	as this word was indeed spoken,
iw ẖbw ḫft-ḥr [n ḥꜣty-ꜥ nfr sꜣ inni]	while a dancer was opposite [the mayor Nefer's son Ineni]
[ꜥḥꜥ.n ḏd.n.f? n] ẖbw pn ptr rn.k	[and he? said to] this dancer said: what is your name?
ꜥḥꜥ.n ḏd.n ẖbw pn [...] ḏꜣr [...].f	Then this dancer said [...] need [...] of him
ꜥḥꜥ.n ḏd.n ḥꜣty-ꜥ nfr sꜣ inni	Then the mayor Nefer's son Ineni said
[...] sꜣ-sbk	[...] Sasobek:
mk tw sfḫ.ti m sprt nt ẖ[bw pn ...]	Now you are released by the petition of [this da]ncer [...]
[...] mnw.i nn wn.i	[...] my pain, I cannot exist,
ꜥnḫ.k n.i nfr sꜣ [inni ...]	as you live for me Nefer's son [Ineni ...]
ḫr m-ḫt kt pḫryt swꜣ[.ti ḥr nn ...]	After another round had passed [by ...]
pr n.f ḫtmw r ḏd	as the sealer went out to him saying:
mk wḏ pr-wr sf[ḫt.k ...]	now the palace man (?) is commanding that [you be rel]eased [...]
ꜥḳ pw ir.n ḫtmw pn	This sealer made his entry
r wḥm mdt tn n ḥꜣty-ꜥ pn [...]	to repeat this word to this mayor [...]
[...] ḫtmw pn n sꜣ-sbk pn	[...] this sealer to this Sasobek:
mi r st.k [...]	come to your place [...]
iw.k tr m-m n nṯr	What are you then to the god?
wn.i[n] sꜣ-sbk [pn ...] .. [...]	Then [this] Sasobek was [...]
[...] ḫnty r rnpt md-ḫmn	a period amounting to eighteen years,
ḫft tpt-r nt ḥfꜣw [...]	in accordance with the utterance of the snake [...]

Fragments A, lines 17-29

mdt ḏdt.n sš ḥwt-ḥr-ḥtp sꜣ sꜣ-sbk	**The word spoken by the writer Hathorhotep's son Sasobek**
pḫr r.f ḫft ḫprt	**as his speech circled over what had happened,**
rdit m-bꜣḥ ḥr rmṯ (?)	**to be placed in the Presence before people (?)**
ꜥnḫ pn n ꜥḥꜥw n rḫ ḫprt [im.f ...]	This life of mortals, it was not known what happens [in it ...],
ḫpr ḥr ꜥ pḥwy.fy sk ḥn[...] r.s	happens at the instant of its end, .. is destroyed [...] to it.
iw ḫr [...] ḫpr r srwd n m-ḫt	.. [...] happens to make growth for the future,
irt.n [...] nḥḥ	what was done by [...] eternity
nn ṯn.s sn n ktt r.f n k[...]	it will not distinguish them for a small thing (?) indeed, .. [...]
ḥns ꜥ ḥr ḫrt ib n [...]	meanness over joy, not [...]
ḳi pw mwt sks pw m ꜥnḫ	it is the serpent of death, it is ruin (?) in life,
wnm-ib pw [...] wḏꜣ ḫft sꜣw	it is self-denial (?) [...] prosperity in front of caution (?)
i[..] nṯr [...] ḥḥ	.. the god [...] quest.

n sṯn.n.s n.f šnʿ[...]	It does not match him in repelling (?) [...]
iw twt.n.f n itn ib	He has become like (?) the fractious man ,
[...] *r ḳn.f ib.f mḥ* [...]	[...] to demolish (?) him, his heart filled [...]
[...] *sꜣ.f r ḏd m-ʿ nf (?)*	[...] his son to speak from that (?).
mk nfr sꜣ inni [...]	Now Nefer's son Ineni [...]

Fragments B, group i

ḫpr ḥmww m ii n ḥr.f sn.t[w].f [...]	The skilled may become one toome forward, he is passed (?) [...]
rḫ pw snn r ḫprt ḥꜣm [...]	the one who copies the past (?) is a wise man, netting [...]
ḥtp.k im.f ḏfꜣw.k n.k	May you be content with it, your food is yours
m ḫrt hrw [nt rʿ nb]	in the course [of every day]
ḫrt.k n.k pw gmḥ wꜣ	Farsightedness means your portion is yours,
swh.f ib [...] *di.f ʿ*	it causes the heart to miss [...] he gives an arm (?),
n rḫ nty n.f sꜣḳ iit.n.s	the one who has self-control would not know its outcome

sf siw* [...] *m-ʿ.f	**Yesterday is passed [...] with it**
dwꜣ ḫpr n ḏt nn rḫ sḫr.f	Tomorrow is forever coming, its manner cannot be known,
m pw n.f sb ḫpr	what is it to him, passing and coming to be?
[...] *m pr* [...]	[...] what issue (?) [...]
[nn] rḫ sḫr.f kꜣ.f dwꜣ	[noone] can know its manner, as he considers tomorrow,
iw wn wr [...] *hꜣy*	the great [man?] is [...] fallen,
tm ir m nb ḫrt	the one who did nothing is now owner of the goods.
[...] *m ḏd hꜣ sḥḥ ʿwꜣ*	[...] when the robber (?) says snare the catch (?),
ʿwꜣ ntyw [...] *šnt ḳb ššp*	those who are [...] robbed (?) [...] the plotter has relaxed by dawn (?)
twt-wy n.f pw ḏdw r ir m sḫrw [...]	'How like him that is' people say of one who acts by the ways [...]
[... *p*]*tr n ḫpr n iw ḫpr.f r.s (?)*	What [...], not happening, does it happen at all (?)?
imn sḫrw nṯr ptr ḫpr m mn r [...]	The ways of the god are hidden: what happens in more pain than [...]
[...] *dd nṯr iwt nn ḥr r.s*	[...] of the gift of the god to come, without attention being paid to it,
srs.f sḏrw [...]*h iwt hr[yt]*	he wakes the sleeper [...] .. one with no fear,
ḥtp m fḳꜣw nṯr	content with the rewards of the god.

di n.k ʿwy.k *r nfrt*	**Your arms are given to you** for good,
smꜣ[...] *mkḥꜣ ḏwt wrt*	renewing (?) [...] warding off evil greatly.
n ʿr.s n.k ḥꜣ [...]	It has not risen to you behind (?) [...]
n sšr irt nt nhꜣ-ib	The eye of the furious has not dried,
dmi pw n hrw [...]*.f* [...]	it is home (?) for the contented (?) [...] of him
iit.n nfr whʿw (?)	when the good of (?) the releases (?) is arrived (?).
in ib smꜣr nb.f	It is the heart that makes his owner miserable,
dd r ḫr p[...]	the gift of the mouth bearing ..[...]
ir r nmtt rmṯ	acting according to the ways of people.
wꜣḥ-ib mnḫ sšrw	The patient man is the one who excels in behaviour,
in [...]	it is the [... who ...]
ḥtmyt pw nt mdt wḥd dꜣir [...]	Suffering the oppressor is the destruction of speech [...]
iw ṯs ʿḥʿ ir.f dḳr	The phrase arises to make pressure,
wn n.f mrwt [...]	love of [...] hastens to it [...]
n psš ḥnʿ nb ḳd m st nbt	without sharing with a man of character anywhere.
ʿwn [...] *iwt* [...]*.f*	Greed [...] one without [...] of him,
ḥs ḥr ib.f iḳr m-bꜣḥ	vile upon his heart, excellent in the presence.
wn pḥty mr[wt ...]	Strength of lo[ve] would be [...]
mnw pw ḳd msd sw swt mry	Character is the monument, but the favourite hates it.

is ib *is* [...]*.f*	**The light-hearted** is the one who is light [...] of him,
ʿḳ r iwty ʿḳw.f	the easy-talker is without his circle
mdw m stwt ḥr ʿšꜣ [...]	One who speaks by likening (?) many faces (?) [...]
sꜣww n.f sf m st isi .. [...]	the humble is prostrate before him in the place of ... [...]
spd ksmw ḥtp ibwy n.sn[-imy?...]	One who is sharp in defiance (?), both of their (?) hearts are content
[...]	
ʿšꜣ ḫrw ʿnd hnw sb ḫr sp[...]	One who is over-talkative has few adherents, for they pass under
..[...]	
[...]*.f* [...] *ḫw ḳd.f ꜣ*[...]	[...] he [...] void his character ..[...]

ḫt pw *mdt šmt*	**A fire is** a word that moves,
iw.s wbd.s [...]	it scalds [...]
mdt iḳrt di.s r ḥꜣt	An excellent word propels foreward,
iṯ.s nw[*ḥ?...*]	it seizes the ro[pe? ...]
[*n*] *wnt wn m ḫt.f*	with no being in his body,
wꜣḥ ib [...]	patient [...]

Fragments B, group ii

[... *ḫ*]*nws pf n m-ḫt mn ḥn* [...]	[...] that fever for the future, pain .. [...]
m wḫd dwꜣ m rḫ nn [...]	in the suffering of tomorrow in knowing, not [...]
gm.k m bw iḳr	You find in excellence,
bsy.k ir [*n*]*frt* [...] *swt sp sn*	your entry is that good is done (?) [...] doubly though,
ir [...] *hr-ib*	doing [...] the contented man,
ḏd iw ꜥnd	saying: the poor is come,
ḫsf šm [...] *ḫr rmṯ*	repelling the one who goes (?) [...] before people.
šm.n.k m ḫnw wꜣḥ [*ib?* ...]	You have gone within pati[ence? ...]
nfr pr h[*ꜣ*] *ḫft ḥmwt*	it is good to come and g[o] according to skill.
ir sšmw.k mi dwn [..].*k ḫwyt*	All your conduct is done as you extend (?) protection,
wꜣḥ-ib m ḫrt-hrw nt rꜥ nb	patient in the course of every day.
ir.k ḫt ḫft.f	May you achieve the case before him,
wnn sꜣ.f ṯs [*r ḫḫ*].*k*	and his protection be, bound, [at] your [neck],
k[...] *swt nḥm.f* [*tw*	so then it may rescue [you
n]*n* (?) *ḫsf m-ꜥ dwt nbt*	without?] warding off all evil,
nn wn ḥn [...]	there will bc no .. [...]
[*d*]*ꜣir srf nn wn twt n wꜣḥ* [...]	[sup]pressing the meek, there will be none like the pati[ent man? ...],
mꜣꜣ.f iy n.f pḥwy	as he says that the end is coming to him,
n wnt ḫftyw [...]	not enemies [...]
tm n ḫrt ib n wꜣḥw [...]	complete (?) for desire, no additions [...]
[...] *iwtw* .. [...]	[...] without .. [...]
ḳd.n n.f ib.f ḫnrt ḥꜣ.f	His heart has built him an enclosure behind him,
ḫ[...] *pḥwy ḫr.f ꜥnw r.f*	.. [...] end before him, turned away (?) from him,
iw m ḫt n rḫ pr [...]	in the body, not knowing the way out (?) [...]
ḫm.n.k *tmt.n.k sḏm m sḏm*	**You are ignorant** of what you have failed to hear in hearing,
n sḏm.k sḏmt.n.k m [...]	you have not heard what you have heard in [...],
[...].*k r.s ḥnꜥ gr m šnt ḫft ḏdw* [...]	[...] you to it and cease from plotting before the speaker [...]
rḫ ḥr ḏd n.k mr r.k n.k nḏ r.f i[...]	The wise says to you: prefer then for yourself advice on it ..[...]
mḏr.k r ḫnnw ḫsf mdwt m [...]	you fortify against turmoil, speech is turned down in [...]
[...].*k nw.f*	you [...] his cord,
ib.f n.k di.f dmi ib.k nf [...]	his heart is yours, he makes your heart unite .. [...]
ḏḥwty pw swḏꜣ ib pꜣ wꜣ [...]	He is a Thoth who cheers the heart that had fallen [...]
snnw pw snnw [...] *m wfꜣ*	he is a second companion [...] in flattery,
ḫsf ḥr iyt gmḥ [*šn*]*ty*	punishing for wrongdoing, perceiving the [plot]ter (?)
sḥm.f [...]	and forcing him back (?) [...]
sbꜣw m srwdt [...]	teacher in planting [...]

Fragments B, group iii

[...*nt*]*k swt iꜥ ibw*	Y[ou] though are one who satisfies,
šms bit s nw[...]	follower of talent, a man who .. [...]
iꜥnw wr-wy *ꜥꜣ-wy*	**Lamentation great** and mighty,
ḫw rḫ [...]	If only there was known [...],
dr ḫw iry ḫpr rwty n m-ḫt [...]	Its evil suppressed, the outsider arisen for the future [...]
[...]*t* .. *sḫm.f r irr* [...]	[...] ... he is more powerful than the doer [...]
[...] *m ḥnwty ḥmww* [...]	[....] with the piercing-word (?) of the skilled man (?) [...]
ḏꜣ šnꜥty iwn [...*t*]*ꜣ*	crossing the coin, hue [...]-heated
m mty n sḥw [...]	as the exact man of the councils [...]
snm r snm tw [...]	the slanderer is the one who slanders you (?) [...]
mṯn [...]	All, see [...]
ꜥnḫ n.i s pn r ḫm rn.f	This man lives for me more than one who does not know his name

[...] *r ḏd iw*	[...] saying: it is over
***mṯn** inḥ ḏw ẖrt[-ib? ...] snd*	**All, see** evil encloses des[ire? ...] fear,
sẖm-ib [m] rẖ st.f	The powerful of heart is the man who knows his place,
spr mdwt r sfnw	the word hits home to the humble,
[...]y r šntt nt ḳꜣ ẖrw	[...].. than the dispute of the loud-mouthed,
di.s šfwt.f	it instils (?) respect (?) of him.
grw ẖnw [...] sntt im ḥr bš r speech,	The silent man is speaker [...] founded there on the one ejecting
šr mṯn.f n pḥ.n.tw.f .. [...]	his way is narrowed, he cannot be reached .. [...]

Fragments B, group iv

[...] *ptr ir m irt sẖrw nw irt.f*	[...] what is done in doing matters of his doing
ḥr .. [...] *ḥr* [...]	on .. [...] on [...]
sbꜣ.f r wsf iwtw šsp.f sḥ [...] *r ḥr*	he teaches to delay one who can receive no advice [...] to attention,
swꜣ.n.f btꜣ [...]	he has passed by the fugitive [....]
sbꜣ.f n ik iw m .. [...]	he teaches the supplicant (?) ... [...]

Fragments B, group v

[...]*w*	[...]-man
***mṯn** hꜣb* .. [...] *m imy-bꜣḥ*	**All, see** there is sent .. [...] as the one who is in the presence,
iʿ ib n iyt [...] *ḫpr*	cleansing the heart of evil [...] happening,
nn ḏr ʿ sẖrw snmy[...]	without restraint on matters of sorrow (?) [...]
mꜣʿt r nb mḥ m [...]	what is Right, every mouth is filled with [...]

Fragments C, group i

[...] *isft ḫprt ḥr.s snmw* [...] *ḥtm*	[...] evil that arose by it, sorrow [...] destroying,
sb sḥbw n wn n.s irw ḫt ḫft.s	the ..-wind passes, she (?) has nothing active before her (?),
ḥm [...] *ḥnʿ hꜣkw-ib*	the [...] are turned back with the rebellious,
pgꜣ-ḥrw ḥr mdt twt [...]	the open-faced are speaking, assembled (?),
ẖt pḥꜣt bnri snsn	clear-bodied, sweet in brotherliness,
ḥꜣg ḥnm[...]	glad and joyful [...]

Fragments C, group ii

[...] *n m-ḫt ḫpr pḥr*[...]	..[...] for the future, when (?) there happens ..[...]
iryw mdt ... [ẖ]m [... r]ḫ sḏm.f	**Masters of speech ... [ign]orant [... w]ise when he hears**
ʿšꜣ pw ib [...] *irt mꜣʿt*	He is plentiful in wish (?) [...] to do what is Right,
iw nfr [...] *nn irt mi iw* [...]	there is good [...] without doing the like .. [...]
ir s m ḳd.f	a man acts by his character,
nn pr[t ...] *iꜣmt wr ḫrt im.f*	without going [out ...] favour, great in share by it,
ḥs[...] *m wḥʿ ib*	praise [...] in unleashing the heart,
ṯn-r ḥꜣw [...] *nfr* .. [...]	distinguished in speech, abundance (?) [...] good .. [...]
mnḫ rḫ [...]	excelling, knowing [...]

Fragments D, group i

***ḥn ʿ.k** sꜣḳ ib.k ḫtm* [...]	**Tauten your arm**, gather your heart, lock [...]

Fragments D, group ii

[...] *swt mnḫ irw ḫt [ḫ]ft.s*	[...] but [...] is excellent, those who act [be]fore her (?)
[...]*.f gr.f šr mꜣn.f* .. [...]	[...] him he is silent, little, he may see .. [...]

Fragments E

[...] *mdt šw m in r*	[...] speech, free from superfluous talk (?),
rdi m [...] *nb nfr ḫrt*	placed in [...] all good [...] condition (?),
swꜣ ḥr ḥr.f n nḏrw [...]	passing by in front of him for the strength (?) [...]
šw sw m ḥꜣt ib r i[..]*ꜣ*[...]	he is free from distortion (?) more than (?) ..[...]

Fragments Fi

[...] *r.f n wnt is wnwt.f iw.f r* [...]	[...] even, there is no hour-duty of his when he is to [...],
n wnt iꜣt.f wnwt [...]	there is no office of his the hour [...]

Fragments Fii

[...] *ḫꜣm rmn*	[...] bending the arm
[...]*.f iw n.f r.f ḥnꜥ irty.f*	[...] of him, he has his mouth and his eyes,
sḏm [...] *in* [...]	hearing [...] bringing [...]

Fragments Fiii

[...]*.f* [...]*.k* (?) [...]*.f*	[...]of him [...] of you (?) [...] him,
ḫft mꜣꜣ.i ꜥpr [...]	as I see equipped (?) [...]

Fragments Gi

[...] *ḏw* [... *n?*] *is ḥtp.f im*	[...] evil [...] he does [not?] rest there,
iw ḥmww r mh.f [...]	the skilled shall neglect him [...]

Fragments Gii

[...] .. [... *n?*] *ꜣḫ.f pw*	[...] .. [...] is his talent (?);
ir wḫꜣ n ḥmww [...]	the depth-line (?) of the skilled man

Fragments Giii

[...]*.tw r.f* [...] *ḥr ḥst.f* [...]	[...] (is done) to him (?) [...] praising him [...]

There are 71 unplaced fragments with scant traces (Barns 1956, pl.5-6), the largest being as follows:

Fragment 8

[... *ḥꜣty*]-*ꜥ inni ꜥḥꜥ.n* [...]	[... the may]or Ineni. Then [...]

Fragment 9

[...]*w im.f* .. [...] *mḥ m wn ḥr*	[...].. with him (?) .. [...] full of enlightenment,
nfr [...] *tm rḫ sw* [...] *pḥ* [...]	good [...] did not know him [...] .. [...]

Fragment 10

[...] *ḫnws ib dy* [... *s*]*mrw*	[...] fevered heart, given [... co]urtiers
[...]*t ib* [...]	[...] .. of heart [...]

Fragment 12

[... *sm?*]*ḫ.t*(*w*) *ḥmww m ḫrt* [...]	[...] the skilled man is forg[otten?] in the course [...]

Fragment 13

[...*m*]*ꜣꜣt nfr sšmw* [...]	[...s]een, good in guidance [...]

Fragment 14

[...]*r š*[...]*.f sꜣ.i sꜣw* [...] *btꜣ*	[...] ... [...] of him, I notice the guard [...] fleeing,
iw wn.s rs [...]	she/it was awake (?) [...]

The Lament of a Fowler?

On the back of one copy of the Tale of Khuninpu, there survive thirty-nine vertical lines from a similar composition (Griffith 1892, British Museum 10274 = Papyrus Butler). Pending a first edition by Richard Parkinson, this version follows the available facsimile copy by Newberry and Griffith, and transcription by Griffith. Unusually, over each tenth line was written its number; at line 12 is the ancient number 20, line 22 ancient 30, and line 32 ancient 40, demonstrating that the present first line was originally the ninth in this copy of the composition. Posener tentatively raised the possibility that this might belong with the title referring to a Fisherman of the Southern City, if that title was ever put to full use (see above, Two Literary Titles).

[…] …[…]	[…] … […]
[…] *ḥry-tp tꜣ ꜣw* […]	[…] overlord of the land, extended […]
wsẖ tꜣšw wr ẖrt m šꜣw …	broad in borders, rich in provisions in the fields …
ꜥ.k ḥr wḥꜥw.k	your arm upon your hunters.
m rdỉ .. sꜣw sn n kwy	Do not cause .. lest others pass us.
n pḥ.sn n.n n.tn	They have not passed us, or all of you,
grg ḏr rk ḥr	established since the time of Horus.
ḫpr n.tn sḫt	The Marsh Goddess comes into being for all of you,
smnḫ ỉrt m rḫt.n.k	action is embellished by what you have known.
mk sḫrw.n ḫft-ḥr.k	Our condition is before you,
šꜣ stỉ r tꜣ nn rwỉ.f ỉm	The fields are shot to the land, without it stirring from there.
spt.f ḳꜥḥt ẖr mnỉw ḫꜣswt	Its corner fringes are under the herdsmen of the hill-lands,
sgr ẖr sꜣw nw kꜣw	Silence is under the stalls of the bulls,
kꜣpw ỉmnw ẖr wꜣḥyt nỉwtyw	The hidden huts are under the grain of the city-dwellers.
ḥr smḥ.f n ỉrt (?)	The face neglects the action (?).
n gm.n.tw … gꜣw mty	There is not found … lack of the righteous.
ꜣr wr ḥr ḫt ỉt.f	The elder is deprived of the property of his father,
ḥtp n hꜣy nst.f	The plaintiff is content in his place.
bṯ.n sꜣ.f ḥr gnbt	His son is vilified before the council
… twꜣw	… beggars.
šꜣ.f ḏrḏrỉ .. ḥryw	His field is hostile .. the masters,
ḫmt.n.f ḥry	he had forgotten terror
wꜣ st r ỉr mꜣꜥt	It is fallen to the doer of what is Right,
n sḏmt.n sḫtyw ỉs pw	and that is even before the marshdwellers heard (?).
kss ꜣpdw ḥr ꜥnwt.f	The birds stumble (?) onto his claws,
prt ỉb ẖr nwḥw	Boldness (?) is ensnared (?).
mnḫ ḥr.s ẖr bgsw	It goes well on it with weariness
ỉr.t(w?) ꜥ n ḏw	The act of the evil man (?) is done (?),
sḫt m nwdw m ḥr-ỉb sḥnt	a blow with the lash amidst the decoys,
shtht ṯꜣ (?) ḳꜥt šꜣ	the quivering of the chick (?), the violence of the field,
n ỉs r ỉnt tm wḫd	but not to bring the one who does not suffer,
ḥꜣg n rdỉ.n.k spr [...]	.. you are not to let […] arrive,
[…]*.k wỉ m prwy šꜥ*	you [...] me from the fighters (?) of the sands (?)
[…]*.k wỉ m sꜣ wꜣw*	you [...] me after the intruder (?)
n ḥwt.n sꜣ n ḫr	before the stall (?) of defeat (?) has struck.
wḫd.k ꜣ wỉ r ḫprt	You injure me though at events
sp.ỉ r rḫt.k sḫr […]	My case is in your knowledge, […] condition […]
ꜣpdw.ỉ .. swdn m ꜥḥꜥ	My fowl .. burdened in standing
nn bỉk ḫft … šꜣšꜣ … […]	With no falcon before … […]
mk wỉ rdỉ r š[…] *ḥr.k*	I am given over to ..[…] over you,
ḳꜥt.k wỉ […] *.. mk ..* […]	You reject me […] .. See .. […]

2d. sets of small fragments tentatively identified as separable by content, literary by hand/content

Fragments from the Theban necropolis

1. About forty Middle Kingdom literary papyrus fragments were retrieved during the Austrian Institute excavation of the tomb-temple of Ankhhor in the Asasif area of Thebes West (Parkinson 2003, 133).

2. Papyrus Ramesseum fragment (if not part of Sasobek Lament): transliteration not available (Parkinson 2002, 310-311)

Fragments from the town at Lahun

1. UC 32107E+H

Two joining fragments, with red interval-point at right of end of second line: line-spacing and hand typical of literary manuscripts.

[...] .. *m* [...]	[...] ... in [...]
[...] .. *n* ... [...]	[...] ... not ... [...]
[...] *m wṯs ẖnw* [...]	[...] in raising rebellion [...]

Fragment UC 32117E possibly comes from the same manuscript: its recto bears the ends of three vertical lines of hieratic, in hand and spacing recalling literary manuscripts, the second with the word *ḥḏw* ‘onions’.

2. UC 32110C

A single fragment with parts of five horizontal lines of hieratic, possible literary by the word *wḫꜣ*.

[...] *wḫꜣ* [...]	[...] foolish man [...]
[...] *ḥr.f r* .. [...]	[...] on him/it to [...]
[...] ... *ḥt* (?) [...]	[...] ... [...]
[...] *mnmn* (?)	[...] moving (?) [...]
[...] ... [...]	[...] ... [...]

3. 32110F

Two fragments of papyrus, with parts of horizontal lines of hieratic in black, and red interval-points, on recto only; the larger also has a black point below the second of its three lines. The points in red, sign form and size, and the sole decipherable word of the larger fragment (*ꜣir* wretched?) indicate literary content.

4. UC 32111B

A single fragment with parts from the centre of eight horizontal lines with red interval-points.

[...] *s m pt* (?)[...]	[...] man in .. [...]
[...]· *sbt* [...]	[...]-people, .. [...]
[...]*rdit* · *ḥꜥ*(?) [...]	[...] man in .. [...]
[...] *ỉšst ỉr*[...]	[...] what is done (?) [...]
[...*r*]*wỉ* (?).*n* ·[...]	[... de]parted (?) [...]
[...] *ḫrw* ..[...]	[...] voice [...]
[...]*w* · *ỉm* .. [...]	[...] .., .. [...]
[...]*m.k wpwt* [...]	[...] of you a message [...]

5. UC 32117G

A single fragment with part of one vertical line of hieratic, in literary hand and with literary vocabulary

[...] *tꜣ-ꜥ m ỉrt ḫt ḫsf ḫt* [...]	[...] fiery-armed (?) in doing things; the one who prosecutes (?) [...]

Part Two, Section Three
At the Boundaries of Literature: eulogies for gods and kings

3a. compositions substantially preserved
The Hymn to the Nile Flood
A cycle of Hymns to king Senusret III
3b. compositions preserved in fragments
In praise of the king in the Fayum ('Sporting King' and 'Fishing and Fowling')
In praise of the king Papyrus British Museum EA 10475

Introduction
On the problems of identifying eulogies as 'practical' (liturgical compositions for recitation at ritual) or 'literary' (written to be read, without functional setting), see Parkinson 1999b, 187-190. Here only the most literary of Middle Egyptian 'hymns' attested on papyrus mansucripts are presented, with acknowledgement of the problems in defining a boundary to literature.
Classical Arabic literature might yield productive comparative material in the poetic *madih* 'eulogy' (Allen 2000, 84-90), and, for the praise of the king in the Fayum, in the genre of *tardiyya* 'hunt-poetry' (Allen 2000, 117-119), though there the setting for a hunt is the desert, and desert-game its prey, rather than the Nilotic motifs of fishing and hunting river-birds.

3a. Compositions substantially preserved
The Hymn to the Nile Flood
The longest surviving hymn to the Nile flood is a literary composition in Middle Egyptian, of uncertain date. All surviving copies were written in the New Kingdom (about 1550-1069 BC), and some scholars have argued that it was composed in the New Kingdom. However the style of language and echoes of other literary compositions, such as laments of the order overturned, suggest that it may date to the Middle Kingdom (about 2025-1700 BC). No author is named on the surviving sources: on the attribution by some Egyptologists to a writer Khety, see above, Part One, Question Three.

The Nile flood, named Hapy (*ḥʿpy*) in Egyptian, was the central event of the agricultural year in the Nile Valley, depositing fine silt from the south over the fields flooded. There is no surviving temple dedicated to the Nile flood, though there might once have been such a cult centre at the place named Per-Hapy 'domain of the Nile flood', in the area now covered by Old Cairo. Instead, other written sources refer to festivals at which great quantities of produce were offered to the flood (Caminos 1982). Possibly, such a festival could have included occasions for the singing of this hymn. However, none of the surviving copies includes directions or dates, and the survival of numerous extracts on ostraca points rather to a literary appreciation or educational use, with copying, individual reading or public recital of the composition at least in the New Kingdom.

The transliteration follows Helck 1972, using the copy on Papyrus Chester Beatty V as principal source. The section divisions are those of Helck 1972.

1.	
dwꜣw ḥʿpy	**Hymn to the flood**
ỉ.nḏ ḥr.k ḥʿpy	Hail flood!
pr m tꜣ ỉy r sʿnḫ kmt	emerging from the earth, arriving to bring Egypt to life,
ỉmn sšm kkwy m hrw	hidden of form, the darkness in the day,
ḥs n.f šmsw.f ỉwḥ šꜣw	the one whose followers sing to him, as he waters the plants,
ḳmꜣw rʿ r sʿnḫ ʿwt nbt	created by Ra to make every herd live,
ssꜣꜣ ḫꜣst wꜣw r mw	who satisfies the desert hills removed from the water,
ỉdt.f pw hꜣ m pt	for it is his dew that descends from the sky
mry gb ḫrp nprỉ	- he, the beloved of Geb, controller of Nepri,
swꜣḏ ḥmwt nt ptḥ	the one who makes the crafts of Ptah verdant.
2.	
nb rmw sḫnty *ḳbḥw*	**Lord of fish, who allows south** marsh fowl,
nn ꜣpdw hꜣy ḥnwy	without a bird falling from heat
ỉr ỉt sḫpr bty	Maker of barley, grower of emmer grain,
sḥb rw-prw	creator of festivals of the temples.
wsf.f ḫr ḏbb fnd	When he delays, then noses are blocked,
ḥr nb nmḥw	everyone is orphaned,

ỉr ḫb.tw m pꜣwt nṯrw
ḫr s ḥḥ ꜣḳ m rmṯ

and if the offerings of the gods are diminished,
then a million men perish among humankind

3.
ỉr ʿwn-ỉb *mn tꜣ r-ḏr.f*
wr šri ḫr nmi
šbb rmṯ ḫft ḥsf.f
ḳd.f sw ḫnmw
wbn.f ḫr tꜣ m ḥʿʿwt
ḫr ḫt nbt m ršwt
ṯst nbt šsp.n.s sbit
ibḥ nb kfꜣ

If he act in greed the whole land suffers,
great and small fall moaning
People are changed at his coming,
the one who creates him is Khnum.
When he rises, then the land is in joy,
then every belly is glad,
every jaw has held laughter,
every tooth revealed.

4.
ỉn kꜣw *wr ḏfꜣw*
ḳmꜣw nfrw nb
nb šfšfyt nḏm sty
sḥtpy ỉy.f
sḫpr smw n mnmnt
rdi sfṯ n nṯr nb
sw m dwꜣt
pt tꜣ r-ḫt.f
mḫ wḏꜣw swsḫ šnwt
rdi ḫt n nmḥw

Bringer of food rich in provisions,
creator of all goodness,
lord of reverence, sweet of scent,
the one whose coming makes peace,
creator of plants for the herds,
provider of butchery for every god.
While he is in the underworld,
sky and earth are in his charge.
Filler of storerooms, enlarger of granaries,
the one who gives plenty to the orphan.

5.
srwd ḫt *ꜣby nb*
nn ktkt r.s
sḫpr imw m pḥty.f
nn mḏḥ m inr
ỉṯ.tw ḏww ḫr ḥwt.f
nn gmḥ.tw.f
nn bꜣkw nn ḫrpwt.f
šdw m štꜣw
nn rḫ.tw bw ntf
nn gmḥ.tw tpḥt.f m sšw

Grower of trees for every desire,
without any cutting for it;
creator of boats by his might,
without any carpenter with stone (tools).
The mountains are quarried by his flooding,
without him being glimpsed,
without workers, without management for him.
One who carries off in secrecy,
and the place that is his is not known,
nor can his cavern be glimpsed in writings

6.
nn nʿyt nt tnw.f
nn sšm n ib.f
šms sw ḏꜣmw ḫrdw
tw nḏ ḫrt.f m nswt mn hꜣw.f
ii r tr.f mḥ šmʿ mḥw
swri.tw mw irt nbt im.f
rdi ḥꜣw nfrw.f

Without sailings of his selection
without a follower of his desire,
(yet) youths and children follows him,
and he is greeted as a king firm in his reign,
arriving in his time, filling Upper and Lower Egypt.
When drinking water, every eye is on him,
the giver of surplus in his goodness.

7.
wn m gꜣw *pr m ḫntš ib nb ḫntš*
ibḥ sbk ms nt
psḏt nty im.f ḏsr
bš sswri sḫt
sḳnn tꜣ-tmm
swsr wʿ m ir n ky
nn wpt hnʿ.f
ir ḥtp nn ks.n.tw.f
tmm ir n.f tš

Whoever is in want emerges in joy, every heart in joy
Sobek child of Neit bares his teeth
and the ennead within is parted.
The one who spouts and causes the marsh to drink,
the one who strengthens everybody.
One man is made powerful by the doing of another,
without any dispute with him.
Maker of peace who cannot be bowed,
and none can set a limit to him.

8.
sḥḏ *pr m kkwy*
ʿnḏ n mnmnt.f

Illuminator coming out of the darkness
fat for his cattle,

pḥty.f pw sḫpr nb
nn wn ꜥnḫ m-ḫmt.f
ḥbs.tw rmṯ m mḥ šꜣw.f
iry ḥḏ-ḥtp bꜣk n.f
ir.n šsm mrḥt.f
nn ḏrw ptḥ m ḳi.f
sḫpr bꜣk nb im.f
sšw nb n mdw-nṯr
ḥnw.f m mḥy

it is his might that creates everyone,
and none can live without him.
People are clothed by the flax of his fields,
he who makes Hedjhetep work for him,
Shesem has made his oils,
and there is no limit to Ptah in his form.
All work is possible by him -
all writings of hieroglyphs,
his produce in the land of reeds.

9.
ꜥḳ m imḥt pr m ḥry
ꜣbb pr m štꜣw
dns ꜥnd rḫyt
ḫdb snm rnpt
mꜣꜣ.n.tw wsr mi mḥy
tny s nb ḫr ḫꜥw
nn iry m pḥ iry
nn ḥbs ḥbsw
nn sḫkr.tw msw šps sw
nn msḏmt ḥr
wš n šnt n gꜣw.f
nn wrḥ n bw nb

He who enters into the cavern, and comes out on top
constantly striving to emerge, in secret;
when heavy, the populace shrinks,
the food for the year is killed,
and the mighty is seen anxious,
everyone distinguished by the weapons they carry,
noone able to do their tasks,
noone to cover what should be covered,
the children of the rich cannot be adorned,
no eye-paint for the face,
a want of hair (?) for lack of it,
no anointing for anyone.

10.
smn mꜣꜥt m ibw rmṯ
ḏd.tw grg r-sꜣ šwꜣw
šbn ḥnꜥ wꜣḏ-wr
tm ḫrp npri
dwꜣ.tw nṯrw nbw
nn ꜣpdw hꜣy ḥr ḫꜣswt
nn sḫt drt.f m nbw
nn s tḫ n ḥḏ
nn wnm.tw ḫsbd mꜣꜥ
it ḫr-ḥꜣt rwd

What is Right is fixed in the hearts of men,
but falsehood is said after poverty
A man who mixes with the marshwater
is not one to master grain,
and even if you praise all gods,
there is no bird who will descend on desert lands.
There is noone who beats his hand with gold,
there is no man who is drunk on silver,
you cannot eat steadfast lapis lazuli:
barley is the foremost for strength.

11.
***šꜣꜥ.tw n.k** ḥsy m bnt*
ḥsy.tw n.k ḥr drt
nhm n.k ḏꜣmw ẖrdw
ꜥpr.tw n.k wpwt
iy ḥr špsy sḫkr tꜣ
swꜣḏ inw ḥꜥw rmṯ
sꜥnḫ ḥꜣty bkꜣ
mr ꜥšꜣt n mnmnt

For you are started songs with the harp
For you they sing with hand-claps,
For you youths and children shout out,
For you the crowds are assembled.
One who comes with riches, adorning the land,
one who makes fresh the hue of the bodies of men,
who enlivens the heart of the pregnant woman,
who loves the multitude of herds.

12.
wbn.k m niwt ḥḳr
ḫr sꜣꜣ.tw m inw.k
ḥnw m r sšn m šrt
ḫt nbt ṯtf ḥr-tp tꜣ
smw nbw m-ꜥ ẖrdw
smḫ.n.sn wnmw
bw nfr ḫꜣꜥ ḥr iwyt
pꜣ tꜣ r-ꜣw ḥr ftft

When you rise in the city of hunger
then people are sated on your supplies
with stalk in the mouth, lotus at the nose,
everything to sprout upon earth,
all vegetables in the hands of children -
they can forget the meals,
goodness cast over the streets,
and this entire land leaping for joy.

13.
ḥw ḥꜥpy
wdn.tw n.k
sft.tw n.k iwꜣ

When the Flood strikes,
offerings are made to you
cattle are butchered for you,

ỉry.tw n.k ꜥꜣbt ꜥꜣt	great offering piles are made for you,
wšꜣ.tw n.k ꜣpdw	birds are slaughtered for you,
grg.tw n.k mꜣiw ḥr ẖꜣst	lions are snared for you in the desert,
ḏbꜣ.tw n.k nfrw	goodness is returned to you.
wdn.tw n nṯr nb	offerings are made to every god
mi ỉr.n ḥꜥpy	according to what the Flood has created,
m snṯr tpy ỉwꜣ wnḏw ꜣpdw nsry	in first quality incense, cattle large and small, birds for the flame.
ḥꜥpy m tpḥt.f wsr	The Flood in his cavern is the mighty one.
nn rẖ.tw rn.f m dwꜣt	His name is not known in the underworld,
nn pr nṯrw ẖr.f	the gods cannot emerge with it.

14.

tmm *wṯs psḏt*	**All people** raise up the Nine Gods,
snd n šfyt ỉr.n sꜣ.f nb-r-ḏr	Have fear for the awe made by his son the Lord of All
r swꜣḏ ỉdbwy	to make the Two Riverbanks flourish
wꜣḏ kꜣpw	Flourish, shelter,
wꜣḏ kꜣpw ḥꜥpy	Flourish, shelter, O Flood
wꜣḏ kꜣpw	Flourish, shelter,
mi r kmt	Come to Egypt,
sẖpr ḥtp.f	make its happiness,
swꜣḏ ỉdbwy	Make the Two Riverbanks flourish,
wꜣḏ kꜣpw.f	Flourish his sheltering,
wꜣḏ kꜣpw.f ḥꜥpy	Flourish, his sheltering, O Flood
wꜣḏ kꜣpw.f	Flourish, his sheltering,
sꜥnẖ rmṯ mnmnt m ỉnw.k n šꜣ	Men and herds are brought to life by your supplies from the fields,
wꜣḏ kꜣpw	Flourish, shelter,
wꜣḏ kꜣpw ḥꜥpy	Flourish, shelter, O Flood
wꜣḏ kꜣpw	Flourish, shelter

Manuscripts with the last part preserved end with extended versions of the note *ỉw.s pw* 'this is its end'.

Hymn to the Nile Flood: sources used in Helck 1972
1. Hieratic papyri of Ramesside date:
Papyrus Chester Beatty V
Papyrus Sallier II
Papyrus Anastasi VII
Turin Papyrus (according to Helck 1972)

2. Writing-boards
Louvre 693
Hieratic writing-board Ashmolean Museum, Oxford

3. Ramesside hieratic ostraca
Deir el-Medina 1027, 1034, 1050-3, 1094, 1176, 1190-3
Gardiner 313
Leipzig 29
Michaelides 30
Ramesseum 90, 92
Wilson collection

A cycle of hymns to king Senusret III (UC 32157, Lahun Papyri lot LV.1)

Description

The hymns are preserved on the front ('recto') of a papyrus roll measuring in height 29.4 cm and in length in its present condition 110.4 cm. The reverse bears the end of a narrative tale called by Griffith 'the story of Hay' (see Part Two, section two above)
First edition: Griffith 1898, 1-3, pl.1-3. Re-edition Collier and Quirke 2004

Part One: the king as protector of Egypt

(column 1)

ḥr [nṯr] ḫprw nbty nṯr mswt	Horus [divine] of forms, He of the Two Ladies, divine of births
ḥr nbw ḫpr	Horus of Gold, who has come into being
nswt bity ḫꜥ-kꜣw-rꜥ	Dual King Khakaura
sꜣ rꜥ snwsrt	Son of Ra Senusret
iṯ.[n.]f tꜣwy m mꜣꜥ-ḫrw	He has taken up the two lands as the one true of voice

(columns 2-3)

i.nḏ ḥr.k ḫꜥ-kꜣw-rꜥ	Hail Khakaura
ḥr.n nṯr ḫprw	Our Horus, divine of forms
mk tꜣ swsḫ tꜣšw.f	Protector of the land, extender of its boundaries
dꜣir ḫꜣswt m wrrt.f	He who defeats foreign lands by his Great Crown
inḳ tꜣwy m r-ꜥw ꜥwy.fy	He who embraces the two lands with the action of his arms

(columns 4-6)

[...] *ḫꜣswt m rmnwy.fy*	He who [...] the foreign lands with his two arms
smꜣ pdtyw nn sḫt ḫt	Who slaughters the bowmen without a blow of a weapon
sti šsr n itḥ rwd	Who fires the arrow without the string being drawn
ḥw.n nrw.f iwntyw m tꜣ.sn	Dread of whom has smitten the nomads in their land
smꜣ snd.f pḏt psḏt	Fear of whom slaughters the nine bows,
rdi.n šꜥt.f mwt ḫꜣw m pdwt	whose massacre causes the death of thousands of bowmen,
[...] *pḥw tꜣš.f*	who [dare?] to reach his border

(columns 7-8)

sti šsr mi ir sḫmt	He who fires an arrow as Sekhmet does,
sḫr.f ḫꜣw m ḫ[mw] bꜣw.f	he fells thousands of those unaware of his power
ns n ḥm.f rtḥ sti	The tongue of His Power is the restraint on the Bow-land
ṯsw.f sbhꜣ stiw	and his commands are what set the nomads to flight

(columns 8-10)

wꜥ rnp [nḫt?] ḥr tꜣš.f	Unique and youthful one [who fights?] at his border,
tm rdi wrd mrt.f	who never lets his workers grow weary,
rdi [s]ḏr pꜥt r šsp	who enables the nobles to sleep to daybreak,
ḏꜣmw.f n ḳddw.sn	with his troops in their sleep

(columns 10-11)

ḥꜣty.f m mkty.sn	His heart is their protector,
ir.n wḏw.f tꜣšw.f	his decrees have drawn up his borders,
sꜣḳ.n mdw.f idbwy	his words have assembled the two riverbanks

Part Two: rejoicing over the king ('page' 2, 1-9)
ḥꜥꜥ-wy [... s]rwd.n.k p3wt.sn
ḥꜥꜥ-wy [...].k ir.n.k t3š.sn
ḥꜥꜥ-wy i[...] imy-b3ḥ sꜥ3.n.k [ps]šw.sn
ḥꜥꜥ-wy km [...] ḫpš.k mk.n.k iswt[.sn?]
ḥꜥꜥ-wy pꜥt m sḫr.k iṯ.n b3w.k ḥ3w[.sn?]
ḥꜥꜥ-wy idbwy m nrw.k swsḫ.n.k ḫrt.sn
ḥꜥꜥ-wy ḏ3mw.k sṯst rdi.n.k rwd.sn
ḥꜥꜥ-wy im3ḫyw.k rdi.n.k rnpy.[s]n
ḥꜥꜥ-wy t3wy m pḥty.k mk.n.k inbw.sn

How the [...] rejoice, for you have made their offerings flourish
How the [...] rejoice at your [...], for you have drawn up their border
How the [...] in the presence rejoice, for you have enlarged their shares
How the Egyptians (?) rejoice at your strong arm, for you have protected [their ?] traditions
How the nobles rejoice at your activity, for your power has grasped [their?] prosperity
How the two riverbanks rejoice at your dread, for you have extended their domain
How your recruits at levy rejoice, for you have caused them to flourish
How your revered ones rejoice, for you have caused them to be young
How the two lands rejoice at your might, for you have protected their walls
refrain ('page' 2, 10)
inyt.f *ḥr swsḫ t3š.f wḥm.k nḥḥ*
its refrain: Horus extender of his border, may you repeat eternity

Part Three: the king as the shelter of Egypt ('page' 2, 11-20)
wr-wy nb n niwt.f ꜥwy ḥḥ pw nḏs pw kwy ḫ3 rmṯ
wr-wy nb n niwt.f isw ꜥ pw dni itrw r wḏnw.f nw mw
wr-wy nb n niwt.f isw mnḳb pw rdi sḏr s nb r šsp
wr-wy nb n niwt.f isw imḏr pw ḥsmn šsm
wr-wy nb n niwt.f isw ibt pw tmm š3š drt.f
wr-wy nb n niwt.f isw nht pw nḥmt snd m-ꜥ ḫrww.f
wr-wy nb n niwt.f isw šwt pw 3ḫt ḳbt m šmw
wr-wy nb n niwt.f isw kꜥḥ pw šm šww r tr n prt
wr-wy nb n niwt.f isw ḏw p[w] mḏr ḏꜥ r tr n nšnn pt
wr-wy nb n niwt.f isw sḫmt pw r ḫryw ḫndw ḥr t3š[.f?]

How great is the lord for his city! he is a million arms, a thousand men are little beside
How great is the lord for his city! indeed he is the dam that stops the river at its torrents of water
How great is the lord for his city! indeed he is the cool room that allows every man to sleep to daybreak
How great is the lord for his city! indeed he is a rampart, in the bronze of Shesem
How great is the lord for his city! indeed he is a refuge, unwavering his hand
How great is the lord for his city! indeed he is a shelter, rescuing the fearful from his enemy
How great is the lord for his city! indeed he is a sunshade at Flood, cool in Summer
How great is the lord for his city! indeed he is a warm corner, dry in Winter time
How great is the lord for his city! indeed he is a mountain resisting the storm at the time the sky rages
How great is the lord for his city! indeed he is Sekhmet against the enemies who tread on [his?] border

Part Four: the arrival of the king ('page' 3, 1-10)

iỉ.n.f n.n ỉṯ.f tꜣ šmꜥ ẖnm.n sḫmty m tp.f
iỉ.n.f smꜣ.n.f tꜣwy ꜣbḫ.n.f šwt n bỉt
iỉ.n.f ḥḳꜣ.n.f kmt rdỉ.n.f dšrt m ꜥb.f
iỉ.n.f mk.n.f tꜣwy sgrḥ.n.f idbwy
iỉ.n.f sꜥnḫ.n.f kmt ḫsr.n.f šnw.s
iỉ.n.f sꜥnḫ.n.f pꜥt srḳ.n.f ḥtyt rḫyt
iỉ.n.f ptpt.n.f ḫꜣswt ḥw.n.f iwntyw ḫmw snd[.f]
iỉ.n.f [..]ꜣ.n.f tꜣš.f nḥm.n.f ꜥwꜣ
iỉ.n.f [..] ..f imꜣḫ n ỉnn n.n ḫpš.f
iỉ.n.f [..] ẖrdw.n ḳrs.n iꜣw.n ḥr (?)

He has come to us, grasping the land of Upper Egypt, the Double Crown has joined his head
He has come, he has united the Two Lands, he has merged the reed with the bee
He has come, he has ruled the Black Land, he has placed the Red Land in its midst
He has come, he has protected the Two Lands, he has calmed the two riverbanks
He has come, he has given Egypt life, he has dispelled her woes
He has come, he has given the nobles life, he has given breath to the throats of the people
He has come, he has trampled the foreign lands, he has struck the nomads ignorant of [his] fear
He has come, he has [..] his border, he has rescued the oppressed
He has come, he [...] the revered by the bringing of his strong arm to us (?)
He has come, [...] our children, we may bury our old .. (?)

Part Five: final sections ('page' 3, 11-20)

[...] ... [...]	[...] ... [...]
mr.tn ḫꜥ-[kꜣw]-rꜥ ꜥnḫ ḏt r nḥḥ [...]	May you love Khakaura, alive for ever and eternity [...]
wdd ỉr.f kꜣw.tn nḥm [...]	He who is ordained to create your sustenance, who rescues [...]
sꜣw.n rḫ snfy ꜥpr (?) [...] [...]	Our guardian who knows how to make (us) breathe, equipped (?)
ḏbꜣ.tn n.f m ꜥnḫ wꜣs ḥḥw n [...]	May you reward him with life and power and millions of [...]
(space)	(space)
ḥst ḫꜥ-kꜣw-rꜥ ꜥnḫ ḏt r n[ḥḥ]	Praise of Khakaura, alive for ever and eternity [...]
fꜣt ꜥ nfw m wỉ[ꜣ?]	raising the arm of the captain in the [bark? ...]
ẖkry m ḏꜥm r [...]	adorned with electrum more than [...]
[..]*.n idbwy r s..s* (?) [...]	the two riverbanks have [...] at ... (?) [...]
[..]*.n.sn mtnw* [...]	they have [...] the paths

3b. Compositions preserved in fragments

In praise of the king and/as hunter: one or two compositions

Introduction: the Moscow literary papyri

The fragments presented here belong to a set of broken manuscripts introduced in Part One, Question One as 'Group Four'. The group comprises a copy of the Tale of Sanehat (Papyrus Moscow Pushkin 4657), a copy of the Teaching for King Merykara (Papyrus Moscow Pushkin 4658), a copy of the Teaching of Ptahhotep (main part in London, Papyrus British Museum EA 10509), and a residue of broken pages identified by Caminos as belonging to three separate compositions, named by him 'Pleasures of Fishing and Fowling', 'Sporting King', and a 'Mythological Story' (Caminos 1956). Shortly after, Korostovtsev published another set of fragments from the 'Mythological Story' (Papyrus Moscow Pushkin 167), and argued for a date in the 18th Dynasty on the basis of the occurrence of the word *ḥmt* 'Power (female)' (Korostovtsev 1960a); it would be the only composition dated later than the Middle Kingdom, in this group of New Kingdom literary papyri. The contents of the other fragments not from known compositions concern the hunting of wild birds and fishing in papyrus-marshes of Fayum and Nile Delta, the ancient Egyptian equivalent of medieval and later aristocratic pastoral idylls. One set is marked by red points at intervals ('verse-points'), and presents a king, his courtiers, and deities; the other has no red points, and presents non-royal characters (an anonymous woman, a man named as Inuseni). Reasonably enough, the first editor distinguished these as two works, but the two sets of fragments have similar physical properties (texture, colour, height of papyrus sheets, and their fragmentary condition leaves open the possibility of a closer relationship between the two. On the one hand, it might argued that they are written in two different hands (uncertain) and two formal styles (presence or absence of 'verse-points', though such variation occurs within a single manuscript in some collections of Ramesside Period 'Literary Miscellanies'). On the other hand, even if the fragments come from two separate manuscripts, the group might have contained two copies of the same work, for example to ensure its complete coverage; large-scale duplication is attested for later larger manuscript libraries (the multiple copies of the Book of the Temple in the Tebtunis Library: Quack 2000), and one late Middle Kingdom group representing probably a single find included two manuscripts with copies of the Tale and Laments of Khuninpu (Part One, Question One, Group One). The Tales of Wonder at the Court of King Khufu demonstrate the scope for moving between and mixing royal/non-royal/divine levels of action, within one cycle of late Middle Kingdom narrative. Given the fragmentary condition, the question seems open: the thematic overlap between the manuscripts might readily be explained on other grounds, such as the 'taste' of the owner, or broader currency of the theme.

Hartwig Altenmüller and Ahmed Moussa noted an unexpected and unexplained echo or antecedent in an inscription from the reign of Amenemhat II, recording apparently in chronological sequence income and expenditure at the royal court (Altenmüller and Moussa 1991, 17-18):

ḥtp nswt m ꜥḥ n tꜣ š rsy	Repose of the king in the palace of the Southern Lake Land,
ỉw n nswt bỉty ḫpr-kꜣ-rꜥ	in the island-domain of the dual king Kheperkara (Senusret I).
sḫt ḥm.f ỉꜣdt mḥ mdt-sn	Weaving by His Power of a net of twelve cubits
m ꜣw n sbꜣ.s ḏs.f ḥnꜥ špsw.f	in the extent of its span, himself with his nobles.
ỉnt st 3000 […]	Bringing 3000 fowl […]
ỉꜣdt mdt mḥ sỉsw m ꜣw n sbꜣ.sn	ten nets of six cubits in the extent of their span.
m sḫt wꜥ m-ꜥ ḥw wꜥ	in a single catch with a single harpoon,
ḫft sry ỉr.n ḥm.f ỉr.s	in accordance with the prophecy made by His Power concerning it.
n sp ḫpr mỉtt ḫr nṯrw ỉmyw-bꜣḥ	Never had the like occurred under the ancestral gods .
ỉnw nbty wḥꜥ m ỉꜣdt mdt-sn	Deliveries of He of the Two Ladies Hunter in twelve nets
n ꜥḳw ꜣpdw 11350	of supplies: fowl 11350
ỉnw n […] *rmw 459*	Deliveries of […] fish 459

Shared features are the throne-name of king Amenemhat II, Nubkaura; the reference to the king (presumably) as "He of the Two Ladies the Hunter" ('king as hunter' Section C); the palace in the Land of the Lake (Fayum); the weaving of the net; the miraculous catch of fish; the involvement of Seshat, Action (Ir) and Hearing (?) (in the inscription present at the vertical year-marker three lines after the episode of the miraculous catch) and the Millions of Sed-festivals (in the inscription, 'millions of years'). The highest title mentioned in the papyrus fragments is "Secretary of Documents of the King, of the Presence"; in the Middle Kingdom that title is not attested before the late 12th Dynasty (Grajetzki 2000, 168-177). On that evidence, the compositions on the papyrus might relate to some reign later than Amenemhat II, perhaps inspired by the model of the event recorded on the hieroglyphic inscription, or both drawing inspiration from a kingship ceremony that produced momentous effect in the reigns of Amenemhat II and a successor. The Fayum monuments and final resting-place of Amenemhat III at

Hawara, on the entrance to the province, might loosely support an ascription of the compositions to the reign of Amenemhat III.

Series of fragments on 'the king as hunter' (with 'verse-points')

The first editor of the papyrus, Ricardo Caminos, pronounced harsh judgement on the contents of the fragments with verse-points, as a "parody of literature" (Caminos 1956, 25). Implicitly if unwittingly he thereby raised the question as to whether it might in fact have been intended as parody, and, more basically, whether we would today be able to identify parody of a genre for which few examples survive. On this problem Mikhail Bakhtin made the following comments, with an allowance for the role of philologists that contrasts with his observations elsewhere on the impact of their deadening hand:

> Стилистический анализ встречается с целым рядом трудностей, особенно там, где он имеет дело с произведениями далеких эпох и чужих языков, где художественное восприятие не находит опоры в живом языковом чутъе. В этом случае, говоря образно, весъ язык, вследствие нашей отдаленности от него, кажется лежащим в одной плоскости, третъе измерение и различие планов и дистанции в нем не ощущаются. Здесъ лингвистическое историко-языковое изучение наличных в данную эпоху языкових систем и стилей (социалъных, профессионалъных, жанровых, направленческих и др) существенно поможет воссозданию третъего измерения в языке романа, поможет дифференцироватъ и дистанцироватъ его.

> "Stylistic analysis meets with a whole series of difficulties, especially where it concerns compositions of distant ages and foreign languages, where the artistic conception finds no support in a living linguistic scent. In this case, figuratively speaking, the whole language seems to lie on one plane, as a result of our distancedness from it, and the third dimension and differentiation of planes and distances in it cannot be felt. Here linguistic historical-communicative study of the language systems and styles present in the given period (social, professional, generic, factional and others) may provide the help essential for reconstruction of the third dimension in the language of the novel, and to reactivate its differentiation and distancing."
>
> (Bakhtin 1977, 228)

Caminos assigned letters to the sections of fragments: the original sequence of these sections is not clear.

Section A, page 1

[…] .. […] .. […]

Section A, page 2

[…] *ỉn špsw.f ỉpn*	[…] by those notables of his.
ḫtmw bỉty sš r ꜥ n nswt n ḫft-ḥr	King's sealbearer , secretary for documents of the king of the Presence
sḥtp-ỉb-rꜥ-[ꜥnḫ …].f	Sehetepibra[ankh], he [said?]:
ỉw mꜣꜣ.n.ỉ ỉty ꜥnḫ wḏꜣ snb nb.ỉ	I have seen, sovereign, life! prosperity! health!, my lord.
ḏd.ỉn ḥm.f ꜥnḫ wḏꜣ snb	Then His Power life! prosperity! health! said:
mỉ-sy ỉšst […].n.k st	what is it like, that which you have [seen?]
ḏd.ỉn sš r ꜥ n nswt n ḫft-ḥr	Then the secretary for the documents of the king of the Presence said:
[ỉw m]ꜣꜣ.n.ỉ wnm ꜣpdw	I have se[en] the feeding of birds,
sf[…] .. tp-ꜥ ṯꜣw wrt	.. […] .. before a great wind,
pt […] ḥwyt ꜥꜣt	the sky […] heavy rain
[…] *ꜣpdw*	[…] birds
mỉ hꜣw […] *n.f*	like the time […] for him/it
[...] *sḏm.n.ỉ ḫrw tꜣ*[...] *nw wꜣḏ* […]	[…] I have heard the sound of .. […] of the Green […]
ỉw m ḥꜣw nbt […]	coming from the fringelands […]
mꜣꜣ.n.ỉ wnm […] *nḥsy*	I have seen the eating […] Nehesy/Nubian
mỉ […] *nt wsrw* […] *m ẖꜣwt tꜣ mḥw*	like […] waters, oars (?) […] in the pools of Lower Egypt
[...] *ḥr gswy ỉꜣdt.k*	[…] each side of your net
ỉw.s mỉ [...] .. *ẖkr* […]	**It is like** […] .. adorned […]

Section A, page 3

.. iw rẖyt m pr-nsr [...]	.., the populace being in the House of Fire [...]
.. ẖnsȝyt ḥtm.ti m spd [...] *ẖkrw*	.. Khonsayt effaced on Sepd[u (?) ...] ornaments,
mȝtryt nt[yw ...]	the wandering-women (?) which are [...]
.. r tnw	**Where [...] going?**
iw [...] *bit mrw* [...]	.. [...] Red Crown, of bulls (?) [...]
sẖȝt [...]*w tpw šsp* [...] .. *sw šb*[...]	Sekhat [...] ..heads receiving [...] ...

Section B, page 1

[...]*.k m iȝd[t* ...]	[...] of you in the net [...]
ẖnty-ẖm [...] *nbty whʿ*	Foremost of Khem [...] He of the Two Ladies, Hunter,
ẖntt [...]*n bit m sʿḥ iswt*	foremost [...] to the Red Crown as noble of the crew
[...] *ʿnẖ wḏȝ snb nb.n*	[...] life! prosperity! health!, our lord,
ḥrt.k m šȝ ḳb [...]	your setting is in the cool field [...]
dmd m ḏt [...] *m inw* [...]	united with eternity [...] in supplies [...]

Section B, page 2, upper part

[...] *ḥmwt*	[...] women
msw nswt ḥr ihhy	the children of the king shouting delight,
šsp [...] ..	receiving [...] ..
wḏȝ m ḥtp [...]	proceeding in peace [...]
m sint nt s[ȝbt ...] *mȝʿy* [...]	in a ferry for cro[ssing? ...] shore [...]
tȝ m ʿḥ tȝ š sȝkw [...] *msw*	land, in the palace of the Land of the Lake, assembled [...] children
***mdw* [...]** *tp rdwy st*	**Words [...]** on the legs of the throne
ḫtmw bity sš r ʿ n nswt n ḥft-ḥr	king's sealbearer, secretary of king's documents of the Presence
sḥtp-ib-rʿ-[ʿnḫ ...]*.f*	Sehetepibra[ankh], he [said?]:
min.k mȝwt.k twy dšrt	Take for yourself this your red harpoon,
timst irtyw [...] *ḥm.k ʿnẖ wḏȝ snb*	red pigment and blue [...] Your Power life! prosperity! health!
stp.s sȝ.s r.k	May it exert its protection over you,
iw.s mi nt diw ḥʿw.s	for it is as Neit when her armour is in place.
šsp n [...] *ẖȝs imy p*	Receive for [...] the coil which is in Pe
ẖȝs imy dp	and the coil which is in Dep,
mi ẖȝw ẖt n gbty	like the horns of the frame of the Coptite
mi [...]*p irt šnbt.f*	like [...] .. which is for his neck,
mi ȝẖty di.f sw m dwȝyt	like the Dual Horizon God when he gives himself in the morning.
n ḥtm [...] *bȝḳt* .. [...] .. [...] *ḥʿ* [...]	Not destroyed [...] shining .. [...] .. [...] armour (?) [...]

Section B, page 2, lower part

[...] *m pr nsr*	[...] in the House of Flame
hrww [...]*t* [...] *pẖr*	days [...] .. [...] circling
msw nswt hrw [...]	the children of the king, the day [...]

Section B, page 2, lower part, to page 3

[...] *mnw m ḥrst ẖntt*	**[...] quartz and carnelian of the Palace (?)**
[...] *ḏbʿw nw* [...]	[...] fingers of [...]
mi ẖnt m ḥwt pʿt	like the hide in the Domain of the Nobles
smȝ.n.s sẖm tpy ḏw	when it has joined the power of the one who is on the mountain
mi špsw m [...] *m imw.f*	like the noble fruit (?) in [...] in his grief,
sbt.f m tmȝt.f	his laughter in his matting,
mi ẖnkt [...]	like the robe [...]
psdw nw mȝtryt	the backs of the wandering-women,
mi mȝsw m ḥtr [...]	like the *mȝsw*-beasts on the yoke [...]-boat,
pẖr.f inb iṯw	when it circles the wall of Itju,
mi iwn [...]	like the pillar [...]
[*wr*]*ḥyw m r ntryt*	[an]ointed with the formula of natron,
mi šmȝw [...]*bȝw ẖr ḳs-msḥw*	like the nomads [...] .. under crocodile-bone,
mi ms[...]	like .. [...]
hrw ip bit mrw	on the day of counting of the Red Crown of bulls,

mi ṯꜣw m ḥˁw wꜣ[...]	like wind on the body ..[…]
[ˁn]tyw sḏt tp nwy	[my]rrh of the fire of the Start of Flood,
mi wnmy m sḫt [...]t	like the right-hand in the marshes […] ..
iw.s mi mꜣmꜣw m ḫnt ḫm	**It is like the dom-palm trees in the foremost of Khem**
[...] *iryw.sn*	[…] their keepers,
mi ibḥ ḳs[…] ..	like the tooth of bone […]-foreigners
iw.s mi mw imy […]*p ḥḏ* […]	it is like the water that is in […] .. white […]
mi […] .. […] .. […]	like […] .. […] .. […]

Section B, page 4

[…] *rḫ* […] *nbwy*	[…] knowing […] the Two Lords
[…]*ꜣt n nswt s*[…] ..	[…] .. to the king .. […] ..
smꜣyt ḥr […]	the confederacy of Horus […]
nfr ḥr nw[…]*.s*	the fair of face .. […] of her/it
ḥtr […]*ipt.n* […]	yoked […] counted by (?) […]
nwt.s […] *ḫˁw* [.. *hꜣ*]*b.n.k sy m-ˁ.k*	her/its bonds […] armour [...] you [se]nt her by your hand (?)
[…] *rˁ*	[…] Ra
di.n […] .. […]	[…] has given […] .. […]

Section C, page 1

[…]*.f*[…]*.k* […]*.s mꜣꜣ*	[…] him/it […] you […] she/it seeing
[…] *wḏ ḫnt* […] *nswt m ˁwy dpt.f*	[…] ordering the sailing […] the king in the arms of his boat,
stp-sꜣ […] *dšrw psḥ.f šn.f*	the palace […] red fish, when it bites its ..
nwḥw […]*.f stꜣw iry*	ropes […] of him/it the towing of it (?)
ḥsr.n […] *ˁnw.n wḥˁw*	[…] removed […] the hunters returned
[…] *wrt*	**[…] the great […]**
ḥw.n.s tpw[.sn] m ˁw.s	She has struck the[ir?] heads with her arms (?)
ḏd […] *ip.tw st.k tn nri ri n t*[…]	saying […] this place of yours is reckoned time upon time (?) ..[…]
iw ḥr.k n.n m ḥḥw pn n ḥb sd	the sight of you is ours in this millions of Sed festivals
[...] *mk ib.k r nw* [...] *nswt n ḏd.s*	[…], your heart is set on the moment (?) […] of the king that she says,
wd mꜣwt ḥr mhnw.sn	cast the harpoons on their coffers,
sḳdwt […] *n* […] *tꜣ m ˁḥ tꜣ š*	sailing […] .. […] the land in the palace of the Land of the Lake,
m-ḫt nn snmt […] *ˁ n nbty wḥˁw* hunter	after these pastures (?) […] the arm of he of the Two Ladies the hunter
min.[k …] .. *irtyw* […] *kꜣ* […]	**Take for [yourself …]** .. blue pigment […] the Bull […]

Section C, page 2

[...]*mw nw nhꜣ swnw*	[…] tents (?) of the brackish pool, of the clearwater pool (?),
mi kꜣꜣw gnw […] *šnw*	like the blocks of the stands […] ringstones,
mi mny r ḥˁw nṯrw	like the .. on the bodies of the gods,
mi bwꜣwt bꜣḳ[...] ..	like the lairs shining (?) […] ..
hrw ṯꜣmw wḏꜣt	the days of the bandages of the Whole Eye,
iw.s mi gm […]	it is like .. […]
ꜣbdw r-sfy [… *dr?*]*ww* […]	the months of the catch [..fl]anks (?) […]

Section D, pages 1 to 2

[...]*fndw ḥḏ*[…] *ˁḥ n ḥwt-nbw*	[…] noses .. […] the palace of the Domain of Gold
[…] *ḫm*	[…] Khem,
ḥry st ḥr wrt ḥkꜣw	the one bearing the throne and the Great Goddess of Heka-Power,
ḳnt r ḥw[…] *rs inb.f*	complete for protecting (?) […] south of his wall,
sšꜣt nn ḫˁ.ti r.s	There is Seshat is risen up,
r-rwty […]	outside […]

Section D, page 2

[…]*ꜣ imw.s*	**[…] .. her *imw*-birds**
šbn.n.s ir sḏmy	she has mixed Action and Hearing,

di͗.f ḫꜥ[…] ꜣpdw tꜣ š	that he may cause to appear […] the birds of the Land of the Lake
r ḫdḏw i͗myw ḳb[…]	more than the waterbirds which are in the catara[ct-region …]
[šsm]w nwdty	[Shesm]u the ointment-maker,
m mrḥt ẖrt ꜥ.f	with the oils which are under his charge,
sḏꜣt […] snsnyt m pr-wr	crossing [..] she who joins in the Great House,
sẖkrt.n wrḥw ꜥw	she whom the anointings have adorned ..
[…] mḏꜣwt.s	[…] her pegs (?),
r šnw nw i͗ꜣdt.k tn	to the lines of this your net,
di͗.s šs.s[…]mw ḥḏt	that she may cast her rope […].. white cloth,
nwt nt rnwtt	the cords of Renutet,
ẖrt-ꜥ […] sꜣ i͗dḥy	the equipment […] son of the Marsh-god,
bꜣnnt [..] sšꜣt	.. […] Seshat,
sḥḏt.n fḫt .. […] bi͗t	she whom the unleashed (?) has illuminated .. […] the Red Crown
wi͗ꜣt n […] grg m i͗ꜣdt.k tn […]	separated .. […] snare with this your net […]
nmtt r ꜥwy rḫtt […] r smnt r ꜥḥꜥw	paces in the arms of fullers (?) […] to fasten the mouth of ..
[…].k	[…] of you
r ḏd sft […] r msw ẖt.s	saying: slaughter […] more than the children of her flock (?)
ti͗[…]	.. […]

Section E, page 1 to page 2

[…]h r […]	[…] .. […]
ꜥrtyw […] r sḫt	those who ascend […] to the marsh
m si͗nt nt sꜣbt sš	in a ferry for crossing (?) the nests,
di͗w r […]	placed at […]
ḳꜣ.n ḫrw sšmw.sn	the voice of their leaders was loud,
tp nfr mni͗ […]ḥty m i͗rt nt ḥḏw (?)	a good start in mooring […] .. in the eye of the white pens (?)

***ḏd mdw i͗n ẖr[…]**.f*	**Words spoken by the bearer […]** of him,
ḫꜣwy m trwt wbꜣy[…]	the columns (?) of willow, … […]
hꜣw m […] ..	wild fowl in […] ..
s[…] šnt [..].s wnwt w[…]	..[…] .. […] of her/it the hours .. […]
ꜥ rsy n mꜣnw	the southern reach of Manu,
pẖr […] i͗ꜣbty pt	circling […] the eastern […] of the sky,
rwd.ti͗ […].wy.sy	in strength […] her/its two […]
špssy.s wrt ḥr i͗b […] sy	her/its fare great on the heart […] her/it,
grg.n.f hrw […] ḥr ꜥwy	he has trapped days […] at once,
sḳdwt ꜥḥꜥw […]	sailing of boats […]

***[…m?]nw** nbw-kꜣw-rꜥ*	**[… monument]s (?)** of Nubkaura
[…] ḥtp m ẖnw kꜣp	[…] resting within the shelter

Section E, page 3

[…]mw m st tꜣ š	[…] .. in the place of the Land of the Lake
rs.ti͗ ẖr.s r <n>ḫbw.sn	awakened bearing her/it towards their joining (?),
mꜣ[…] ꜥnt mꜣi͗w	see[…] claws of lions,
[s]ḫpr.n.s ꜣpdw n mrw	she has [cre]ated the birds of the canals,
ꜥpr […]bꜣyt […] n tpw ḥr.s	equipping […] .. […] to the heads of her face (?),
sḫpr.n.s ꜣpdw […]	she has created the birds […]
mꜣꜣ i͗rt […]	the eye seeing […]
sḥḏ wr r-rwt[y …]	illumined and great outsi[de …]

***[…] wnmw h[…]** ḫr […] m ꜥw.k*	**[…] fattened birds (?) ..[…]** fallen […] in your arms,
šni͗t […] ḏꜥ (?) n ꜣpdw	rain […]spearing at the birds
[…w]dn rw ḥr ꜥ […]	[… he]avy are the geese on the arm […]
r-ꜥ sḫt […]	activity of the marshes […]

Twelve unplaced fragments assigned in the first edition to the 'sporting king':

Fragment 1

[...] *sy m* ˁ*.k imnty* [...] *wnty*	[...] her/it in your western reach [...] Wenty
sd [...] *mꜣꜣ.n.k sẖt*	Sed (?) [...] you have seen the Marsh Goddess
iw.s ḥr tp [..]*.k* [...]*bꜣw.s*	when it is upon your [...] her [...]-fish
sip.s n.k ḫntyw [...] .. *mrw*	and she assigns you the fore-lands [...] .. bulls
hꜣw nfr n mꜣwt.k	**Good fortune to your lance**
[...] *in smr pn*	[...] by this courtier
mk sy r ˁ*fꜣ*[...]	She/It is at the encamp[ment (?) ...]

Fragment 2

[...] *rmṯ nw* ..[...]	[...] people of ..[...]
[...] *rnwy.f* ***dd.in*** ..[...]	[...] his calves **Then [...] said** [...]
[...] *bit wḥ*ˁ*w* [...]	[...] Red Crown, hunter [...]
[...] *ꜣḥwt pẖr.n*[...]	[...] fields, there circled [...]
[...] ... [...]	[...] ...[...]
[...] *.f iw s*..[...]	[...] of him, ..[...]

Fragment 3

[...]*tyt m* [...]	[...] ... [...]

Fragment 4

[...]*w ẖrt-*ˁ[...]	[...] ... equipment (?) [...]

Fragment 5

[...] *sḏm* [...]	[...] hearing [...]

Fragment 6

[...].. *m ḥwt* [...]	[...] .. in the Domain [...]

Fragment 7

[...] .. *nb pt* [...]	[...] .. lord of the sky [...]
[...] .. *irw* [...]	[...] .. form [...]
[... *sfḫ*]*t* ˁ*bwy nbt nrw* [...]	[... Sefekh]etabwy lady of terror [...]
[...] ... [...]	[...]-jars (?) [...]

Fragment 8

[... *š*]*m.s r.s ḫft wḏ* [...]	[...] she goe[s], her utterance by the decree [...]
[...].. *tꜣ*[*š*...]	[...] .. bor[der ...]
[...].. *mi šm* [...]	[...] .. like going (?) [...]

Fragment 9

[...] *m* [*mꜣ*]*nw* [...]	[...] in [Ma]nu [...]
[...] *pt* [...]	[...] .. sky [...]

Fragment 10

[...] *iw ir.n* [...]	[...] made/did [...]
[...] ... [...]	[...] ... [...]

Fragment 11

[... *iꜣ*]*dt.s tp* [...]	[...] her [n]et, head [...]

Fragment 12

[...] *ẖrw* ˁ*ḥ*ˁ [...]	[...] lower, then (?) [...]

Series of fragments on ‘the hunt’ (no verse-points)
The first editor of the papyrus, Ricardo Caminos, assigned letters to three fragmentary sections, separable but in a highly tentative order; the sections are given here in order of size (B, C, A), to leave open the question of their original sequence.

‘Section B’ with parts of five pages (the fifth with one word only preserved)

Section B, page 1

[…] *mḥ wꜥ* […] *sḫt*	[…] 1 cubit […] the Marsh Goddess
ms […]*šrw-ḫt mr* […]	bring […]… love […]
sḏr.n ḥr ḥꜥm […]	we may spend the night fishing […]
ꜥb n ỉn.n ḏs.n [...]	a meal of our own bringing [...]
nfr-wy ḥr.k ỉn-sn.ỉ	**How fair the sight of you, Inseni,**
ỉw šsp […]	Received […]
ꜥnḫ m kꜥhw ꜥnḫ.n ỉm m ḥny	Living in the regions, where we may live, on water-plants
[*... ḥn*]*y wꜥty r gswy bḫny.ỉ*	[… water]-plants, alone beside my towerhouse,
wš […]	wasted […]
ỉr ḫd.k ỉb.k ꜣw ỉst.k ḥꜥ […]	If you travel north, your heart is glad, your crew equipped (?) […]
smḥy ḫdy.n ỉm.f r bḫny[*.ỉ …*]	The papyrus-boat in which we travel north to [my] towerhouse […]
[…]*w nn r sḏr ỉmnw* […] *m* [...]	[…].. without entrance, asleep and hidden […] .. […]
ḳny […]*w* […]	brave […] .. […]

Section B, page 2

[…] *ỉr.n šmw.n ỉm*	[…] we spend our summer there,
swr[*ỉ …*] *nšmyt*	drin[k …] fish-scales,
wpt.ỉ ḫr bkk	my forehead with the bekek-lock.
ỉry.ỉ n.ỉ wꜣḥw.ỉ n m[…]	I make myself my garland of ..[…]
ḥr.ỉ n[*.ỉ*] *ỉꜣmw.ỉ m wꜥn*	I prepare (?) for [myself] my tent out of juniper,
kꜣp.ỉ sw m ꜥš […]*w*	and cover it with pine […]..
[…]*wy sbꜣ*[…] *r sḫt*	[…]-land … […] the mouth of the marshes,
mꜣꜣ.ỉ msw ḥwt-ỉḥyt ḥr ḳmꜣ wỉꜣyt	so that I can see the children of Hutihyt beating out the marshbirds
st nbt [*ḥr*] *snhy ꜣpdw.s r ḥr n ḫnt.f*	every woman clamour[ing] its wildfowl upwards, unable to alight.
ḥms.ỉ r ssy	**I settle down (at) the mouth of the opening,**
[*ḥr*]*.ỉ n.ỉ kꜣp smn.n.ỉ ḥꜣrw.ỉ*	I [prepare] myself a cover, after I have fastened my decoy-bird.
ỉw.ỉ n ḳbw rmw.ỉ n šw	I am in the cool air, my fish are in the sunlight.
ḥms ḥr ḥm.ỉ	One settling at my patch,
ỉw.ỉ ḥr mꜣꜣ.f n mꜣꜣ.n.f wỉ	I can see it, it cannot see me.
rm ḏꜣw ḥr stw ỉw.ỉ ḥr ḫdb r tnw sp	The fish are pierced on the spear, I kill at each chance,
nn ꜣbw n mꜣwt[*.ỉ*]	There is no stopping [my] harpoon,
ỉry.ỉ kꜣrw m ỉnt ḥḏt	I make bundles of white bulti-fish
n ḫnm.n wỉ wgs ssm.ỉ šꜣbw […]	Slitting does not delight me, my business is … […]
m ꜥb n dỉw.n (?)	As a meal of our giving (?)
nb.ỉ nb.ỉ sḏr m kꜣp	**My lord my lord, spend a night in the cover,**
sḥny wꜣḏ n ỉtḥ ḥḏ-tꜣ […] *ḥry-ỉb*	success is assigned to one who draws in at dawn […] in the midst
ỉw ỉꜣm.n n.k sḫt	The Marsh Goddess has favoured you,
ỉꜣm.n n.k ꜥw.k	your arms have favoured you.
wꜣḏ šꜣ nb snm.n.k sḫt	Every field flourishes, you have nourished the marshes,
mnỉ […] *ỉww wdn n.k ỉm*	mooring […] the islands, laden down for you there,
ỉn.n.n sp skꜣs.n.n ky	we brought in one chance, we bound in another.
sḫtyw tpyw-ꜥ […] *nb ḥr*	The marshdwellers of the past [...] every […] saying:
ḥꜣ wỉ m-ḫt.f sḫty pn ỉḳr	If I could only be in his following, this excellent marshdweller!
kꜣ ḥꜥy nṯr.k ỉm.k	Then your god would rejoice over you,
wbn.k sḥḏ.k ỉmyw ỉꜣyt.sn	you would rise, you would illumine those in their snake-mounds.
kꜣ mꜣꜣ.k srwd sbꜣw	Then you would see the strengthening of the doors
nw sdw ḥryw-rw	of the tails of the primeval snakes.

***ḥms* [...]**	**Spend time [...]**
***s3w ḥry-ib n mw ḥry r* [...]**	**... in the midst of the water over the mouth [...]**
nsw m itrty isw ḥr s3.i n inw ẖry.i	with the shrubs in two lines, reeds at my back for matting beneath me,
k3p [... *3*]*pdw ḥr nmi n ii.n ḏrw.f*	the cover [... b]irds roaming, with no end to their passing,
sp3w ḥr [...]	the disturbed fowl [...]
st.f wʿtt nt sš imt mr [...]	its lonely goose of the nest, within the canal [...]
mtr.i n.i ḫrw.s wḥʿ iry [...]	I may witness for myself its cry, as its trapper [...]
[...] *n 3pdw.f rdy.ty.fy ḳmy*[*t*] *n ʿš3*	[...] of his birds, one who will give pellets (?) to the throngs of birds

Section B, page 3

[... *nw*]*ḥ smn.n.i tpty.i ḥ3* .. [...]	[... ro]pe, when I have tied my ... [...]
šs3 m sḫt mitt ib.i ḏs.i	skilled in the marshes, the like of my own heart,
ṯrm [...] *w3w* .. [...]	blinking [...] distant .. [...]
ʿw.i n dns ẖr stk[*n?* ...]	with my arms on the net-sinker (?), drawing in (?) [...]
w3w.i šw ḥr [... *m*]*šrw ḥr stkn.i*	in my distance, the sunlight on [... ev]ening at my drawing in.
wrš.i im ḥr i3ʿš n nty m š3	I spend the day there calling out to the one who is in the field,
wḏf [...] .. *nwḥ.i swḏb ḥr ḳʿḥ.i*	delaying [...] .. my rope coiled over my shoulder,
ii.n.i n ksm [...] *srw n r* [..] *ḏw*	I have come, not opposed [...] the geese of the mouth [..] mountain
***wrš.i ḥr s*[*ḳ3*]*s r ḫr ḫ3w* [...]**	**I spend the day ty[ing] up to fell thousands [...]**
[...] *ḫft-ḥr.i*	[...] facing me,
wnn nbt ḥr sšnt n.i mi [...]	while the lady is weaving for me as [...]
in iw m33.n.k [...] *inw*	have you ever seen [...] catches?
wr wḥm inw r [...] *sḫt*	Great is the repeater of catches, more than [...] the marshes
n rḫ.f tnwt int [...] *ḥr trp*	he has been unable to count the catch [...] and geese
hrw* [*nfr nw*]*ḥ.i ḥr mtnw *k3p* [...]	**[Happy] day when my r[ope] is on the paths** the cover [...]
[...] *r sfy n ḫpr.n* [...]	[...] the catch, there has not happened [...]
[...] ...*n sšw* [...]	[...] we [...] the nests [...]

Section B, page 4

[...] *sw ḥmsw ḥnʿ ist.f m ẖnw k3p*	[...] him, sitting with his crew within the shelter
[...] *w3ḏ*	[...] fresh,
ir wḥʿ tm pr r niwt ʿnḫ.f m ʿdy	as for the hunter who does not go to the town, he lives on fat.
***ḥ3 wi m* [...]**]*wnw m 3byt ib.i*	**If only I were in [...]** that were my heart's desire,
m wnn niwt.i pw sḫt [...] *pw tpy š3*	as when the marsh was my city, and the one on the field was [...]
n [...] *rmṯ 3by ib.i ḫnmsw.i*	and not [...] people of my heart's desire, my friends,
wrš[*.i*] *m st snkt* [...] *mḥt*	and [I] might spend the day in the place of the crocodiles [...] papyrus,
ḥḏ-t3 wšʿ.i w3y.i šm.i 3 m st-ib.i	at dawn I might have a bite, and be remote, and go just by my choice
šm.i* [...] *itry *m 3bd mddint*	**I might go [...] rivers** on the month- and fifteen-day- festivals,
h3.i r š sṯsw ḥr rmnwy.i	and go down to the Lake, the supports on my shoulders,
ʿw.i r-s3.i mḥ sn šsp diw m ḥṯt.i	my kit behind me, two cubits five palms in my armpit,
ḥr.i r itḥ mḥ diw w3rt m-ʿ.i	my attention on drawing in five cubits of cord in my hand
sf3t mw wmt m mḥ drt r sš pn	The deep water slows down the pulling of the hand at this nest.
m33.n ḫr.f [*m?*] *sḏm.n.n hmhmt.f*	We see him fall [as?] we have heard his roar,
grg.n sw m i3dt bw3wt	we snare him in the net of the hiding-place,
dbḥyt nt [...] *n.n wnwt psdt*	supply-ground (?) of [...] for us nine hours,
pḥwy iy ḫpr	and the end has come and gone.
m ʿm ib.k ḥms m [...] *mk 3* [...]*it*	Do not consume your heart, dwell in [...] see then [...] ..
wnm.f m š3 wr [...] .. [...]	as he eats in the great field [...] .. [...]

Section B, page 5

[...] *nḫt* [...]	[...] strong [...]

‘Section C’ with parts of four pages (page 4 starts of two words only)

Section C, page 1, upper part

[...] *bꜣt* [...] *ḫꜣnsyt ḥms*	[...] reeds [...] *ḫꜣnsyt* -plants sitting
[...] *nt šꜣw ḳb* [...]	[...] of *šꜣw*-plants, cool [...]
[...] *ỉr wḫꜣ.ỉ sḏr.ỉ m mḫꜣw*	[...] as for my night-time, I spend the night in the sleeping-shelter
[... *ḫ*]*tyw n prt šny m kꜣwtyw*	[... ter]race of *prt šny*-plants with apes
[...] .. *n fdḳ.n wꜥt ṯsw* [...]	[...] .. one woman (?) does not sever what is joined [by another? ...]

[...]*n*.. *ḥr.ỉ n hnw*	**[...].. my face to the waters**
pt [...]*ꜣt sw kt ỉꜣdt*	the sky [...].. it another dew-cover
ꜥḳ [...] *n ỉꜣdt nt*	entering [...] of the dew (?) of Neit,
wrš.ỉ m bꜣ[...] *pns*	I spend the day in ..[...] clay
dỉ.ỉ sw ḫr tp gꜣy[...]	I place it under the head ... [...]

Section C, page 1, lower part

[...] *d* [...] *rḥw* [...]	[...] .. [...] companions [...]
smꜣw snnw.f mꜣ[...] *ḥr ps*[...]	killed by his fellow, seeing [...] upon .. [...]

Section C, page 2, upper part

[...] .. *m-ꜥ* [...]*b nt* [...]*t gmw sḫtw*[...]
[...]*t m ssꜣw.n wḥꜥ ꜣw* [...].*sn n.ỉ m ḥny*
rmn [...]

[...] .. from [...] ... [...] *gmw*-plants ... [...]
[...] when the hunter has taken his fill (?), laid out [...] they [...] to me with *ḥny*-plants,
shoulder [...[

[...] *mḫꜣt.ỉ m nỉwt* *ḏꜣt mꜣꜥ* [...].*sn ꜥḫ* [...]
šntyt mỉ ḥꜣrw [...] *m ẖnw* [...]*y.ỉ r* [...] *mrw ỉ*[...] ... [...]

[...].. my pair in the city pressing the forehead [...] they [...] .. [...]
herons as decoys [...] within [...] I [go?] to [...] ... [...] ... [...]

Section C, page 2, lower part

[... *b*]*ꜣt ḫd* [...]*w nn* [...] *n.k s*[...] *sḏr.ỉ ḥnꜥ.k* [...]
rdwy r rs [...] *ḏꜣḏꜣw r mḥty pt m ꜣỉw* [*s*]*mḥ* [...] ..

[... bu]shes, going north [...] ... not [...] to you [...] may I spend a night with you [...]
legs to the south [...] head to the north, sky in .. , the papyrus-boat [...]

mỉ ḥnꜥ* [...].*ỉ *r ꜥfꜣy ꜥ mḥty dỉ.ỉ wnmt*
[...] *n.t dỉ.ỉ wnmt rmw nn* [...] *ꜣpdw nn šwt.f*
ꜥḏꜣ-wy tw ỉnw-sn.ỉ [...] *mỉ ꜣ*[*pd*]*w nn šwt.f*

Come with [...] my [pair?] to the camp of the northern reach, that I may give a meal
[...] to you, that I may give a meal of fish without [...] of fowl without its feathers
How violent you are, Inuseni [...] as of fo[w]l without its feathers

Section C, page 3

[... *m?*] *wrw mrḥt m ꜥb* [...]*ꜣ pẖr sḏryt* [...]
mst ḫꜣw ḳmꜣ [...] *ḥmt.s*
ꜣww [...] *ḥr mkḥꜣ ḫr.k*

[...] ... and oil in the meal (?) [...] .,, the night-birds (?) going around [...]
chicks ... creating [...] her servantwoman,
extended [...] on the back of the head before you

[…].*s mšrw* […] *stt dbt ir kꜣ* […]
[…] *m šꜣ rmw ḳriw r* […]*p*
smḥ.n ḥr pr[*t* …] *iyt rn.s m-ꜥ* […]
r-tp bw […] *rmw wrw* […].*k ḳb m mšꜣ.f*
wgs.k m ḥmty wgs.k […]

[…] of it/her the evening […] harpooning hippopotami, making the bull […]
[…] in the field, fish … to […] ..
our papyrus-boat in going [out ...] arrival of (?) her name with […]
in front of the place […] great fish […] of you, cool in his slitting-bay,
you slit with metal, you slit […]

[…] .. *tp im.i*
sbꜣ.i tw š n sbk tꜣ imnty
[…]*w mtwnyt iꜣt šꜣ n tp-ny* […*šꜣ ws*]*fꜣt ḥr šꜣ mnyt*
ẖꜣsw […] *ḏꜥw ḥwt wꜥrt rḫtt ḥwt ḥrt ḥwt ẖrt*
wꜣtt ḥr […]*w nẖ mnt iry wn.t(w) ẖn n wḥꜥ* […] *nbw*
n wḥd.n wḥꜥ mꜣꜣ h[…]

[…] before me
Let me teach you of the Lake of Sobek, the Western Land,
[…]-u, Metunyt, Iat, Field of Tepny [… Field of Wes]fat and Field of Menyt,
Khasu […] Djau, Hutwaret, Rekhtet, the Upper Domain, the Lower Domain,
the Ways of Horus […].. its pain is small, the tent is opened to the hunter […] all […]
the hunter does not suffer seeing ..[…]

[… *in-iw-*]*sn.i* (?) *šꜣ.k pw st nbt*
r-ḥꜣt mḥ sy ẖr wḥꜥ […] *n nw.i n.k*
mk iww ḥryw-ib ẖr mnyw.k dpt […]

[… Iniu]seni (?) – everywhere is your field
the river mouth is full of hunters […] which I snare for you.
The islands in the midst bear your herdsman, the taste […]

Section C, page 4
[…] *iꜣ*[…] *mrw* […]

[…] .. […] .. […]

'Section A' with parts of three pages

Section A, page 1
[…]*t.i mi-m* *wrt šꜣꜥ im.s*
ḏd.n.tw […] *pr m* […]
sn[*w*].*i wn m-ꜥ wst iꜣdt* […]
ꜣyt n.i prt […]

What is the […]of my […] like – a great matter is grown from it.
It is called […] coming from […]
My brothers who were in the hand of decay and disease […]
Heated for me, coming […]

Section A, page 2
hrw nfr iw.n m hꜣt r šꜣ
grg.n ẖnnt […]*-nw ḥr mwy sn*
iw n.n wḥꜥ msnw itḥ.n m ẖꜣw
[…] *smḥ.n mni.n n bꜣt*
di.n ḥr ẖt n sbk nb š […]
ity ꜥnḫ wḏꜣ snb

Happy day when we arrive going down to the field!
We snare the alighting birds […] many […] on the two waters.
The fisherman and harpooner come to us, we drag in the nets
[…] our papyrus-boats as we moor at the rushes.
We offer on the fire to Sobek lord of the Lake […]
the sovereign, may he live, prosper, be well!

hrw nfr sbk nb š
sꜣ snwy ꜥꜣ imy-r ẖnt
wr rmw ꜥꜣ ḥtpt
mr […] *hrw nfr*
rdi.n im.f n bw nb
sḥt.n ḥtpti iw.n r int iw.n r […]
[*iw*].*n r sḥt m ẖꜣw*
iw.n r irt ꜥḥ n sbk
swsẖ sꜣw […]
ꜣšrt ḥr.f m wḏyw ḥr srw
srw ḥr ẖt dšrw ḥr […]
ḏbꜥw (?) *n šwt nšmyt*

Happy day for Sobek lord of the Lake,
Son of the Two Brothers, the great one, governor of the canal,
Rich in fish, full of offerings,
Loving […] the happy day
on which we give to all people.
Our Marsh Goddess is content, and we can catch, we can […]
We [can] snare thousands of birds,
We can make a burnt offering to Sobek,
Extended and lengthened […]
Roast meat upon it, of slit fish and geese,
Geese on the fire, red fish on […]
Tens of thousands (?) of feather and scale.

nn wn nkꜣy m ꜥḳw	**None will think of food**
m-ḫt h[ꜣt …]	After the des[cent (to the field)? …]
ꜥnḫ[t].n.ỉ ỉm m sf	on which I lived yesterday,
ꜥb n ỉn.n.ỉ	a meal of my own bringing.
ꜥnḫ.ỉ m swḥt ḥr bỉt	I live on eggs and honey
[...]	[…]
rmw n mꜣwt.ỉ ꜣpdw [n] ỉꜣd[t].ỉ […]	fish to my harpoon, birds [to] my net […]

Section A, page 3

ḫt.ỉ r […]	my staff to […]
ꜣḥt ḥḏt […]..	shining fields […]-fish
ỉnḥꜣs [...]	lotus-leaves […]
m nỉwtỉw.s [...]	from its townspeople […]
ḥr ẖꜣꜥ nw[ḥ ...]	**casting a line […]**
[..]*ꜣw pr* [...] *nt ḳsn r .ỉ m* […]	[…]-birds come from […] too hard for me in […]
rmn.ỉ ẖr sḥy […] *dn[s …]*	my shoulder bearing the .. […] heav[y …]

Unplaced fragments assigned in the first edition to the 'pleasures of fishing and fowling':

Fragment 1

[…] *m ḥrty* […]	[…] in climbing (?) […]

Fragment 2

[… *wḏ*]*yw ꜣ*[…]	[…]-fish ..[…]

Fragment 3

[…] *ẖr ꜥḥꜣ* […]	[…] Kheraha […]
[…] *m ḫt wꜥt* […]	[…] in one piece (?) […]

Fragment 4

[…] *ḥny sšw wr* […]	[…] rushes nests .. […]
[…] *r šꜣ wdn* […]	[…] to the field, offering […]
[…] … *ꜥ nbd m* […]	[…] of arm, braided with […]

Fragment 5

[…] *ꜣsb* […]	[…] licking (?) […]
[…] *n.n t ḥḏ dỉw ḥr ꜥ* […]	[…] to us white loaves, placed on the arm […]
[…] *mḥyt ḏbꜥ ḫt* […]	[…] north wind, finger of wood (?) […]

Fragment 6

[…]*t nt š* […]	[…] .. of the lake […]
[…] *ḥḏ ḥr wdb* […]	[…] shining on the shore (?) […]
[…] *smw* […]	[…] plants […]
[…] .. *ỉr.ỉ nꜣ* […]	[…] .. I make these […]
[…] *mt.ỉ* […]	[…] … […]
[…]*ꜣ n s*[…]	[…] … […]
[…] … […]	[…]-jars (?) […]

Fragment 7

[…] *ḥꜣt m ỉꜣb*[…]	[…] front from the east […]
[…] *.n sw ꜥ* […]	[…] .. it/him […]
[…]*..f m* […]	[…] .. of him in […]
[…] *mn* […]	[…] .. […]

Fragment 8

[...].*n ḥr ṯꜣ*[...]	[...] of us upon .. [...]
[...].*n n* [...]	[...] of us to [...]
[...].*n ḥr bꜣḥ* [...]	[...] of us on the foreskin (?) [...]
[...] *ḳbḥw* [...]	[...] the cataract-region (?) [...]

Fragment 9

[...]*w n hm*[...]	[...so]und (?) of a ro[ar (?)...]
[...] *n smḥy* ***mt ỉw*** [...]	[...] of the papyrus-boat **See the arri**[**val**...]
[...] *m pꜥrwt g*[...]	[...] with *pꜥrwt*-birds .. [...]

Fragment 10

[...] *sꜣꜣw šꜣ* [...]	[...]-land, satisfied by the field [...]
[...]*ỉt rdyt*[...]	[...] ... [...]
[...] .. [...]	[...] .. [...]

In praise of the king Papyrus British Museum EA 10475

The composition survives in part only, on a series of fragments from the lower quarter of a papyrus roll (British Museum EA 10475: for the narrative composition on the back of this papyrus, see above, A tale at the palace). The provenance is not known, and it was probably 'Old Collection' already at the time that it received its museum number around 1888. The manuscript has not been fully published at present, but Richard Parkinson has provided a comprehensive account of its contents and a transcription with translation of the main sections (Parkinson 1999b), and the following is based on that preliminary edition.

Column 1 fragmentary

Column 2, line 5

[…] *n ḫnn.n tp-rd n ꜥḥ*	[…] the regulations of the palace are not disturbed
***ḥḏ.n tꜣ ỉw th*[…] ..**	**At daybreak .. […] ..**

Column 3, lines 2-4

[…]*nb šdšḏ* […] *ḥnwty*	[…] lord of the *shedshed* […] of the two horns
[…]*w ḫnty ḥsrt ḥr ib ḥwt-ibṯt* […]	[…].. foremost of Hesret, amid Hut-ibtjet[…]
nb in […] *wr* […]	lord of .. […] great […]
nb tny ḳꜣ ḥr […]	lord of Tjeny, high upon […]
wtt ḫprw n nḥḥ imy ꜣbḏw […]	who begets the forms of eternity, the one who is in Abydos […]

Column 4 fragmentary

Column 5, lines 3-4

[…] *šnw itn*	[…] whom (?) the sun-disk encircles
im(?)[…*s*]*ḥḏ.f tꜣwy*	.. […] he illumines the two lands,
srwd.f ḥꜥw m nwt.f […]	he makes limbs flourish by his rays […]

Column 6, lines 4-6

[…] *in.f* […] *n rḫyt*	[…] .. he brings […] to the populace
[…]*swꜣḏ.f šny tꜣ wšr*	[…] he makes flourish the vegetation that had dried out,
sbnri.f ḫt srwd.f npri	he sweetens the trees, he makes the grain grow,
sḫpr.f rnpyt sb.ti	he brings into being the plants that had perished flourish by his rays
in.f ꜣpdw ḳbḥw	he brings the fowl of the Cataract Region,
ip.n ẖt.f imt.f […]	his body has calculated what is in it […]

Column 7, lines 3-6 with vertical line 1 after a thick vertical dividing-line

[…] *swꜣḏ.n.f tꜣ ti-sw wšr.n.f*	[…] he has made the land green when it had been dry
..ḥ.n.f ṯꜣw m fnd n rmṯ	he has .. air in the noses of people
ṯs.n.f pꜥt ḥsr.ti	he has raised up the nobles who were impoverished (?)
gm.n.f kmt sb.ti m r-ꜥ	he found Egypt wasted by action
[…] *stpy šꜣt.n nṯrw ḏr-bꜣḥ*	[…] (towns) sacked (?), what the gods ordained before
ḥḏ.n st nbdw-ḳd	the evil-natured had destroyed it.
in ꜥwy.fy nḥm pꜥt	It is his arms that rescue the nobles
pḥty.fy mk […]	his strength that protects […]
mk.n.f tꜣ ti-sw […]	he has protected the land when it was […]

References

D. Abouseif, La conception de la ville dans la pensée arabe du Moyen-Age, in C. Nicolet, R. Ilbert and J.-C. Depaule (eds.), *Mégapoles méditerranéennes*, Paris 2000, 32-40

B. Adams, Petrie's manuscript journal from Coptos, in *Topoi* Supplement 3, 2002, 5-22

J. Allen, Coffin Texts from Lisht, in H. Willems (ed.), *The World of the Coffin Texts. Proceedings of the Symposium held on the occasion of the 100th Birthday of Adriaan de Buck*, Leiden 1996, 1-15

J. Allen, *Middle Egyptian. An introduction to the language and culture of hieroglyphs*, Cambridge 2000

J. Allen, *The Heqanakht Papyri*, New York 2002

R. Allen, *An Introduction to Arabic Literature*, Cambridge 2000

H. Altenmüller and A. Moussa, Die Inschrift Amenemhets II. aus dem Ptah-Tempel von Memphis. Vorbericht, in *Studien zur Altägyptischen Kultur* 18, 1991, 1-48

P. Andrassy, Überlegungen zur Bezeichnung s n njwt tn "Mann dieser Stadt" und zur Sozialstruktur des Mittleren Reiches, in C. Eyre (ed.), *Proceedings of the VIIth international congress of Egyptologists, Cambridge 3-9 September 1995*, Louvain 1998, 49-58

A. Angeli, Lo svolgimento dei papiri carbonizzati, in M. Capasso (ed.), *Il rotolo librario: fabbricazione, restauro, organizzazione interna*, Lecce 1994

D. Arnold, Grab, in W. Helck (ed.), *Lexikon der Ägyptologie* II, Wiesbaden 1977, 826-837

Do. Arnold, Amenemhet I and the early Twelfth Dynasty at Thebes, in *Metropolitan Museum Journal* 26, 1991

J. Assmann, *Ma`at. Gerechtigkeit und Unsterblichkeit im Alten Ägypten*, Munich 1990

J. Assmann, Gebrauch und Gedächtnis. Die zwei Kulturen des pharaonischen Ägypten, in A. Assmann and D. Harth (eds.), *Kultur als Lebenswelt und Monument*, Frankfurt am Main 1991, 135-152

J. Assmann, Kulturelle und Literarische Texte, in A. Loprieno, *Ancient Egyptian Literature. History and Forms*, Leiden 1996, 59-82

J. Assmann and M. Bommas, *Altägyptischen Totenliturgien I. Totenliturgien in den Sargtexten des Mittleren Reiches*, Heidelberg 2002

Z. Bahrani, Conjuring Mesopotamia: imaginative geography and a world past, in L. Meskell (ed.), *Archaeology under Fire. Nationalism, politics and heritage in the Eastern Mediterranean and Middle East*, London and New York 1998, 159-174

J. Baines, Literacy and Ancient Egyptian Society, in *Man. New Series* 18, 1983, 572-599

J. Baines and C. Eyre, Four notes on literacy, in *Göttinger Miszellen* 61, 1983, 65-96

M. Bakhtin, Слово в романе, in M. Bakhtin, Вопросы Литературы и эстетики, Moscow 1977, 72-233

L. Baqtar, *Tamilat fi al-adab al-misry al-qadim*, Cairo n.d. [1990-]

C. Barbotin, L'inscription de Sésostris Ier à Tôd, in *Bulletin de l'Institut Français d'Archéologie Orientale*
au Caire 91, 1991, 1-32

J. Barns, *Five Ramesseum Papyri*, Oxford 1956

J. Barns, A New Wisdom Text from a Writing-board in Oxford, in *Journal of Egyptian Archaeology* 54, 1968, 71-76

W. Barta, *Das Gespräch eines Mannes mit seinem BA (Papyrus Berlin 3024)*, Berlin 1969

M. Bárta, *Sinuhetův Útěk z Egypta. Egypt a Syropalestina v době Abrahamově*, Prague 1999

R. Barthes, The Death of the Author. Translation in S. Heath (ed.), *Image, Music, Text*, New York 1977

H. Beinlich, Gauprozession, in W. Helck (ed.), *Lexikon der Ägyptologie* II, Wiesbaden 1977, 417-420

O. Berlev, Один из способов датировки стел Среднего царства (формула «О живые на земле...»), in Краткие сообщения института народов Азии 46, 1962, 45-87

O. Berlev, Трудовое население Египта в эпоху Среднего царства, Moscow 1972

O. Berlev, Общественные отношения в Египте эпохи Среднего царства, Moscow 1978

O.Berlev, Two kings - two suns: on the worldview of the ancient Egyptians, in S. Quirke (ed.), *Discovering Egypt from the Neva. The Egyptological legacy of Oleg D Berlev*, Berlin 2003, 1-18 (Russian), 19-35

O. Berlev and S. Hodjash, An Early Dynasty XII Offering Service from Meir (Moscow and London), in *Warsaw Egyptological Studies I. Essays in honour of Prof.Dr. Jadwiga Lipińska*, Warsaw, 1997, 283-290

A. Blackman, *Middle Egyptian Stories*, Brussels 1932

A. Blackman, *The Story of King Kheops and the Magicians transcribed from Papyrus Westcar (Berlin Papyrus 3033)*, Reading 1988

E. Blumenthal, Die "Klagen des Bauern" als Rechtserzählung, in S. Quirke (ed.), *Discovering Egypt from the Neva: the Egyptological legacy of O.D. Berlev*, Berlin 2003, 37-46

J. Bloom, *Paper before print. The history and impact of paper in the Islamic world*, New Haven and London 2001

A. von Bomhard, Le conte du naufragé et le papyrus Prisse, in *Revue d'Egyptologie* 50, 1999, 51-56
Botti 1959

N. Bosson and S. Aufrère, *Egyptes: l'égyptien et le copte*, Lattes 1999

P. Bourdieu, *La distinction. critique sociale du jugement*, Paris 1979

J. Bourriau, Patterns of change in burial customs, in S.Quirke (ed.), *Middle Kingdom Studies*, SIA, New Malden 1991

G. Burkard, Bibliotheken im alten Ägypten: Überlegungen zu Methodik ihres Nachweises und Übersicht zum Stand der Forschung, in *Bibliothek. Forschung und Praxis* 4, 1980, 79-115

K. Butzer, *Early Hydraulic Civilization in Egypt. A study in cultural ecology*, Chicago and London 1976

R. Caminos, *Literary Fragments in the Hieratic Script*, Oxford 1956

R. Caminos, Nilopfer, in W. Helck and W. Westendorf (eds.), *Lexikon der Ägyptologie* IV, Wiesbaden 1982, 498-500

P. Caron, *Des "Belles Lettres" à la "littérature". Une archéologie des signes du savoir profane en langue française(1680-1760)*, Louvain and Paris 1992

J. Černý, *A Community of Workmen at Thebes in the Ramesside Period*, Cairo 1973

B. Cerquiglini, *Eloge de la variante*, Seuil, Paris 1989

R. Chartier, Labourers and voyagers. From the text to the reader, in *Diacritics* 22:2, 1992, 49-61

W. Clarysse, Literary papyri in documentary "archives", in E. van `T Dack, P. van dessel, W. van Gucht (eds.), *Egypt and the Hellenistic World*, Louvain 1976, 43-61

M. Collier and S. Quirke, *The UCL Lahun Papyri. Letters*, Oxford 2002

M. Collier and S. Quirke, *The UCL Lahun Papyri. Religious, Literary, Legal, Mathematical and Medical*, Oxford 2004

D. Crawford, The good official of Ptolemaic Egypt, in H. Maehler and V. Strocka (eds.), *Das ptolemäische Ägypten*, Mainz-am-Rhein 1978, 195-202

G. Daressy, La découverte et l'inventaire du tombeau de Sen-nezem, in *Annales du Service des Antiquités d'Egypte* 20, 1920, 145-158

P. Derchain, Auteur et Société, in A. Loprieno, *Ancient Egyptian Literature. History and Forms*, Leiden 1996, 83-94

M. Dewachter, Nouvelles informations relatives à l'exploitation de la nécropole royale de Drah Aboul Neggah, in *Revue d'Egyptologie* 36, 1985, 43-66

S. Donadoni (ed.), *L'uomo egiziano*, Rome 1990

T. Eagleton, *The Ideology of the Aesthetic*, Oxford 1990

R. Engelbach, *Harageh*, London 1923

H. Fischer, *L'écriture et l'art de l'Egypte ancienne*, Paris 1986

H.-W. Fischer-Elfert, Die Arbeit am Text: Altägyptische Literaturwerke aus philologischer Perspektive, in A. Loprieno, *Ancient Egyptian Literature. History and Forms*, Leiden 1996, 499-513

H.-W. Fischer-Elfert, *Die Lehre eines Mannes für seinen Sohn : eine Etappe auf dem "Gottesweg" des loyalen und solidarischen Beamten des Mittleren Reich*, Wiesbaden 1999

H.-W. Fischer-Elfert, Quelques textes et une vignette du Papyrus magique no 1826 de la Bibliothèque nationale d'Athènes, in Y. Koenig (ed.), *La magie en Egypte: à la recherche d'une* définition, Paris 2002

H.-W. Fischer-Elfert, Representations of the past in New Kingdom literature, in J. Tait (ed.), *Never had the like occurred: Egypt's view of its own past*, London 2003

M. Foucault, What is an Author? Translation of the 1969 essay, in R. Davis and R. Schleifer (eds.), *Contemporary Literary Criticism*, 2nd edition, New York 1989, 262-275

D. Franke, *Das Heiligtum des Heqaib auf Elephantine. Geschichte eines Provinzheiligtums im Mittlern Reich*, Heidelberg 1994

D. Franke, Kleiner Mann (*nḏs*) – was bist Du?, in *Göttinger Miszellen* 167, 1998, 33-48

D. Franke, Middle Kingdom hymns and other sundry religious texts – an inventory, in S. Meyer (ed.), *Egypt – Temple of the Whole World. Studies in Honour of Jan Assmann*, Leiden 2003, 95-135

J. Galán, *Cuatro Viajes en la Literatura del Antiguo Egipto*, Madrid 1998

C. Gallorini, A reconstruction of Petrie's excavation at the Middle Kingdom settlement of Kahun, in S. Quirke (ed.), *Lahun Studies*, Reigate 1998, 42-59 with editorial corrigenda sheet for nn.26-86

A. Gardiner, *The Admonitions of an Egyptian Sage from a hieratic papyrus in Leiden*, Leipzig 1909 (cited in this volume as Gardiner 1909a)

A. Gardiner, *Die Erzählung des Sinuhe und die Hirtengeschichte*, Leipzig 1909 (cited in this volume as Gardiner 1909b)

A. Gardiner, *Hieratic Papyri in the British Museum Third Series. Chester Beatty gift*, London 1935 (cited in this volume as Gardiner 1935a)

A. Gardiner, A lawsuit arising from the purchase of two slaves, in *Journal of Egyptian Archaeology* 21, 1935, 140-146 (cited in this volume as Gardiner 1935b)

A. Gardiner, The Instruction addressed to Kagemni and his brethren, in *Journal of Egyptian Archaeology* 32, 1946, 71-74

A. Gardiner, *Ancient Egyptian Onomastica*, Oxford 1947

A. Gardiner, *The Ramesseum Papyri*, Oxford 1955

A. Gardiner and K. Sethe, *Egyptian Letters to the Dead*, London 1928

G. Genette, *Seuils*, Paris 1987

O. Goelet, Kemet and other Egyptian terms for their land, in R. Chazan, W. Hallo and L. Schiffman (eds.), *Ki Baruch Hu: Ancient Near Eastern, Biblical and Judaic Studies in Honor of Baruch A. Levine*, Winona Lake 1999, 23-42

J. Gorak, *The making of the modern canon: genesis and crisis of an idea*, London 1991

W. Grajetzki, *Die höchsten Beamten der ägyptischen Zentralverwaltung zur Zeit des Mittleren Reiches*, Berlin 2000

W. Grajetzki, *Two Treasurers of the late Middle Kingdom*, Oxford 2001

W. Grajetzki, *Burial Customs in Ancient Egypt: life in death for rich and poor*, London 2003

W. Grajetzki, Zu einigen Titeln in literarischen Werken des Mittleren Reiches, in press

P. Grandet, *Le Papyrus Harris I*, Cairo 1994

F.L. Griffith, Fragments of Old Egyptian Stories. From the British Museum and Amherst Collections, in *Proceedings of the Society of Biblical Archaeology* 14, 1892, 251-472

F.Ll. Griffith, *The Petrie Papyri. Hieratic Papyri from Kahun and Gurob (principally of the Middle Kingdom)*, London 1898

F.Ll. Griffith and W.M.F.Petrie, *Two Hieroglyphic Papyri from* Tanis, London 1889

W. Hayes, *Ostraka and Name Stones from the Tomb of Sen-Mut (No.71) at Thebes*, New York 1942

W. Helck, *Der Text der "Lehre Amenemhets I. für seinen Sohn"*, Wiesbaden 1969

W. Helck, *Die Lehre des dwꜣ-ẖtjj*, Wiesbaden 1970 (cited in this volume as Helck 1970a)

W. Helck, *Die Prophezeiung des nfr.tj*, Wiesbaden 1970 (cited in this volume as Helck 1970b)

W. Helck, *Der Text des "Nilhymnus"*, Wiesbaden 1972

W. Helck, *Die Lehre des Djedefhor und die Lehre eines Vaters an seinen Sohn*, Wiesbaden 1984

K. Hirschkop, *Mikhail Bakhtin, an aesthetic for democracy*, Oxford 1999

E. Iversen, *The Myth of Egypt and its hieroglyphs in the European tradition*, Princeton 1993

K. Jansen-Winkeln, Das Ende des Neuen Reiches, in *Zeitschrift für Ägyptische Sprache und Altertumskunde* 119, 1992, 22-37

R. Jasnow, Recent trends and advances in the study of Late Period Egyptian literature, in *Journal of the American Research Center in Egypt* 39, 2002, 207-216

G. Jéquier, *Le Papyrus Prisse et ses variantes*, Paris 1911

A. Kilito, *L'auteur et ses doubles. Essai sur la culture arabe classique*, Paris 1985

R. Koch, *Die Erzählung des Sinuhe*, Brussels, 1990

M. Korostovtsev, Египетский Йератический папирус № 167 Государственного Музея Изобразителъных Исскуств им. А.С. Пушкина в Москве, in V. Struve et al (eds.), *Древний Египет*, Moscow 1960, 119-133 (cited in this volume as Korostovtsev 1960a)

M. Korostovtsev, Путешествие Ун-амуна в Библ. Египетский Йератический папирус № 120 Государственного Музея Изобразителъных Исскуств им. А.С. Пушкина в Москве, Moscow 1960 (cited in this volume as Korostovtsev 1960b)

G. Lapp, *The Papyrus of Nu*, London 1997

P. Le Guilloux, *Le Conte du Paysan éloquent*, Angers 2002

B. Leach and J. Tait, Papyrus, in I. Shaw and P. Nicholson, *Ancient Egyptian Materials and Technology*, Cambridge 2000

M.A. Leahy, *Excavations at Malkata and the Birket Habu, 1971-1974. The inscriptions*, Warminster 1978

B. Legras, *Lire en Egypte, d'Alexandre à l'Islam*, Paris 2002

L. Lesko, Literacy, in D. Redford (ed.), *The Oxford Encyclopedia of Ancient Egypt*, Oxford 2001, 297-299

J. López, Felsinschriften, in W. Helck (ed.), *Lexikon der Ägyptologie* II, Wiesbaden 1977, 159-162

A. Loprieno, *Ancient Egyptian. A linguistic introduction*, Cambridge 1995

A. Loprieno, Defining Egyptian literature: ancient texts and modern theories, in A. Loprieno, *Ancient Egyptian Literature. History and Forms*, Leiden 1996, 39-58

Yu. Lotman, Структура художественного текста, Moscow 1970

U. Luft, Illahunstudien I: der Chronologie und den Beamten in den Briefen aus Illahun, in *Oikumene* 3, 1982, 101-156

J. Malek, assisted by D. Magee and E. Miles, *Topographical Bibliography of Ancient Egyptian Hieroglyphic Texts, Statues, Reliefs and Paintings VIII Objects of Provenance Not Known, Part 1 Royal Statues, Private Statues (Predynastic to Dynasty XVII)*, Oxford 1999

A. Mariette, *Les papyrus égyptiens du Musée de Boulaq II*, Paris 1872

H. de Meulenaere, Papyrus Brooklyn, in W. Helck (ed.), *Lexikon der Ägyptologie* IV, Wiesbaden 1982, 693-695

P. van Minnen, Literature in Egyptian villages in the Fayum in the Graeco-Roman Period, in *Journal of Juristic Papyrology* 28, 1998, 99-184

D. Morse, Author-Reader-Language: reflections on a critical closed circuit, in F. Gloversmith, *The theory of reading*, Totowa 1984, 52-92

I. Munro, *Untersuchungen zu den Totenbuch-Papyri der 18. Dynastie*, London and New York 1988

I. Munro, Der Totenbuch-Papyrus des Veziers Weser-Jmn, in *Göttinger Miszellen* 116, 1990, 73-78

W. Murnane, *The Boundary Stelae of Akhenaten*, London 1993

A. Niwiński, Les périodes whm-mswt dans l'histoire de l'Egypte: un histoire comparatif, in *Bulletin de la Société Française d'Egyptologie* 136, 1996, 5-26

J. Osing, *Hieratische Papyri aus Tebtunis I*, Copenhagen 1998

J. Osing and G. Rosati, *Papiri Geroglifici e Ieratici da Tebtynis*, Florence 1998

R. Parkinson, *The Tale of the Eloquent Peasant*, Oxford 1991 (cited in this volume as Parkinson 1991a)

R. Parkinson, Teachings, Discourses and Tales from the Middle Kingdom, in S. Quirke (ed.), *Middle Kingdom Studies*, New Malden 1991, 91-122 (cited in this volume as Parkinson 1991b)

R. Parkinson, Individual and Society in Middle Kingdom Literature, in A. Loprieno, *Ancient Egyptian Literature. History and Forms*, Leiden 1996, 137-155 (cited in this volume as Parkinson 1996a)

R. Parkinson, Types of literature in the Middle Kingdom, in A. Loprieno, *Ancient Egyptian Literature. History and Forms*, Leiden 1996, 297-312(cited in this volume as Parkinson 1996b)

R. Parkinson, The Teaching of King Amenemhat I at el-Amarna: British Museum EA 57458 and 57459, in A. Leahy and J. Tait (eds.), *Studies on ancient Egypt in honour of H.S. Smith*, London 1999, 221-226 (cited in this volume as Parkinson 1999a)

R. Parkinson, Two new "literary" texts on a Second Intermediate Period Papyrus? A preliminary account of P. BM EA 10475, in J. Assmann and E. Blumenthal (eds.), *Literatur und Politik im pharaonischen und ptolemäischen Ägypten*, Cairo 1999, 177-196 (cited in this volume as Parkinson 1999b)

R. Parkinson, *Poetry and Culture in Middle Kingdom Egypt. A dark side to perfection*, London 2002

R. Parkinson, The missing beginning of 'The Dialogue of a Man and his Ba': P. Amherst III and the History of the Berlin Library, in *Zeitschrift für Ägyptische Sprache und Altertumskunde* 130, 2003, 120-133

P. Pestman, Who were the owners, in the ‚Community of Workmen', of the Chester Beatty Papyri?, in R. Demarée and J. Janssen (eds.), *Gleanings from Deir el-*Medîna, Leiden 1982, 155-172

W.M.F. Petrie, *Tanis Part I. 1883-4*, London 1885

W.M.F. Petrie, *The Labyrinth, Gerzeh and Mazghuneh*, London 1912

G. Posener, *Littérature et Politique dans l'Egypte de la XIIe dynastie*, Paris 1956

G. Posener, Le Conte de Néferkarê et du Général Siséné (Recherches Littéraires, VI), in *Revue d'Egyptologie* 11, 1957, 119-137

G. Posener, Une nouvelle histoire de revenant (Recherches Litteraires, VII), in *Revue d'Egyptologie* 12, 1960, 75-82

G. Posener, Fragment littéraire de Moscou, in *Mitteilungen des Deutschen Archäologischen Instituts Abteilung Kairo* 24-25, 1969, 101-106

G. Posener, *L'enseignement loyaliste*, Geneva 1976

J. Quack, *Studien zur Lehre für Merikare*, Wiesbaden 1992

J. Quack, Das Buch vom Tempel und verwandte Texte: ein Vorbericht, in *Archiv für Religionsgeschichte* 2, 2000, 1-20

J. Quack, Aus einer spätzeitlichen literarischen Sammelhandschrift (Papyrus Berlin 23045), in *Zeitschrift für Ägyptische Sprache und Altertumskunde* 130, 2003, 182-185

J. Quibell, *The Ramesseum*, London 1898

S. Quirke, "Townsmen" in the late Middle Kingdom. On the term s n njwt tn in the Lahun Temple Accounts, in *Zeitschrift für Ägyptische Sprache und Altertumskunde* 118, 1991, 141-149

S. Quirke, Archive, in A. Loprieno, *Ancient Egyptian Literature. History and Forms*, Leiden 1996, 379-401

S. Quirke, Two Thirteenth Dynasty Heart Scarabs, in *Jaarbericht Ex Oriente Lux* 37 (2001-2002), 2003, 31-40

A. Roccati, *Papiro ieratico n.54003. Estratti magici e rituali del primo Medio Regno*, Turin 1970

E. Said, *Orientalism. Western conceptions of the Orient.* Reprint with new afterword, London and New York, 1995

M. Salama-Carr, *La traduction à l'époque abbasside*, Paris 1990

S. Schott, *Bücher und Bibliotheken im Alten Ägypten. Verzeichnis der Buch- und Spruchtitel und der Termini technici*, Wiesbaden 1990

A. Schwab-Schlott, *Die Ausmasse Ägyptens nach altägyptischen Texte*, Wiesbaden 1981

W.K. Simpson, Papyrus Lythgoe: a fragment of a literary text of the Middle Kingdom from el-Lisht, in *Journal of Egyptian Archaeology* 1960, 65-70.

W.K. Simpson, *The Terrace of the Great God at Abydos: the offering chapels of Dynasties 12 and 13*, New Haven 1974

W.K. Simpson, The Memphite epistolary formula on a jar stand of the First Intermediate Period from Naga ed-Deir, in W.K. Simpson and W. Davies (eds.), *Studies in Ancient Egypt, the Aegean and the Sudan. Essays in Honor of Dows Dunham on the occasion of his 90th birthday*, Boston 1981, 173-179

W.K. Simpson, *Inscribed Material from the Pennsylvania-Yale Excavations at Abydos*, New Haven and Philadelphia 1995

H. Smith, The story of 'Onchsheshonqy, in *Sarapis* 6, 1980, 133-157

A. Spalinger, Dates in Ancient Egypt, in *Studien zur Altägyptischen Kultur* 15, 1988, 255-276

A. Spalinger, *The Transformation of an Ancient Egyptian Narrative: P. Sallier III and the Battle of Kadesh*, Wiesbaden 2002

W. Spiegelberg, *Hieratic Ostraka & Papyri found by J.E.Quibell in the Ramesseum, 1895-6*, London 1898

A. Varvaro, Review of Cerquiglini 1989, in *Medioevo romanzo* 14, 1989, 474-477

U. Verhoeven, Ein historischer "Sitz im Leben" für die Erzählung von Horus und Seth des Papyrus Chester Beatty I, in M. Schade-Busch, *Wege Öffnen. Festschrift für Rolf Gundlach zum 65. Geburtstag*, Wiesbaden 1996, 347-363

U. Verhoeven, Von hieratischer Literaturwerken in der Spätzeit, in J. Assmann and E. Blumenthal, *Literatur und Politik im pharaonischen und ptolemäischen Ägypten*, Cairo 1999

P. Vernus, Langue littéraire et diglossie, in A. Loprieno, *Ancient Egyptian Literature. History and Forms*, Leiden 1996, 555-564

V. Voloshinov, Марксизм и философия языка, 1929 reprinted 1995 as V. Voloshinov, Философия и социология гуманитарных наук, St Petersburg 1995, 216-380

W. Waddell, *Manetho*, London 1940

W. Ward, *An Index of Egyptian Administrative and Religious Titles of the Middle Kingdom*, Beirut 1982

E. Wente, *Letters from Ancient Egypt*, Atlanta 1990

M. Woodmansee, The Genius and the Copyright: economic and legal conditions of the emergence of the 'author', in *Eighteenth-Century Studies* 17, 1984, 425-448

M. Woodmansee and P. Jaszi (eds.), *The Construction of Authorship: Textual Appropriation in Law and Literature*, Dunham NC and London, 1994

K.-T. Zauzich, P. Carlsberg 21 und 22. Zwei Briefe von Bücherfreunden, in J. Quack and P. Frandsen, *A Miscellany of Demotic Texts and Studies. Papyri Carlbserg 3*, Copenhagen 2000, 53-57